# GEORGE HARRISON
# ON GEORGE HARRISON

OTHER BOOKS IN THE MUSICIANS IN THEIR OWN WORDS SERIES

# GEORGE
# HARRISON
# ON GEORGE
# HARRISON

## INTERVIEWS AND ENCOUNTERS

### EDITED BY ASHLEY KAHN

CHICAGO
REVIEW
PRESS

An A Cappella Book

ISBN 978-1-64160-051-4

Library of Congress Control Number: 2020932900

A list of credits and copyright notices for the individual pieces in this collection can be found on pages 553–556.

Interior layout: Nord Compo

Printed in the United States of America
5 4 3

For Hal Willner, who grasped the balance
between a bright light and a dark horse,
for Eric and Heidi, whose gift of a Beatles
8-track introduced me to George Harrison,
and for all who continue to evolve and look for answers

# CONTENTS

## Part IV • 1982–1989

## Part V • 1992–2001

# PREFACE

Back when the Beatles first exploded onto the popular radar, there came the need to separate and identify each of the four. In the pop firmament, that hadn't been necessary before—not for Frank Sinatra or Elvis, nor would it be required for Michael or Madonna. But in 1964, the succession of singular stars had been interrupted by plurality, and in the desire to define each from the other, George Harrison became the "Quiet Beatle."

*Quieter* would have been more accurate. At the outset, relative to his bandmates, Harrison was more thoughtful and more sincere—as this anthology of interviews, essays, and statements shows. Ironically, *George Harrison on George Harrison* also reveals that, at the time he received that tag, he was also being called upon to be a spokesman of the group, interviewing his fellow Fabs for the BBC radio program *Public Ear* in 1964 or writing a column for Manchester's *Daily Express*. Amid the mocking group banter the Beatles excelled at, Harrison held his own, throwing out lines that kept the others—and his fans—in stitches. Before stardom or spirituality, humor was his first line of defense.

"Were you bored by all that?" a television host asked him, in 1988, of the unending barrage of encounters the Beatles faced while circuiting the globe. "Well, sometimes it was boring, sometimes we'd just make fun of them. We'd have our own little in jokes, you know, to get through," recalled Harrison. "It's like a survival kind of thing."

Harrison survived, thrived, and became many things beyond his moniker. He was thoughtful *and* he was quick *and* he was enduringly curious. He grew and evolved from the quiet to the questioning Beatle. He became the spiritual seeker of the group, the one most dedicated to meeting the shamans of the day, the one most determined to find his guru, and he wove that search into his music. At the height of their popularity, the Beatles broke apart and Harrison was the first to step out and top the charts—praising the divine in numerous ways and with numerous names—while asking the biggest of the big questions: what is Life?

Harrison made that query rock loudly and ring true for an entire generation. He made pop music a tool of spiritual exploration and of God-awareness. In the years that followed, he examined various paths but was most attuned to the way of Krishna consciousness espoused by Sri Prabhupada, founder of the Hare Krishna movement and the International Society for Krishna Consciousness (ISKCON). He balanced his inner pursuit with a solo career that covered what was expected of a rock star from the '70s through the '90s—albums, collaborations, and all-star concerts. He wrote books and dove into the movie business. He defied expectations as well, developing an aspersion for touring (one can count the number of George Harrison tours on one hand) and, for many years, a preference for staying home and gardening.

*George Harrison on George Harrison* covers his biographical sweep as fully as an autobiography would, detailing Harrison's life as he remembered and reported it. It's all in here, all phases and stages, triumphs and travails, even if the telling is not perfectly chronological. How could it be? In 1963, as Beatlemania gathered steam, the group was regarded largely as a fad soon to fade—even the Beatles themselves could not see their popularity lasting more than a few years. And at that time, Harrison couldn't possibly unpack the Beatles experience; he was too busy being Fab. Some of the best stories and revelations about his years as a teenager and young adult—his Liverpool days, his rock and roll apprenticeship in Hamburg—are to be found in conversations in the '80s and '90s. With distance and clarity came a deepened understanding, as well as newly remembered details.

The through line in *George Harrison on George Harrison* is a marked guilelessness. At the age of 24, on national British television, he's open to answering questions about his sense of success and wealth. "By having the money, we found that money wasn't the answer," he said. "And it was good really, because we learned that that wasn't it. We still lacked something." What sounded to some like faux, show-biz humility has proven over time to be reflective of his true nature, of priorities that were musically oriented and spiritually driven. Yes, he was a business-man, unapologetically so. Yet he regarded his success as a means to an end. This anthology is rife with evidence of that balanced sensibility.

In *George Harrison on George Harrison*, his evolution—as a man and a musician, as a producer and instigator of projects—reveals itself through a virtual roundtable of multiple Georges, from the greasy-haired teenager to the gray-haired man of the manor—and all the others in between. There are inevitable overlaps: over the years, journalists revisited the same questions—about the Beatles days, for example. About reunion rumors. About his ongoing relationship with Paul and Ringo and John. And Yoko. What changed over time was how Harrison chose to answer these questions and others that tended to cycle repeatedly, his responses serving as a measure of a man growing more comfortable with—and even amused by—his own legacy.

*George Harrison on George Harrison* works as a window into the burgeoning role of music journalists, from the celebrity watchers of the '60s to successive generations of reporters with an expanded knowledge of the world and deeper curiosity for music and its makers, who regarded their journalism as a means to delivering messages of social relevance. (Of course, this means that audiences were similarly evolving, expect-ing more from their music stars—a trend that the Beatles, and Harrison especially, were greatly responsible for initiating.) I'm pleased that many pioneering writers from this proud tradition are featured, from *Melody Maker*'s Nick Jones and Alan Walsh and TV hosts David Frost and Dick Cavett; to the *Village Voice*'s Howard Smith, *Crawdaddy*'s Mitch Glazer, *Billboard*'s Timothy White, *Rolling Stone*'s Anthony DeCurtis, and *Musician*'s Mark Rowland—among many others.

A number of never-published gems were unearthed and are featured in *George Harrison on George Harrison*. This anthology marks the first time the *Daily Express* columns he wrote in 1964 have been compiled, offering a peek inside the bubble of the band's ascendancy. Also among these finds: Harrison's first US interview ever, conducted while visiting his sister in southern Illinois in '63 and printed in a high school newspaper; his initial US interview following the Beatles breakup, weeks before the release of his groundbreaking album *All Things Must Pass*; and a forgotten encounter with Michael Jackson on a BBC radio program from 1979, weeks before the release Jackson's breakout solo album *Off The Wall*.

There are a few TV appearances that had to be part of this as well: Harrison speaking with John Lennon on David Frost's show in '67 and with Ringo Starr on Michael Aspel's program in '86. Other must-haves point to significant moments in his timeline, like the press conference before his ill-fated '74 tour and a rock radio interview a few months later, bristling with disappointment at the critical drubbing he had received. There were discussions on spirituality—Harrison conversing with his swami Sri Prabhupada, digging into the verses from the Bhagavad Gita, applying the timeless Vedic ideas to modern Western life—and on his movie production career, Harrison sharing both his passion for film and his concerns about the business in '87.

Harrison may have been focused on God-consciousness, but he was never more than human. On occasion he felt disrespected, and he reacted. In 1988 he shared his unfiltered disappointment at Paul McCartney missing the Beatles' induction into the Rock & Roll Hall of Fame. In an interview with MTV News in '89, Harrison chafed at the inanity of a line of questions, determined nonetheless to deliver what's expected of him. In an expansive, ninety-minute conversation for a 1990 *Musician* cover story, Harrison's rage was palpable as he spoke about worldwide political corruption and the environmental impact of governmental policies.

Yet Harrison never lost his love for a "good larf," often at his own expense; there's a dry, self-deprecating wit in the brusque toast he gave at the tenth-anniversary fete for HandMade Films, the company he first established to save Monty Python's *Life of Brian*. But Harrison wasn't afraid to speak candidly either; included is a telling missive sent with deep sincerity in early 2000, just weeks after an attempt on his life.

Harrison survived that attack because of his wife Olivia, who fought off the deranged fan. In *George Harrison on George Harrison*, she's mentioned a few times, and in a more expansive way she's in here, between the lines. She's the reason George made it through the '70s as positively as he did. Their union and the birth of their son Dhani in 1978 are primary reasons he avoided the spotlight through much of the early '80s. In turn Olivia shared many of George's passions and projects and initiated a few herself, like the Romanian Angel Appeal, established in 1990 to support abandoned orphans after the overthrow of Communism. Her devotion to meditation and a spiritual life validated Harrison's. It made their home at Friar's Park a sanctuary. Her role in Harrison's life kept him steady, free from darkness, living in the light—even as life challenged him with more than enough reasons to retreat and disengage: unnerving lawsuits, business squabbles with his old mates, undue criticism from the media, the death of John Lennon, and a knife-wielding attacker.

"You're optimistic," remarked John Fugelsang in a conversation aired on VH1 in 1997, four years before Harrison would pass away from cancer. George pauses. The quiet Beatle has grown more thoughtful, more complex than ever. One can see it in his eyes, still bright and piercing, and feel it in the rougher texture of his voice, despite the years that have passed. There's that familiar energy but also a hint of fatigue. The world has changed around him, even as he once served as an agent of change.

Today the Beatles do not cast the tremendous shadow they once did, nor are they as ubiquitous as they once were—a point Harrison anticipated, and undoubtedly welcomed. Yet the Fabs remain a necessary part of any level of musical literacy or general cultural awareness. They are celebrated and their songs are sung, listened to, and studied. These days—if streaming platforms can be looked on as a measure—"Here Comes the Sun" is shining brighter than ever; of the foursome's legendary discography, Harrison's tune from *Abbey Road* is either the number-one or number-two song that a multigenerational music audience clicks on when the Beatles come to mind. Harrison's uplifting ode to positivity, his "burst of joy" as *Rolling Stone* calls it, has become an exemplar of the Beatles sound and message.

"You *have* to be optimistic, yeah," was Harrison's crisp, matter-of-fact reply to the VH1 host.

———————

At its core, Harrison's story is about gifts and gratitude. The opportunity to assemble and edit it brought forth the same. The list of those meriting appreciation starts with Olivia and Dhani Harrison and their representatives—Richard Radford in the United Kingdom, stateside curator Don Fleming, Apple Corps's Jeff Jones, as well as old friends Hal Willner and Dave Brendel who helped facilitate the connections. Much thanks are due to my agent, Dave Dunton, and Yuval Taylor, founding editor of A Capella's Musicians in Their Own Words series, and those at Chicago Review Press who helped bring this book home: Cynthia Sherry, Kara Rota, and Benjamin Krapohl.

Thanks as well to a force of friends, fellow writers, and music-biz veterans for sharing information and guidance: Josh Feigenbaum, Ira Robbins, Bill Flanagan, Holly George-Warren, David Fricke, George Gilbert, Craig Inciardi, Anthony DeCurtis, Jason Fine, Jeff Burger, and Chris DeVito. And also to the individuals at the institutions, archives, and collections where much of George's words now reside: Barney Hoskyns and Katie Sainsbury at Rock's Backpages; Andy Leach, Jennie Thomas, and Shannon Erb at the Rock & Roll Hall of Fame Library and Archives; Ranjit Das and Eddy Gaasbeek at Bhaktivedanta Archives; Chris Robertson at Global ImageWorks; Johnny Palumbo at Entercom; Bruce Gillmer, Curtis Conroy, Lorne Mitchell, and Clayton Grayum at ViacomCBS; Richard Latto at BBC Radio Solent; Alexis Singh, Kara Ioconus, and Angela Giannacopolous at BBC New York; Natalie Jones and Emma Radford at Reach PLC; Laura Scougall at ITV; and Georgia Wright, Sean Bridgeman, Ryan Henderson, and Lisa Simmons at Nine Network.

I am indebted as well to those who went beyond the call of duty by updating and reviewing text that originally appeared in more limited form—Judy Garlan White, Elaine Dutka, Mark Rowland, Charles Bermant, Anthony DeCurtis, and Ezra Bookstein—and by describing their respective encounters with George—Mitch Glazer, Nick Jones, Mick Jones, Marcia Schafer Raubach, Jenny Boyd, and Andy McConnell.

Finally, praise to those whose personal support made the way easier: Lynette Coburn, Eric Weiss, Tom Grant, Shyamasundar Das, Larry Kane, Cynthia Colonna, Abby Royle, and Giselle Robledo.

———————

"So what are you working on?"

"A George Harrison book," I'd say. "His words, not mine."

That's how it's been going for two years. Often my comment elicited the same reply, something along the lines of: "Harrison wasn't my favorite Beatle at the start, but he is now." I didn't consider it too much at first, but over time, I encountered it more and more. Increasingly it made sense.

It made me think of how it was the early 1970s when I first became aware of Harrison and his music—the era of Watergate, oil shortages, and, for a teenager growing up in Cincinnati, the Big Red Machine. I was part of the generation that came to appreciate the Beatles not as they first appeared but as they were dividing into four separate, still-active parts—each developing their own distinct identity. For a few years, George Harrison was as ubiquitous as any of them, one Top 40 hit following another—"Give Me Love," "Dark Horse," and "Ding Dong, Ding Dong." As I hit adolescence and popular music grew to a personal, need-to-know obsession, I pursued my studies with the help of a small bedroom stereo and a used record store. Harrison's history revealed itself; as brief a gesture as his closing guitar part on the Beatles' "The End" would glisten like a flawless gem, urging me to know and pay close attention to the no-longer-Quiet one.

Through the '70s, the comparisons between John, Paul, Ringo, and George were ongoing. I reached adulthood at the close of the decade. Ringo's run on the charts trailed off, and in 1980 John was tragically, unfairly taken from us. Paul remained productive well into the MTV era and for years after, collaborating with the likes of Stevie Wonder and Michael Jackson and touring often.

In the long run, it was George who stood out and held our attention. We watched Harrison the longest because he gave us the most reasons to. He was the Beatle who carried their collective dream forward, who attained what Apple Corps, the joint partnership the group established in 1968, first set out to do. His collaborations were more enduring. His music, films, and good works reached as many ears and hearts and minds as those of any former Beatle, in more extensive, generous ways. What he achieved through skill and good fortune was amplified by a deep inner strength. Carlos Santana, another spiritual seeker who looked Eastward in the '60s and '70s for inspiration—and like Harrison, held to that path—describes the rare breed of rock musicians forged in that age as "multi-dimensional warriors."

Harrison was a shining example of that ideal. In a day when there seems to be a dearth of musical warriors who are able to match stardom with a sense of service and lead that same charge, there's little surprise many would now claim George Harrison as their Beatle of choice. For those who already do, this book holds much confirmation. For the rest, read his words and know the man. Read, and know a life well-lived.

—ASHLEY KAHN
8 Sep 2019

# PART I
# 1961–1966

# RADIO INTERVIEW

**Monty Lister | October 28, 1962 | *Sunday Spin*, Radio Clatterbridge**

This interview took place almost immediately—just a few weeks—after the Beatles's first UK single, "Love Me Do," was released. The group was still performing in Hamburg, West Germany, and Ringo Starr was so new to the lineup he measured his involvement in weeks. Monty Lister was both a fan of the group and producer of two local Liverpool radio programs—*Music with Monty* and *Sunday Spin*. Noted Beatles historian Mark Lewisohn has identified this discussion as the foursome's first-ever radio interview. The two excerpts below focus on Harrison. —Ed.

**Monty Lister**: Then there's George Harrison.

**George Harrison**: How d'you do.

**Lister**: How d'you do. What's your job?

**Harrison**: Uhh, lead guitar and sort of singing.

**Lister**: By playing lead guitar does that mean that you're sort of leader of the group or are you . . . ?

**Harrison**: No, no. Just . . . well you see, the other guitar is the rhythm. Ching, ching, ching, you see.

**Paul McCartney**: He's solo guitar, you see. John is in fact the leader of the group.

---

**Lister**: George, were you brought up in Liverpool?

**Harrison**: Yes. So far, yes.

**Lister**: Whereabouts?

**Harrison**: Well, born in Wavertree, and bred in Wavertree and Speke. Where the airplanes are, you know.

**Lister**: Are you all Liverpool types, then?

**Ringo Starr**: Yes.

**John Lennon**: Uhh . . . types, yes.

**McCartney**: Oh yeah.

**Starr**: Liverpool-typed Paul, there . . .

# FILM AND RADIO INTERVIEWS

**The Beatles | August–October 1963 | *The Mersey Sound, The Public Ear,* BBC Radio**

Harrison was as instrumental to the Fab Four's reputation for witty irreverence and humorous asides as any of the other three. Many interviews during this period found all bandmembers handling the spokesperson role together, speaking among and often over each other, and Harrison holding his own. Through the end of 1963, the Beatles remained primarily a British phenomenon, still performing in various cities around the country, then zipping back to London to make guest appearances on various TV and radio programs like *Juke Box Jury.*

The following excerpts trace the Beatles on the rise in the United Kingdom in late '63. One of the more commonly asked questions during this period was "How long can this phenomenon last?"—followed by "What will you do then?" Harrison had fun explaining how the band learned to put on a good stage show in Hamburg ("maching schau"), discussed the mania that had begun to follow members of the group in their daily lives (to his mother's dismay), and confessed to not being as focused on his guitar as he could be. —Ed.

## August 28, 1963

*[The Beatles were interviewed in their dressing room and filmed in perfor-
mance in Manchester for the BBC documentary* The Mersey Sound. —Ed.]

**John Lennon:** The best thing was "Love Me Do" came to the charts in two days. And everybody thought it was a fiddle because our manager's stores send in these . . . what is it . . . record things.

**George Harrison:** Returns.

**Lennon:** Returns. And everybody down south thought, "Oh, aha! He's buying them himself or he's just fiddling the charts," you know. But he wasn't.

**Harrison:** Actually we'd been at it a long time before that. We'd been to Hamburg. I think that's where we found our style . . . we developed our style because of this fella. He used to say, "You've got to make a show for the people," and he used to come up every night, shouting, "Mach schau! Mach schau!" So we used to "mach schau," and John used to dance around like a gorilla, and we'd all, you know, knock our heads together and things like that. Anyway, we got back to Liverpool and all the groups there were doing Shadows type of stuff. [*The Shadows were a popular guitar-based instrumental group of the period. —Ed.*] And we came back with leather jackets and jeans and funny hair, "maching schau," which went down quite well.

**Lennon:** We just wore leather jackets. Not for the group—one person wore one, I can't remember—and then we all liked them, so it ended up we were all on stage with them. And we'd always worn jeans because we didn't have anything else at the time, you know. And then we went back to Liverpool and got quite a few bookings. They all thought we were German; you know, we were billed as [*being*] from Hamburg and they all said, "You speak good English." So we went back to Germany and we had a bit more money the second time, so we wore leather pants and we looked like four Gene Vincents, only a bit younger, I think. And that was it, you know. We just kept the leather gear till Brian [*Epstein*] came along.

**Paul McCartney:** It was a bit, sort of, old hat anyway, all wearing leather gear, and we decided we didn't want to look ridiculous going home because more often than not too many people would laugh. It was just stupid. We didn't want to appear as a gang of idiots. And Brian suggested that we just, sort of, wear ordinary suits. So we just got what we thought were quite good suits and got rid of the leather gear. That was all.

**Harrison:** We do like the fans and enjoy reading the publicity about us, but sometimes you don't realize that it's about yourself. You see your pictures and read articles about George Harrison, Ringo Starr, Paul, and John, but you don't actually think, oh, that's me. There I am in the paper. It's funny. It's just as though it's a different person.

**Ringo Starr:** When we go home, we go in early in the morning when we've finished a job, and the kids don't know you're at home. But if they find out where I live, they get the drums out and beat it out! Because it's a play street and, you know, there's no traffic or nothing bothering them. Once when the boys came for me—they popped in to see me Mum and me Dad, you know—we had to go out the back because there were twenty or thirty outside. And they wouldn't believe me mother, you know, knocking and saying, "Can we have their autographs?" So it built up so much. There was about two hundred kids all around the door, peeping through the window and knocking. In the end, me mother was ill, you know—terrified out of her life—with just all these kids and boys and girls, you know.

**Harrison:** They send us a lot of jelly babies and chocolates and things like that, just because somebody wrote in one of the papers about presents and things that we'd had given to us. And John said he'd got some jelly babies and I ate them. But ever since that we've been inundated. We get about two ton a night. But the main trouble is they tend to throw them at us when were on stage, and once I got one in my eye which wasn't very nice. In fact, I haven't been the same since.

**Lennon:** It all sounds like we're complaining, but you know, we're not. We're just putting the point that it affects your home more than it does yourself, you know, because you know what to expect but your parents and family don't know what's happening.

---

**Lennon:** "How long are you going to last?" Well, you can't say, you know. You can be bigheaded and say, "Yeah, we're going to last ten years."

But as soon as you've said that you think, "We're lucky if we last three months," you know.

**McCartney**: Well, obviously we can't keep playing the same sort of music until we're about forty, sort of, old men playing "From Me to You"! Nobody is going to want to know at all about that sort of thing. You know, we've thought about it, and probably the thing that John and I will do, uhh, will be to write songs as we have been doing as a sort of sideline now. We'll probably develop that a bit more we hope. Who knows? At forty, we may not know how to write songs anymore.

**Harrison**: I hope to have enough money to go into a business of my own by the time we, umm, do flop. And we don't know—it may be next week, it may be two or three years. But I think we'll be in the business, either up there or down there, for at least another four years.

**Starr**: I've always fancied having a ladies' hairdressing salon. You know, a string of them, in fact. Strut around in me stripes and tails, you know. "Like a cup of tea, Madam?"

### October 3, 1963

[*This brief discussion was recorded for radio in Brian Epstein's North End Music Stores (NEMS) offices in London for the BBC program* The Public Ear. *At the time, the group was busy in the studio, recording tracks for the* With the Beatles *album which would be released in the United Kingdom on November 22, the day President Kennedy was shot. —Ed.*]

**McCartney**: It wasn't so much that we foresaw a big success. We just never thought that anything particularly bad would happen to us. We never felt . . . never sat down at one particular point at all and, sort of, worried about anything. We've always thought that something would turn up sometime.

**Harrison**: We have been misquoted. People saying we make seven thousand a week, and all that.

**McCartney**: I wish we did.

**Harrison**: We probably do make quite a bit, but we don't actually see it because record royalties, things like that, take months before they come in. And anyway . . .

**Lennon**: Hotels cost a fortune.

**Harrison**: Yeah, my mother costs a fortune. But we've also got an accountant and a company—Beatles Limited. They see the money. The thing is, indirectly, we are and we aren't doing it for the money, really, because don't forget, we played for about three or four years or maybe longer just earning hardly anything. Well, we wouldn't have lived on that. If we were doing it for the money, we wouldn't have lasted out all those years. But the money does help, let's face it. Yeah, we all love being onstage and . . .

**Lennon**: I haven't got the patience to practice to become a perfect guitarist, you know. I'm more interested in the combination of my voice and the guitar I know, and to write songs, than I am in the instrument. So I never go through a day hardly without playing it whether I'm performing or not, you know.

**McCartney**: George is the one of us who is interested in the instrument.

**Harrison**: Well, I don't *practice.*

**McCartney**: But the other three of us are more interested in the sound of the group.

**Harrison**: To be a guitarist, you're supposed to practice a couple of hours a day. But, I mean, I don't do that.

**Starr**: To be *anything,* you're supposed to practice a couple of hours a day.

**McCartney**: Yeah.

**Harrison**: Well you know, I mean, the thing is . . . individually we're all . . . I suppose we're all crummy musicians, really.

## HARRISON AND THE BEATLES ON

### "Kiss Me Quick" by Elvis Presley

**McCartney**: The only thing I don't like about Elvis now is the songs. You know, I love his voice. I used to love all the records like "Blue Suede Shoes" and "Heartbreak Hotel"—lovely. But I don't like the songs now. And "Kiss Me Quick," it sounds like Blackpool on a sunny day.

**Starr**: I didn't like it at all, no.

**Harrison**: I must admit I didn't like it very much. Not at all. It's an old track. And I think, seeing as they're releasing old stuff, if they release something like "My Baby Left Me," it'd be number one because Elvis is definitely still popular. It's just the song's a load of rubbish. I mean, Elvis is great. He's fine. But it's not for me.

**Lennon**: Well, I think it'll be a hit because it's Elvis, like people said. But I don't think it'll be very great. [*Clownish voice*] I like those hats, though, with "Kiss Me Quick" on it!"

—from *Juke Box Jury*, BBC, December 7, 1963

## HARRISON ON

### Post-Beatles Plans

**Dibbs Mather**: You are one of the reputed deep-thinkers in this group. How do you see this as a peak in your life? What happens to you after this is over?

**Harrison**: Well, I suppose we'll stay doing this sort of stuff for a couple of years. Whether we're . . . I mean, naturally we won't be able to stay at this level. But, we should have another two years at least, I think.

**Mather**: What happens to George Harrison then?

**Harrison**: I don't know. I'll know by the time that comes along. Probably I'll have a little business or something like that.

**Mather**: You don't want to go on in the profession?

**Harrison**: Probably, yeah. I'd like to make records, you know, with other artists. I don't mean perform. I mean as a producer.

—from BBC interview with Dibbs Mather on *Dateline London*,
Gaumont Theater, Brighton, UK, December 10, 1963

# HIGH SCHOOL PAPER ARTICLE

Marcia Schafer | September 1963 | *Redbird Notes*

Media specialist Marcia Schafer Raubach, through a simple twist of fate, has the distinction of being the first member of the American media to welcome a Beatle stateside. She interviewed Harrison when he was twenty and she was seventeen; here's what brought them together.

Harrison's older sister Louise had married a designer of mining equipment whose skills were prized—first by a company in Toronto, Canada, and then in the small town of Benton, in southern Illinois, across the river from St. Louis. She kept in touch with the family in Liverpool, avidly following her baby brother's success. She received copies of the Beatles' earliest singles and got the local radio station, where Schafer had a weekly show, to play them. In September 1963 both Harrison brothers—Peter and George—flew over to see their sister and get their first taste of the US.

Apparently there's a home movie of their visit, Peter having bought an 8mm movie camera for the occasion. They lived in and explored Benton for almost two weeks, staying with their sister, camping for a few days, and meeting people their own age. They played boccie ball and stopped by a music instrument store, where Harrison purchased a Rickenbacker 425 electric guitar, and a small record shop, where he picked up the obscure single "I've Got My Mind Set On You" by James Ray, which he would cover in 1987. Harrison also ate his first T-bone steak and sat in with a local group, the Four Vests, at a nearby VFW hall, playing Hank Williams songs.

On a Saturday in late September—Raubach can't recall the exact date—she had finished her weekly show, *Saturday Session,* and left the station when she received a call telling her all three Harrison siblings were at the radio station, hoping to thank her for playing the Beatles, and that they had a new single for her: "She Loves You."

"In 1963, music was all across the board. I was playing Elvis, Frank Sinatra, some Motown," recalls Raubach. "The Beatles music was so totally different than anything else." Harrison himself did not look or act like the guys she knew. "He was unusual-looking. He dressed differently than the guys here. He was very soft-spoken and polite."

Raubach interviewed Harrison briefly, welcoming him to southern Illinois, asking him a number of questions—primarily about being in America for the first time and about this new group, the Beatles. Their discussion was not recorded, but she did describe it in an article she wrote for her high school newspaper. It's an impressive effort at reporting for a teenager in '63, an unusual story with references to many things British. In the last few paragraphs one can hear an excited Harrison explaining and sharing stories in a country that had inspired his musical path from the outset.

"Back then, I had no idea how significant the Beatles would be for my own generation and so many generations to follow," Raubach adds. For many, Harrison's Atlantic crossing—the first Beatle to do so—is more than a footnote. Today there's a historic marker in Benton commemorating the visit and an entire book, *Before He Was Fab: George Harrison's First American Visit*, by local historian Jim Kirkpatrick, examines it in detail. —Ed.

This past summer I was fortunate enough to meet George Harrison, a member of England's sensational new "beat Music" quartet.

Harrison, a brother of Mrs. Gordon Caldwell of Benton, was visiting his sister, whom I had met earlier at the local radio station. During his U.S. stay, I met him at WFRX. George Harrison turned out to be a down-to-earth person, very easy to talk to. A former apprentice electrician, he began singing at the age of 15 in his native town of Liverpool, England. After playing in ballrooms and strip clubs, they out grew this and became a super charged quartet, calling themselves "the Beatles." Their first song "Love Me Do" soared to the hit parade in its first 48 hours.

Two of the boys, John Lennon and Paul McCartney, write their tunes and have enough self penned numbers to keep them in original numbers until 1975. The four boys are "Do-it-yourselves" from the beginning, working out their vocal arrangements and lyrics. Their music is wild and uninhibited and outsells the worlds [*sic*] greatest recording artists although not one of the Beatles can read music. Last week 80,000 tickets were sold in two hours for a Christmas concert to be given during Christmas week.

Back to George Harrison, he likes the United States very much, except for the hot weather. He is now 20 years old and so naturally one of his likes is small blondes, since he is short himself. He likes driving, sleeping, television, Eartha Kitt, eggs and chips and Alfred Hitchcock movies. He plays the lead guitar with the group and was delighted with the variety of records he found in a music store in Mt. Vernon. He was also fascinated with the car hops on roller skates working at a Mt. Vernon drive-in. He enjoyed drive-in theatres, since they do not have them in England.

He told of some of his experiences at the personal appearances of the Beatles. At one appearance, 100 screaming teenagers were carried from the Bank Holiday Fete, fainting in the heat.

Another time, the group [*was*] smuggled into the theatre in a garbage van. Girls climbed the guy ropes to get a glimpse of their idols.

The Beatles say they play beat music whatever that is[,] and whatever it is . . . it's catching.

# *DAILY EXPRESS* COLUMNS

**George Harrison and Derek Taylor | January–August 1964 |** *Daily Express*

In late 1963, as the Beatles came to the end of their first year conquering Great Britain, Manchester's *Daily Express*—one of the first newspapers to positively report on and support them—asked Brian Epstein if one member of the group would be interested in penning a series of columns for the *Daily*. The idea was cooked up by Derek Taylor, the staff writer who had written a rave review of the band the previous summer. Taylor would eventually leave the paper to become the Beatles' groundbreaking press officer, a guiding force in the group's history for many years.

Harrison was nominated to write these columns, of which only a dozen or so appeared between January and midsummer of 1964. They were in fact cowritten by Taylor, who at first imagined he'd be ghostwriting them alone. But as he later wrote, he almost lost the gig before it had even begun.

> I was pleased when George's *Daily Express* column fell to me, but I started on the wrong foot. I did a real ghosting job. George's father was a bus driver, so I invented a conversation between his father and him in typical popular newspaper style. It went like this: "So my dad said to me, 'Don't worry about me son, you stick to your guitar and I'll carry on driving the big green jobs.'"

"What are big green jobs?" Harrison asked after Taylor read his first effort; Lennon was just as mystified. Taylor confessed he'd invented the term to describe Liverpool buses. That he freely admitted his invention impressed Harrison. "George said, 'I'll help you write the column—we can do it together.'"

Harrison took on an active role, choosing the focus of the reports. He collaborated with Taylor and later another staff reporter, Ivor Davis, providing *Daily Express* readers reports from inside the Beatles's comet-like ascent in the first half of 1964, capturing the buildup to and their first days in America: *The Ed Sullivan Show*, Washington Coliseum, Carnegie Hall, Miami. Harrison's *Daily Express* columns established a friendship and partnership between Harrison and Taylor that endured for decades. —Ed.

## January 16, 1964

Swamped in Mid-Champs (Paris, Wednesday)

The Yeah-Yeahs—that's what the Parisians are calling us. Cute title!
The only cloud over the trip so far has been Ringo's disappearing act in the fogs of Liverpool.
But he flew in from London this afternoon and it's nice to have him back.
Three Beatles are not the same as four. It's like losing a limb.
We stopped the traffic in the Champs-Elysées today, or rather hordes of girls did, clamouring for autographs.
John, Paul, and I had gone for a mid-afternoon stroll in the gentle sunshine when we were spotted.
Beautiful girls ran from gown shops waving paper and pens. French cabbies cursed and waved their fists as we were engulfed.
Next we tried to sit at a kerb-side café for a drink, but it was impossible.
We ran for a taxi, a crowd followed, and a new traffic jam started.
The gendarmerie dragged people off the bonnet of the taxi and we escaped to our hotel.
Is Beatlemania starting up here? There are signs . . .
A 13-year old English girl, Jeanne Collinson, told me as I signed my name for her: "Paris is getting ready to go crazy. The English over here have made sure of that."
John and Paul slept until 3 p.m. today—reinforcing themselves for tonight's try-out opening in Versailles.
They didn't go out on the town last night. I did. Night-clubbing in the Place Pigalle and didn't get to bed until 5am.
I would have slept through, but the phone rang at about 10 a.m. and an English girl's voice said: "I'm ringing from London. Is Paul there?"

I said: "No. He's kipping. Who's that?" She giggled a bit and I realised it was a fan.

There are hundreds of marvelous chicks here—neat, very much in control of themselves.

If you look at a French girl she looks straight back and smiles. It simply means, "Thank you."

Otherwise a smart French girl is very much like a smart girl the world over. I think girls are here to stay.


## January 31, 1964

We've Lots More Songs to Sing You

How long will the Beatles last? How long will we be "hot" as we are now? Is Beatlemania over?

I'm not asking these questions. Nor are John, Paul, or Ringo. But others are. So many people want to know what the distant future holds for us.

We don't. We live for the present or, at the most, for the day after tomorrow.

This doesn't mean we're saying the future doesn't matter. Just that we don't go peering into 1965 or 1984, looking for trouble. Well, how long will we last then? We can't expect in 10 years time to come on stage singing "Twist and Shout" or "She Loves You" or their 1974 successors. We can't all stay single forever. And I don't think the Beatles' image could stand another marriage.

John's did no harm. One married Beatle is O.K. But two or more, no. Still, how long will we last?

You ain't seen nothing yet. Remember we've not yet travelled beyond Northern Europe. A month ago we were totally unknown in America. Then suddenly, it all happened. We became top of all the charts. And we've yet to appear in person. There's a huge continent to conquer when we land at Idlewild on February 7.

And there's Australia, the Middle East, Africa, Canada.

All these places to visit and it's a mere 16 months since our first British record crept into the charts at No. 17.

We thought once that a broadcast would be the greatest things that could happen. We got one. Then we thought TV would be fab. That happened. Then we wanted a series. Got one.

The pace increased. Top of the bill at the Palladium knocked us out with excitement. But the Royal Show capped the lot and we thought nothing bigger could happen.

We went to Paris and found they liked us. Then we learned we topped the U.S. hit parade.

This, we thought, was the ultimate. What was there left to do? What? Carnegie Hall. The greatest concert hall in the world.

Is there anything bigger for us? The answer is probably Yes.

We start our film in March and this opens up all sorts of opportunities. It could be a big success with more to follow.

We've years of life and great hopes as a foursome. And though we will, one day, lose the position of number one teenage rave, though we may have to leave Liverpool and base ourselves in London, and though we all may marry, there's still a lot of work to be done and a lot of songs to sing.


**February 7, 1964**

Can the Beatles Beat New York?

Today we fly to New York on the most vital journey of our lives. We have one aim: to conquer the United States.

We know we may be knocked and knocked hard. No nation likes to be taken by storm by foreigners. And the U.S., birthplace of pop music, isn't going to give us an easy run.

Our records are selling in the millions over there. Our act—on film—has been seen on television. Our faces and our haircuts are now well known. The build-up in curiosity value has been tremendous and we hope this will be an advantage. But there's a chance that the advance publicity may act against us.

We're totally exposed—naked you might say—and the Americans are going to look very long and very hard at us.

"So O.K.," they'll be saying with their shrewd showbiz eyes. "You're here. So what's so good? Show us."

We hope to show them. We will step into the piercing spotlight on the great stage at Carnegie Hall and we will sing and play as well as we can, as hard as we can as we always do and always did.

More than that we can't do and we believe it will be enough. From Cavern to Carnegie is 3,000 miles and as many dollars but, ultimately, they are both show business.

John, Paul, Ringo and I are full of confidence. For once we're knocked out with excitement and anticipation.

It's a nice change, because with so much happening during the last year we've built a defence mechanism to keep things in perspective.

We've become blasé deliberately because if we hadn't we'd have gone round the bend with nervous excitement.

We've been getting most of our kicks from soft things—like singing the wrong line or nearly missing a plane.

When you're together as much as the four of us are—and often under pressure—you get to laughing at simple things. We play life on a low key and this way we avoid rows.

We never have bad arguments, which is surprising because there's a lot of artistic temperament under the surface and not one of us is like the other.

A lot of rubbish has been written about our personalities. John is supposed to be a relaxed, laconic comedian. But this isn't the whole picture or even the right one.

John is a little shy, defensive, always aware of people, interested in their motives and not always pleased by what he finds.

In public, Ringo sings little and says less. But in private he is the star—far and away the party boy of the four of us.

He talks plenty, wittily, in a dry, throwaway style. He's the one the girls want to dance with. The life and soul. Paul, easy-going, wide-eyed. Paul has concealed depths.

He has strong views on everything, great belief in himself, and immense ambition.

He is a born leader, though within the Beatles no one leads.

As a foursome we are aware of our success: grateful and pleased but no more than that.

We never boast and try not to think boastfully, because we know there is a cliff-edge at the point where vanity takes over from self-confidence. And we are not yet ready to die. Not nearly ready.


**February 11, 1964**

How Those Girls Love Ringo! (New York, Monday)

Well, we did it—made our first live appearance on American TV. And it went fine.

Mind you we had something great going for us—the audience. And something else.

About half an hour before we were going to go on the Ed Sullivan Show our Press agent, Brian Sommerville, handed us a telegram.

"You might be interested," he said.

Interested! It was from Elvis Presley and his manager Colonel Tom Parker, welcoming us to America and wishing us the best for the show. It was a terrific gesture and made us feel wonderful. So we went before the cameras in great form.

The audience was fabulous. They started screaming from the second we appeared. Mind you, Ed Sullivan had given us a great build-up. The fans shouting and cheering like crazy. Especially over Ringo. He really seems to have something big for the American girls.

But he doesn't know what it is. He just shakes his head and they go mad. People have asked me here, "Are the American fans any different to the British?"

They're not really. They still react in the same way and shout the same things, except it's in an American accent.

They use different phrases in their letters. I had a note today from a boy who wrote that he had no father and no brothers and asked: "Will you be my big brother?"

That's a new one. And it's new, too, the way the fans telephone. In England if they get on the phone they'll go on talking and talking for ever. The Americans are quicker and straight to the point. They say: "I just want to welcome you to America. I think you're great. I know you'll enjoy it here. Goodbye."

Anyway, tomorrow we're off to Washington [*D.C.*] and the first of our big concerts, and that night we're going to a masked charity ball at the British Embassy—which could be a gas.

Then it's back to New York and Carnegie Hall. That's what we're really looking forward to.

Footnote by Frank Sinatra: "I thought the Beatles would die in New York. I was very surprised by the reception they got. I guess I was wrong."

**February 13, 1964**

The Tingling Effect of the Fans! (Washington, Wednesday)

I suppose millions of words have been written on the effect we have on fans. Psychiatrists get into the act everywhere we go. And sociologists. And psychologists.

The facts, as we always say, are that we don't know why we make audiences react the way that they do. They just do it.

What's never been discussed is what the audiences do to us. This emotional reaction is not just a one-way thing—it's a communication.

Last night at the Washington Coliseum we played to the biggest and the best audience ever to attend a Beatle show. There were 8,600 there and they let us know it every second.

It is really an electric thing. The emotion coming from the fans hits you right in the stomach and then practically takes over.

A lot of people say that we played as we have never played before last night. It could be true. We really hooked in and let go.

Ringo told me afterwards that he could feel the excitement of the audience going right through him.

It's very hard to explain this physical thing. It isn't a pain. But a feeling, a tingling, a vibration that hits you, spreads all over your body until you're glowing. It's elation and it generates its own vitality and honestly takes you over.

You feel you could go on and on for ever. Time stands still. There's only the moment and you're living it. That's how we feel and maybe that's how the fans feel.

Afterwards you're tired but you feel great.

So much has been happening here that it's hard to remember where and when.

The hotel switchboard in New York has been flooded with calls. And although we've given them the names of people who should be put through it doesn't always work out.

Yesterday Brian Epstein, our manager, tried to phone me and they wouldn't put him through!


**February 14, 1964**

They All Ask What Makes a Beatle Tick (New York, Thursday)

Ever since we've been here the Americans have been trying to find out what makes us tick—particularly me. The newspapers, as well as sending reporters and photographers to our press conferences, have been sending psychiatrists and psychologists.

Actually, we thought it might be interesting if there was some explanation for our success. But we're no nearer finding that out from the psychiatrists than from anyone else.

John says he isn't reading any more of what they are writing. "It's a load of old rubbish," he said. "Enough to send you to a psychiatrist."

Still, they keep trying. The other day one of them got up and asked: "Ringo is known for his rings. Paul obviously for his looks, and John for his marriage. Then there's you, Mr. Harrison—what are you known for?"

I told them: "Just as long as I get an equal share of the money I'm willing to stay anonymous."

In fact, we all have a good giggle at the labels that are pinned on us. They are a long way removed from the truth.

There's no real shy one, no real sexy one. But as long as the money comes on and they go on liking us, they can call us what they want.

The big point in this business is to take it how it comes and be flexible. It's no good being swept away by your own publicity man. That way you're done for.

And it's no good thinking all the girls screaming and shouting when you play are in love with you.

And quite honestly none of us does. We love our fans, but we have adapted ourselves to them. And that's why I think they still like us.


## February 15, 1964

Manners? The Parents Need a Few Lessons! (Miami, Friday)

Sunny Florida at last! The temperature is 75degs and when I looked out of my hotel window this morning I could see the bluest sea I ever set eyes upon.

Marvellous! And now we want to relax—if we get a chance. For the crowds here when we Beatles flew in were even bigger than in New York. It was a great welcome. And the girls—they were great.

There was a line of bathing beauties all tanned and blonde waiting with welcome gifts for us and we hardly stepped off the plane before we were kissing them for the photographers.

It's a great place for show business. Bob Hope and Red Skelton stayed in our hotel. Carol Lawrence is here too appearing in the supper club.

But the main things that interest us are sunshine and privacy. Although we had a fabulous trip it has been exhausting.

The worst thing about America, despite what some commentators have said, is not the teenage fans but their parents.

It's the adults who come to us in hotels, trains, and planes who have given us a rough time. They're so rude.

Last night outside a Miami restaurant an expensively dressed man came up to Paul with a piece of paper in his hand to ask for an autograph. This is the way he did it: "I have two teenage children who listen to your records. God only knows why. I wouldn't. But they are going all day long in my house. So sign this."

It was the same in the plane coming down here. The first-class passengers asked for so many autographs you might have thought they were going into the business of selling them. One man wanted 13 of each.

They talk about teenagers, but some of the so-called adults could take a few lessons from their kids in the case of manners.

Still, that's just a minor moan of what has been the greatest trip ever—for all of us.


## February 21, 1964

Miami Beach—This Is the Life for Me! (New York, Thursday)

We all fell in love—with Miami Beach. We think it's the greatest place we've ever seen. We had a fabulous time.

We love our work but it was great not having to do any for a few days. And it was only while we were relaxing that we suddenly realised that we had had practically five months without a single day off.

One day we went deep-sea fishing. And I was the only Beatle to get a catch. It wasn't very big but it was mine.

Paul had a bash at water skiing—he's tried it before. And we all had a marvellous time dashing around the bay in our own speedboats.

On land it was just as good. I was lent a blue MG and the roads were great. Whipping along in the sunshine with the hood down is my idea of a holiday.

Mind you, it wasn't all holiday. We were out in a yacht the other day, a whopping great thing almost as big as the Queen Mary. For a while we just lay on the deck with cool drinks in our hands. But Paul's a worker. He wandered off and a few minutes later we heard the notes of a piano. He'd found one in the saloon.

So we all got up and gathered round. John got a pencil and paper and we started to work on some new songs. Not a bad way to compose, cruising along off the coast of Florida.

We got a start on a couple of numbers. They need polishing—but we hope you'll be listening to them soon. We'll be recording when we get back to England.

The Americans love to jump into things with great excitement and enthusiasm. That's why our merchandising has gone over so big. Every fan has a Beatle button, a Beatle badge, hat or sweater. It's fantastic.

And us—we're wearing sweaters too, with "Stamp out the Beatles" on them. They come from Detroit and we think they're great. But we're also getting another set of sweaters with "Stamp out Detroit" on them.

Right now they're talking about bringing us back in the autumn. This time to see the Mid-West and California.

Suits us. As far as we're concerned, it's a great life.

And here we are back in New York. Then on to London to arrive on Saturday morning.

Be seeing you.

[*A few more reports bore George Harrison's byline in June, filed from the Beatles's first tour of Asia and Australia. His final Daily Express column appears to be this one, from the kickoff date—August 19, 1964—of the group's second, equally chaotic American tour. —Ed.*]

## August 21, 1964

We Are Bombarded By 18,000 Audience (San Francisco, Thursday)

Even the cops went wild. They ringed the stage at San Francisco's massive Cow Palace. Behind them, close to 18,000 happy young Americans. This was by far the biggest audience that's ever seen us and it was one of the most thrilling experiences of our lives. And one of the most painful. I lost count of the number of times those hard little jellybeans were showered upon us from four sides of the gigantic arena. I got hit on the back of the neck, on the face, on the nose, and on both hands, and also on my guitar. Performing in the Cow Palace is like playing in the Mersey Tunnel. Its huge, arched ceiling seemed to extend to the heavens. People in the back seats looked like little black ants.

But the place has atmosphere, and although there were scores of uniformed sheriff's men to control the crowd and the houselights went on, the excitement was terrific.

We were glad Sheriff Whitmore's men managed to hold back the surging, screaming crowd. Many of them were caged-in behind a nine-foot mesh fence only a few inches from Ringo's expensive head.

We flew into Las Vegas on our 70-seater charter plane early today. This city is just another world. We are staying on the Strip at the Sahara Hotel in the centre of the desert.

I am writing this on the balcony in the hot, dry morning sun. Ahead lie two Vegas concerts and a night on the town. There are worse lives than this.

# RADIO INTERVIEW

**Carroll James | February 11, 1964 | WWDC**

Beyond the impromptu and chaotic press conferences the Beatles gave during the first US tour in early 1964—sparring with reporters and making fun of any straight or uninformed questions—there were a few interviews that were friendlier and more supportive. One was conducted by WWDC disc jockey Carroll James in Washington, D.C. James, as the Beatles learned during the interview, was reportedly the first stateside deejay to play the Beatles on a commercial radio show the previous December, honoring the request of Marsha Albert, a teenage listener who was aware of the band and had asked James to play "I Want to Hold Your Hand." (Harrison kept it to himself that he had been interviewed the previous September on a small Illinois station that played the Beatles.)

 "I Want to Hold Your Hand" soon proved to be the Beatles' first number one hit in the US. James spoke to the band after the performance in a remote studio at the Washington Coliseum, the venue that housed the Beatles' first-ever show in America; during the conversation, he introduced the group to Albert. In this excerpt from the interview that focused on Harrison, the quiet one again proves himself on par with his mates in his comic inventiveness and taste for the nonsensical. What, really, is a "baggy sweeger"? —Ed.

**Carroll James**: You, George, are the only Beatle who had been in America before this trip. Is that correct?

**George Harrison**: Yeah. That's correct.

**James**: Went to visit your sister a few months ago.

**Harrison**: Yeah. September.

**James**: At that time, did anybody out there know of the Beatles?

**Harrison**: Nobody had here, either. In New York, I went into a record shop to ask if they'd ever heard of us and they hadn't. No, that was October.

**James**: That was October. And then we started hearing things in this country, I guess, first around November. And in December, WWDC flew your record "I Want to Hold Your . . ."'

**Harrison**: You did?

**James**: Yes.

**Harrison**: Thanks, that was great.

**Paul McCartney and Ringo Starr**: Thanks.

**John Lennon**: Thank you very much.

**James**: Well, you're very welcome. I'd like you to meet the young lady, right after we're finished talking here, Marsha Albert is . . . Come on in here very quickly, Marsha.

**Starr**: All right, Marsha.

**McCartney**: Hello, Marsha.

**Lennon**: Good ol' Marsha!

**Harrison**: Marsha Mellow.

**Starr**: Thank you, Marsha.

**James**: [*To Lennon*] They call you the chief Beatle . . .

**Lennon**: Look, I don't call *you* names. Why do you have to call me names?

**James**: Who is responsible for the haircut?

**Lennon**: Well, I think it's . . . bigger than both of us, Carroll. That's all I can say.

**Starr**: Nobody, really.

**James**: When you went to high school—grammar school—what did you have in mind as a career?

**McCartney**: I don't know. At that time I thought of being a teacher, actually. But luckily I got into this business, because I would have been a very bad teacher.

**James**: George?

**Harrison**: I was going to be a baggy sweeger.

**James**: I beg your pardon?

**Harrison**: A baggy sweeger.

**James**: And what is that?

**Harrison**: Well, you see, in every city there are twenty-five baggy sweegers. And their job is to go out to the airport each morning . . .

**McCartney**: [*Laughing*] Baggy sweeger!

**Harrison**: . . . and baggy sweeging all along the line, man.

# TOUR INTERVIEWS

**Larry Kane | February 1964–August 1965 | *Ticket to Ride***

Larry Kane, the sole broadcast journalist to witness every one of the Beatles' appearances on their historic 1964 and '65 American tours, was just twenty-one when he met them for the first time. He traveled with the band, on the same planes and in the same hotels, having convinced his higher-ups at Miami radio station WAME to invest the $2,500 to do so. Among the three books Kane later wrote of his experience in the center of the Beatlemania bubble—*Ticket to Ride*, *Lennon Revealed*, and *When They Were Boys*—he included the letter he received from Derek Taylor's office, confirming his press credentials for the Beatles' first tour of the US. (He also later released the audio of his interviews and actualities from their tours.)

Kane's youth helped him appreciate the music and the phenomenon, but he was no cub reporter. He had been at it since the age of sixteen, already distinguishing himself by being one of the first to report on the thwarted Bay of Pigs invasion in 1961. But applying skills honed on political and hard news stories to the Beatles was a challenge. As one listens to Kane chatting with each Beatle—usually one at a time—it's clear the young journalist was striving to find the right questions to ask, though they are often leading. The interactions were brief—he caught them backstage or midflight—and reveal him earnestly trying to understand their craft, respecting their talent and dedication, and being dismayed by the dismissive manner many in the US media treated them with.

Kane admired the four, and Harrison in particular, whom he described in *Ticket to Ride* as "one of the most unaffected people I ever met, in show business or out . . . [he was] clearly and simply the most honest Beatle." —Ed.

KANE: There are a lot of fan magazines that have rumors. Does that ever bug you?

HARRISON: It drives you up a wall sometimes. Since we've been over here they've been asking us, "Is John leaving?" Well, the new one today is it's me leaving. You know, that's just because some idiot in Hollywood has written in the papers that I'm leaving, so now I will have for weeks people coming up time after time and asking, "Is it true you are leaving?"

---

Q: George some in the press say your music is bad. [*The question is from an unnamed individual; Kane recorded other question-and-answer exchanges with the Beatles that he witnessed besides his own. —Ed.*]

HARRISON: It is, don't you think?

Q: Will you get married?

HARRISON: Do you think anybody will have me?

---

KANE: George, we've been hearing things, and reading about this woman who's predicting plane disaster [*popular psychic Jeane Dixon, who made the prediction that the Beatles' plane would crash after a concert in Philadelphia in 1964. —Ed.*].

HARRISON: Uh, normally, I just take it with a laugh and a smile and a pinch of salt. Thinking, you know, she's off her head. But, y'know, it's not a nice thing to say, especially when you're flying almost every day. But, just hope for the best, and keep a stiff upper head, and away we go. If you crash, you crash. When your number's up, that's it.

---

KANE: Have you ever had trouble replicating your sound onstage?

HARRISON: No way, Larry. From the beginning, when we were taping, we always did it in one take. We never did any of that overdubbing and that stuff. We are what we are.

---

KANE: Do you have any individual plans for songwriting in the future?

HARRISON: Well, I am still trying to turn out a couple. My main problem is trying to write lyrics, and I don't think it is worth writing songs and getting someone else to write lyrics because you don't feel as if you have done it, really. So I have written a few more songs I've got taped at home, but if I get something going, then I'll tape it. I'll leave it for about five weeks, then I'll suddenly remember. Then I'll add a bit more to it, and so it will probably take me about three months before I finish one song. I'm so lazy it's ridiculous, but I'd like to write more.

---

KANE: Okay. The guitar that you have, right—I should say the guitar that you're playing—has twelve strings. Now why, the song "If I Fell" during the act, you change guitars. What is the reason behind this?

HARRISON: Uh, 'cause it's got a different sound, y'see. With a twelve-string, it's two sets of each—I mean, there's two lots of each string, y'see. Only, instead of it being tuned the same, they're in octaves, y'see, so instead of getting this note [plays a note] like you would on a normal one, you get [plays same note an octave higher]. So you get [high note] and [low note] both together, so it gives you that noise, y'see. It's—it's a higher sound. And with it being electric, it's a good sound, and I, so the one's I've used, um, when I've used this on a record, I use it onstage as well, y'see, that's why I'm always swapping 'round.

---

KANE: How did you react inside? [*regarding a harrowing midflight fire the Beatles and Kane had experienced* —Ed.]

HARRISON: Well, the first reaction was, What smoke? When I looked and saw it, and we all ran to the back where we were far away from the flames—cowards as we are, you know—all sat around the emergency door and even tested the emergency door, ready to jump out. Of course, I said, "Beatles and children first."

KANE: What are your immediate reflections on your visit last night with Elvis Presley?

HARRISON: Great actually, I liked it a lot because I didn't expect him to be half as nice as he was.

KANE: I understand he gave you guys a whole box full of records.

HARRISON: Yeah, we asked the Colonel [*Tom Parker, Elvis's manager*] when we saw him the other day for Elvis's very early albums which are deleted right now in England. But they're the ones we liked so [he] gave us a parcel each.

KANE: Did he live up to your expectations as far as a person . . . ?

HARRISON: He was more . . . he was a bit more than I anticipated.

KANE: In what way?

HARRISON: Well, uhm, I expected him to be quieter and for him to not have such an amount of noise in his house. In fact when we walked into his house it was exactly like going into ours. It was great—it was the record player, TV, and electric guitar, all playing all at once, you know . . .

KANE: What did you do over there?

HARRISON: Well, we had drinks, some played pool, some were playing roulette, we were playing electric guitars and playing records and watching TV—everything, you know.

KANE: Did you have any serious discussions about music?

HARRISON: We talked a little about, asking him why he didn't record some of the older stuff or something in the old style, because we thought that was much better. And he seemed to want to do something like that himself. But we didn't really talk that much about business things, because it's quite hard meeting people like that— hard for him or for us—it's a bit embarrassing. But you know, so we laid off and talked about different things altogether—like about other people and other records.

KANE: On your first U.S. visit, George, you were known as the quiet Beatle, the somber, thoughtful, and pensive one, and suddenly here in 1965 you've kind of, according to most people's way of thinking, opened up. You're talking a lot at the press conferences, a lot of questions are directed at you. What's the reason for all of that?

HARRISON: Actually, I did talk about the same amount on the last tour. It's just that, you know, first of all, when we first came over here they didn't know us all that well. People, like, hang tags on you. Ringo was the cuddly one or something. Paul was the lovely one and I was the quiet one, and John was the shouting one. I've been the same all along. I talk when I feel like it. I shut up when I don't feel like talking.

# RADIO INTERVIEWS

**George Harrison | March 22, 1964 | *The Public Ear*, BBC Radio**

Back in the United Kingdom, during the filming of *A Hard Day's Night*, the Beatles' first full-length feature film of many to come, Harrison was asked to conduct a number of short interviews with his band members for the BBC radio program *The Public Ear*. The program's producers chose wisely, as the results below show. —Ed.

**George Harrison**: Well this week, we have a special person for you on our program—none other than John Lennon of the Beatles. Well John, I believe you've written a "bewk." And this "bewk's" called *John Lennon in His Own Write*, folks. W-R-I-T-E, you see. It's a larf. It's a larf a minute with John Lennon. Some of you might find it a bit difficult to understand, because you see it's in a sort of funny lingo. Well, we get it, you see. It's full of larfs. I don't really know how you could describe it. But, it's sort of rubbish. Maybe that's one way. Well, sitting on my left I have another person of the Beatles called Ringo Starr. What, Ringo, do you think of this book by John Lennon?

**Ringo Starr**: Well, I think it's marvelous. I mean, I've never read anything like it.

**Harrison**: You've never read before, though, have you?

**Starr**: No. I can't read, you see. That's why I've never . . . I mean, the stories are so funny, I just . . . Ha-ha! I mean, the titles are so funny. "Partly Dave," and what else have we got here? We got many a nice story. "Sad Michael"—that's a sad story. "The Famous Five through Woenow

Abbey"—that's a well-known place. "Randolf's Party," I mean, that's one not to be missed by anybody. We also have "The Wrestling Dog." Many little drawings which will make you laugh.

**Harrison**: Larf . . .

**Starr**: George is trying to lose his accent, you see.

**Harrison**: Well thank you, Ringo. So I'd just like to hand you over to John Lennon. And what are you going to read for us?

**John Lennon**: Well just so happens, George, I've got a copy of me book here, and I'll read a poem what is called "Alec Speaking."

> "He is putting it lithely when he says
> Quobble in the Grass
> Strab he down the soddieflays
> Amo amat amass
> Amonk, amink, a minibus
> Amarmylaidie Moon
> Amikky mendip multiplus
> Amighty midgey spoon
> And so I traddled onward
> Caring not a care
> Onward, Onward, Onward.
> [*Loudly*] Onward my friends, and glory for the fifty-ninth!!"

Actually, it's the thirty-ninth, but I goofed.

**Harrison**: Well thank you, John, thank you. This is the last program, isn't it, Ringo?

**Starr**: Aww. They're awfully . . .

**Harrison**: Because we like doing *Public Ear*. We think it's a great program because when we're on tour, we listen to it. Don't we, Ringo?

**Starr**: Yeah, it's a fab show.

**Harrison:** Well, we just have been out for dinner at the Dorchester. And, Paul McCartney, would you like to say a few words to the listeners of *Public Ear*?

**Paul McCartney:** Uhh, yes. What about them, George?

**Harrison:** How are you enjoying filming? This is your first film, isn't it, Paul?

**McCartney:** Yes. The first film we ever made, and we're having a good time. We're not very good actors, but we're trying hard. That's the most important thing, really—having a try, isn't it?

**Harrison:** Yes. I suppose it is, Paul. Well, are you having any trouble learning your lines, or anything like that?

**McCartney:** Well actually, George, I'm a bit lazy about that. I normally learn them about ten minutes before we do the scene, actually. I feel it gives an air of impromptu-ity.

**Harrison:** I see. How's the director of the film?

**McCartney:** Well, yes. Dick Lester's directing the film . . . uhh, what's your name? George?

**Harrison:** George, yeah. BBC! I'm from the BBC, you see. *Public Ear*.

**McCartney:** Anyway, his name is Dick Lester. He's a good fella. He's bald, but don't hold that against him. He's one of the nicest fellows I've met, and he's a great director. I think he's going to save the film in the cutting rooms. Great fellow, he is.

**Harrison:** What do you mean, "He's going to save it in the cutting rooms?" What exactly do you mean by that, Paul?

**McCartney:** Well you see, George, the acting may not be very good, but if he can cut it up and slice it around and slop bits in here and slop bits in there, he may make it into a good film, you see.

**Harrison:** I see. Well thank you, Paul. And you'll receive your three-shilling fee at a later date.

**McCartney:** Don't mention it, George. Thank you.

# TELEDATE: SYLVIA STEPHEN TALKING TO GEORGE HARRISON

**Sylvia Stephen | June 13, 1964 | *Fabulous***

What better magazine to cover the Beatles than one which began publishing in January 1964, bearing the same epithet as the Fab Four. *Fabulous* was established to cover the explosion of music groups then stealing the fire from other celebrities—screen idols and such. Like most fan zines of that era, it focused more on lifestyle details and puff pieces: color centerfolds of the leading faces of the day suitable for pinning up and limited discussion of music or music making.

This brief chat with Harrison in early summer '64 took place a month after principal photography—a grueling seven weeks—of the group's debut film *A Hard Day's Night* had been completed. In his reply about the hurry-and-wait process of moviemaking, one can feel him starting to grow a bit weary of the celebrity bit, wanting to speak of how things actually were. But a journalist bent on including herself in a Beatles story (Stephens was not the first and certainly not the last) and a distracting knock on the door from other band members denied Harrison the chance to speak about anything more significant than waterskiing. —Ed.

Y'know, I'd like to adopt George Harrison. (Sit down those girls who yelled "So would we.") I don't have a favourite Beatle, they're all FAB, but George is the one I always want to take home to Mum so she can feed him, especially when he tells me, as he did when he 'phoned recently, that he usually only manages to grab a spoonful of cornflakes for breakfast. What else did he say? What, you mean you're interested? I'll tell you then.

**SYLVIA** *(picking up 'phone)*: 'Lo.

**GEORGE:** Hello, missis.

**SYLVIA** *(grinning)*: George Harrison, don't be cheeky.

**GEORGE:** How did you know it was me?

**SYLVIA:** 'Cos you're the only person in show business who calls me 'Missis.' Anyway, how are things?

**GEORGE:** Great, couldn't be better. We've finished the film now.

**SYLVIA:** So I gather. How did you enjoy working on it?

**GEORGE:** Marvelous, except that they made us get up at the crack of dawn every day. Terrible, it was. We're not used to getting up that early.

**SYLVIA:** Well you usually start work about the time most people are going to bed. What time did you finish in the evening?

**GEORGE:** Six, usually. Filming was fun, really, especially as half the time you don't know what's going on.

**SYLVIA:** Now, that I do not believe!

**GEORGE** *(laughing)*: But it's true.

**SYLVIA:** Come off it, George. You and the boys always know what's going on.

**GEORGE** *(serious again)*: Well you know what I mean. On a film, you don't shoot from the beginning of a story through to the end. You do a bit from the end, a bit from the middle, a bit from the beginning. Dead confusing. I can't wait to see it.

**SYLVIA:** Norman Rossington, who plays your road manager Neil in the film, told me it was unlike working on any other film. He said he did nothing but laugh.

**GEORGE:** Yeah. Well, we like to laugh.

**SYLVIA:** I had noticed that before, actually. How did you feel about all the hanging around—there's an awful lot of that when you're filming?

**GEORGE:** Oh, 'orrible. Boring. You'd be at the studio maybe eight hours and be lucky if you worked one. We like to keep going.

**SYLVIA:** Is there any country you'd prefer?

**GEORGE:** Let me see. I like places that are really hot. I love the sun.

**SYLVIA:** Oh, then you'd really dig the Canary Islands.

**GEORGE** *(amazed)*: You're joking! We went there last year and it rained all the time.

**SYLVIA** *(more amazed)*: I was there for *FAB* awhile back and I got a gorgeous tan.

**GEORGE:** Well, either you were very lucky or we were very unlucky. Y'know, I think I'd like to go to Egypt.

**SYLVIA** *(grinning at the thought of a Beatle among the Pyramids)*: Yes. I'm sure that would be very interesting. Or you could go back to Miami.

**GEORGE** *(regretfully)*: Did I tell you I tried some water skiing while I was out there?

**SYLVIA** *(enviously)*: Lucky you! What was it like?

**GEORGE** *(enthusiastically)*: Great. I came a cropper once, though. I told the man at the helm of the boat to go real fast. He did, and I lost my balance. And they rescued the skis first—just left me there. "Never mind them," I yelled. "Come and get me out!"

**SYLVIA:** Poor George. Are you a good swimmer?

**GEORGE:** I can swim. But I couldn't go for long distances, like some people. Ringo's here, and he heard us talking about places to visit. He says to tell you he'd like to go to Basuti.

**SYLVIA:** To where??!??!

**GEORGE:** Basuti.

**SYLVIA:** Where's that?

**GEORGE:** I don't know. Where's that, Ringo? Huh? He says he doesn't know either, but he's going there.

**SYLVIA** *(helpless)*: Tell him I hope he has a very nice time.

**GEORGE** *(to Ringo)*: Stephens hopes you have a nice time. But you want to watch out for elephants, you know. Tigers, too. What? Of course there are tigers in Basuti. Everyone knows that. What d'you mean, I don't know what I'm on about?

SYLVIA (*yelling*): George!!

GEORGE (*innocently*): Yes, missis? Can you hang on a minute please? There's someone at the door. Ringo! Answer the door.

SYLVIA: Is it anyone interesting?

GEORGE: I don't know yet. (*Pause*) Oh no, not very. Only John and Paul.

SYLVIA (*weakly*): *Only John and Paul* the man says.

GEORGE: How's everyone on *FAB* by the way? Paul wants to know which of you I'm talking to. (*To Paul*) Sylvie. Let go of the 'phone, I haven't finished talking to her yet. I don't suppose she wants to talk to you anyway.

SYLVIA (*yelling again*): George! I'd love to talk to Paul.

GEORGE (*obviously not to Sylvia*): Ow! Watch it, Paul!

SYLVIA (*hearing a scuffle*): George, what's going on? George!

But that was the end of that conversation. I still don't know quite what happened. I don't suppose George does, either.

# MAGAZINE INTERVIEW

**David Hull and Derek Taylor | April 7, 1965 | *KRLA Beat***

This seaside interview took place as the sun beat down and the waves crashed on New Providence Island in the Bahamas. The Beatles were on location, filming scenes for their second movie *Eight Arms to Hold You*—eventually retitled *Help!*

Radio deejay Dave Hull (aka "The Hullabalooer") and Derek Taylor (the Beatles' former press officer who had recently relocated to California) both contributed to *KRLA Beat*, a music publication established by Los Angeles's popular rock radio station in 1964. The two traveled to the Bahamas to record interviews with the band, catching up with Harrison as he lounged in jeans and a shade hat on the beach. Their conversation became the second of a four-part series aired by KRLA, was published in the station's magazine, and was eventually syndicated to a number of other stations around the US.

Harrison is cordial to his old mate and writing partner from '63 and '64 and to one of America's leading deejays. But there seems to be a tired note in Harrison's responses, even in his excitement about Kinfauns, his new home southwest of London, in Surrey. One can also detect the stirrings of future habits: gardening, cooking, and a preference for domesticity over traveling to exotic destinations (certainly not beaches). The questions posed were still largely focused on celebrity issues—the handling of fame and the juggling of old, new, and newer projects—with the remarkable comment on the band's work ethic: the eleven tracks for their next album *Help!* (seven of which would be heard in the film) were all recorded in one week. —Ed.

DEREK: With the gentle swish of the Caribbean behind me, this is Derek Taylor sitting thankfully in the sun on the beach of Nassau with George Harrison, who's wearing a straw hat and blue jeans, and looks extremely well. His long, dark hair is curly. He's, of course, one of the two single Beatles and I think the first to buy a house. He bought a house in Surrey which he takes considerable interest in. Anyway, George, let's say first it's nice to see you after about three months away.

GEORGE: Nice to see you again, Derek.

DEREK: How do you like it here?

GEORGE: I like it fine except that we're up at 7:00 in the morning every day on the set filming. It's good really because if you're off work there's nothing much to do. It gets boring just sitting in the sun and we'd all prefer to be up and working.

DEREK: I asked you because it may seem like a paradise to people who can't get into the sun to think of spending two or three weeks in the Bahamas. But of course you are working very hard all day.

GEORGE: Yeah, that's right. Well, we get up at 7:00 and we usually start about 8:00 or 8:30, right through and then have lunch for about a half hour, and then we work right through until the sun goes and there's no more light, which is usually about 5:30.

DEREK: The pattern of your life now seems to be with not so much touring. Now that you can record 11 numbers in five days you can have an awful lot of leisure. Do you have too much leisure, do you find?

GEORGE: No. We haven't had a great deal, really. This year, maybe, because after the film I'm not too sure what we're doing. I think we may have a week or so and then we go to Europe for about a week.

DEREK: Are you touring Europe?

GEORGE: I think we're doing six concerts—two in France and two in Italy and two in Spain.

DEREK: You've been in France. You haven't been to the other places before?

GEORGE: We've been to Spain—Paul, Ringo and I went.

DEREK: You didn't play there, though.

GEORGE: No.

DEREK: When that tour is over you presumably will then have a lot of time before visiting America.

GEORGE: That's August. I think in the meantime we'll have a new record out, doing TV and things in England. And then with a bit of luck the film will probably be out around about that time. So then we'll have the film songs out to plug and we'll have a premiere. And then I think it'll be the American trip. Or maybe the premiere will be after the American trip, which is in August.

DEREK: So in fact the pace in life seems to be almost as hot as it was. It appears deceptive.

GEORGE: We can't tell, really, because we haven't really been told exactly what's happening. We just vaguely know that it's America, and then for all we know we may start on our third film after the American trip, in which case, you know, we'll be . . .

DEREK: I notice that . . . you seem to be doing two films in one year.

GEORGE: We're trying to. I hope so because we enjoy it so much more than anything else.

DEREK: You prefer films?

GEORGE: Yeah, it's great. And when the film's finished you get more satisfaction from it. You feel as though you've done something worthwhile, more so than a tour.

DEREK: Brian Epstein did say once—I don't want to commit you to anything that you don't want to talk about—but he did say once that it might be you'd go more and more into filming, and into isolated shows. Is this going to be sooner than we expected?

GEORGE: I don't know. This depends on when we expected it.

DEREK: He meant in terms, I think, of next year.

GEORGE: We'd like to do more films and naturally a little less touring because . . .

DEREK: Touring's tiring.

GEORGE: Yes, it is. People don't realize that each day you jump out of bed onto an airplane and fly two thousand miles to do a show . . . You know that's not much fun, really.

DEREK: The American trip destroyed almost everybody. Everybody was a bit off their heads when it was over.

GEORGE: Yeah.

DEREK: Now going back to leisure, how do you spend your free time when you're home? Like spend a Sunday off?

GEORGE: On Sunday I have a lie-in, I suppose, and then . . .

DEREK: You're a great sleeper . . . a sleep worshipper, really.

GEORGE: Yeah, but I do like it if I can. It's just trying to get up. Since I've gotten my house I used to just lie around in the backyard last summer when it was quite hot. But now, as it's sort of freezing cold in England, on a Sunday I just get up and have a late breakfast about 12 o'clock.

DEREK: Have you got help in the house?

GEORGE: I've got a woman who comes in each day. She cooks dinner for me and keeps the place tidy.

DEREK: What's her name?

GEORGE: Margaret. Mrs. Walker. I read the Sunday papers and go out for a drive, and sometimes go out for lunch with some people.

DEREK: Do you eat more out than you do in?

GEORGE: Uh . . . I think so because I usually just eat in on the week-ends. I usually, on a Sunday, have friends over and just stay in and have dinner and watch TV.

DEREK: You've got a pretty good garden. You don't do it yourself, do you?

GEORGE: No.

DEREK: Do you like gardening?

GEORGE: Well, I like a sort of nice garden but it's too much trouble really. But the good thing about my garden is that most of it [is] just lawn. It's just lots of big lawn with trees and things.

DEREK: It's a new house though?

GEORGE: It's a bungalow, actually, just a big long bungalow.

DEREK: Bungalow it what we call a one-level house, I think.

GEORGE: Anyway, originally the fellow who built it is the fellow I bought it from [and he] was an Australian. He built it like an Australian ranch bungalow. It's about ten years old. Two years ago he had a new part built on the end so it's ten and two years old.

DEREK: Do you take an interest in the house in improving it or is it simply a place to live?

GEORGE: I like it.

DEREK: Are you a house-proud man? Do you talk about your house to other people?

GEORGE: Well, to friends and things I suppose. I like the idea of it looking great in the way I like it.

DEREK: Are your tastes in interior decorating simple?

GEORGE: Really being the first house ever of mine I've just tried to get it so that it pleases me. At first I got some fellow to get some furniture and he bought a lot of rubbish. Since then I decided I didn't really like it. He just bought odd stuff just so I could move in straight away. Since then I've changed it around a lot. Things I'd like to do if ever I buy another house is stay in this one until I get the new one furnished just how I like it and then move. I'm not a great believer in interior design and all that because it ends up you're living in the designer's house and I'd much rather do it myself.

DEREK: Yes, I quite agree. You were going to have a pool put in, I think, the last time I saw you. Is that still happening?

GEORGE: They started about two weeks before we left England, and actually the morning we left the airport there was a massive great hole dug out and mud all over the place, and one of these big diggers in the backyard. The workmen have got sheds built up. Every time I go out there I just hear music in the little shed and they're all playing cards and singing. They never seem to do any work. I'm hoping by the time I get back most of the mess will gone.

DEREK: Have you spent a lot of money on the house since you got it?

GEORGE: Uh . . . not really, no.

DEREK: What's it called, by the way, has it a name or a number or what?

GEORGE: It has a name but somebody pinched it.

DEREK: The fans know where it is, do they?

GEORGE: Well, some of them do. Actually there's a girls' school right next to it but the head mistress was good and she told the kids to give me a bit of privacy.

DEREK: Pursuing the point of leisure but now forgetting about the house, it has for a long time been quite easy for you in certain places to move around London as a normal human being in your own car. Can you explain how you've been able to do this because I've never never [sic] known how you managed it, how you park and how you get from the car to the theatre?

GEORGE: The thing is, if we're doing a show then that's the only time there is going to be thousands of people, really. If we're not doing a show and just going out for the night somewhere, there's not liable to be millions of people waiting for you to arrive at the restaurant because they don't know where you're going.

DEREK: But you still have the autograph books.

GEORGE: Oh, yeah.

DEREK: How do you avoid that? Do you go to selected places?

GEORGE: Now, you know, through experience, you just do it by . . . if you go to a place and have quite a good time and you're treated all right, then naturally you go back again. And usually the managers of places like you to go there so it's in their own interest, really, to make sure you're having quite a good time. But generally in London it's quite good.

DEREK: You're very fond of London, I think?

GEORGE: Yeah, I thing [sic] it's fabulous.

DEREK: Do you go home very often?

GEORGE: To Liverpool? I went there about three weeks ago. I was up there for a week . . . my brother got married.

DEREK: I saw the picture in the paper.

GEORGE: Yes. Really, there are so many people and friends to see in the short time I was there.

DEREK: You're like most people[:] you left the place you were born and you've grown very fond of London. It happens in most countries of the world. You probably grow away from places and grow up a bit. Never been any suggestion of your living outside England?

GEORGE: No.

DEREK: This is a good place to live here, of course.

GEORGE: Thing is, with a place like, say this beach we're sitting on now, I think it's marvelous and I'd love a house . . . but probably after two or three weeks of this I'd get fed up. I wouldn't mind living in a place like this . . . nice beach, nice sea, and sort of hot climate. But it's so boring after two weeks. But still I wouldn't mind a place like this say . . . every time I got fed up with the cold in England you could just fly out here. But still I prefer to live in a place like London anytime.

DEREK: Well, there's an awful lot happening in London and in Los Angeles, where your voice will be heard pretty soon—as soon as Dave Hull and I get back there. Los Angeles has a climate similar to this only cooler in winter and always much drier. Well, George, I won't keep you any more because I know you have to get on the set. It's been nice to see you and I'll see you later on today. I'll turn you over to Dave Hull now.

GEORGE: Okay, see you, Derek. Bye, Bye.

DAVE: How're you, George?

GEORGE: Hello, Dave, how're you?

DAVE: Good. You look comfortable, you've got on a pair of faded blue Levi's and an old straw hat . . .

GEORGE: They're not Levi's.

DAVE: Well they're jeans. In America we call them Levi's. That's what we call anything that's blue and faded. You got a straw hat on. Where'd you find that straw hat?

GEORGE: Just bought it here.

DAVE: I see you stole my dark glasses.

GEORGE: They're yours, are they?

DAVE: Yeah.

GEORGE: No they're not . . . I bought them.

DAVE: No you didn't, you just stole them from me. I just set them on the sand.

GEORGE: No you didn't, they're mine.

DAVE: No they're not.

GEORGE: They're not . . . I've had these on for days.

DAVE: Listen . . .

GEORGE: Don't believe this man . . . they're mine.

DAVE: Listen, this idol out there in the water that we're watching, is going to be a one-shot take, and it comes up and it's got ten arms. What has this got to do with the movie?

GEORGE: This is Kali, and . . . it's the sacrificial god or something. It's a bit involved. I'll wait until they finish making the film and then I'll go and see it and then I'll know what's happening.

DAVE: How come it has to be a one-shot take?

GEORGE: This thing is 20-foot high and it's taken them two hours to submerge it under the water. They can do it again but they'll have to wait another two hours before they can get the thing down on the bottom again. It's a lot of work, so if they can do it in one take it saves a lot of time and trouble.

DAVE: How do you feel about this movie compared to "A Hard Day's Night"? Is the script different? Is there a lot of spontaneity?

GEORGE: The only thing, really, that's the same as "A Hard Day's Night" is the fact that we're still playing ourselves. But I mean, this has got a story line to it whereas "A Hard Day's Night" didn't really. It was more or less like a documentary.

DAVE: You mean this one's got a plot?

GEORGE: Yeah, this one's got a plot.

DAVE: Are you ad-libbing a lot of lines? A lot of scenes that were in "A Hard Day's Night" were spontaneous and when you had to go back and cut the scene came out completely different from the way it was before. Is this happening now or not?

GEORGE: Yeah, there's lots of things that if we think of on the actual day of shooting—if the director can think of something or we can—that will make it a little bit better, then well change it a little bit. But, you know, so far we seem to be sticking to the script.

DAVE: I didn't ask John or Paul or anyone about the songs in the movie, but can you give me an idea . . . You have seven new ones, is that correct?

GEORGE: Well, we recorded 11 the last week before we left England.

DAVE: But you're only using seven, are you?

GEORGE: We'll only use about seven in the film, but even if we use only about five in the film, we'll still have about 10 or 12 tracks on the LP.

DAVE: Can you tell me what the titles are . . . I bet you can't, can you?

GEORGE: I can't, no.

DAVE: Can you give us a hint, then, what they're like?

GEORGE: It's so hard, really, because when you record eleven all in one week, you just work on one until you've finished it then completely disregard that and go on to something else. By the time the week's over, you've forgotten, really, what you've done. You know vaguely, but not until we start doing the songs do we remember them one at a time. It's a mixture.

DAVE: I want to ask you a question about your mother and father, if I may for a moment. They had planned on coming to America and to Hollywood. Do you know if your mother and father have continued with their plans?

GEORGE: I don't know . . . don't think so. I think they'd like to go for a holiday. They've mentioned to me that they may go. I don't think they've made any sort of definite plans.

DAVE: You probably haven't seen them for some time anyway.

GEORGE: I saw them three weeks ago when I went to Liverpool for my brother's wedding.

DAVE: Oh, that's right. Your brother Peter, is it not?

GEORGE: That's right.

DAVE: You were best man?

GEORGE: That's right.

DAVE: When did that all take place?

GEORGE: It was January.

DAVE: Well, you've been a best man now. What about your plans? Do you have any plans for the future as far as Pattie Boyd or anything like that, can you say?

GEORGE: Well, you know, I wouldn't make sort of long arrangements long before hand. At the moment I have nothing in mind at all.

DAVE: Have you talked to Pattie recently?

GEORGE: Not since I was in England.

DAVE: You haven't called her then?

GEORGE: No, not yet.

DAVE: We'll be seeing you tonight. I see you've got your feet buried in the sand. It'll cool you off a bit.

GEORGE: Okay, see you then, Dave.

DAVE: Thank you very much.

# HOW A BEATLE LIVES PART 3: GEORGE HARRISON

**Maureen Cleave | March 18, 1966 | *Evening Standard***

This article—not an interview per se, though Harrison's words drive the flow—offers an early glimpse into Harrison's shifting personal priorities, from the music itself to larger questions of self-purpose. It also serves to show how some journalists were beginning, by 1966, to ask deeper questions that required Harrison to discuss more meaningful topics.

With more insight than most, Maureen Cleave wrote about pop music and culture for London's *Evening Standard* in the 1960s. She had first written about the Beatles during their meteoric rise in '63, quoting Liverpool housewives ("They look beat-up and depraved in the nicest possible way") rather than the usual teen fans and describing the band's energy as part of a continuum: "It takes you back doesn't it? To the early days of rock 'n' roll." It was Cleave who spoke with John Lennon a few weeks before Harrison and reported his infamous remark that engendered widespread backlash: "We're more popular than Jesus now."

As Cleave's conversation with Harrison shows, she benefitted from unusual access, dining and hanging with him at his home only weeks after his marriage to Pattie Boyd. While her writing tends to overguide the reader, she did allow Harrison's words to reveal his priorities and passions at this point: his love for Pattie, his burgeoning interest in Indian music, his focus on living well and eating healthy, his desire to grow as a songwriter, his left-leaning political stance (specifically, opposing the Vietnam War—soon to become the wedge issue of the day), the economic policies of British Prime Minister Harold Wilson, and (after watching a televised debate on religion between two leading humanist thinkers of the day, the Reverend Lord Doinal Soper and Ludavic Kennedy) questions about his own Catholic upbringing.

About the "Mr. Hovis" Harrison claimed to have made popular: the wry reference is to Hovis Ltd., a long-established British producer of baked products. Harrison seems, in a sense, to compare the popularity of the Beatles to the ubiquity—perhaps even banality—of a well-known brand of sliced bread. *Ouch.* —Ed.

George Harrison is 23, the youngest Beatle and the least well-known. He isn't one of the two who sing and he isn't Ringo; indeed some people like him best because they think (wrongly) that nobody else does. "Good old George," is how he used to see himself, "good average old George, plodding along, a mere morsel."

He is in fact a strong-willed and uncompromising character with a strict regard for what he considers to be the truth, and an even stricter regard for his own rights.

"I asked to be successful," he said. "I never asked to be *famous*; I can tell you I got more famous than I wanted to be. I never intended to be the Big Cheese." There then followed a typical piece of Harrison logic: "People keep saying, 'We made you what you are,' well, I made Mr. Hovis what *he* is and I don't go round crawling over his gates and smashing up the wall round his house. I can't understand some of them being so aggressively bad-mannered; I suppose they feel belittled wanting something from four scruffy louts like us."

He is pretty independent; the others often think George is out on some kind of limb but, though they laugh at him, they often end up doing the same thing themselves. He was the first to move out of London, the first to become interested in Indian music. He does not watch television during all its waking hours and he thinks Rolls-Royces look dreadful. He likes to rise at 10:30 and has got hold of the revolutionary idea that Beatles should take exercise. "Just swimming," he said hastily, "not exercise you'd notice. I want us all to be healthy and that, not going to clubs."

Any self-consciousness seems to have been drummed out of him in the early days in Liverpool when he would stand at the bus stop wearing his black leather suit, white cowboy boots and very pale pink flat hat. When the bus arrived, he would board it with guitar, amplifier and often tea chest bass. George likes to be himself and bitterly regrets having abandoned his early habit of eating and sleeping on the stage. "We should have stuck out for all that," he said, "eating toast and chips and chickens. We only cut our hair and said all the yes-sir-no-sir three-bags-full-sir bit to get in."

He lives in Esher with his young wife Pattie in a large white sunny bungalow surrounded by an old brick wall. "Part of Queen Victoria's country pad," he said grandly, "and Clive of India had it for a bit. It's a National Trust wall—you're not allowed to chop it up or anything." He added poetically that it glowed red in the setting sun.

He has a housekeeper called Margaret, a Ferrari, two Minis; 48 so far unread leather-bound volumes on natural history in French, a Sidney Nolan print that he loves, a conservatory; and a music room with tape recorders, a little juke box and walls covered in guitars.

## Incense After the Wedding

In this setting he was a curiously elegant figure in black velvet with his long thin legs, his cavernous cheeks and his wild head of hair. It was George who chose to be married in a coat of Mongolian lamb; and after the wedding they came home and burnt incense. He wears a watch that is the last word in watches: it is elliptical in shape and it came in white gold at vast expense from Cartier. The point of it to George is a sophisticated one: it looks a toy watch. "Or one of Salvador Dali's soft watches," he said, "flowing all over the place."

His acquaintances are as decorative as himself; George and Pattie showing their young, long-haired, slender friends round the strange pink plants in the conservatory is a happy sight of what would be period charm if it were not for the trouser suits.

"I want to get the house so that every little bit is pleasing," he said enthusiastically. "This"—he patted the modern dining room table, "this was me two years ago. It'll have to go. The natural thing when you get money is that you acquire taste. I've got a lot of my taste off Pattie. You get taste in food as well; instead of eggs and beans and steak you branch out into the avocado scene. I never dreamt I would like avocado pears. I thought it was like eating bits of wax—fake pears out of a bowl—when I saw people shoving it down." Now he shoves it down like the rest.

He is hospitable, charming and good company. It is his enthusiasm that is so engaging—you can see why they all like George. He is proud of his house, proud of his wife. Pattie (Boyd as she used to be) is 22. She is a successful model and runs her house most capably. She is quiet, dainty, pretty and an excellent cook. "Tuck in," George said, in front of one of Pattie's dinners. There seems to be an inexhaustible supply of pretty Boyd girls; her sister Jenny is a model and her younger sister Paula is the girl too much in love to eat her Shredded Wheat.

George met Pattie two years ago making a film. This is her background, according to him. She was born in Taunton, went to East Africa to live and came back. "I married her," he said, "because I loved her and because I was fed up not being married. 22 is the normal age for people to get married. That's when a petrol pump attendant gets married though he hasn't got all these people looking at him.

"The great thing about getting married, you see, is that everything's different. Before I used to think—there's Pattie cooking my dinner in my pots and pans. Now, they're *her* pots and pans and this house is a home.

"We're a match for each other," he went on. "People should know everything about each other before they get married; I'd like you to put that in my article. Not almost everything, but really everything. You must spill it out and get it off your chest like going to the psychiatrist. That's the great thing about a wife, you see. She's your best friend."

The other romantic passion in George's life is music. He says it is his religion and he worries a lot about it. He wishes he could write fine songs as Lennon and McCartney do, but he has difficulty with the words. "Pattie keeps asking me to write more beautiful words," he said. His own voice came over on the tape with a new composition: "Love me while you can; before I'm a dead old man." George was aware that these words were not beautiful.

He has been given Roget's Thesaurus to help. "I wanted another word for 'thick'," he said. (By *thick* he means stupid). He looked it up and was thrilled with the list of synonyms. You have heard the one he used on the LP: "Although your mind's opaque; try thinking more if just for your own sake."

He plays the guitar for hours, taking it up like a piece of knitting. Out comes Bach, 'Hello Dolly', anything. "Was that the Trumpet Voluntary?" he asked suspiciously, his memory stirred. It had been.

## A Seat on the Carpet, like Ravi

When it isn't the guitar, it's the sitar. For George this instrument of Indian classical music has given new meaning to life. He went to hear Ravi Shankar play it at the Festival Hall. "I couldn't believe it," he said. "It was just like everything you have ever thought of as great all coming out at once."

He went to Indiacraft and bought some sitars, several sitars. He sat on carpets and twisted his legs round like Ravi did in the picture; his legs went to sleep and when he stood up he fell over. "I wish I could sit on the floor like Ravi," he said earnestly.

The instrument is complicated and George's enthusiasm—while it does not increase understanding—is infectious. He insists you count with him the 16 beats in certain passages; he twists his mouth about to sing with the old Indian lady of 70 on the record. He has considered going to India for six years to play it properly, but thinks he would miss his friends. "Just before I went to sleep one night, I thought what it would be like to be inside Ravi's sitar."

But there is a practical side to George, a side that admits no mysteries, no contradictions in life. He is firm where he believes himself to be right—which is most of the time. Take the war in Vietnam.

"I think about it every day," he said[,] "and it's wrong. Anything to do with war is wrong. They're all wrapped up in their Nelsons and their Churchills and their Montys—always talking about war heroes. Look at [the Granada Television series on World War II] All Our Yesterdays. How we killed a few more Huns here or there. Makes me sick. They're the sort who are leaning on the walking sticks and telling us a few years in the Army would do us good."

## Mr. Wilson—Sheriff of Nottingham

His views are disconcertingly simple. He thinks that his, George's personal taxes are going directly to pay for F111's. He sees Mr. Wilson, the Prime Minister of England, as the Sheriff of Nottingham, "Taking all the money," he said, "and then moaning about deficits here, deficits there—always moaning about deficits."

In fact, he approves of nobody in authority, religious or secular. These people are called Big Cheeses or King Henrys. They should practice what they preach, and, according to George, they do not. "Take teachers," he said. "In every class when I was at school there was always a little kid who was scruffy and smelly; and the punishment was always to sit next to the smelly kid. Fancy a teacher doing that."

"And to go on to religion," George said (he was born into the Catholic faith). "I think religion falls flat on its face. All this love thy neighbour, but none of them are doing it. How can anybody get themselves into the position of being Pope and accept all the glory and the money and the Mercedes-Benz and that? I could never be Pope until I'd sold my rich gates and my posh hat. I couldn't sit there with all that money on me and believe I was religious."

And he was furious when the Lord Soper–Ludovic Kennedy discussion finished on television: he had been following it closely.

"That's something I want you to get down in my article," he said. "Why can't we bring all this out in the open? Why is there all this stuff about blasphemy? If Christianity's as good as they say it is, it should stand up to a bit of discussion."

## Babies—And the Evils of Urban Society

He takes a Wordsworthian view of the evils of urban society and the influences of mass media. "Babies when they are born," George said, "are pure. Gradually they get more impure with all the rubbish being pumped into them by society and television and that; till gradually they're dying off, full of everything."

It was a distressing thought. The guitar showed signs of lapsing into the Trumpet Voluntary once more, and George, who had concerned himself with this interview so far, grew anxious about the ending.

"I don't want my article to end up sad," he said. "Me in nowhere land making all my nothing plans for nobody. I don't want the angry young man against the world sort of ending. I tell you what I think: the main thing is to have a good time and do the best you can.

"OK—we're the famous Beatles. So what? There are other things apart from being famous Beatles. It's not the living end, is it?

"On the other hand, I feel I've seen twice as much of life as most people do when they peg out. I'm very pleased that I'm me. Because after all, I could have been somebody else, couldn't I?"

# PART II
# 1967–1970

# THE WAY OUT IS IN: A GEORGE HARRISON INTERVIEW

**Barry Miles | May 19, 1967 | *International Times***

The tag of the "Quiet Beatle" certainly no longer fit Harrison by 1967. He had found not only found his voice but his own message as well: pursuing spiritual enlightenment with a passion that would not be tempered by the years nor the pressures that came with being a rock star living in the material world.

All the interviews Harrison gave, and much of his music as well, began to reflect his new priority. Fortunately a number of journalists and writers were similarly inspired to work on their inner selves and to conduct their work with an open heart and mind.

Barry Miles—best known simply as Miles—was one of those. Born in 1943, he spent four years at Gloucestershire College of Art before moving to London in 1963. In 1966 he cofounded Indica Books and Gallery—where John Lennon first met Yoko Ono—as well as *International Times*, Europe's first underground newspaper. His first four interviews for the publication were with Paul McCartney, Mick Jagger, Pete Townshend, and—famously—George Harrison. Their conversation stands as one of the most illuminating, catching the Beatle in the first few months of his spiritual awakening when, for many, the flame burns brightest. —Ed.

GH: If you could just say a word and it would tell people something straight to the point, then you take all the words that are going to say everything, and you'd get it in about two lines. Just use those. Just keep saying those words.

M: *Like the "Hari Krishna" chants, except the meaning of the words gradually fades away anyway.*

GH: That's right. They get hung up on the meaning of the word rather than the sound of the word. "In the beginning was the word," and that's the thing about Krishna saying Krishna, Krishna, Krishna, Krishna, so it's not the word that you're saying, it's the sound: Krishna Krishna Krishna Krishna Krishna Krishna Krishna and it's just sounds and it's great. Sounds are vibrations and the more you can put into that vibration, the more you can get out, action and reaction that's the thing to tell the people. You see it's all very obvious, the whole thing of life and all the answers to everything are in one divine law, Karma, action and reaction. It's obvious: everybody knows that if they're happy then usually the people around them are happy, or that people around them happy make them a little happier; that's a proved thing, like "I give to you and you give to me"; they all know that but they haven't thought about it to the point of every action that they do. That's what it is with every action that you do, there's a reaction to it, and if you want a good reaction then you do a good action, and if you want a bad one, then you punch somebody. But that's where it is at. Just that one thing. That's why there is the whole scene of heaven and hell; heaven and hell is right now, right at this moment. You make it heaven or you make it hell by your actions . . . it's just obvious, isn't it?

M: People don't realize all of the possibilities, they don't realize how much they are in charge of the reality of their situation.

GH: Well that's because of ignorance; everybody is great really and has got to be great because they're going to be here until they get straight and that's it . . . Everybody would like to be good, that's the silly thing, everybody always likes it when they're having a nice time or when they're happy or when it's sunny, they all dig it; but then they go and forget about it, they never really try to make it nice. They think that it just comes along and it's nice if you're lucky, or if you're unlucky it's bad for you.

M: . . . People act unconsciously at this level, they don't realise that they are purposely going out to stop things from getting any better.

GH: They're all ignorant, they fear new things, they fear knowledge some-how, I don't know why. Everything that I ever learned was always so great. I never thought so at the time, it was just that little bit more in your mind[,] an expansion of consciousness or awareness. Even those of us who are very very aware are still so unaware. Everything's relative so that, the more you know, the more you know you don't know anything . . .

Christ was the one washing the leper's feet so he was very, very humble, but it's not the way they're putting it down now. They feel as though God is that up there and they are that down there and they don't realize that they are God and that Christ was exactly the same as us but he realizes that he was God. That's all it is, we're God too but we don't realize it . . .

I'm a person who's trying to live within divine law, to the best, and it's very hard because it's self-discipline, because the more you realize, the more you've got to get yourself straight, so it's hard, you know. I'm trying and there are a lot of people who are trying, even people who are not conscious that they are doing it, but they are really . . . doing things for the good, or just to be happy or whatever. But then there's those other people, but you've got to have them to have this . . . I'm not a part of anything in particular, because it's not really 1967 and it's not half-past eight, that's still what people have said it is. So it's just a little bit of time out of the cycle. There's this Indian fellow who worked out a cycle like the idea of stone-age, bronze-age, only he did it on an Indian one. The cycle goes from nothing until now and 20th century and then on and right round the cycle until the people are really grooving and then it just sinks back into ignorance until it gets back into the beginning again. So the 20th century is a fraction of that cycle, and how many of those cycles has it done yet? It's done as many as you think and all these times it's been through exactly the same things, and it'll be this again. Only be a few million million years and it'll be exactly the same thing going on, only with other people doing it . . . I am part of the cycle, rebirth death, rebirth death, rebirth death. Some of the readers will know exactly what I mean, the ones who believe in re-incarnation. It's pointless me trying to explain things like rebirth and death because I've just accepted that, you know, I can leave that.

*M: The final death comes when the energy of consciousness reaches a point of complete unity with the universal energy flow and then ZAP, no more rebirth.*

GH: But that's in that book. That is the final release of that bit of you that is God so that it can merge into everything else ("Autobiography of a Yogi"). It's a far-out book, it's a gas. Through Yoga, anybody can attain; it's a God realisation; you just practice Yoga and if you really mean it, then you'll do it. You'll do it to a degree . . . there's Yogis that have done it to such a degree that they're God, they're like Christ and they can walk on the water and materialize bodies and they can do all those tricks. But that's not the point; the point is that we can all do that and we've all got to do that and we'll keep on being reborn because for the law of action and reaction; "What-so-ever a man soweth, that shall he also reap"; you reap when you come back in your next birth, what you've sewn in your previous incarnation, that's why I'm me and you're you and he's him and we are all whoever we are. From when I was born where I am now, all I did was to be me to get this: Whatever you've done, you get it back, so you can either go on, or you can blow it.

**The Buzz of All Buzzes**

*M: Are you concerned with communication?*

GH: Oh, yes, of course, we are all one, I mean communication, just the realisation of human love reciprocated, it's such a gas, it's a good vibration which makes you feel good. These vibrations that you get through Yoga, Cosmic chants and things like that, I mean it's such a buzz, it buzzes you out of everywhere. It's nothing to do with pills or anything like that. It's just in your own head, the realisation, it's such a buzz, it buzzes you right into the astral plane.

Nobody can become a drug addict if they're hip. Because it's obvious that if you're hip then you've got to make it. The buzz of all buzzes which is the thing that is God—you've got to be straight to get it. I'm sorry to tell you (turning to microphone) . . . you can get it better or more if you're straight because you can only get it to a degree. You know even if you get it, you only get it however long your pill lasts. So the thing is, if you really want to get it permanently, you have got to do it, you know . . . Be healthy, don't eat meat, keep away from those Night-Clubs and MEDITATE . . . The clan. The Ku Klux Klan or whatever they are. Do you know, it's stupid, isn't it, they're only little fellows who just put on their outfit, it's like we could be them, you just get your outfit and you go out with your little banner shouting at somebody like that. There was all that thing about the "Klan are coming to get us" at a concert somewhere in the States—and there were about 4 or 5 of them walking up and down, shouting, "Don't go in there . . ." something about that Christ thing, and there was all the kids' shouting at them and laughing at them and that and then the police came around and told them to move away. It wasn't like you imagine . . . people with all fiery crosses and coming to burn us. Oh yes that was silly.

*M: Did you find it easy to communicate with people in India?*

GH: With most of the people you just communicate, you don't have to talk. There are such great musicians; it was so nice and it was really just so . . . straight. They have a whole thing of trying to be humble, you've got to be humble really to be yourself or to get a chance to be yourself. If you're not humble, your ego and your big cabbage head are getting in the way. There were these musicians who are all advanced students of Ravi's and he'd been giving them a lesson. We were there just to watch a bit, and he sat in the middle and sang and they all followed him and went through about two and a half hours . . . improvised the whole lot. He was singing—which was pretty far out. All these people playing knocked me out so much, it was so great yet they were so humble and saying "It's such a pleasure to meet you," which was horrible because I was trying to be humble there. I was there for that, not for anything to do with being a Beatle. Ravi Shankar is so brilliant and these fellows, as far as I was concerned, were very far out . . . with people you com-municate, there is no bullshit, because they don't create it. It's not so much a game as Western thought because they're a bit more spiritually inclined and they just sort of feel . . .

*M: Did you just realize this yourself?*

GH: I felt the vibrations all the time from the people I was with. They've all got their problems but they're just happy and vibrate.

*M: You didn't search out a Guru?*

GH: Ravi's my musical Guru, but the whole musical thing was too much just to be able to appreciate it whether I play or not. I've never been knocked out with anything for so long. But then later I realized that there wasn't the real thing, that was still only a little stepping stone for me to see. Through the music you reach the spiritual but the music's very involved with the spiritual JBS [*a reference to a Hindu holy triad—brothers Jagannath and Balabhadra and sister Subhadra— worshipped by members of the Hare Krishna movement —Ed.*] we know from Hari Krishna we just heard. It's so attuned to the spiritual scene, it depends how spiritual the musician is. Ravi is fantastic. He just sits there with a bit of wire and just does all that and says all that, things that you know and can't say because there's no words and he can say it like that.

*M: Why does it come across best in music?*

GH: Because music is sound, vibrations, whereas paintings are vibrations of whatever you pick up. If not actually an energy vibration you get from a groovy painting, but music and sound seem to travel along vibrations, you know the whole thing with mantras is to repeat and repeat those sounds . . . it's vibrations in everything like prayers and hymns. They don't know about this over here. Prayer is to vibrate, do the devotion, whatever it is, to whoever you believe in, Christ or Buddha or Krishna or any of them. You get the response depending on how much you need it. Those people become that because they give it out, they want it so much, they give out so much, they get back so much, it snowballs until you're Christ. You know we're back to that again. I'm not really hip to too much of the Zen or the Buddhist point of view, but you see I don't have to because I just know that they're all the same, its [*sic*] all the same, it's just which ever one you want to take and it happens that I'm taking the Hindu one . . . Be straight with yourself just to maybe save a few more people from being stupid and being ignorant. That's what we're doing here now, talking, because we've got to save them, because they're all potentially divine.

*M: Does that concern you much?*

GH: I couldn't cut off from everyone, because I'm still leaning on them, so if I'm leaning on them then there's someone leaning on me, only very subtly. I'm part of a structure that's going on and rather than cop out now, just at the moment, because I'm not ready, I'll wait. Maybe later on I'll get into where it's peaceful. We're already getting going, so that we'll have somewhere nice to be, because that's what it is you know, everybody should just stay at home and meditate and they'd be so much happier. That'll all come for us, because we are going to make it. "You make and preserve the image of your choice." But still we've got to communicate. We've got to be doing things because we're part of it and because it's nice. You've got to have an outlet. It's like having a big intake in the front of your head and there's so much going on, and it's going through all this, and there's a little exhaust pipe on the back, that goes POW and lets a bit out. The aim is to get as much going out the back as is coming in. You've got to do that because for everything you get in you've got to give something out. So The Beatles, and whatever our own personal interests are, what we're doing from day to day, then that's like our little exhaust, coming out the back.

*M: Which seems to be getting bigger and bigger?*

GH: Well it's got to be but it's great, just the realisation of it all, everything feasible because its all only a dream anyway and that gives you infinite scope. You just go on and on and on until you go right rut there. The thing is we could go; there's times, I'm sure, where we hold back a lot with things like "Strawberry Fields." I know there's a lot of people who like that who probably wouldn't have liked us a year ago. And then there's a lot of people who didn't like it who did like us a year ago. It's all the same really. Just some people pretend it's not happening. But they know, they simply must know. Because we're all together on this thing, we're just part of it and we'd like to get as many people who want to be a part of it with us. And if we really freaked out . . .

*M: Do you think you're bringing most of them along with you?*

GH: Well, we're losing a lot but we're gaining a lot too, I think. I dunno. But what I think, whatever it is, it's good. When somebody does something which everybody really wants to do, then it makes everyone else try a bit harder and strive for something better, and it's good. If ever we've done something like that then everybody's been there. We're as much influenced by everybody else as they are by us, if they are. It's just all a part of the big thing. I give to you and you give to me and it goes like that into the music you know.

## Guru and Disciple

GH: The Guru and Disciple relationship is where the person has a 100% belief in the Guru and that way you put your trust in the Guru, that he's going to get you out of this mess. If you are a Christian, then Christ is your Guru, and they're all disciples of Christ. If they are. So to put your full belief in your Guru, because it's for your own good, because you've decided that . . . It's just having a lot of respect for the person and it's like that with music as well . . . You should love your instrument and respect it. Whenever Ravi does a concert he'll put his special thing on, and get nice and clean, and washed up and get his joss-sticks going. He's very straight, he doesn't drink or smoke or anything like that and by his real devotion he's mastered the thing. By his own discipline. He's playing for 18 hours a day for about 15 years, that's why he's that good. I've got no illusions about being a sitar player, I mean it's nothing like that. I really see it in perspective because he's got about 10,000,000 students who are all so groovy playing the sitar and yet he's only got hope for one of them to really make it, so that's me out for a kick-off. But that's not the important thing you see. The thing is, that however little you learn of it, it's too much, it's too much. Indian music is brilliant and for me, anyway, (this is only personal) it's got everything in it. I still like electronics and all sorts of music if it's good but Indian music is just . . . an untouchable; you can't say what it is, because it just is.

Your religion, or whatever you're doing, so if your're [sic] putting out something to make people happy and something that's a bit devotional. It's got to be. If you spend all your life in a studio; you can't last out if it's not. Stockhausen (he's the one we mention in IT, Stockhausen, he's really IT) and all the others, they're just trying to take you a bit further out or in, further in, to yourself. The way out is in. It's since the newspapers started the drug craze. That's it, you see, isn't that a bizarre scene, I mean you're the only paper that can say this because you're the only honest paper, really, when you get down to it. What I mean is, that thing about the sales, that's all they're concerned with how many . . . all this bullshit, on the front page how many papers we've sold today, and we're selling more than the *Daily Express*, hup yer. All their silly little games, all that crap. And another thing they're always saying, "*The Daily Mirror* carried 13,000 inches of advertising"—and fuck-all to read, just a lot of shit. Actually bragging about how, it's stupid isn't it, it's a newspaper, anyway, we forgive them, as always. But this is the great thing. When you've got yourself to a point where you've realized certain things about life and the world and everything like that, then you know that none of that can affect you at all because you know it's the same thing now with those newspaper people they were always writing all that, just making it up. The thing is we know what the scene is, and we know them, they're all those little fellows. They'd all really like to be happy and they try to be happy but they're in a nasty little organisation and it's great really. The whole thing of hate, anybody who hates, I feel sorry for them you know, that they are in that position and the newspapers are like that. I feel we got away from the point, whatever it was. The point was, you can print your paper, you know that they can't touch you because you know more than them and its obvious because they'd be the ones to puzzle about it. On our side of the fence there's no puzzling to it. We know what it is.

The policemen are people as well. All those nasty people aren't really nasty if they'd realize it. All those policemen can't be themselves and they've got to do that game and pretend to be a policemen and go all through that shit about what's in the book, they've got to make themselves into a little part of themselves which is a lie and an untruth. The moment they put a uniform on they're bullshitting themselves, just thinking that they're policemen, because they are not policemen. They think that they created a thing called policemen and so then they try and enforce their creation on others and say "Now we've made a thing and it's called The Police and we want you all to believe in it and it's all for your own good and if you don't look up to it you'll get your ass kicked and you'll go in the craphouse."

You just keep changing the subject onto what you think we should be talking about and I'll just talk it back out of it again onto this . . . to people who look at the scene negatively, then it is, and they stay in their drab world. We've got to get it back again, after the war, and get it back to how it should be—everybody's happy and smiling and leaping about and doing what they all know is there that they should be doing. There's something happening. If everybody could just get into it, great, they'd all smile and all dress up. Yes—that'd be good. "The world is a stage." Well he was right, because we're Beatles, and it's a little scene and we're playing and we're pretending to be Beatles, like Harold Wilson's pretending to be Prime Minister and you're pretending to be the Interview on IT. They're all playing. The Queen's the Queen. The idea that you wake up and it happens that you're Queen, it's amazing but you could all be Queens if you imagined it . . . they'll have a war quickly if it gets too good, they'll just pick on the nearest person to save us from our doom. That's it, soon as you freak out and have a good time, it's dangerous, but they don't think of the danger of going into some other country in a tank with a machine-gun and shooting some-one. That's all legal and above board, but you can't freak out—that's stupid.

# THE GEORGE HARRISON INTERVIEW

Alan Walsh | September 2, 1967 | *Melody Maker*

Alan Walsh was born at the right time and in the right location to experience Beatlemania in its local, nascent stage. Hailing from Liverpool, he grew up close to the action and, in fact, worked part-time at the now-legendary Cavern Club. Starting in 1963, Walsh climbed the ladder of music journalism, from contributor, to staff writer, to top editorial positions at several British publications: *Disc* and, within a year, *Melody Maker*, where he eventually became news editor. His seven-year run at that position placed him directly in the middle of the UK pop music scene, affording him the opportunity to speak with many of the moment's most important music makers at key junctures in their careers. Being a fellow Liverpudlian, he spoke with each of the Beatles numerous times and accompanied them on many tours, including their first return to Hamburg and on their visits to America.

Walsh's 1967 interview, which ran in two consecutive issues of *Melody Maker*, caught Harrison immediately after his return from a jaunt to the US without any fellow Beatles or gigs to perform—his first trip to the States of that sort since visiting his sister in southern Illinois in '63. This time Harrison made California his destination, visiting former Beatles press officer Derek Taylor in Los Angeles and then—with entourage in tow—journeying up to San Francisco to get a firsthand look at ground zero of the hippie movement. To many, the burgeoning spiritual and chemical experimentation of the age were a direct result of what the Beatles had wrought with their music and their messages, their lyrics and their lifestyle, their wardrobe and their hair.

At the time, Harrison was well along his own path of inner reflection and self-discovery—he had learned to chant and meditate and was exploring the Hare Krishna movement. As such, he

71

had the means to perform his own litmus test, to gauge the spiritual veracity and efficacy of what he encountered in Haight-Ashbury. As his words with Walsh reveal, he was less then enthused. Walsh—who went on to found a number of other music publications in the '70s and died in 2015—is remembered in part for this conversation, in which Harrison pulls no punches. –Ed.

"You may think this interview is of no importance to me," said George Harrison across a table in NEM's Enterprises [*sic*] Mayfair offices. "But you'd be wrong. It's very important. We have realized that it's up to everyone—including the Beatles—to spread love and understanding and to communicate this in any way we can." George, radiant in flowered shirt and trousers, long flowing hair and bushy moustache, lit up a dismal wet London day by his clothes, his friendliness and the warmth of his replies. George spoke quietly but frankly about many subjects—from God to LSD—and the 90 minute conversation examined the whole existence of the most introspective Beatle.

**You have just returned from Haight-Ashbury. What were your impressions of life there?**

Well, we were only in Haight Ashbury for about 30 minutes, but I did see quite a bit. We parked our limousine a block away just to appear the same and walked along the street for about a hundred yards, half like a tourist and half like a hippie. We were trying to have a look in a few shops.

**Who was with you?**

Pattie, her sister Jenny, a friend of Jenny's, Derek Taylor, Neil Aspinall, our road manager, and Magic Alex, who's a friend. We walked along and it was nice. At first they were just saying "hello" and "can I shake your hand" . . . things like that. Then more and more people arrived and it got bigger and bigger. We walked into the park and it just became a bit of a joke. All these people were just following us along.

**One of them tried to give you STP, I believe?**

They were trying to give me everything. This is a thing that I want to try and get over to people. Although we've been identified a lot with hippies, especially since all this thing about pot and LSD's come out, we don't want to tell anyone else to have it because it's something that's up to the person himself. Although it was like a key that opened the door and showed a lot of things on the other side, it's still up to people themselves what they do with it. LSD isn't a real answer.

It doesn't give you anything. It enables you to see a lot of possibilities that you may never have noticed before but it isn't the answer. You don't just take LSD and that's it forever, you're OK.

A hippie is supposed to be someone who becomes aware—you're hip if you know what's going on. But if you're really hip you don't get involved with LSD and things like that. You see the potential that it has and the good that can come from it, but you also see that you don't really need it.

I needed it the first time I ever had it. Actually, I didn't know that I'd had it, I'd never even heard of it then. This is something that just hasn't been told. Everybody now knows that we've had it but the circumstances were that somebody just shoved it in our coffee before we'd ever heard of the stuff. So we happened to have it quite unaware of the fact.

I don't mind telling people I've had it. I'm not embarrassed. It makes no difference because I know that I didn't actually go out and try to get some.

**You've never deliberately set out to take LSD?**

No, not really. For me, it was a good thing but it showed me that LSD isn't really the answer to everything. It can help you to go from A to B, but when you get to B, you see C. And you see that to get really high, you have to do it straight. There are special ways of getting high without drugs—with yoga, meditation and all those things. So this was the disappointing thing about LSD.

In this physical world we live in, there's always duality—good and bad, black and white, yes and no. Whatever there is, there's always the opposite. There's always something equal and opposite to everything and this is why you can't say LSD is good or it's bad, because it's good AND it's bad. It's both of them and it's neither of them all together. People don't consider that.

Haight-Ashbury was a bit of a shock because although there were so many great people, really nice people who only wanted to be friends and didn't want to impose anything or be anything, there was still the black bit, the opposite. There was the bit where people were so out of their minds trying to shove STP on me, and acid—every step I took there was somebody trying to give me something—but I didn't want to know about that. I want to get high and you can't get high on LSD. You can take it and take it as many times as you like but you get to a point that you can't get any further unless you stop taking it.

Haight-Ashbury reminded me a bit of the Bowery. There were these people just sitting round the pavement begging, saying, "Give us some money for a blanket." These are hypocrites. They are making fun of tourists and all that and at the same time, they are holding their hands out begging off them. That's what I don't like.

I don't mind anybody dropping out of anything, but it's the imposition on somebody else I don't like. The moment you start dropping out and then begging off somebody else to help you then it's no good. I've just realized through a lot of things that it doesn't matter what you are as long as you work. It doesn't matter if you chop wood as long as you chop and keep chopping. Then you get what's coming to you. You don't have to drop out. In fact if you drop out you put yourself further away from the goal of life than if you were to keep working.

**Have you any defined idea of what your goal in life is?**

We've all got the same goal whether we realize it or not. We're all striving for something which is called God. For a reunion, complete. Everybody has realized at some time or other that no matter how happy they are, there's still always the unhappiness that comes with it.

Everyone is a potential Jesus Christ, really. We are all trying to get to where Jesus Christ got. And we're going to be on this world until we get there. We're all different people and we are all doing different things in life, but that doesn't matter because the whole point of life is to harmonize with everything, every aspect in creation. That means down to not killing the flies, eating the meat, killing people or chopping the trees down.

**Can we ever get it down to this level?**

You can only do it if you believe in it. Everybody is potentially divine. It's just a matter of self-realisation before it will all happen. The hippies are a good idea—love, flowers and that is great—but when you see the other half of it, it's like anything. I love all these people too, those who are honest and trying to find a bit of truth and to straighten out the untruths. I'm with them 100 per cent but when I see the bad side of it, I'm not so happy.

**To get anywhere near what you are talking about, do you believe you have to be a hippie or a flower person?**

Anybody can do it. I doubt if anyone who is a hippie or flower person feels that he is. It's only you, the press, who call us that. They've always got to have some tag. If you like, I'm a hippie or a flower person. I know I'm not. I'm George Harrison, a person. Just like everybody else, but different to everybody else at the same time. You get to a point where you realize that it doesn't matter what people think you are, it's what you think you are yourself that matters. Or what you know you are. Anyone can make it. You don't have to put a flowery shirt on.

**Could a bank clerk make it?**

Anyone can, but they've got to have the desire. The Beatles got all the material wealth that we needed and that was enough to show us that this thing wasn't material. We are all in the physical world, yet what we are striving for isn't physical. We all get so hung up with material things like cars and televisions and houses, yet what they can give you is only there for a little bit and then it's gone.

**Did you ever reach the point where you considered getting rid of the material wealth?**

Yes, but now that I've got the material thing in perspective, it's OK. The whole reason I've got material things is because they were given to me as a gift. So it's not really bad that I've got it because I didn't ask for it. It was just mine. All I did was be me.

All we ever had to do was just be ourselves and it all happened. It was there, given to us. All this. But then, it was given to us to enable us to see that that wasn't it. There was more to it.

**Where do these beliefs fit in with the musical side of the Beatles?**

I'm a musician. I don't know why. This is a thing that I've looked back on since my birth. Many people think life is pre-destined. I think it is vaguely but it's still up to you which way your life's going to go. All I've ever done is keep being me and it's just all worked out. It just did it all . . . magic . . . it just did it. We never planned anything. So it's obvious— because I'm a musician now, that's what I was destined to be. It's my gig.

**George, can you tell where the Beatles are at musically today? What are you trying to do?**

Nothing. We're not trying to do anything. This is the big joke. It's all Cosmic Joke 43. Everyone gets our records and says "wonder how they thought of that?" or "wonder what they're planning next?" or whatever they do say. But we don't plan anything. We don't do anything. All we do is just keep on being ourselves. It just comes out. It's the Beatles.

All any of us are trying to do now is get as much peace and love as possible. Love will never be played out because you can't play out the truth. Whatever I say can be taken a million different ways depending on how screwed up the reader is. But the Beatles is just a hobby really . . . it's just doing it on its own. We don't even have to think about it. The songs write themselves. It just all works out. Everything that we're taking into our minds and trying to learn or find out—and I feel personally it's such a lot, there's so much to get in—and yet the output coming out the back end is still so much smaller than what you're putting in.

Everything is relative to everything else. We know that now. So we've got to a point where when people say "there's nothing else you can do," we know that's only from where they are. They look up and think we can't do any more, but when you're up there you see you haven't started.

Take Ravi Shankar, who is so brilliant. With pop music, the more you listen to it, the more you get to know it, the more you see through it and the less satisfaction it gives you whereas Indian music and Ravi Shankar as a person . . . it's exactly the opposite because the more you're able to understand the music, the more you see there is to appreciate. The more you get back out of it. You can have just one record of Indian music and play it for the rest of your life and you'd probably still never see all the subtleties in it. It's the same with Ravi Shankar. He feels as though he hasn't started and yet he's doing so much, teaching so many people, writing film music, everything.

**Have you any idea what the Beatles will do the next time you go into the recording studios?**

No idea. We won't know until we do it. We're naturally influenced by everything that's going on around us. If you weren't influenced, you wouldn't be able to do anything. That's all anything is, an influence from one person to another. We'll write songs and go into the studios and record them and we'll try and make them good. We'll make a better LP than *Sergeant Pepper*. But I don't know what it's going to be.

**If you had a child, do you know what you would try to do as a father?**

I haven't and I can't really know what I'd do. But I do know I wouldn't let it go to school. I'm not letting Fascist teachers put things into the child's head. I'd get an Indian guru to teach him—and me, too.

**I believe the Beatles are thinking about making a film in which you create the visual as well as the sound and music?**

Yes. We've got to the point now where we've found out that if you rely on other people, things never work out. This may sound conceited but it's not. It's just what happens. The things that we've decided ourselves and that we've gone ahead and done ourselves have always worked out right—or at least satisfactorily—whereas the moment you get involved with other people, it goes wrong.

It's like a record company. You hand them the whole LP and the sleeve and everything there on a plate. All they've got to do is print it. Then all the crap starts: "you can't have that" and "you don't do this" and we get so involved with trivial little things that it all starts deteriorating around us.

And it's the same with a film. The more involved we get with film people the less of a Beatles film it's going to be. Take that *Our World* television show. We were trying to make it into a recording session and a good time and the BBC were trying to make it into a television show. It's a constant struggle to get ourselves across through all these other people, all hassling.

In the end it'll be best if we write the music, write the visual and the script, film it, edit it, do everything ourselves. But then it's such a hell of a job that you have to get involved and that means you couldn't do other things.

But we'll have to get other people to do things because we can't give that much time to just a film because it's only a film and there are more important things in life.

**Do you think the film will come off in the near future?**

Yes. I think it'll probably all happen next year sometime.

# TELEVISION INTERVIEWS

**David Frost | September 29 and October 4, 1967 | *The Frost Programme,* ITV**

In May 1967 the Beatles released *Sgt. Pepper's Lonely Hearts Club Band*, and the world itself began to change. In the stories it told and the sounds it employed, the album became the soundtrack for the Summer of Love, the rise of flower power, and the arrival of the hippies.

That August George Harrison and John Lennon appeared on the British television talk show *The Frost Programme*, hosted by David Frost, one of the more popular and in-tune commentators of the day. In his autobiography Frost wrote about the program, quoting Harrison ("By having the money we found that money wasn't the answer,") and stating: "George Harrison could have been talking there on behalf of an entire generation. The Beatles may have been '60s heroes, '60s icons, but they shared with their contemporaries the same sometimes frenzied search for inner peace."

In August 1967, the Beatles attended various lectures in Wales given by the Maharishi Mahesh Yogi. He spoke on the benefits of Transcendental Meditation, or TM, and the spotlight that shone so brightly on the band now included this visiting mystic from India. Frost's instinct was to dive deeper into a topic everyone was aware of and had an opinion about, yet few fully grasped. He devoted two consecutive programs to TM and asked the Beatles to both. In the first, Frost spoke with the Yogi in a taped interview, then Lennon and Harrison together. The follow-up program a week later included the two again and added a few pro-and-con voices to the mix: lawyer, writer (and later successful playwright) John Mortimer—an "atheist for God" and an Eastern spirituality denier—plus two exponents of TM, John Allison and Nick Clark. Frost invited audience members to participate as well.

Some of the results are rather predictable, like the semantic mismatch as different generations grappled with words like "God" and "religion" and "spirituality." There's a lot that can be unpacked here, such as the role of television journalism in the '60s, keeping up with the cultural leaps at hand. And the contextual issue of how Western and Eastern thought—varying takes on life values and priorities—collided and left many confused, and Harrison himself frustrated with Mortimer's contrariness and overuse of the word "mystical." (Mortimer does throw in an ominous warning about the recent election of actor Ronald Reagan to the governorship of California!)

It's encouraging in a way to see Lennon and Harrison working together in support of their experiences with TM. Harrison was not alone when he began his search along Eastern paths; at first all four Beatles made that trek to Wales—and later India—to listen and learn. Many rock stars and cultural heavyweights of the time followed suit, choosing from among various gurus and swamis. Yet very few remained as dedicated or public about that commitment as Harrison; for him, his lessons in TM were the first steps on a lifelong journey.

(A word about the "good news/bad news" jokes sent in to the show by viewers and read by Frost at the start of the second show: as off-color and politically incorrect as some are, they serve a contextual purpose, helping to frame the time and place in which this discussion on spirituality was taking place.) —Ed.

## September 29, 1967

**David Frost:** Earlier this evening we managed to abduct John Lennon and George Harrison. The film of the Maharishi was still being processed at the time but we started by taking up a point that the Maharishi had first made at the end of his conversation. The two things that the Maharishi said this morning were the results for people who meditated and followed this system of meditation. The two things he claimed for it were: serenity and energy. [*To Lennon and Harrison*] Have you found that?

**John Lennon:** I've got more energy. I mean, I've got the same energy, but I know how to tap it sort of.

**Frost:** How do you mean, exactly?

**Lennon:** Well, you know, the energy that I found through doing it, I know damn well I've had it there before. I just haven't, I've only used it on good days, when everything is going well. And then I found more energy, because it's been going well. So with meditation, I find that, if it's not too good a day, I'll still sort of get the same amount of . . .

**Frost:** And can you link the two in any way? I mean, is it true any day of meditation is equally good?

**Lennon:** Well, the worst days I have on meditation are better than the worst days that I had before without it.

**Frost:** Have you found that, George?

**George Harrison:** It's all . . . the energy is latent within everybody. It's there anyway. The meditation is just a natural process of being able to contact that, so by doing it each day, you contact that energy and give yourself a little more. Consequently, you're able to do whatever you normally do, just with a little bit more . . . happiness, maybe.

**Frost:** How do you come to reach this stage of meditation? The Maharishi this morning was very clear about how he gave to everyone or his teachers gave to everyone a specific sound, and that each person had a sound that was—tried to be—in rhythm with the person.

**Harrison:** Each person, the individual life, sort of co-relates with their own rhythm, so they give a word or a song, a mantra which co-relates with that rhythm. So by using the mantra rather than a thought, because the whole idea is to transcend to the subtlest level of thought. So you replace the thought with the mantra, and the mantra becomes more subtle and more subtle, until finally you've lost it in the mantra. And then you find yourself at that level of pure consciousness.

**Frost:** What I was, in fact . . . is the mantra something you use to get back to the subject, if you find earthly or irrelevant thoughts [*indistinct*] . . . or is it more than that?

**Lennon:** Yeah, it's also like that. You just sort of sit there, and you let your mind go, wherever it's going, it doesn't matter what you're thinking about. Just let it go. And you just introduce the mantra or the vibration, just to take over from the thought. You don't will it or use your willpower.

**Harrison:** If you find yourself thinking, then the moment you realize you've been thinking about things again, then you replace that thought with the mantra again. Sometimes you can go on, and you find that you haven't even had the mantra in your mind, it's just a complete blank.

But when you reach that point, because it's beyond all experience, then it's down there and that level is timeless, spaceless, and you can be there for five minutes and come out. You don't actually know how long you've been there, because it's just the actual contact of that, and then coming back out to the gross level, like this level, and you bring that with you.

**Frost:** But I mean, in fact, then the aim, as opposed to sitting and thinking or anything, is to reach a point in a sense when you have no thoughts, is it?

**Lennon:** Yeah, but you're not even conscious of that sometimes. You just know that, the only time you're conscious is when you suddenly, it's like you don't know you're awake or something, asleep until you're awake, most of the time, you know. You just aren't asleep before. You come out in twenty minutes. Sometimes you come out and it's been twenty minutes sitting there, and other times you come out and it just seems as though no time has gone at all.

**Frost:** And can you look back at the end of that period and recap what's happened in the last . . .

**Lennon:** That's why you go and see these people. So they sort of say, "What were you doing?" And you say, "Well, nothing, I haven't done anything," and they say, "Well, what about this?" And you say, "Oh, it did seem very short," or "That seemed to happen."

**Harrison:** You can't really tell anybody what it is, because it's . . . the teaching is all based on the individual experience. But if you were to do it, then you get instruction, which leads to some sort of experience, and upon having experience you're taught the next part. But really . . .

**Lennon:** It's like we're trying to tell you what chocolate tastes like.

**Harrison:** Or how it is to be drunk, you know. They've got to be drunk themselves before they know what it is.

**Frost:** I can see that, I mean you're doing very well in fact, in expressing something that probably is inexpressible. Because, I mean, the thing is, at the end of it, do you feel more relaxed? Do you feel you know more about yourself? Do you feel you know more about something else or someone else?

**Lennon:** You don't feel you have more knowledge or anything. Well, maybe you do, but I can't feel that exactly. You just feel more energetic, you know, just simply for doing work or anything. You just come out of it, it's just "Let's get going!" you know, it's a real thing.

**Harrison:** It takes a lot of practice to arrive at the point, if you can remain there permanently. But the whole thing, we've only been doing it for a matter of six weeks maybe. But there's definite proof, I've had, that it is something. It really works. But in actual fact, if you take a long time to arrive at the point where I'm able to hold that pure consciousness on this level or to be able to bring that level of consciousness into this level of consciousness, which is the aim of it.

**Frost:** You mean the aim is to carry on the state you're in, in meditation, when you're here, when you're in your rec room.

**Lennon:** You know, we practice. He said . . . one of his sort of analogies or whatever, is that it's like dipping a cloth into gold. So you dip it in, and you bring it out, and you dip it in and you bring it out. And if you leave it in, it gets soggy, you know, like if you're sitting in a cave all your life—

**Harrison:** And if you bring it out it's the same.

**Lennon:** And if you bring it out then it's the same. But the meditation is going in and going out and going in, so that when, after how many years or whatever, when you bring it out, it's the same when it's out as it's in. So when you do it in this, you really zap in all the time inside. But that's something else.

**Frost:** But I mean, the thing is, you said permanently. One of you, I think it was Paul, said in fact that this feeling that meditation gives is the sort of permanent version of what drugs can give temporarily, is that true?

**Harrison:** Well, not really, because drugs, it's still all on the relative level. Like this, sleeping and dreaming and waking, all those three states that people live through, is all only relative, which is on this level. Whereas this is on a subtler level, so really you couldn't compare it. With drugs you do have a glimpse of a few things like that.

**Frost:** Is it as deep?

**Harrison:** The thing is, you could take drugs, which would heighten perception a little, and then maybe to try and get into that subtle level with the drug. But just to take the drug and hope it's going to bring that subtly onto this gross level is a mistake, you know, it's never worked.

**Frost:** I mean, you experimented with drugs, is that why you put them on one side?

**Lennon:** Well, we dropped them long before the Maharishi.

**Frost:** Oh, it wasn't . . .

**Lennon:** Yeah, we just, you know, we'd had enough acid. It had done all it could do for us, you know, there was no going any further. It only does so much.

**Frost:** What does it do?

**Lennon:** Well, what it does mainly is that is more finding out about yourself, you know, and your ego, and that kind of scene, so it's more psychological than anything else.

**Frost:** Whereas this is not psychological? I mean, it seems . . .

**Lennon:** Well, it will be in the end. But I mean, with acid, it is just all about yourself, it's all that, but this [is] just sort of a bit gentler. Or more gentle.
[*Laughter*]

**Frost:** See, you're on the ball even there. But do you think that with acid in fact that what you discover is yourself or just a fantasy?

**Lennon:** No, it's yourself more, but obviously you will have hallucinations as they call them. It's only a sort of state, but it is about yourself, you know. You don't find out, I mean you could find out about other people, but they're only mirrors of yourself anyway. But you find out about yourself, you know, instead of taking a hundred years, or maybe you never find out.

**Harrison:** People can look at themselves objectively, you know, instead of thinking that you are the big cheese.

**Lennon:** Or even you're not the big cheese, whatever you think.

**Harrison:** Yeah, or whatever you think, you can see yourself from a different point of view. So consequently, it shows you a bit more truth than you've seen. Only, of course, truth depends on the person's feelings. The thing is, you see certain things that have been there all the time, and yet you've lived with such a narrow concept of just general things, just like the trees or the grass, or anything.

**Frost:** But I mean, presumably when you gave up those experiments with drugs, it wasn't because you felt you knew everything about yourselves, but because of the disadvantages of the thing as well.

**Harrison:** Because the thing is, your true self isn't on this level; again, it's on a subtler level. So, whatever the true self is, the way to approach it is through that meditation or some form of yoga. We're not saying that this meditation is the only answer; it's obviously not. Yoga incorporates lots of different techniques, but the whole point is that each soul is potentially divine, and yoga is a technique of manifesting that, to arrive at that point that is divine.

**Frost:** You've had six weeks of this, and it's already had a tremendous impact on you. Do you find that this sort of tremendous concern with meditation and one's own self and so on is now starting to impose, not necessarily rules, but a difference to your conduct of the rest of the day, I mean towards other people or anything?

**Lennon:** No.

**Frost:** Or rules of any kind?

**Lennon:** It doesn't, you see. It's just something you add. If you haven't been treating your teeth all your life, it's just suddenly that somebody says, "Hey, it's a good idea if you clean them." So you try it, and it seems quite good. You just add it to your routine, you know. So you're just the same, just with that, the little difference of doing it. You add to your religion, you don't have to change your religion or anything.

You know, whatever you are, you carry on. But this is something that is a plus.

**Harrison:** And you're surprised your teeth are suddenly shiny.

[*Laughter*]

**Frost:** But I mean, in fact, if you'd compare this with, say, something like Christianity, which is concerned to try and find serenity, to give energy through the Holy Spirit or whatever. At the same time, a good fifty percent of that is concerned with, then, one's responsibility to other people. There doesn't seem to be any of that in this.

**Lennon:** Because it's, you know, if you go, if you asked Maharishi or any of the people, give us a few rules for living by, well, they'd be the same as Christianity. You know, Christianity is the answer as well as this. It's the same thing, just . . .

**Harrison:** Christianity, how I was taught it, they told to believe in Jesus and God and all that; they didn't actually show me any way of experiencing God or Jesus. So, the whole point of to believe in something, without actually seeing it, well, it's . . . it's no good. You've got to actually experience the thing, you know, if there's a God, you must see Him. And that's the point, you know, the whole thing, it's no good to believe in something, you know, just . . .

**Lennon:** And the whole thing about "the kingdom of heaven is within you," you know, that's all it means, to have a peace inside. There's nobody to see in there, you know, some old fellow. It's still just like electricity, you don't see it.

**Frost:** But I mean it's the same in the sense that you now have evidence, you personally feel of this thing; equally Christians feel they have experience of that thing. But in both cases, it's impossible to prove it to anybody else, isn't it?

**Lennon:** Yeah, but having been—I'm still, I'm really a Christian—I've done this; I know the difference between being fifteen and just being, "Oh, it's very nice," and all that, and had I been told meditation at fifteen, now I would be pretty groovy.

**Frost:** Yes, but I mean, the word, for instance, the word God, does it mean something different to you now than it did before Maharishi?

**Harrison:** It means all sorts of things to me. I mean, the first concept of a man in the sky, well, I kicked that one a few years ago, but I've got back to that now, because it's a man in the sky as well, if you like. It's just everything, the whole thing, that it's just everything, every aspect of creation is part of God.

**Lennon:** I think of it just as a big piece of energy, you know, like electricity, just a bigger piece, a big powerhouse.

**Harrison:** The energy that runs through everything, that holds everything together and makes everything one. One big piece of energy.

**Frost:** But yes, I'm still concerned about the outgoing part. I mean, how does it, is it solely concerned with oneself, or does it in any way, make one feel more responsible for other people or more responsible for people that are depending on you or . . . ?

**Harrison:** Well, you realize that your actions are going to lead to whatever the reaction is. And so, that's like the only thing about your attitude to other people. If you treat other people good, they'll treat you good. If you kick them in the face, they'll probably do the same thing. And that's the easiest thing to do with religion. Action and reaction, that's the thing that Christ was saying about you sow, you reap. It just means, whatever you do, you get it back. And that's why it doesn't really matter what people say or think because they get it back just like you'll get back what's coming.

**Frost:** That's Old Testament.

**Lennon:** Everything you read about all the religions, you know, they're all the same. It's just a matter of people opening their minds up, to allow the, yeah, all right, Buddha was a groove. Jesus was all right. They're all saying exactly the same thing.

**Frost:** How would you, what differences would you say there were between Jesus, say, and the Maharishi, for instance?

**Lennon:** Well, I don't know, you know. Maharishi doesn't do miracles, you know, for a kickoff. [*Laughter*] I don't know how divine or how you know, super-human or whatever it is, he is, that's all. But I mean Jesus was . . .

**Harrison:** A divine incarnation. Like some of the people, like Christ and Buddha and Krishna and various others, are divine the moment they're born. That is, they've achieved the highest thing, and they choose to come back to try and save a few more people. Whereas others manage to be born just ordinary and attain their divinity in that incarnation.

**Lennon:** So Maharishi was probably one of them, you know, who was born quite ordinary, but he's working at it.

[*Laughter*]

**Frost:** How do you think in fact, this, the Maharishi, this meditation can, for instance, help the world's problems?

**Lennon:** Well, if everybody was doing it, it would just be . . .

**Harrison:** It's the same thing that Jesus said about go and fix your own house, and it's solved, everything's fixed up then. If you sort yourself out, everybody needs to go home and find out for themselves, and fix up all their personal problems. Then no other problems exist, because they only cause the problems that exist in the world. It's all each person, individual. It's just up to him to do it.

**Frost:** And as each person does that, as each person goes deeper and deeper within themselves, is each person going to find good, and good thoughts below? I mean, or is there such a thing in this definition as . . .

**Lennon:** It doesn't matter what you're thinking when you do it. I mean, you could be thinking the most awful things in the world, I suppose. The point is to get down there, and then you're not thinking anything. It's when you come out you might be thinking quite the same, you know, after a few weeks. I mean, we don't really know what happened to a sort of, a killer or somebody that did it, you know; maybe he changed his mind, we don't know about that; you should have asked him that side of it. But, it's for the good, you know, and it's simple, that's the main bit about it. So they're bound to be a bit better than they were, whatever they were before they did it.

**Frost:** And each person, you're saying, each person, there's no one to which it's not possible.

**Lennon:** Anybody. All you've got to do is be interested in it, whether you're interested in it to knock it, or to do an anything. But if you just want to try it to find out, that's all you need, you know. Because the fellow that runs it here in London was a real sort of, you know, trying to knock it down for months before he got it. You know, he was a real cynical whatever you call it.

**Frost:** I mean, even so, as you look at this thing, I mean, you find that you say on the one hand there's no *rules* for how it will affect people or anything, but I mean, looking back in your last work in *Sgt. Pepper's*, there the music was affected by the experiments with all of the drugs and so on that you'd been doing. Are you finding now—we've grabbed you in the middle of this day of a recording session—are you finding a difference in yourselves as you work, in what you work at, and how you work?

**Lennon:** All the differences in *Pepper* and all that were in retrospect, you know. It wasn't, sitting and thinking, "Oh, we had LSD, so we'll make a little tinkle on this." You know, it all . . .

**Frost:** Oh no, as you look in retrospect to what you did yesterday . . .

**Lennon:** We can't see what we've done now.

**Harrison:** I feel that we're all a little more tolerant; we've been learning that over the past four or five years. But I . . . just lately, I think we are very much more tolerant than we have been. And I hope that we'll get even more tolerant.

**Frost:** One of the last things I asked the Maharishi was what he thought that people were on earth for. After six weeks of his teachings, what would you say?

**Harrison:** To create more happiness, to fulfill all desires—the personal things, that everybody's going to be here until they have fulfilled all desires. I mean, this gets into other things that may take up hours of argument.

**Frost:** How do you mean they're still going to be here?

**Harrison:** Well, I believe in reincarnation. I mean, it's just something that I feel exists, that what you sow you reap, so when you die, life and death are still only relative to thought—there's no such thing really, you just keep going. I believe in rebirth, and then you come back and go through more experience, and you die and you come back again and you keep coming back until you've got it straight. That's how I see it.

**Frost:** And then what?

**Harrison:** Well, the ultimate thing is to manifest that divinity so that you can become one with the Creator. I mean, it sounds pretty far out, talking about things like that, but that's just what I believe.

**Lennon:** I believe the same, but it's just when we're talking about meditation and that, it's frightening, really, for people that haven't done it or still, that still fancy the meditation but they hear about coming back and all that up there. So, you know, I'd sooner put it over and forget about that.

**Harrison:** Because that's not really important.

**Lennon:** That happens anyway.

**Harrison:** The whole point of his meditation is for now, you know. Because it's now all the time. It's present, and past has got nothing to do with it.

**Lennon:** Not to live to get into heaven by being a good boy, or to go to hell, just to live better as you're living, do whatever you're doing better. And live now, you know, not looking forward to the great day, or whatever it turns out to be.

**Frost:** And there we must leave it. John and George, thank you very much indeed.

**Lennon and Harrison:** Thank you.

## October 4, 1967

**Frost:** Thank you, thank you and good evening. We're returning to a subject we dealt with last week. Before that, we return to one other subject we dealt with last week. Namely, the "bad news—good news" jokes we asked you to send in. I've got bad news for you and good news, the bad news first.

Mrs. I.M. Lancaster of Ilford said I've got bad news for you and good news. The bad news first. Here's a letter from our son's principal. He's being sent down for having a girl in his room. And now the good news: he's passed his biology exam. G.W. Pilson of Upper Warlingham. R.S.M. to soldier: the bad news for you, you've been posted abroad. The good news: she's a cracker. [*Laughter.*] Anthony—I never know whether this is "Tiggy" or "Tige" [*Thyge*]—of Bushey is right up to the minute. Policeman to motorist after crash: the bad news first, the doctor says you have ten crushed ribs. Now the good news: you passed the breathalyzer test.

Some of them went further than that and wider. From Oswestry, we had this. Doctor after examining woman: I have good news for you, Mrs. Smith. Woman: No, Miss Smith. Doctor: Well, I have some bad news for you, Miss Smith. You're going to have a baby. Woman: That's impossible, I have never ever been with a man. At this, the doctor takes a pair of binoculars from his drawer and looks out of the window. Woman: What are you doing? Doctor: Last time this happened, three wise men came over the horizon and I don't . . . [*Laughter.*]

And Alan Iliff of Keele, the bad news first: the Chinese have landed on the moon. The good news: all of them. [*Laughter.*]

And now we return to the subject we dealt with on Friday when we talked to the Maharishi, and then we talked with John Lennon and George Harrison, and we welcome them back very much indeed, again tonight. We said we were going to deal with the letters that you sent in and so on, and that's what we want to do.

First of all though, one subject that lots of people have referred to, and we talked about a little, in fact, after the program, talking about meditation and the Maharishi in general, after the program on Friday, is the whole area is . . . what would you say—would you say that your lives have altered since the Maharishi, that they've got more meaning and purpose, or more fun or something?

**Harrison:** I think our lives have been altering all the time, that's what life is. It's one continuous alteration, and you keep altering until you've made yourself perfect, or as near perfect as you're capable. But, we have altered a little more, probably, since meeting Maharishi, because we've got something more to work on now. I mean, before we've known . . . I've been under the impression that meditation and yoga, things like that, have held the answer, personally, and yet I haven't actually had any formal teaching, whereas when Maharishi came around, there he was, ready to teach us.

**Frost:** But in fact, from what you were saying, it would seem as though, that before meditation and before the Maharishi, there weren't enough answers, or, from what John was saying last week . . .

**Lennon:** Go on.

**Frost:** . . . that life—[*laughing*] I'm implicating you here—that, I mean, that life, you had bad days and good days. That now, there are more good days, that life has more purpose, that things like money and so on weren't enough before.

**Lennon:** Yeah, well I mean we said that last week. It's just that the good days are very good and the bad days are okay, you know. It's just through tapping me source of energy.

**Frost:** And I mean, has it altered your attitude to something like money, was money ever satisfying and it isn't now, or what?

**Lennon:** No, it's not all . . . what I meant about the money last week was, before we sort of made it, as they say, money was partly the goal but it still wasn't a, sort of, "Let's get some money." But, we sort of got, suddenly had money, and then it wasn't all that good, you know.

**Harrison:** By having the money we found that money wasn't the answer. Because we had lots of material things that people sort of spend their whole life to try and get. We managed to get them at quite an early age. And it was good, really, because we learned that that wasn't it. We still lacked something, and that something is the thing that religion is trying to give to people.

**Frost:** And now that you've got meditation, would you . . . now you have that plus, would you be as happy now if all the money were taken away?

**Harrison:** Yeah, I'd probably be happier actually, because it's the . . . if you have some income, then you have some income tax, and if you have a big house, you have all the other things, headaches, that go with it. So, naturally, for every material thing you gain, there's always a little loss, whether it's mental or in some other way. You get a headache for everything you own, so if you don't own anything, you've got a clear mind.

**Lennon:** You'll get them all saying, "Give it away," now.

[*Laughter.*]

**Harrison:** Yeah. You see that's like . . .

**Frost:** Yes, a lot of people seem to think that, that this was one of the things that was sort of too easy about meditation, that where Jesus Christ said, "Give everything away to the poor," the Maharishi says, "Just give one week's wages." I mean, do you think that's too easy?

**Lennon:** No, I mean, why is it too easy? It's better than not doing anything. Isn't it? You know, what's easy about it?

**Frost:** Well, I'm quoting them, I'm not sure really.

**Harrison:** You see, his meaning for this meditation is to . . . so that people don't alter their day-to-day routine, but through the meditation their routine will naturally become influenced by the meditation experience, so they can keep all their material wealth and things like that that they have. It's just that this gives them some spiritual wealth to go with it, and with that you're able to put the material wealth more into the true perspective. Instead of, I mean, you can use all the material things, like we've got them and it's nice to have them, but we don't really believe in them, whereas some people, who haven't the material things, they tend to believe in them.

**Frost:** But if you were to choose at this moment between having meditation and all that goes with it, and having all your possessions, you would choose to give up the possessions?

**Harrison:** Yes.

**Frost:** Jay Gadney writes, from Plumstead, London, about a friend of his, who is a compulsive gambler. And he says that this friend is married with two children. And he says, "Could meditation stop the friend gambling?" Now does it . . . because he says that it was implied on Friday night that meditation helps people to do the right thing. Now does it? Is it a practical aid like that?

**Lennon:** I don't know whether it could just do . . . I mean, you'd have to ask John that, sort of. It would help him, you know. He might see what he's doing a bit better. Maybe he wouldn't have so much time for gambling.

**Harrison:** You see, with the meditation, the natural thing, it comes: consciousness expansion. And once a person's consciousness has been expanded, then things that they used to do, they probably have less meaning for them, because they're just able to see themselves a little bit more, a bit clearer. So, consequently, things like gambling, probably the person would just see that it was pointless himself.

**Frost:** Yes. A lady writing from Gosport goes further. She's been practicing transcendental meditation for some time, and she says that you become more and more aware of all the dangers that exist in present living. And she finds that she avoids social things and withdraws because you find it such a strain to have patience with a senseless conversation, apart from it being an aimless waste of time. Well, thank you for coming. But the . . . now, can you see yourself getting as impatient as that . . .

**Harrison:** No.

**Frost:** . . . with life on the superficial level.

**Lennon:** Is she doing the same one?

**Frost:** Well, she calls it TM, but I mean, which I assume is . . . but she says . . .

**Harrison:** There's various forms of meditation. And as we're trying this one, we're not able really to comment on hers. Obviously, hers isn't much cop, otherwise . . .

[*Laughter.*]

**Harrison:** Otherwise she'd be happy and able to go through society with whatever she need do, I mean, it's . . . this is part of this thing, is to stay and be able to do everything that you normally do, just to be able to do it easier.

**Frost:** Can you—you explained sort of after the program was over on Friday that, I mean, I was . . . what the eventual aim of it is and the eventual aim of life is and the eventual point with meditation that you hope to reach. Scribbling on there again if you like, what were you saying there?

**Harrison:** Well, with this expansion of consciousness, these three states that we live in at the moment, like sleeping and waking and dreaming. They're all known as relative states, because it's all relative. Transcendental meditation takes you to that transcendental level of pure consciousness. But by going there often enough, you bring that level of consciousness out onto this level. Or you bring this level onto that level. But the relative plus that level becomes cosmic consciousness. And that means that you're able to hold the full bliss consciousness in the relative field, so you can go about your actions all the time with bliss consciousness.

**Frost:** Yes . . . and can you go . . .

**Harrison:** And there's a higher one, yes, they go higher and attain what's known as God consciousness and then higher still to one known as supreme knowledge where the people who know about supreme knowledge know about all the subtle laws that control the universe. Consequently, they're able to do all those things that are called miracles. In actual fact, a miracle is just having knowledge of supreme law.

**Frost:** And so these people are able to do miracles, are they, when they reach this point, also able to live longer and do this?

**Harrison:** Yes, well there's lots of cases, there's a book I've been reading about a yogi known as Shivapuri Baba. He lived to be 136, and when he was 112, he got cancer of the mouth and started smoking cigarettes and got rid of it. [*Laughter.*] And there's another one, [*laughs*] there's one who's in the Himalayas at this very moment and he's been there since . . . I mean, it sounds pretty far out, you know, to the average person who doesn't know anything about this, but this fellow's been there since before Jesus Christ, and he's still here now in the same physical body.

**Lennon:** Same suit.

**Frost:** So, from before Jesus Christ. He's still there?

**Harrison:** They get control over life and death. They have complete control over . . . everything, having attained that higher state of consciousness.

**Frost:** And this is eventually the aim of anyone who takes that meditation?

**Harrison:** Yeah.

**Frost:** But a long, long time ahead?

**Harrison:** Well, I think Maharishi's . . .

**Lennon:** I mean, they don't mean this life. You can be at that miracle scene. That happens later, a few more lives, maybe, you might get . . .

**Frost:** When you've returned a number of times.

**Lennon:** Yeah.

**Frost:** Yeah.

**Harrison:** But his plan is so that people from the age of say, fifteen, practice it. By the time they're our age they've already attained cosmic consciousness, that is, the state of bliss.

**Frost:** Stage three, as it were. Yeah.

**Harrison:** And then, they're at an age where they can go and act, and manage to change the world a little bit for the better. Rather than sort of waiting, till you're almost dying, then thinking, you know, "What is it? We've got to find out where we're going, what's all this thing about death?" And then they start panicking, and then it's a bit late. The whole point is to try and find it out at this age and then you've got your whole life to go and act upon it.

**Frost:** And then you set about doing something about the world around you.

**Harrison:** Well, obviously, if you believe in certain things, and other people aren't, as it were, harmonizing with these laws. It's all the thing about the Ten Commandments, all that, it's that sort of thing that certain people have laid down laws, or they've said that these laws exist and we live within these laws anyway, whether we like it or not. We're controlled by these divine laws. So if you harmonize with the laws, then everything's much nicer, and nature tends to support you.

**Frost:** Right. At that point can we throw it open to our audience here. I can see in the audience a number of people who are leaders in the practicing of meditation, who have come along here tonight, including John Allison and Nick Clark and also John Mortimer, who's expressed his views in print on the subject of meditation, so if we could turn our cameras around to the audience . . . John, have you got some comment to make at this point?

**John Mortimer:** Yes. [*Indistinct.*] First of all, I don't accept universal divine laws, so that's a difficulty, but I think you've really got to judge these beliefs by their pragmatic effect, and the amount of good they're going to do in the world. And what worries me very much about this attitude is that it seems to be tremendously self-involved and, finally, tremendously selfish. And the idea of sitting very quietly perfecting yourself, while everybody else goes to hell around, you seems to be not really . . .

**Lennon:** For twenty minutes a day?

**Mortimer:** . . . the most, well, but it seems to me there is a great deal of very important things happening in the world. We're in a great crisis of history, and if we all wait to perfect ourselves, nothing will be done about it.

**Lennon:** But it's twenty minutes in the morning, so's you can go out and do something about all the . . .

**Harrison:** You're not listening to what we said, I mean . . .

**Mortimer:** But you see, this kind of doctrine of universal love, in a way seems to me to end up by not really caring about anybody very much.

**Harrison:** Well, that's *your* point of view.

**Mortimer:** What I think one needs is a little well-aimed loathing of things like President Johnson and Ronald Reagan and so on, and not sitting in San Francisco watching the flowers grow and letting Governor Reagan be elected perhaps for the presidency of the United States.

**Lennon:** Well, that's not the same thing, you know, I mean, that's . . . watching the flowers grow in Haight-Ashbury is not what we're talking about.

**Mortimer:** No, but I think that everything, nothing that you've said has seemed to me to have any real consciousness of the historical crises in which other people are getting . . .

**John Allison:** This is the whole point of this whole situation. This is in order to expand the conscious capacity of the mind for right action. And if the intelligence is increased, and if the contentment is increased, and if the energy is increased, this all comes to bear upon whatever the moment may be. The whole purpose of this teaching is for action.

**Mortimer:** But with great respect, that hasn't happened in India. What's happened in India is an enormous acceptance of disaster and the kind of placid . . .

**Allison:** Precisely, now this whole point is what is wrong with spiritual teaching, it has been wrong for centuries.

**Mortimer:** Well, that may be wrong with the Maharishi himself.

**Allison:** No, because this is precisely the situation which he has come to reform. His position is exactly the position that you're taking up.

**Frost:** How do you mean?

**Mortimer:** Well, I'm very pleased to hear it.

**Frost:** How do you mean?

**Nick Clark:** May I say a word?

**Frost:** Yes, of course.

**Clark:** A few moments of silence every day, of deep silence, can only be good, do good to us all, in this world of noise, first. Second, in these moments of silence, once we are conscious of something deep in us, which is our own being in eternity, independent of our becoming in time, then we have had the greatest and deepest experience of our life. Third, if in that moment we can feel that our object is to receive the love of the universe that brought us here and to give something of this love to all, at all times, in all places if we can—and if not, we struggle to do it—it can only be good.

**Frost:** John.

**Mortimer:** Well, again, it's very, very self-involved. You want to get peace, you want to enjoy peace, you want to enjoy placidity. You think the universe is something which has independent love for you, I don't happen to agree. I think the universe is a soulless, biological thing, and it's up to us to improve it. And we're not going to improve it if we're going to stay quite still, enjoying peace and perfection.

**Lennon:** But nobody's saying stay still all day, are they?

**Allison:** I'm not doubting your sincerity about this, John [*Mortimer*], but do you think you're capable of doing a right action from a state of unlovingness?

**Mortimer:** Oh yes. I'm sure you are. I don't think there was much love in Lenin, or much love in many, many people who have enormously advanced the happiness and the progress of humanity. If Lenin had stopped quite still and had twenty minutes silence, and then contemplated his navel, we'd still have czars.

**Allison:** You might not have had the purges in the 1930s.

**Mortimer:** Exactly, it's a very difficult choice.

**Audience Member:** What is the basis, what is the motivation of your action and your social concern? You're a man who is socially concerned. On what basis?

**Mortimer:** I think that you must try and do an imperfect best to improve a lot of other people.

**Audience Member:** But you don't seem to know why.

**Mortimer:** Because I think that it's finally a kind of evolutionary necessity. I think that we must advance.

**Clark:** Must you not improve yourself first? Take the problem of war. We all want peace, I mean except idiotic people who . . . or evil people. But first, if we work for peace, we cannot truly work for peace unless we have peace in ourselves, unless we have love in ourselves. Then you can work for peace, and you can be crucified if necessary, it is. But you cannot suffer and work, finally, and this is the solution of the modern world, what we might call Christian communism.

**Frost:** At that point, let me go back to John and George. I mean, is this fair, the parallel that's being drawn here, between your sort of getting very involved with meditation and that somehow being very, very selfish and not caring about the world.

**Lennon:** No, what they're saying about selfishness is it sounds as though you're going to sit down in silence all the time. You know, you do it in the morning, say, to do your day's action, whatever it is, better. But you're putting it down, saying, "We can't sit down contemplating our navels, while all this is going on." The whole point of doing it is to have more energy and more control over yourself, to be able to do whatever action you want to do.

**Mortimer:** I never thought any of that for a moment.

**Lennon:** What were you saying then?

**Audience Member:** Some of us here are Quakers, and we've been practicing what some people would call a form of meditation, which has driven the Society of Friends into action. Now, after last week's wonderful program, we're very impressed, and people have been saying to us, "There's a couple of lads there who are natural Quakers." [*Laughter.*] Now, do they think they're Quakers?

**Harrison:** Well, it's all the same. This is the point we've got to try and get over to people, that religion, there's only one God and they're all a branch of the same thing. And the sooner people get over this sectarianism, the better, you know. I mean, I'm a Quaker, I'm a Christian, and I'm a Buddhist, and I'm a Hindu. And it's all the same.

**Audience Member:** Well, that's what Quakers have been saying for the last three hundred years . . . the divine in all of us.

**Allison:** I want to come back onto this thing of action. It's a commonplace that we live very much on the surface of our minds in relation to the surface of events. This is a very . . . weak situation. Now, it's also commonplace that there's a great depth in every human mind. All this transcendental meditation is, is a simple technique of coming to the deepest aspect of that, having established oneself in that state to come out and act, like pulling an arrow back on a bow. If you don't know about shooting an arrow, you say, "Well, what are you pulling it back for?" But this is the whole technique of shooting the arrow.

**Mortimer:** Yes, but then you see there is in this belief a kind of faith in a transcendental will in the universe, which I don't happen to share. But I think you can waste a tremendous lot of time trying to get into a state of bliss, in communion with that.

**Frost:** There's no faith at all, John Allison?

**Allison:** This is a perceptual method. It's absolutely unconcerned with conceptual apparatus.

**Mortimer:** I don't think the Maharishi made it that clear to us really.

**Frost:** Do you find, John and George, that your beliefs have altered as a result of meditation?

**Harrison:** No, they've been strengthened. But I've always believed this for the last couple of years, but through the meditation, it's just strengthened it. You see, all these doctrines and beliefs that have been laid down by great prophets, they've been put down there because these people have actually experienced it. And by their experience with some form of truth, they've tried to put it out for all the rest of the people to take up. But his argument is just based on no experience at all.

**Frost:** You said just now that you're a Hindu, you're a Buddhist, you're a Christian. You're all of these.

**Harrison:** Yes.

**Frost:** People think of those things normally as different. What is it . . . in what way is it that they're all the same?

**Harrison:** Well, because it's teaching the people through various forms how to approach God. And God being the one and only creator. They're all different—

**Audience Member:** But is this experience driving our friends into some kind of community? This is what's bothering us a bit. Is this something you must do on your own, or does it lead you into community action?

**Harrison:** Well, you must do it on your own to attain your own bliss state, naturally. It's something that Jesus said, something about, "Go and fix your own house first," and that's what you've got to do. Everybody goes and fixes themselves up, and when they're all straight, then they're all able to act together, because we're all one anyway whether you like it or not.

---

**Frost:** We've got about three more things to do in this second half tonight, but it's quite clear talking to the audience and so on during the break that there's a lot more to be said on this subject. So, we'll scrap the rest and we'll carry on with this. Do you think it's fair, what's been said so far by John Mortimer and so on, suggesting that meditation is selfish?

**Lennon:** I don't see how it's selfish, if we've no need to be here. You know, I mean we don't sort of dig doing TV for the fun of it. We're here just because we want, you know, we believe in meditation. So that's not very selfish.

**Harrison:** And we can sort of maybe help a few other people to understand that it's, you know, that it's easy.

**Mortimer:** But we've got no need to be here either, really.

[*Laughter.*]

**Lennon:** We're not claiming you're selfish, though.

**Mortimer:** And I would like to understand, I think that perhaps we should try and get it a little clearer, what we're talking about. If we're talking about a mystical religious belief, which I think that George Harrison is, because he talked about the divine laws . . .

**Harrison:** It's not mystical. . . .

**Mortimer:** Well, let me just finish this. Then that's one thing, which I would dispute, but I would like to ask John Allison, whether really this has got anything to do with a belief in God at all. Because if all we're talking about is a technique of self-examination that you can perform over shaving in the morning and then go out and help mankind more as a result of having done it, then nobody in their senses would dispute that it was a very excellent thing to do. Are we talking about that, or are we talking about a universe which has some hidden laws and a hidden creator, who manifests himself only to people like Mr. Harrison and the Maharishi when they get into a state of trance, that's what I want to know.

**Harrison:** Well, let's face it, these laws that you say, hidden laws, they are hidden, but they're only hidden by our own ignorance. And the word "mysticism" is . . . just been arrived at through people's ignorance. There's nothing mystical about it, only that you're ignorant of what that entails.

**Mortimer:** Everybody with any religious belief has always thought that everybody else was ignorant about its mystical value. But are we really talking about mysticism, or are we talking about a technique of improving yourself, which is totally scientific and rational?

**Allison:** You can take it either way, you can take it either way. This is because it is a perceptual method. If a man has got a great conceptual apparatus and he meditates, he will begin to understand the nature of the conceptual apparatus, and if he's wrong about it, he will begin to understand where he's wrong about it. If he's got no conceptual apparatus, he simply perceives an abstract experience. Now, when he's had an abstract experience, he may wish then to give himself explanation for it. But it's primarily a perceptual method.

**Frost:** And how, for everybody, do you define the word "perceptual"?

**Allison:** Experience, rather than thinking about something. Not an idea, not an attitude, not a belief—an experience. It's the difference . . . conceptual is a biological textbook; going for a walk in the country is an experience. They refer to each other, but they're in different situations.

**Mortimer:** But why should this abstract experience be any more valuable than the other experience, you see. George Harrison talked about a bliss experience. Well, you can have a bliss experience by drinking a bottle of whiskey. Why is his bliss experience . . .

[*Laughter.*]

**Frost:** A hell of a non-bliss experience the next morning.

**Mortimer:** How is his abstract bliss experience in any way more valuable than anybody else's bliss experience?

**Audience Member:** You are notoriously an anti-God man, but if you told me the God that you don't believe in, I'm sure we'd all say we didn't believe in Him either. But one isn't talking about belief, one is talking about experience. And this experience is an inner experience, and having had this experience or having this experience you then have to describe it. And certainly there is a language to describe it. But it's something that can be talked about, it's something that is actual, it happened as much as the historical.

**Frost:** Yes, but look, but I mean the thing is that, what is the difference then, what is the difference between the two things that John has just said. What is the difference between a bliss experience through meditation and, assuming it's possible, a bliss experience through drinking—as I sound as though I'm doing at the moment—a bottle of whiskey?

**Harrison:** Because the bottle of whiskey one is relative. It could be relative bliss depending on how intoxicated you got, whereas the meditation, you go beyond this ordinary experience that's on the relative level of experience, it's beyond that. And this is why you can't tell the people about it really; it's something that if they did it themselves, then they'd know because they'd actually experience the thing. You can't talk about an abstract experience, you can't really put it into words.

**Mortimer:** You see, that's what Dr. Allison has talked about, he says it's an abstract experience. Well that sounds to me a very blurred conception, and as uninteresting really as abstract art. Why isn't it better to have an experience which is related to the actual world we live in?

**Lennon:** What's wrong with abstract art?

**Allison:** Well, this is the point. Could I make this point? John, the thing is, that, in the last resort, people can talk about meditation until they're pie-eyed, as if you're a public meal on television. And in fact, it won't convince you or anybody else at all, it's just simply something you have got to try. I cannot tell you what a strawberry tastes like. The last resort if you want to know what a strawberry is like: eat it. You may like it at the end of it, or you may not. Now, the point . . .

**Mortimer:** It doesn't give the strawberry some translucent, mystical . . . [*Laughter.*]

**Allison:** No, look, let's . . . well, speak for yourself, I adore strawberries, they're one of the most delicious things in the world, but I mean, let's get on . . . a side track. Yes.

**Frost:** Now let's get on to your restaurant.

[*Laughter.*]

**Allison:** No, but the point is this, the point is this, John if I could just finish. It's the reason that all of us who practice meditation feel it's so important for people to know about it, is because you do come to a state where you can find total serenity, total peace. And this is desperately what the world is needing.

**Mortimer:** There are many, many ways of achieving total serenity.

**Lennon:** How do you do it?

**Mortimer:** I've never have had it.

**Lennon:** Well, why don't you try it then, instead of talking about it?

**Mortimer:** I don't honestly know whether it's something I'm particularly interested in. You can achieve total serenity by going mad, you can achieve marvelous serenity by going to sleep. What one has got to decide is whether the serenity which you are seeking is, A, of practical value to the world, and B, particularly enjoyable to yourself. You say it's enjoyable, we don't know.

**Allison:** Don't worry about whether I personally enjoy this, it's totally irrelevant. Do you believe there is such a thing as evil and sin in the world? . . . Something unpleasant?

**Mortimer:** I certainly believe there are very many unpleasant things in the world, yes.

**Allison:** Now, I believe it is true to say that all sin is fear-motivated. I believe fear is the central enemy of mankind, whether it's neuroticism, whether it's actual active aggressive evil, it doesn't matter what it is. Fear, fear, fear, this is our heritage. I think for original sin you can read original fear. Now, paradoxically, society, for countless generations have been trying to fight fear with more fear. Fear of hellfire and damnation. Fear of what society will say, what people will say. Fear of the hell, of the cat, fear of the galleys, fear of prison, fear of this, fear of that. Piling fear upon fear upon fear.

It's not surprising that, in fact, society is in a ghastly terrible state. Now, where the Bible says "perfect love casted out fear," this is just what we're talking about. You arrive at a state of peace, of serenity, of joy, inside yourself. You are no longer afraid, therefore you are able to give out love to other people.

**Mortimer:** Nobody is going to argue that it is not a good thing to cast out fear. Nobody's going to try and pretend it's not a good thing to love people and have goodwill as much as possible. The only thing that I'm venturing to question is whether the pursuit of your own serenity is the best path towards achieving all these excellent . . .

**Lennon:** Well, if you're happy, you're more likely to make other people happy, that's all it is, you know.

**Mortimer:** Not necessarily.

**Lennon:** Why?

**Mortimer:** I can imagine a very happy husband giving his family absolute hell.

**Lennon:** Well, he's not really happy then, you know. I'm talking about true happiness.

**Frost:** How would you characterize true happiness?

**Lennon:** Well, as opposed to happiness from a bottle of whiskey, and happiness from going in there. You know, same again.

**Clark:** Is it not a difference of words? A bottle of whiskey, I would say, gives us pleasure—if there's something transient, if I drink it, somebody else cannot drink it. But an experience of joy, even the experience of a poem or music, of contemplation of nature, we all can have it. And therefore, that higher experience, and we call it joy, is the joy, and this joy grows higher and higher until we can find a joy in the very center of our souls. The joy of being and the joy of love. If for a moment we all have this feeling of love now, here, universal love, the millions or thousands of people who hear us would feel it.

**Frost:** Yes, but what is a feeling?

**Harrison:** What is a feeling, right. This is it, you see. It's all . . . it's vibrations that people give off. I mean, if somebody's happy then he gives off a good vibration as opposed to being annoyed, he'll give off a bad vibration, it's something like that. If you get a lot of people like when we first went to Bangor, we met all these meditators, and it's so obvious just by seeing the people because they give off this peace and happiness. And that's the thing, the more people who do it, the more the vibration, and that's the influence for everybody else. The bigger the vibration, the more people receive it, and the more the other people will believe it.

**Mortimer:** You see, there were a lot of Christian saints who spent their time up in convents, carefully cultivating their innocent serenity and the grooming the perfection of their own soul. And there were other saints, I suppose, who went out into the world and tried to improve a lot of other people. I think you simply have to choose which you admire the most.

**Harrison:** But sometimes you don't . . .

**Allison:** A cake-and-eat-it scene, John, this is literally a cake-and-eat-it scene. I agree with you, there have been techniques, and there probably still are techniques of people withdrawing totally from the world and living in a cave or sitting on the top of a pillar and doing absolutely nothing at all, apparently doing nothing at all. Maybe they feel *wonderful* and quite fairly you say, "What good do they do?" Now, all Maharishi has come to do in the West is to teach every single one of us, what . . .

[*Crashing sound.*]

**Lennon:** [*Shouting in a funny voice*] Look out, Charlie!

**Frost:** Oh, the end of the world, this.

**Lennon:** It's a miracle.

**Frost:** No, somebody's just drunk a bottle of whiskey.
[*Laughter.*]

**Allison:** This is cosmic consciousness at work, obviously. Now, what was I saying?

**Frost:** You're not expected to remember.

**Allison:** No, this whole point is that it is a technique whereby somebody, whatever you're doing or maybe frightfully busy, you just meditate for twenty minutes, twenty-five minutes, half an hour, twice a day and you come back slap-bang on with very much more energy to get on and do things. It is an increase in energy.

**Audience Member:** Are you claiming this is something new?

**Harrison:** No, no, it's ancient.

**Audience Member:** You are expressing in a new way something that has been with us all the time?

**Harrison:** Yes, yes, and it'll always be here.

**Audience Member:** But it had to be rediscovered from time to time because our society, as it goes on, overlays it with materialistic concerns, we build a nice structure for ourselves, we're getting at the money, we're building ourselves a nice career, and we're kicking our people in the teeth while we're doing it.

**Frost:** The thing that people were concerned about after Friday's thing, was that, that this meditation, while it may do something for the individual, was not also concerned with the other fifty percent stopping us, or other people kicking each other in the teeth. Now, today it's clear that the way John Allison, George, and John see this thing, it equally then reacts on the way you live and the way you behave and the way you care about other people. But I don't think it is the meditation that does that, is it? We're rather fortunate to have three exponents here who do care; you could be an exponent and not give a damn, couldn't you? What you just said is that . . .

**Allison:** It's not this matter at all, you see, one thing that Halliman said, that state of pure consciousness, which is what the tension is led to, is the same in everyone. You come to that state, this is union with the whole creation. Having established that in the mind, you come out of it. Little by little as you go on, year after year meditating, more and more and more of that comes out. So in the midst of your dynamic, frenzied activities, that is not overshadowed, and that becomes automatically expressed by your actions.

**Mortimer:** Then you're back on a mystic faith and a universal conscience.

**Harrison:** "Mystic, mystic," all the time! You know, there's nothing mystic about *mystic*, you know, it's just a word that people have invented because they don't understand it.

**Frost:** But all right . . . then, John, what is then the difference would you say between John Lennon before meditation and John Lennon after a few weeks of meditation?

**Lennon:** Well, before I wouldn't have been here. I've got more energy and more happiness. I don't know about intelligence. I'm just happier, you know, I'm just a better person. And I wasn't bad before.

**Harrison:** I'll second that.

[*Laughter.*]

**Lennon:** Thank you, George, thank you.

**Frost:** And that, there, with personal testimony, is where we must leave it. Until tomorrow night, good night.

# BEATLE GEORGE AND
# WHERE HE'S AT

Nick Jones | December 16 and 30, 1967 | *Melody Maker*

Nick Jones joined *Melody Maker*— "the *MM*," as those in the know called it—as a sixteen-year-old junior reporter in 1965, introduced by his father Max, the paper's veteran jazz and blues writer. From the late 1930s to early '70s, the *MM*'s coverage had spanned dance and swing bands; rock 'n' roll; pop chart hits; traditional, modern, and avant-garde jazz; country blues to urban R&B; and traditional to electric folk music. With its concert and gig news, "musicians wanted" advertising, and instrument and equipment advice, *Melody Maker* had a secure, symbiotic relationship with the music industry and the artists who fueled it.

Soon after joining the publication, Jones embedded his own youthful enthusiasm for the Who, the Action, the Small Faces, American soul, Motown, and psychedelia into the paper. In November '67—after the Beatles' summer sojourns with the Maharishi, the death of Brian Epstein, and the filming of *Magical Mystery Tour*—the group's London office unexpectedly proffered an exclusive preview of their new single and promotional film "Hello, Goodbye," specifically requesting the presence of young Nick. Jones recalls the rest:

> Hooking up in a Soho cutting room where they were editing *Magical Mystery Tour* footage, John casually tossed out quotes from a recent review I had written with characteristic gusto and good humor. After this chastening experience, I accompanied Paul to a nearby preview theatre to view the completed "Hello, Goodbye" sequence, succeeded by a flurry of visits to some Carnaby Street fashion emporiums, where he was getting fitted out. If the morning's whirlwind activity was a test of my mettle, I

must have passed because next came the invitation to meet George at the famous 2i's Coffee Bar in London's Old Compton Street.

In understated denim, George spoke passionately of his recently focused spiritual journey and love of Indian music. We sat opposite each other in the 2i's, completely undisturbed and unnoticed, as the world outside rushed past. It was as if a cloak of invisibility and peacefulness had embraced us both, whilst the message was delivered. All I did was listen. George did not require much prompting at all. I transcribed the interview exactly as it transpired, and to their eternal credit, the *MM* editors published every word.

It was my very last contribution to the paper. I resigned to pursue a different muse and never met a Beatle again. But, as with so many others, they had already changed my life forever . . . and I still listen to Ravi Shankar.

—Ed.

## December 16, 1967

For many people, the Beatles have long passed the stage where they are merely a pop group. The first indication of this development was probably when George Harrison began to take an interest in Indian music and consequently Indian culture. It was George who introduced John, Paul, and Ringo to the Maharishi and it is George's passion for his teaching that affects almost all Beatle thinking at the moment. In this exclusive *Melody Maker* interview, conducted by Nick Jones, George dwells on his new-found philosophy of life; how he arrived at it; what it means to him; and what it will mean to the directions the Beatles are now taking. Music hardly entered the conversation—but then, the Beatles are much more than music alone now.

**The Maharishi Mahesh Yogi is already being criticized, as are the Beatles, in connection with your studies in transcendental meditation.**

It's easier to criticize somebody than to see yourself. We had got to the point where we were looking for somebody like the Maharishi, and then there he was. Most other people had never thought about this before and suddenly there he is being thrust down their necks.

**You didn't just suddenly get on to a meditation "kick"?**

No, it's been about three years thinking, looking for why we're here—the purpose of what we're doing here on this world, getting born and dying. Normally people don't think about it and then they just die, and then they've gone and missed it—because we do come here for some purpose.

And I've found out that the reason we come here is to get back to that thing God had, whatever you might call God, you know, that scene. The thing is everybody is potentially divine, every human being is potentially a Christ.

**So you all were in this scene before the Maharishi and all the publicity came along?**

Yeah. When you're young you get taken to church by your parents and you get pushed into religion in school. They're trying to put something into your mind. But it's wrong you know. Obviously, because nobody goes to church and nobody believes in God. Why? Because religious teachers don't know what they're teaching. They haven't interpreted the Bible as it was intended.

### Acid

This is the thing that led me into the Indian scene, that I didn't really believe in God as I'd been taught it. It was just like something out of a science fiction novel.

I think it was really after acid, because acid was the big sort of psychological reaction. It's really only after acid that it pushes home to you that you're only little—really. And there's all that infinity out there and there's something doing it, you know.

It's not just that it's us doing it or the Queen doing it, but that it's some great power that's doing it.

Then the music, Indian music just seemed to have something very spiritual for me[,] and it became a stepping-stone for me to find out about a whole lot of other things. Finding out all about Hinduism and all those sort of religions made me realize that Christianity is that as well—every religion is just the same scene really.

For Christianity, it's the people who profess to be the religious teachers who screw the whole thing up. They're the people who create the sectarianism, the prejudices and the hate that goes on. You know, those people who are supposed to be propagating the Lord's word—they're screwing it all up.

You're taught to just have faith, you don't have to worry about it, just believe what we're telling you. And this is what makes the Indian one such a groove for me and I'm sure for a lot of other people, because over there they say, "Don't believe in anything . . . if there's a God we must see him, if there's a soul we must perceive it," and so on.

## Cringe

It's better to be an outspoken atheist than a hypocrite, so their whole teaching is don't believe in nothing until you've witnessed it for yourself. I really feel and believe very much in this whole sort of scene, you know, God. You know when you say the word "god" people are going to curl up and cringe—they all interpret it in a different way.

The Maharishi is a monk and he hasn't got a penny, and he doesn't want to have a penny. He doesn't want any money and obviously you get the Press saying he's staying in the Hilton and he does this and he does that—but in actual fact he didn't stay in the Hilton but in a meditator's house.

## Nature

And he's been here for nine years and for eight of those years he never had a word said or written about him until the Beatles got interested in it and then he gets all this.

So we know where the Press are at and all those people who are putting him down—because they're only writing about him because of us.

**But how do these realizations fit into your actual everyday existence? You're saying that everything really is predestined?**

Well, yes. This is what the Maharishi says. The more you meditate and the more you harmonize with life in general then the more nature supports you. Nature has supported you since you were born if you come to think about it.

I mean, why did I go to that school at that time, and meet that fella, who met this fella, and we did this, you know, why?

Why did I meet Ravi Shankar? And the difference between the thing of me meeting Shankar is that people will see this from their point of view, but actually it's much different.

When I met him and got to know him, it was like I'd known him for a thousand years—and the same response back from him.

The more I've got into it, the more you find out about the truth, then the more you see this thing we call reality isn't reality at all—this is all an illusion.

And this is the big drag because everybody lives their lives thinking this is reality and then say to people like us, "oh, you're just escaping from reality."

## Joke

They seriously term this scene of waking up, going out to work, going home again, going to sleep, dreaming, waking up again and all that—reality! But in actual fact you're into illusion—it's nothing to do with reality because reality is God alone. Everything else is illusion.

Those people in the Himalayas, the Yogi who are very advanced spiritually, and all the ones on other planets, well it's just a joke to them all this that we do and call reality. I mean it's even a joke if you just take yourself out of it and watch all the things going on.

It's a joke. And the joke's on all the people who take it seriously. There's so much more to it.

You see every so often somebody comes to the earth, like Jesus did, and they've been coming every so often, these people, divine incarnation, like Buddha, Jesus, and all that.

## Miracle

There's always, these people coming and they are the truth, like God, this great force whatever it is, manifesting itself into a physical form.

And there are quite a few people walking around on earth this minute who have attained that—all over the world, in the Himalayas, in America, everywhere—and they just look like funny little old men. I mean, like Maharishi, they look like that.

People of course don't take much notice of them or put 'em down, when all these people are doing is telling the truth—they're always there.

I read somewhere that the next fella like that, the next Messiah like, he'll come and he'll just be too much. Anybody who doesn't believe that he's the one then he'll just show 'em, you know. He's just gonna come down and zap them all.

Miracles, like. That's why this whole thing is getting better and better. It's building up to a great peak. It's the cycle moving on. The majority of people are going to believe and they'll be digging everything and he'll come and say "yeah baby, that's right," and all those other people who are bastards, they're gonna get something else. Instead when they die, they won't reincarnate on this earth, they'll get put down on another planet that's still got to come through the evolutionary thousands of years that we've just been through. It's just fantastic you know.

Really it's all too much because everybody who's becoming involved and realizes it is part of the plot.

## Cycles

I don't like to use the word "religious" but when you get into whatever that is, that scene, when you go through yoga and meditation it's just . . . self realization.

And the next world that's coming along is going to bring us into this age that's known as the Golden Age.

You know that scene about the Iron Age, the Stone Age, the Ice Age, and that's this thing of evolution, the cycles that it goes through—and the Golden Age is when everything is really nice.

A pleasure to be here.

## December 30, 1967

**We were talking about how meditation and yoga leads to self realization.**

Yes, that's the whole thing why people have missed God. They haven't been able to see God because he is hidden in themselves. All the time people concentrate their energies and activities outwards on this surface level that we live on.

But it's only by turning your concentration and directing it inwardly, in a form of meditation, that you can see your own god in there. When you realize that then you can realize a lot more things about this surface level—because you're now looking at it from a more subtle point of view. I mean really there's people on every planet, but going on different planes. Not necessarily in a physical form as we know it, but in a different form. Like Venus. They've gone to Venus and they come back and say: "Oh, very sorry, it's too hot to live there, and there's none of this," and all that scene, but they're looking for people as we know them, people like us. Really what they're saying is, you can't live on Venus in the physical body as we know it. As we understand people to be the same as us, then they couldn't possibly live there—but in actual fact, you won't see anybody if you go there unless you're on their frequency.

**But how important do you think positive music is in this huge evolutionary cycle?**

Yeah, very important. I think there is spiritual music. This is why I'm so hung up on Indian music and from the day I got into it till the day I die I still believe it's the greatest music ever on our level of existence. It's really so, so subtle and that's the whole thing. This level of consciousness now that we're on is the gross level, which is the opposite to the subtle level.

Everything those Indian musicians do—it's just indescribable. It's an inner feeling, yeah, soul. It's like saying "It's soul man!" You know all this spade music that's going—it's just the first thing people getting into, the soul kick, but when you really get into soul, then—it's God.

### Brainwashing with Music

But the music is very important because of the "mass media" point of view. I think music is the main interest of the younger people. It doesn't really matter about the older people now because they're finished anyway.

There's still going to be years and years of having all these old fools who are governing us and who are bombing us and doin' all that because, you know, it's always them. But it's no good getting hung up about them because the main thing is to get the kids. You know, this is the Catholic trick—they nail you when you're young and brainwash you, and then they've got you for the rest of your life. In actual fact, do this sort of thing—but brainwash people with the truth—turn them all onto music and books at that age, then they'll live a better life. Then it's the next generation that does it more, and after that . . . so it doesn't matter if we see the perfection of the Golden Age or not.

I don't expect to see the world in a perfect state of bliss—you know, like 100 per cent—but it doesn't matter, it's on the way now.

So really, with Maharishi, we've gone into all these things and scenes, and I've learned a hell of a lot about Hinduism from being in India, things I've read, and from Ravi Shankar, who's really too much. So great. Not only in his music but in him as well.

This is the thing. He is the music, and the music is him. The whole culture of the Indian philosophy, the background and all that.

Mainly it's this thing of discipline. Discipline is something that we don't like, especially young people where they have to go through school and they put you in the army and all that discipline. But in a different way I've found out it's very important because the only way those musicians are great is because they've been disciplined by their guru or teacher, and they've surrendered themselves to the person they want to be.

It's only by complete surrender and doing what that bloke tells you that you're going to get there, too. So with their music they do just that. You must practice twelve hours a day for years and years and years. And Shankar has really studied every part of the music until he just improvises the music until it is just him, he is the music.

**Was this the point you were trying to make in your ads, which said "*Sergeant Pepper* IS the Beatles?"**

I feel this is something we've been trying to do all the time. Keep that identification with people. It gets harder and harder the more famous you get.

## Down from the Pedestal

People see you, they put you up on that pedestal and they really believe you're different from them. With *Sgt. Pepper* we've always tried to keep this identification and tried to do things for those people, to please those people, because in actual fact, they're us, too, really.

It's no good us doing it all for ourselves, it's for them. With *Pepper* it's just that anybody who feels, anybody who wants to be in Pepper's Band is in it. Anybody who feels any identification. And this all gets back again to God.

But at the same time we're all responsible in a way because a lot of people are following us, we're influencing a lot of people, so really, it's to influence them in the right way.

**A lot of people, though, never realise what you're giving them?**

Well, lots of people do, but then there's always the other ones who write in saying "Why the fuck do you think you are doing that." There's always that, you see, and it all gets back to the thing of the Maharishi and God.

The Maharishi says this level that we're on is like the surface of the ocean, which is always changing, chopping and changing, and we're living on the surface with these waves crashing about.

But unless we're anchored on the bottom we're at the mercy of whatever goes on on the surface. So you go into meditation and your thoughts get smaller all the time, finer and finer, until you get right down there, until that's just pure consciousness, and you anchor yourself to that—and once you've established that anchor then it doesn't matter what goes on up on the surface.

The more people do it the more they'll realize. You can't tell somebody what it's like until they try it for themselves.

If you can contact that absolute state you can just tap that amazing source of energy and intelligence. It's there, anyway—you've just got to contact it and then it will make whatever you do easier and better. Everything in life works out better because everybody is happier with themselves.

# RADIO INTERVIEW

DAVID WIGG | October 8, 1969 | *Scene and Heard*, BBC Radio

Relaxed and at times somewhat self-amused in this conversation, Harrison was interviewed by BBC Radio 1 host David Wigg, whose *Scene and Heard* program featured conversations with all the Beatles that year. Besides serving as a popular DJ, Wigg was also well known as a music journalist, writing columns for the *Daily Express* and the *London Evening News*. As Wigg recalled:

> We met at the Apple offices in London . . . it was an important time for George as he was emerging as a strong songwriting influence. He explained how "Here Comes the Sun" had come to him while sitting in Eric Clapton's garden, and that "Something" was for [*his wife*] Pattie. He also described what meditation and Hare Krishna meant to him, the Beatles financial problems, and how he came to terms with being a Beatle.

Increasingly through this period, Harrison is remarkably open to speaking about the business of being a Beatle—from financial and personal perspectives, alike. He addresses what that identity means to him and the inequities he felt, being looked at as wealthy while dealing with the unusual machinations of a four-man partnership. He considers the need to balance his business side with his growing focus on spiritual well-being; it's clear that Harrison did not consider the two pursuits to be mutually exclusive.

While there is confusion regarding the exact date of this conversation—March 4 has been posited, as well as October 8—the fact that the two discuss the album *Abbey Road*, which was released on September 26 that year, points to the October date. Their conversation aired in two parts later that month. —Ed.

**George Harrison:** All I'm doing, I'm acting out the part of Beatle George, and, you know, we're all acting out our own parts. The world is a stage and the people are the players. Shakespeare said that. And he's right, you know.

**David Wigg:** Do you expect another part, later?

**Harrison:** Oh, many parts. Yes.

**Wigg:** Is that why you've come to terms with it?

**Harrison:** Yes, because you just do whatever you can do. I mean, even if it's being a Beatle for the rest of my life, it's still only a temporary thing. And, I mean really, all we did was get born and live so many years and this is what happened. I got born seemingly to become Beatle George. But it doesn't really matter who you are or what you are, because that's only a temporary sort of tag for a limited sort of period of years.

**Wigg:** Do you enjoy it now?

**Harrison:** It's the same as any job, you know. It's up and down, you know. Life is up and down all the time. And maybe for us it goes up higher but it comes down lower. Relativity. So, you know, if we have a bad time, it's really bad. And if we have a good time, maybe it's really good. But it's only the same, you know. It's relativity. So the same law operates for everybody.

**Wigg:** Yes.

**Harrison:** But they only . . . it's the same thing, like, they see showbiz, that thing, and all they think of is, "Oh, all that money you've got and you've got a big house and car," and all that sort of thing. But the problems that come along with that, you know, are incredible. And I can tell you, everything material that we have, every hundred pounds we've earned, we've got a hundred pounds worth of problems to balance it.

**Wigg:** Yes.

**Harrison:** It's very ironical in a way, because we've all got, maybe, a big house and a car and an office, but to actually get the money that you've earned is virtually impossible. It's like illegal to earn money. Well, not to earn it, it's illegal to keep the money you earn. "You never give me your money, you only give me your funny paper." You know, that's what we get. Bits of paper saying how much is earned and what's this and that. But you never actually get it in . . . uhh . . .

**Wigg:** . . . pounds, shillings, and pennies.

**Harrison:** Yes. But I think it's another of life's problems that you never actually solve. Oh, it's very difficult to solve and anyway you've just got to, no matter how much money you've got, you can't be happy anyway. So you have to find your happiness with the problems you have and you have to not worry too much about them. And [*smiling*] Hare Krishna, Hare Krishna, Krishna Krishna Hare Hare.

**Wigg:** George, how did you come to record [*the album*] *Hare Krishna*?

**Harrison:** Because the people from the Radha Krishna Temple were over here since about a year. And I got to know a couple of them, because they were in and out of Apple office. And I've known about Hare Krishna Mantra anyway for a number of years. Originally, the Spiritual Master [*Sri Prabhupada*] made a record in America which didn't really sell well. And apparently the people ran off with the money. But I got to know about it. And also in India, you know, they chant those sort of things all over the place. The thing about the word "Hare" is the word that calls upon the energy that's around, from the Lord. Whichever Lord you like, really. But in this case it happens to be Krishna . . . which is like the words that Christ said became the Christian Bible. And the words that Krishna said became the sort of Hindu Bible called the Bhagavad Gita. So it's just by merely the repetition of that. It's the same if you were just to go around chanting "Christ, Christ, Christ, Christ." If you say it long enough then you build up this identification. Whatever you identify with, you become one with it. So it's really a method of becoming one with God.

**Wigg:** I see.

**Harrison:** It's just another process. It's really the same sort of thing as meditation, but this is the thing—it has more effect, I think. Or quicker effect, because music is such a powerful force. And it's like, God likes me when I work, but loves me when I sing.

But it's really the same end as meditation. The response that comes from it is in the form of bliss. The more you do it, the more you don't wanna stop it, because it feels so nice. Peaceful. I believe in the saying, "If there's a God, we must see him." And I don't believe in the idea, like, in most churches they say now, "You're not gonna see him, he's way above you. Just believe what we tell you and shut up." Well, their whole thing is a different way. It's a process of actually having that realization and direct God perception, which is the thing you can attain through chanting and through meditation. And then you don't have any questions. You don't have to ask the vicar about this, because it all becomes clear with the expanded state of consciousness.

But you don't get it in five minutes. It's something that takes a long time. So it's really . . . it's like to "give peace a chance," or "all you need is love." The thing is, you can't just stand there and say, "love, love, love" or "peace, peace, peace" and get it. You have to have a direct process of attaining that. Like, you know, Christ said, "Put your own house in order." Maharishi said, "For a forest to be green, each tree must be green." So the same for the world to have peace, each individual must have peace. And you don't get it through society's normal channels. And that's why each individual must tend to himself and get his own peace. And that way the whole society will have peace.

**Wigg:** George, and what about these rules. Do you support all these things that the Krishna movement support? I mean they don't approve for example of alcohol and drugs.

**Harrison:** I believe in it.

**Wigg:** And they recommend a certain kind of food, vegetarian.

**Harrison:** Yeah. Well, there's certain . . .

**Wigg:** And no sex, unless you're about going to have children, right?

**Harrison:** Yeah. Illicit. Non-illicit sex. Which means . . . So, there are members of this Radha Krishna Temple who are married and now have children. So all that means, you know, not raving around and knocking off everybody. You know, because that's, then, becomes a bit undisciplined. Because all those emotions like that lust and greed are things, emotions that have got to be curbed. I believe in being a vegetarian, because meat's one of the worst things anybody can eat.

**Wigg:** What about the other ones?

**Harrison:** Which ones?

**Wigg:** No alcohol or drugs.

**Harrison:** Yeah, well, I don't drink alcohol personally, because . . . I mean, that's one reason why I smoked pot. When I started smoking pot a few years ago, I hope they won't edit this piece out, because I'm not really . . .

**Wigg:** I hope they won't. I'm sure they won't, I won't let them.

**Harrison:** Ok, the thing was that, as soon as I smoked pot I gave up alcohol, because I realized the only reason I was drinking alcohol was to get high. So I got high much easier without any sickness after it. But the thing is now that to really have pure state of consciousness and good perception that is above the normal state of consciousness that we're aware of, then you must have a perfectly clear mind. So alcohol and any sort of drugs is out. But I haven't taken anything like that personally for a long time. In fact even before I got busted I never took it. It just happened that, you know, that they seem to bring it with them, that day.

**Wigg:** I see.

**Harrison:** So, for that's a different story. Edit, edit! Anyway, yes I agree with that. Because to *really* get high you've got to have a pure system. You know, your mind and body has got to be clear.

**Wigg:** Two of the most beautiful songs on *Abbey Road* are from yourself when we've been so used to Lennon/McCartney compositions and of course people have been commenting this week about "Something" and "Here Comes the Sun," which are your own compositions. How did this all happen? It's so unusual for you to contribute so much to an LP.

**Harrison:** Well, not really. I mean, the last album we did had four songs of mine on it. And, you know, I thought they were all right. So I thought these, "Something" and "Here Comes the Sun" was OK . . . probably, maybe a bit more commercial, but as songs not much better than the songs on the last album. But I've been writing for a couple of years now. And there's been lots of songs I've written which I haven't got 'round to recording. So, you know, in my own mind I don't see what the fuss is, because I've heard these songs before and I wrote them, you know quite a while back. And it's really nice that people like the songs, but . . .

**Wigg:** You don't look upon yourself as a late developer as regards song-writing then? Because it's kind of hit everyone in that way, you know.

**Harrison:** Late, early, you know. What's late and what's early?

**Wigg:** But you hadn't really got the reputation as yet as a songwriter, had you?

**Harrison:** No, no. I wasn't Lennon or I wasn't McCartney. And, you know, I was me. And the only reason I started to write songs was because I thought, well if they can write them, I can write them. You know, 'cuz really, everybody can write songs if they . . . if they want to. If they have a desire to and if they have sort of some musical knowledge and background. And then it's by writing them the same as writing books or writing articles or painting—the more you do it, the better or the more you can understand how to do it. And I used to just write songs. I still do. I just write a song and it just comes out however it wants to. And some of them are catchy songs like "Here Comes the Sun" and some of them aren't, you know. But to me there's just songs and I just write them and some will be considered as good by maybe the masses and some won't. But to me they're just songs, things that are there that have to be got out.

**Wigg:** What inspired "Something," for example?

**Harrison:** Maybe Pattie, probably.

**Wigg:** Really?

**Harrison:** I think—I wrote it at the time when we were making the last double album. And it's just the first line, "Something in the way she moves" which has been in millions of songs. It's not a special thing. But it just seemed quite apt. I usually get the first few lines of lyrics and melody both at once. And then I finish the melody usually first and then I have to write the words. Like, there's another song I wrote when we were in India about two years, eighteen months ago, and I wrote it straight away. And the first verse I wrote just said everything I wanted to say, like that. And then, now I need to write a couple of more verses and I find it much more difficult. But John gave me a handy tip once, which is, once you start to write the song, try and finish it straight away while you're in the mood. And I've learned from experience. Because you go to back to it and then you're in a whole different state of mind and it's more difficult. Sometimes it's easier but on the whole it's more difficult to come back to something. So I do it now, try and finish them straight away.

**Wigg:** Is it the first time that one of your songs has been released as a Beatles single?

**Harrison:** As an A-side, yeah.

**Wigg:** As an A-side.

**Harrison:** They blessed me with a couple of B-sides in the past. But this is the first time I've had an A-side. Big deal, eh? [*Laughs.*]

**Wigg:** Yes, and "Here Comes the Sun." That sounds a more obvious one. You must have been inspired by the sun, but where were you?

**Harrison:** The story behind that was, like, Paul sung "You Never Give Me Your Money." I think, because whatever you're involved with rubs off and influences you. "You Never Give Me Your Money" is, I think, during all these business things that we had to go through to sort out the past, so it came out in Paul's song.

**Wigg:** Was that written as a sort of dig, or was it written as a sort of . . . ?

**Harrison:** No, I don't think so. I think it's just written as that's what it is, you know. That's what we are experiencing, you know. Paul in particular. But "Here Comes the Sun" was the same period. We had meetings and meetings and with all this, you know, banks, bankers, and—you know—lawyers and all sorts of things. And contracts and shares. And it was really awful, 'cuz it's not the sort of thing we enjoy. And one day I didn't come in to the office. I just sort of, it was like sagging off school.

And I went to a friend's house in the country. And it was just sunny and it was all just the release of that tension that had been building up on me. And it was just a really nice sunny day. And I picked up the guitar, which was the first time I'd played the guitar for a couple of weeks because I'd been so busy. And the first thing that came out was that song. It just came. And I finished it later when I was on holiday in Sardinia.

**Wigg:** What was your own personal response to the *Abbey Road* album? How do you feel it—comparing it with previous albums?

**Harrison:** I thought it was quite nice. On the whole I think it's a pretty good album.

**Wigg:** What are your own personal favorites? Which ones that you really do like?

**Harrison:** I like . . . I like—my favorite one is, I think, "Because."

**Wigg:** Oh, yes.

**Harrison:** Just because I like three-part harmony. We've never done something like that for years, I think, since a B-side, [*sings opening line to "Yes It Is"*] "If you wear red tonight, and what I said tonight." So I like that. I like, I dunno—I like lots of them. I like "You Never Give Me Your Money" and "Golden Slumbers" and things.

**Wigg:** That's beautiful.

**Harrison:** You know, Paul always writes nice melodies. In fact, I don't know where he finds them half the time. He's amazing for doing that. I like Ringo's song.

**Wigg:** Yes.

**Harrison:** Because, I mean, most people say, "Oh, well, it's Ringo," or you know, "Ha-ha" or something. But it's great that Ringo should do it. You know, why shouldn't he do it. And it's just like a country and western tune anyway. And it's a happy tune and it's all that. And I like what he's saying about ". . . rest our head on the sea bed," and all that. "We could be warm beneath the storm."

**Wigg:** The little kids are gonna love that.

**Harrison:** Well, yeah. Maybe some big kids like it. I've heard a few people already who are big kids saying that it's their favorite track on the album. So, you know, you can't . . . One person may dislike certain things, somebody else likes it. Which is, makes it difficult doing albums because we're all influenced by different things. And the Beatles has always been, soft of, a lot of different music. It's never been one sort of "bag." [*Laughs.*] But the thing is that you can set a high standard and it doesn't necessarily have to be a hit. You know, this is one thing. I don't know, the market for hits is . . . you know, I just can't figure it out. I know when the Beatles put out a single it's a "hit." But I don't know if . . . sometimes I feel that if somebody else had put out the same thing but done in their way it mightn't be a hit. I don't know. It's very difficult. I've really decided I haven't got a clue what's commercial and what isn't. And that's the problem, you know, trying to decide what is and what isn't a single.

I think the American idea is really good where they just put out an album and the stations over there, you know, they have a lot of independent stations, unlike Britain, you see. That's a problem with Britain, you've got your good old BBC, full stop. You know, maybe Radio Luxembourg if the weather's fine.

You know, this is the thing I don't like. It's the Monopolies Commission. You know if anybody, you know, Kodak, or somebody is cleaning up the market with film, the Monopolies Commission, the government send them in there, and say you know, you're not allowed to monopolize. Yet, when the government's monopolizing, who's gonna send in, you know, this Commission to sort that one out. Britain in a way, you know, it cuts its own throat. Just from my experience of Britain. It's, you know, it's on every level. You know, from your tax right down into every little speck of business. The British government's policy seems to be grab as much as you can now because maybe it's only gonna last another six months. I know personally for me, there's no point in me going out and doing a job, doing a show or doing a TV show or anything, you know. Because in Britain, first of all, they can't afford to pay you. And whatever they do pay you is taxed so highly that it ends up that *you* owe *them* money.

So, you know, why bother working? But if my tax is cut then I'd do four times as much work, I'd make four times as much money. They'd take less tax but they'd make more from me. But they cut their own throat. They do it all over the show, every place you look in Britain it's the same. It's like, I mean, it makes me sick sometimes. It's like, one big Coronation Street. And that's Britain. Now in America, there's more people. And there's more good people, there's more bad people. But just generally, there's just more of everything. So more things get heard, more things get done and, you know, it really pays.

**Wigg:** Yes. Would you like to see the Beatles performing on stage live again?

**Harrison:** Uhh, I don't know. I wouldn't mind playing, you know. I like playing the guitar with people and singing a few songs and stuff. But I don't know as to going on clubs and things like that.

**Wigg:** Yes. You can't split, can you.

**Harrison:** No, well, I think it's mental. It's a mental concept. But to physically or spiritually split is impossible. Well, maybe not physically, I mean, spiritually, it's, you know, you can't split.

**Wigg:** No. So that doesn't bother you.

**Harrison:** Because, if you're listening, I'm the Walrus too. [*Laughs.*]

# ROOM CONVERSATION WITH SRI PRABHUPADA, JOHN LENNON, YOKO ONO, AND GEORGE HARRISON

**September 11, 1969 | Original Transcription**

As things turned out, meeting the Maharishi Mahesh Yogi in 1967 and learning Transcendental Meditation was a relatively small step along the spiritual path—albeit a very public one—for Harrison. A year later, Harrison met the Calcutta-born swami Srila Prabhupada—also known as A. C. Bhaktivedanta—a seventy-two-year-old spiritual teacher and Vaishnava monk whose followers were collectively known as the International Society of Krishna Consciousness (ISKCON), or more familiarly, the Hare Krishna Movement. Prabhupada had founded ISKCON in '66 as a means of spreading his teachings to the West. By '68, his following had proliferated to the point of establishing homes in a number of major American cities and had begun to do the same in London.

Prabhupada's approach and energy captivated Harrison and made sense to him. He became an acolyte, to a degree. Though he eschewed wearing orange robes or shaving his head, he did become a lifelong vegetarian, learned to sing *bhajans* and chants, and supported ISKCON's efforts in spreading their message and approach. He recorded their music and released it on the Apple label; he helped find them a home in London. Harrison and, for a while, John Lennon and Yoko Ono, would periodically host evenings during which Prabhupada—"Swamiji" to his followers—would read from the Bhagavad Gita, explaining his system of devotion ("Vishnuism") to members of the circle. On occasion, those discussions were recorded.

The following excerpt is from a longer lecture followed by questions and comments that took place at the country house Lennon had bought and moved into in the summer of 1969 with Ono. Navigating through linguistic and cultural differences, the three attempt to grasp certain intricacies of the Vaishnava way and the names and teachings of swamis of the recent and distant past (Paramahansa Yogananda, Adi Shankaracharya), while focusing on one of the tenets that would hold an enduring sway on Harrison—that of an unbroken line of discipleship. —Ed.

**Shyamasundar Das:** One thing that Prabhupada was explaining, I think, that didn't quite get cleared up, was how do we discern which translation of the Gita is most authoritative. Well, he answered when he said that Krishna is the authority. So we have to take it in a channel from Krishna, and there are only four lines of disciplic [*sic*] succession that come from Krishna. And of these, only one is existing now. Or is it two?

**Yoko Ono:** What do you mean by "channel"? Is it through hereditary or what?

**Shyamasundar:** Lines of disciplic [*sic*] succession. Yes, it's hereditary. Swamiji's spiritual master . . .

**Sri Prabhupada:** Just like channel you'll understand very easily. You send some money order to your friend. So, from which channel he'll receive? He'll receive through the post office, not through any other channel. So, if the postal peon delivers it, you are confident, "Yes, the money has come." So why you give the importance to the postal peon? Because he's representative of the post office. Similarly, Krishna is the original authority.

So, the Krishna's representative is the authority. And who is Krishna's representative? Who is a devotee of Krishna. So therefore, the devotee of Krishna is authority, at least of Bhagavad Gita. So, you have to receive through the devotee of Krishna about Bhagavad Gita. One who does not know about anything about Krishna, how he can preach Bhagavad Gita? This is common sense.

**Lecture Attendee:** Will you excuse me? I must put my baby to bed. Good night.

**Prabhupada:** [*Chuckles.*] Take some *prasadam*. Give him some.

**Attendee:** Oh, thank you.

**John Lennon:** Well, who says who's in the line of descent? You know, I mean, it's just like royalty. Who's who? Who's claiming . . .

[*Everyone talks at once.*]

**Ono:** That's what I was talking about.

**Lennon:** I mean, [*Paramahansa*] Yogananda claims . . .

**George Harrison:** His guru's guru's guru's . . .

**Lennon:** All his guru's guru's guru's gurus, like that. Maharishi claimed all his guru's guru's gurus went back. I mean, how are we to know? I mean, it's a matter of just deciding, you know.

**Prabhupada:** But Maharishi does not say anything about Krishna.

**Lennon:** Doesn't he?

**Harrison:** No, his guru is the Shankaracharya, which is Shankara's teaching.

**Lennon:** But they all talk about God, and Krishna's just a name for God, isn't it?

**Prabhupada:** Anyway, whatever he may be, he does not go up to Krishna. [*Chuckles.*]

**Harrison:** . . . personality, anyway, of . . .

**Lennon:** Well, that's what he used to say in exactly the same way, about anybody else.

**Prabhupada:** No, no. He cannot be, because he does not speak about anything Krishna. A peon comes, he does not know anything about post office—what kind of peon he is?

**Ono:** No, but his post office . . . He was talking about his post office.

**Prabhupada:** No, you cannot create post office. Post office one: government post office.

**Ono:** Yes, of course. I'm sure there's only one post office.

**Prabhupada:** You cannot create that he is . . . Somebody says, "I belong to another post office," then he is at once unauthorized.

[*Everyone talks at once.*]

**Ono:** No, no. He is saying that his post office is the one post office.

**ISKCON Member:** Then why . . . Obviously not satisfied yet with what they found in that post office. Why have you come here, then? If you have been satisfied with that . . . You have to test.

**Lennon:** Yeah, we've gotta go around. Yoko never met Maharishi. We're asking advice of how to, you know, how to stop. You can go on forever. I know people that have been wandering around for years, seeking gurus and spiritual teachers. I mean it's doing them all quite well.

**Prabhupada:** [*Aside*] Bring *prasadam.*

**Lennon:** I mean, we can only judge on a material level by looking at your disciples and looking at other peoples' disciples and looking at ourselves, you know. And, of course, if there's thirty disciples, seven of them look fairly spiritual, another ten look okay, and the others just look as though they're having trouble, you know. So there's no . . .

**Ono:** It's the same thing.

**Lennon:** We still have to keep sifting through like sand to see whose got the best [*indistinct*], or . . .

**Prabhupada:** Try to understand this, that regarding authority, you say that how to find out the authority. To answer this question: Krishna is authority. There is no doubt. Because if Krishna is an authority, Maharishi takes also Krishna's book and Aurobindo takes Krishna's book, Vivekananda takes Krishna's book, Dr. Radhakrishnan takes Krishna's book. So Krishna is authority.

Shankaracharya also takes Krishna's book. You know Shankaracharya's commentary on Krishna? And in that commentary he accepts, *Krsnas tu bhagavän svayam, sa bhagavän svayam Krsnah* "Krishna is the Supreme Personality of Godhead." He accepts. You say that Maharishi accepts Shankaracharya. Shankaracharya accepts Krishna as the Supreme Personality of Godhead.

**Harrison:** Yes, but it's like the Bible, which came . . .

**Prabhupada:** Now, don't go to Bible. We're talking of Krishna. [*Laughter.*] Just try to understand.

**Ono:** Yes, but, you see, the religion is bringing out [*indistinct*].

**Prabhupada:** Just see that Krishna is the authority. He's accepted by everyone. You say Maharishi belongs to the Shankara *sampradāya*. Shankaracharya accepts Krishna. Not as authority ... He says, "Krishna is the Supreme Personality of Godhead." He says this very word in his commentary.

**Gurudasa:** *Bhaja govindam bhaja govindam bhaja govindam.*

**Prabhupada:** So authority means one who has accepted Krishna as the Supreme Lord. Then he is authority.

**Ono:** Now, who said that?

**Prabhupada:** Everyone says. All authorities. Shankaracharya says. Rāmānujācārya says. Those who are really authorities, those disciplic [*sic*] succession is going on. In India, there are five sects. Actually two sects: Vaishnava and Shankara. So the Vaishnava accept Krishna as the authority, and Shankara accepted Krishna authority. There are no third sect. Practically, actually, there is one sect, the Vaishnava. Anyway, later on, later ages, Shankaracharya established his sect. But Shankaracharya accepts that *Krsnas tu bhagavān svayam*, "Krishna is the Supreme Personality of Godhead," in his writing. And at his last stage of his life he said, "You rascal fools, what you are dealing with? That will not save you." *Bhaja govindam*: "You just worship Krishna." *Bhaja govindam bhaja govindam bhaja govindam mūdha-mate. Mūdha-mate* means "you rascal."

[*Laughter.*]

**Lennon:** Means what?

**Gurudasa:** "You rascal."

**Prabhupada:** "You rascal. You rascal, just worship Krishna and become devotee of Krishna, Govinda."

> *bhaja govindam bhaja govindam*
> *bhaja govindam mūdha-mate*

*präpte sannihite käle*
*na hi na hi raksati dukrn-karane*

"When your death will come, all this grammatical jugglery of words will not save you. Krishna can save you. So you *bhaja govindam*." That is instruction of Shankaracharya.

**Ono:** But every sect says that. But every sect says that . . .

**Prabhupada:** No, there is no question "every sect." Krishna is the center of every sect. If Krishna is the center, then there is no question of "every sect." Only Krishna sect.

**Lennon:** Does "Krishna" mean God?

**Shyamasundar:** Yes.

**Lennon:** Yes.

**Prabhupada:** Yes. Krishna means God, and God means Krishna.

**Lennon:** So for the Bible or any other holy book, they all talk about one God, but they all have many ways of . . .

**Prabhupada:** That's all right.

**Harrison:** Personalities.

**Lennon:** Yes.

**Prabhupada:** That's all right.

**Lennon:** It's still just the one Being everywhere, in all the books. But they all have . . . Why isn't Hare Krishna or something similar in the Bible, then? I mean, that's the only other one I know, because I was brought up with the Bible.

**Gurudasa:** It is. In the 150th Psalm it says, "Praise the Lord with every breath. Praise the Lord with drum and flute."

**Lennon:** But they haven't got very good tunes, you know. I mean, they haven't been passing on any good chants, have they?

**Mukunda Goswami:** They don't have the aural disciplic [*sic*] succession with the Bible. It's broken.

**Lennon:** It's just a matter of that is it. I mean, would it be as effective to chant "Lord Jesus, Lord Jesus. Hail Lord Jesus"?

**ISKCON Member:** If you're sincere, sure.

**Prabhupada:** Lord Jesus . . .

**Lennon:** But it's a waste of time of doing it insincerely, isn't it?

**Ono:** Yeah, it depends on sincerity.

**Prabhupada:** No, no. Lord Jesus says that he is son of God. He's son of God.

**ISKCON Member:** Your cab's here, Shyamasundar. Hare Krishna.

[*Someone enters.*]

**Prabhupada:** What is that? You want to hear? Come on, sit down. So there is no difference. Lord Jesus Christ says that he is son of God. So there is no quarrel between God and God's son. So he says that "Love God," and Krishna says, "Love Me." The same thing. [*Laughs.*] If you say that, "You love me," and your wife says that, "Love my husband," there is no difference of opinion.

**Ono:** But about the knowledge, I'm a bit worried about it, if you have to, you know, learn Sanskrit and all that, and that's the only way to get enlightenment . . . I mean, what do you do about people who are not sort of skillful in learning languages and things like that? I mean, would that not at all . . . I mean, I thought that it . . .

**Lennon:** It's translated, anyway.

**Prabhupada:** Translation is there.

**Lennon:** So you've got to take a risk.

**Ono:** But he said, then why don't you go and . . .

**Lennon:** So then you've got to take the risk of reading a translated one.

**Gurudasa:** So you see many devotees of the authority, and then you decide which is the most sincere devotee. And just like in the ninth chapter he says, "You will come to Me." Now, if I asked you for a glass of water and you poured it on the wall, I'd think you were silly. But if you brought it to me, then I knew you were in knowledge, we were having a reciprocal relationship. Therefore, if the devotee is saying "Worship Krishna" and not putting so much of his own ideas in, but just saying "Worship Krishna" all throughout, as Swamiji does, then you can know he's a sincere devotee.

**Prabhupada:** Now, one thing you try to understand. Why these people, if Krishna is not the supreme authority, why they are taking Krishna's book and translating? Why don't you try to understand?

**Harrison:** I'm not saying Krishna isn't the Supreme. I believe that.

**Prabhupada:** No, no. I mean to say, even there are other sects, as you say, Maharishi, they accept also indirectly Krishna as the supreme authority. Because if we say Maharishi belongs to Shankara *sampradāya*, you said just like . . .

**Harrison:** Yeah, but we had a misunderstanding before about the translation of the Sanskrit Gita into English, and I was saying that there's many versions, and I think we thought you were trying to say that your version, your translation, was the only authority, and that the other translations . . . But we didn't really have misunderstanding as to the identity of Krishna.

**Prabhupada:** That's all right. If you believe Krishna is the Supreme Lord, if that is your version, then you have to see who are much addicted to Krishna directly. For argument's sake. That these people, they are twenty-four hours chanting "Krishna," and another person who has no, not a single word "Krishna," how he can become devotee of Krishna? How he can become representative of Krsna, who does not utter even the name of Krishna? If Krishna is authority accepted, therefore who are directly addicted to Krishna, they are authorities.

# GEORGE HARRISON, MAY 1970

**Howard Smith | May 1, 1970 |** *The Smith Tapes*

Howard Smith was the *Village Voice* columnist who covered the rise of the counterculture in New York City from 1966 into the '80s. His column was titled *Scenes*, and his beat—as he is quoted as saying in *The Smith Tapes*, an anthology of his interviews—was "the cultural revolution—sex, drugs, rock 'n' roll, art, fashion, changing mores and new ideas." He was leader among a new breed of journalists, sharing the deep curiosity, sincerity, and hair length of his readership. Smith's perspective respected the importance and the power of the new Aquarian Age, but he never pandered to it. He chronicled and analyzed the moment as both a participant in and critic of popular culture.

In 1969 Smith was hired to produce a weekly radio show for WABC/WPLJ, re-creating his column for the newly popular FM airwaves, positioning him in the advantageous position of covering the scene both over the airwaves and in print. He was a publicist's dream: two major hits for the price of one. "Because of my column and my radio show," he told Ezra Bookstein in the introduction to *The Smith Tapes*, "I had a lotta clout. And everybody wanted to announce anything new that they were doing in my column, and hopefully on my radio show too."

The leverage afforded him unusual access to rock stars and celebrities, artists and politicians, writers and revolutionaries: John Lennon, Allen Ginsberg, Jane Fonda, Dick Gregory, Mick Jagger, Carole King, Sly Stone, Vidal Sasson, Frank Zappa, Norman Mailer, Lou Reed. The list goes on.

In keeping with the brevity of his *Scenes* column, Smith would edit a few sound bites from his recording of an interview to play during his radio show. The full recordings were not intended to be heard in their entirety, and they laid dormant until his son unearthed the hundreds of reels of audio tape in the back of his West Village loft decades later.

Loose and unscripted, these discussions are valuable time capsules—intimate, uncensored, and unrushed conversations, many catching stars at pivotal moments. Smith had the first conversation with Dennis Hopper and Peter Fonda after the two returned from the premiere of *Easy Rider* at Cannes. He was the last person to interview Janis Joplin, just four days before her death. He caught Eric Clapton on his last US tour before going solo, the same day he recorded *Live at the Fillmore* with Derek and the Dominos.

And—mere weeks after the dissolution of the Beatles was announced in 1970, and days before he returned to England to begin recording his debut solo album—George Harrison spoke to Smith with candor about topics like the balance of creative and financial power in the Beatles. Unflinchingly, Smith asked the questions everyone had on their mind at the time: Why the breakup? Who's to blame? What now?

Smith's career later led him into the film world, the role of documentary producer becoming another part of his legacy. His Oscar-winning, behind-the-curtain portrait of Bible preacher Marjoe Gortner (*Marjoe*, 1972) left an indelible imprint on the truth-seeking mood of that age. In turn, Harrison went on to great things after their conversation; his debut album *All Things Must Pass*—along with its kickoff single, "My Sweet Lord"—topped the *Billboard* charts in late '70, making him the first Beatle to hold both number one spots simultaneously as a solo artist. —Ed.

**SMITH:** Are you going to be doing any recording while you're in town?

**HARRISON:** No. Well, I can't work that sort of work; I'd need a different visa. Anyway, there's not enough time to record. But I am gonna be recording in about three weeks. Gonna start an album of my own, as Ringo and Paul . . . This is gonna be the George album. I start that [in] three to four weeks' time and I hope to do it with Phil Spector.

**SMITH:** Have you written the material?

**HARRISON:** Yeah. I've had songs for a long time and lots of new songs. I've got about enough songs for three or four albums actually, but if I do one, that'll be good enough for me.

**SMITH:** I didn't know you were that prolific as a writer, because there's so few of your songs on Beatles albums.

**HARRISON:** Well, I wrote some songs—in fact, some songs I feel are quite nice, which I'll use on this album—about four years ago. But it was more difficult for me then to get in there, to do it. It was the way the Beatles took off with Paul and John's songs, and it made it very difficult for me to get in. Also, I suppose at that time I didn't have as much confidence when it came down to pushing my own material as I have now. . . . I did write one song on about the second album. And I left it; I didn't write anymore. That was just an exercise to see if I could write. About two years later I recorded a couple more songs, I think *Rubber Soul*, and then I've had one or two songs on each album. There are four songs of mine on the double *White Album*. But now the output of songs is too much to be able to just sit around waiting to put two songs on an album—I've got to get 'em out.

SMITH: How was it decided how many songs you would have on a Beatles album?

HARRISON: It's always been whoever would be the heaviest would get the most songs done. Consequently, I couldn't be bothered pushing like that much. Even on *Abbey Road*, for instance, we'd recorded about eight tracks before I got round to doin' one o' mine. Because you say, "I've got a song," and then Paul, "Well, I've got a song as well and mine goes like this, 'Dit a lit a lit a li,'" and away you go. It was just difficult to get in there and I wasn't going to push and shout. But it was just over the last year or so, we worked something out—which was still a joke really. Three songs for me, three songs for Paul, three songs for John, and two for Ringo.

SMITH: Why did Ringo only get two?

HARRISON: Well, because that's fair, isn't it? That's what you call being fair. No, but even Ringo is writing more songs. We just cut a Ringo song called "It Don't Come Easy." But Paul and John and myself have just got so many songs . . . This is a good way: if we do our own albums, we don't have to compromise. Because in a way, Paul wants to do songs his way, he doesn't want to do his songs my way, and I don't wanna do my songs their way. I'm sure that after we've all completed an album or even two albums each, then that novelty will have worn off.

SMITH: You think the Beatles will get together again then?

**HARRISON:** Well, I couldn't tell if they do or not. I'll certainly try my best to do something with them again. I mean, it's only a matter of accepting that that situation is a compromise. In a way, it's a compromise and it's a sacrifice, because we all have to sacrifice a little in order to gain something really big. And there is a big gain by recording together—musically and financially and also spiritually and for the rest of the world . . . It's the least we could do to sacrifice three months of the year just to do an album or two. I think it's very selfish if the Beatles don't record together.

**SMITH:** But everything looks so gloomy right now.

**HARRISON:** It's no more gloomy than it's been for the last ten years. It really isn't any worse. It's just that over the last year, what with John and stuff and lately with Paul, everything that they've thought or said has come out to the public; it's being printed; it's been for everyone to read and to comment about or to join in on.

**SMITH:** But the feelings had been there all along?

**HARRISON:** In different ways. We're just like anyone else: familiarity breeds contempt, they do say. We've had slight problems, but it's only been recently, because we didn't work together for such a long time, and the Yoko and John situation, and then Paul and Linda. But it's not as bad as it seems.

**SMITH:** There seems such animosity between Paul and . . . It sounds like he's saying it's all over.

**HARRISON:** But it's more of a personal thing that's down to the management situation with Apple. Because Paul, really it was his idea to do Apple. . . . Then it got really chaotic and we had to do something about it. When we started doing something about it, obviously Paul didn't have as much say in the matter . . . because he wanted Lee Eastman, his in-laws, to run it and we didn't. That's the only reason; that's only a personal problem that he'll have to get over, because the reality is that he's outvoted and we're a partnership. We've got these companies which we all own 25 percent of each, and if there's a decision to be made, then like in any other business or group, you have a vote.

And he's outvoted three to one and if he doesn't like it, it's really the pity. Because we're tryin' to do what's best for the Beatles as a group or best for Apple as a company. We're not tryin' to do what's best for Paul and his in-laws.

**SMITH:** You think that's what the key fight is over?

**HARRISON:** Because it's on such a personal level that it is a big problem, really. You imagine that situation if you were married and you wanted your in-laws to handle certain things. It's a difficult one to overcome, because you can think of the subtleties. He's really living with it like that, you see. When I go home at night, I'm not living there with Allen Klein. Whereas in a way, Paul is living with the Eastmans. So it's not really between Paul and us. It's between Paul's advisors, who are the Eastmans, and our business advisor, which is Allen Klein. But it's all right.

**SMITH:** I'm not as optimistic.

**HARRISON:** It's all right. All things pass away, as they say.

**SMITH:** I detected some animosity between Yoko and Linda; is that part of what it's about?

**HARRISON:** I don't think about it. I refuse to be a part of any hassles like that. Hare Krishna, Hare Krishna, Krishna, Krishna, Hare, Hare, and it'll all be okay. Just give 'em time, because they *do* really love each other. I mean, we all do. We've been so close and through so much together that to talk about it like this, we'll never get any nearer to it. But the main thing is, like in anybody's life, we have slight problems and it's just that our problems are always blown up and shown to everybody. But it's not really a problem; it's only a problem if you think about it.

**SMITH:** You don't think there's any great anger between Paul and John?

**HARRISON:** No. I think there may be what you'd term a little bitchiness, but that's all it is. Just being bitchy to each other, childish. But I get on well with Ringo and John and I try my best to get on well with Paul. It's just a matter of time, for everybody to work out their own problems, and once they've done that, I'm sure we'll get back round the cycle again. But if not, it's still all right. Whatever happens, it's gonna be okay. In fact, it's never looked better from my point of view. The companies are in great shape—Apple Films, Apple Records, my song company. . . . We got back a lotta money that a lotta people had that was ours, a lotta percents that different people had. . . .

**SMITH:** Did Klein do all that for you? Were you really broke or were all of you just crying poor?

**HARRISON:** We weren't broke. We'd earned a lot of money but we didn't actually have the money that we'd earned. It was floating around. . . . Right back, that's really the history since 1962; the way everything was structured, none of us knew anything about it. We'd just spend money when we wanted to spend money, but we didn't know where we were spending it from or if we paid taxes on it. We were really in bad shape as far as that was concerned, because none of us could really be bothered. We just felt as though we were rich, because really we were rich by what we sold and what we did. But it was so run together, the business side of it . . . But now it's very together and we know exactly where everything is and there's daily reports on where it is and what it is and how much it is.

**SMITH:** What do you wanna do with all your money? I just saw one of the daily reports and you've got a lotta money.

**HARRISON:** I just want to live as comfortably as I can or as I need, which is really very comfortable, I can tell you. Money is to be used. I try and help different things that I believe in. But I don't believe in just givin' my money away. . . . I'd rather keep my money and make it into more money until I've got so much money and then give it all away. But that's not for a few years. I'd much rather buy something with the money, like buy a house and fill it full of people doing something good and then give that away, rather than just give people dollars.

**SMITH:** On the new album that you mentioned, are you gonna be playing all the instruments?

**HARRISON:** No. I'd much rather play with other people, because united we stand, divided we fall. Musically, it can sound much more together if you have a bass player, drummer, and a few friends, a little help from your friends. . . . But I really want to use as much instrumentation as I think the songs need. It'll be a production album, as opposed to down home on me Nagra [*the top-choice tape recorder for field recordings at the time —Ed.*].

**SMITH:** I guess you've heard Paul's album. What did you think?

**HARRISON:** I thought "That Would be Something" and "Maybe I'm Amazed" are great and everything else I think is fair. It's quite good but a little disappointing. But I don't know—maybe I shouldn't be disappointed. It's best not to expect anything and then everything is bonus. . . .

**SMITH:** I wonder whether that can work again with you guys. I find it very hard to imagine you all staying in a studio again for the months that it takes to produce a record. How are you gonna just work it all out?

**HARRISON:** Well, it's really quite easy. We've done it for years . . . All we have to do is accept that we're all individuals and have as much potential as the other. Having accepted that, it says, "Scan not a friend with microscopic glass, you know his faults, then let his foibles pass." That's written on my house.

If we were all perfected beings, we wouldn't be here in the physical world. The fact that we're all here in these bodies means that we're not perfected. So having accepted we're not perfected, we can allow for each other's inadequacies or failings with a little compassion. I'm certainly ready to be able to try and work things out with whoever I'm with. But if whoever I'm with is full of hassles, then I'm not gonna be with him, am I? I'm gonna go with somebody else. I mean, that's really how things happened for me when I got tired of being with the Beatles. Because musically, it was like being in a bag—they wouldn't let me out the bag. Which was mainly Paul at that time, the conflict musically for me was Paul. And yet I could play with any other band or musician and have a reasonably good time.

**SMITH:** What was the conflict with Paul? I don't understand.

HARRISON: Well . . . Paul and I went to school together, you know? I got the feeling that, you know, everybody changes and sometimes people don't want other people to change, or even if you do change, they won't accept that you've changed and they keep in their mind some other image of you. Gandhi said, "Create and preserve the image of your choice."

SMITH: What was his image of you?

HARRISON: I got the impression he still acted like he was the groovy Lennon/McCartney. There was a point in my life where I realized anybody can be Lennon/McCartney. Because being part of Lennon/McCartney, really, I could appreciate how good they actually are and at the same time see the infatuation the public had or the praise that was put on them. I could see everybody as a Lennon/McCartney if that's what you wanna be. I don't know if I'm explaining. . . . The point is that they're nobody special. There's not many special people around. And if Lennon and McCartney are special, then Harrison and Starkey are special too. That's really what I'm saying is that I can be Lennon/McCartney too, but I'd rather be Harrison.

SMITH: Are you doing things other than recording now?

HARRISON: Just composing and recording and trying to get myself straight. The only purpose for being alive is to get yourself straight. Each soul is potentially divine; the goal is to manifest that divinity. And liberation, that's really what I wanna do—is liberate meself from this chaos and of this body. I wanna be God-conscious. That's really my only ambition, and incidental is everything else . . . .

This is where I really disagreed with John, because I want peace too. But I don't think you get peace by goin' around shouting, "Give peace a chance, man!" For a forest to be green, each tree must be green. You don't get peace by talking about peace. You don't get any sort of peace until you really stop talking and be more on the road to peace.

SMITH: It seems much slower, less direct. I think what Lennon's trying to do is find a quicker way of getting peace.

HARRISON: But it's like trying to take a pill, isn't it? It's like acid: people took acid in order to have some higher state of consciousness, but it doesn't work. To get God-conscious, you have to stop taking pills and stop all that scene. You're not gonna get God-conscious just in half an hour. It takes lifetimes. It takes a million years of healthy life to spiritually evolve like that. It gets boring all those incarnations and stuff. I can understand John wantin' to get it in five minutes, because I'd like it like that too. I wish you could take a pill and it'd just make you disappear, but that's not the way.

# PART III
# 1971–1979

# TELEVISION INTERVIEW

**Dick Cavett | November 23, 1971 | *The Dick Cavett Show***

*The Dick Cavett Show* of the late 1960s and '70s was one of the few programs on American television on which the heroes of the counterculture—Janis Joplin, Jimi Hendrix, John Lennon, Yoko Ono—were welcomed, and spoken to with the same mix of respect and irreverence that the comedy-writer-turned-talk-show-host leveled at politicians, writers, and other mainstream figures of the time. There were fun, historic moments—but it didn't always work. Cavett could be a little too smart for his guests, and when flower power was in full bloom, his subtle, digging humor was sometime a mismatch with the overriding sincerity of the time. There were cringeworthy moments, like when he used the word "gimmicks" to describe Hendrix's groundbreaking instrumental techniques, causing the guitarist to nearly leap from the guest chair, chafing at the implication that his music or stage show was anything but authentic.

Similarly, in Cavett's 1971 encounter with Harrison and Shankar, the host hits a nerve by calling the sound of the sitar "bizarre." Yet it's telling how swiftly and smoothly he recovers, keeping the conversation on an even keel. That was Cavett's skill: to acknowledge his missteps and grow from them, all in front of a television audience. Despite the tension at the start of his conversation with Harrison, he remains positive and respectful—even as Harrison continues to needle him about the number of commercial interruptions and his disappointment with American television in general.

Things do improve as the show progresses. Harrison turns his guns from Cavett to target first various members of the media who dig through the dirt to find salacious stories of rock stars behaving badly. Then there's his lengthy, unfiltered diatribe against Capitol Records—specifically Bhaskar Menon, head of Capitol's parent company, EMI—for delaying distribution of *The Concert for Bangladesh* LP, preventing funds from reaching the organizations helping the needy.

The entire program—including Cavett's opening monologue and his conversation with Shankar—is transcribed below, to provide a fuller sense of context and Cavett's peculiar balance of corny humor and intellectual wit. At its best, his show pushed the limits of the more stilted, old-school comic sensibility that prevailed on television at the time, even while it was itself being pushed to find a way to speak to the rock generation.

Years later, in a public interview conducted at WNYC's the Greene Space in New York City, Cavett was shown a clip from this 1971 conversation, with Harrison seeming to threaten to put the brakes on the entire conversation: "There's really nothing to say these days . . ."

Cavett laughed at the reminder, recalling: "People said, 'You're going to try and do a ninety-minute show with Harrison? Lots of luck!'" But, he added, there was a lesson to be learned. "Some of [the interview] was like that, and then it got better and better and better as the show went on, and that's one the arguments for a long show." —Ed.

**Dick Cavett:** Please, please. I know you're excited. Of course, I can't appreciate it; I see myself every day. Listen, I want to test you—I was trying to see what the audience actually looks like because there's a lot of excitement about tonight's show, and a lot of people wanted to be here, especially tonight. And I'm interested in what kind of audience we get from night to night. I have a little test I'm going to give you to see how much you know, if the crowds actually reflect the kind of show we're doing. Because when we do sports, like I did the other night, we'll get a whole audience of people who like to watch or participate in sports . . . heh, which, like you, killed the joke.

Or like, when we had Mandy Rice-Davies [*a British model —Ed.*] one night, a lot of people were here . . . who like to watch or participate in sports, I suppose, I dunno, anyway . . . we have a lot of . . . it depends on what you have on stage. And there's a certain air about tonight's show, a certain excitement in the air—which is natural. I mean, just the mention of the names of these two giants, Noel Harrison and Albert Shanker, is enough to—

[*Laughter.*]

**Cavett:** [*To side of stage.*] Oh, that's wrong? [*Consults paper.*] Oh.

Let me just ask you just a general, musical knowledge test to see if the people who came tonight to see George Harrison and Ravi Shankar have a general background in this area. Oh, this is an easy question that Miss, uh . . . [*To side of stage.*] What's our research lady's name again? . . . Miss Beesmeyer put in, yeah.

Ringo Starr's real name—everyone knows that.

**Various Audience Members:** Richard Starkey!

**Cavett:** Richard Starkey—wha? Who can name four girls' names made popular in Beatles songs? [*Audience yells out names*]. Michelle . . . Lucy . . . what was the other one? Eleanor Rigby . . . one more. No, you that got already, we have it—I have two Lucys already. [*Audience continues yelling names.*] Martha? No, you know what the one is that you left out? Penny Lane. [*General groan from audience.*] Miss Beesmeyer's idea of a joke.

By the way, I asked, does anyone know who's associated with the famous song "Abba Dabba Honeymoon"? The Andrews Sisters? No. It's Debbie Reynolds. Isn't that amazing?

Here's a multiple-choice question: Zimmerman is the real last name of Ethel Merman, Bob Dylan, or Ravi Shankar? [*Audience yelling.*] Everyone knows that.

Which of the following does not have anything to do with music? Monteverdi, Mantovani, Montenegro, Monty Woolley? [*General laughter.*] These are easy!

This is, wait a minute, this is a good one. Which of the following is not . . . you may not know this—put your hand up if you the answer to this. Which of the following is not a world-famous opera singer? Belle Silverman, Pinkie Perlemuter [*he means Perlemuth —Ed.*], David Barnheiser.

[*Laughter.*]

**Cavett:** How many . . . which one is not?

**Audience Member:** David Barn . . .

**Cavett:** Yes, that's the made-up name. Barnheiser is the made-up name. Belle Silverman is Beverly Sills, and Pinkie Perlemuter is Jan Peerce, I didn't realize that. My staff thinks I would know nothing about music because I come from a farm state—they figure there, if you want to hear music, you back a car slowly over a pig or something. Eastern snobs that they are.

I don't know if this can be done—this is for Rosengarden [*the show's musical director, Bobby Rosengarden —Ed.*]. I'm going to dictate the opening phrases of a song, and you tell me what it is. Now, no help from the band. Why should tonight be any different? If anyone can get this, fine. All the notes are in the same octave, key of C, common time. E quarter note, E dotted eighth, E sixteenth, F dotted eighth, E sixteenth, D dotted eighth, C sixteenth, bar, E whole note.

**Bobby Rosengarden:** One Note Samba.

**Cavett:** Nah. Can—can anyone do that, actually?

**Rosengarden:** One more time.

**Cavett:** Does anyone know from that what it was?

**Rosengarden:** Repeat it again.

[*Cavett repeats sequence as camera focuses on Rosengarden; band pianist plays theme.*]

**Cavett:** That's it! How did you do that? That's not what I said? Well, don't spoil the game for us. Yeah, that is what I said.

**Rosengarden:** You didn't dictate it right—nothing personal.

**Cavett:** Why, I don't even write this! [*Looks offstage.*] Am I going too long? Oh, I have, OK. Let's take one last question then . . . [*to Rosengarden*] I didn't know that could be done.

Which of the following is not true of Ravi Shankar? A., he started his career as a dancer. B., he made a record with Yehudi Menuhin. D., he appeared at the Monterey—I mean, C., he appeared at the Monterey Pop Festival. Or D., he played semi-professional baseball in 1948.

[*Laughter.*]

**Cavett:** There is only one of those that isn't true, you know that? How many have known the answer to everything so far? Anyone? Every so often . . . the man there? The lady? Oh, yes. People don't like people like you who know everything. We will be back with my guests, and, uh, everyone else shortly after this message. The next thirty seconds are brought to you by the Bulova Watch Company. We'll be back. Stay with us.

———————

**Cavett:** Our first guest tonight is actually a group, called Gary Wright and Wonder Wheel. And they're going to do a song written by Mr. Wright himself, called "Two-Faced Man." Will you welcome please, Gary Wright, Wonder Wheel, and . . . *friend.*

[*Gary Wright and Wonder Wheel perform, with Harrison joining them*]

**Cavett:** [*Sitting down with Harrison after the performance*] I guess everyone knows by now that you're Gary Wright.

**Harrison:** Right.

[*Laughter.*]

**Cavett:** Where do you know Gary Wright and this group from?

**Harrison:** From England. He used to be in a band called Spooky Tooth. I met him during my album, *All Things Must Pass.* He came and played piano on the whole album, and so I returned the favor tonight.

**Cavett:** Very nice. How many in the audience knew that George was in the group up there? How many didn't know?

**Harrison:** I'm not in the group.

**Cavett:** I meant that you were up . . . if they recognized you there, the subtle way we had you camouflaged, blending into the background like that. You know, I haven't, uh . . . You're only the second member of your former organization that I've ever met. I know John.

**Harrison:** You didn't meet the other eight.

**Cavett:** Were there that many?

**Harrison:** Yeah, hundreds. Did you ever hear of the eighteenth Beatle?

[*Laughter.*]

**Cavett:** I—there were rumors that the Beatles were not always the same person. In fact, there was once a rumor that it wasn't even the real four of you who came over here on one trip. That they just sent four . . .

**Harrison:** We just sent four dummies out there.

**Cavett:** That and what was the other one? Oh, that you actually were all bald and had no hair; that was so you could go out on the street and not be recognized.

**Harrison:** It's all truth.

**Cavett:** It is?

**Harrison:** Yeah.

**Cavett:** Oh, well then they *aren't* rumors.

**Harrison:** [*Looking off set*] Let's take a little march through the time with Birds Eye Frozen Orange.

**Cavett:** . . . Plus. Well, he's right. You weren't supposed to see that. Let's do take a little march through time—

**Harrison:** He couldn't miss it, really.

**Cavett:** [*Laughing*] I know.

**Harrison:** Well, look.

**Cavett:** [*Sweeping gesture toward off-set prompts.*] That's right, it's in three places. . . . [*To camera.*] Um, with Birds Eye Frozen Orange Plus. [*To Harrison.*] If you'd . . . like—well . . .

[*Harrison raises a glass of orange juice from the table between the two chairs; Cavett signals to cut to commercial.*]

———————

[*Harrison talks indistinctly as cameras come back on.*]

**Cavett:** . . . No, *now* we're here. Is this confusing you a little bit? This set up?

**Harrison:** It is, all these cameras. I don't know which one I'm supposed to be looking at.

**Cavett:** It must be exciting for you to be next to a famous person.

**Harrison:** It is, it's very exciting. [*Audience laughs.*] I don't do this every night you know.

Cavett: No. I do unfortunately. . . . You're probably wondering what we were looking at. George saw the lights go on over the cameras which give me the lead-in to the commercial. Actually, I don't think the audience at home cares what we're looking at. I mean, they're more interested in what we think.

Harrison: I want to know who, what's looking at me really. I'd like to check it out. . . [*Looks around before looking straight into camera.*] There he is.

Cavett: They always say you don't have to worry about what camera is on, that they'll find you.

Harrison: Yes . . . Big Brother is watching you.

Cavett: Whatever. Yoko sat in that very chair.

Harrison: Ah! [*Gets out of chair in mock fear; audience laughs.*]

Harrison: [*Sitting back down.*] Well, I bet many people have sat in this chair.

Cavett: Well, a lot of people have sat in it, but I was just thinking—

Harrison: I saw the show, it was very nice.

Cavett: Did you see that?

Harrison: Yeah. There was one thing they forgot to plug, so . . . so, I thought I'd plug it for them, and that's their new Christmas record— [*looking directly into camera*] "We Wish You a Merry Christmas, War is Over," get yours now. [*Softly.*] Thank you.

Cavett: Is there such a record?

Harrison: Yes, he made it after he was on the show, so he didn't get a chance to talk about it.

[*Laughter.*]

Cavett: Is there a slight undercurrent of hostility between you and, and the other members of the . . . ?

Harrison: No, no, really. John, you know . . .

Cavett: I'm not going to tell anybody.

**Harrison:** No, no, I just thought I'd take the opportunity and promote his record for him. It's "War Is Over If You Want It, Happy Christmas." Emperor Records.

**Cavett:** Well, are you in any sense in contact with each other? I mean—

**Harrison:** Yeah, I saw him last night actually, at the premier of *Raga*, which is . . . what we should talk about, maybe.

**Cavett:** But, I mean, what did you say?

**Harrison:** I said, "Hi, hello!"

[*Laughter.*]

**Cavett:** Do you have writers who think of these things, or do you just have them ready and you can just snap them right out, like that?

**Harrison:** Yeah, yeah, we have writers at home. Rooms full of them.

**Cavett:** What did he come back with right away?

**Harrison:** With, "Hi!"

**Cavett:** Yeah? Gee, this ought to be—was there more, or did that just . . . ?

**Harrison:** You've got real boring people you know, to talk to on your show. I'm probably the biggest bore you've ever had on the show.

**Cavett:** Really? You think?

**Harrison:** Yeah.

[*General sad disagreement from the audience.*]

**Cavett:** I'll be the judge of that. Listen, I'll tell ya . . .

**Harrison:** Well, I don't really . . . You know, they asked me, "Do you want to come on *The Dick Cavett Show*," and I said, "I've got nothing to talk about, really." They said, "Think of something, you know, anything." So, I thought, "Okay, we'll go and talk about *Raga*," which is a . . .

**Cavett:** Film.

**Harrison:** Mm-hm, yeah.

**Cavett:** You mean that's it, when we're done talking about that, then . . .

**Harrison:** Then I go.

**Cavett:** You don't like to talk, then.

**Harrison:** Well, not really. Sometimes, if there's something to say but there's really nothing to say these days. [*Smiles slightly; audience laughs.*]

**Cavett:** You know, I have that feeling too. People think that I must love to talk and that I would love to go to parties and yak my head off, but I could go for months without talking.

**Harrison:** Well, you talk every night, don't you.

**Cavett:** I know, and I've never liked it. I mean, I don't crave conversation. I could sit in an empty room for days and days. I'd have to leave occasionally, but not to talk, I mean . . . [*Audience laughs.*] In other words I don't have a terrific appetite for talking. The reason I'm rattling on like this is that you've just frightened me by telling me that you don't like to talk and I figure I may have to . . . will I have to fill in this last hour of the show?

**Harrison:** You just talk, and I'll watch.

**Cavett:** [*Laughs.*] Okay, well, let's do talk about the film. And then, well—before we get to that . . .

**Harrison:** Let's get to something else.

**Cavett:** If you and John and Yoko meet, you're not really . . . gritting your teeth?

**Harrison:** No, no. We're good friends.

**Cavett:** Well, all of that about her being the problem with the group, is that slightly silly that one woman could be so much of a problem?

**Harrison:** No, the group had problems long before Yoko came along. Many problems, folks.

**Cavett:** Can you remember who was the first to say, "You know I bet we'll break up one day. This won't go on. This is sort of a dream" . . . ?

**Harrison:** Uh, I don't really remember anything about the Beatle days. It seems like a sort of, you know, previous incarnation when I think about it.

**Cavett:** And a long time ago, like another life?

**Harrison:** Yeah.

**Cavett:** Do you regret any of it?

**Harrison:** No, no. I don't regret really anything, you know. That's what happened and it was good, you know. It was good, but it was also good to carry on and do something else. In fact, it was a relief. [*Chuckles.*]

**Cavett:** Sometimes they say you were—

**Harrison:** Some people can't understand that you know, because Beatles were such a big deal. They can't understand why we should actually enjoy splitting up, but there's a time, you know, there's a time when people grow up and they leave home or whatever they do. And they go for a change and it was really time for a change.

**Cavett:** Don't you think a lot of people just envied the idea of being world celebrities, though?

**Harrison:** Well some people, you know, would go around forever singing the same tune and playing the same gig if they were making some money, you know. I think we'd all rather give that up and try going on our own and try doing something that we really want to do, and if we don't make it then hard luck. As it happens we've all got such a lot of good will hanging over from being Beatles. I mean, you probably wouldn't have me on the show if I hadn't been one. Let's face it.

**Cavett:** No, you wouldn't get here on looks alone. [*Audience laughs.*] Now, do you think—

**Harrison:** [*Looking off set.*] We will return after these messages from our local station.

**Cavett:** Oh, now wait a minute! Just 'cause that comes on doesn't mean you have to do it right away.

**Harrison:** Oh.

**Cavett:** Do you feel like doing it now?

**Harrison:** I just did it.

**Cavett:** Oh.

**Harrison:** Oh, I see, [*gesturing toward and reading the off-screen prompt*] "Four or five minutes. Lead in."

**Cavett:** He's right folks. We will return after this message from our local stations.

---

**Cavett:** I'm talking with George Harrison, who wants to know if it's over yet. [*Audience laughs.*] Do you think you might have been the most anxious of the four to get out? I get that impression from reading about you.

**Harrison:** Um, maybe. Maybe, yeah.

**Cavett:** Why?

**Harrison:** Well, because over the years I had such a lot of songs mounting up that I really wanted to do, but I only got my quota of one or two tunes per album, and that way I would have had to have recorded about a hundred Beatle albums just to get out the tunes I had in 1965.

**Cavett:** Were you held down by the other fellows?

**Harrison:** Uh, well very subtly, yes. They didn't really, they didn't strap me down or anything like that, but, um, it was just the way things happened, you know. It started off I didn't write, they wrote, and then I started to write, and it was sort of trying to push in a bit.

**Cavett:** You don't actually read or write music do you?

**Harrison:** No.

**Cavett:** Then, when you say write, if you have a tune that hits you how do you get it down?

**Harrison:** Just keep it in your head, you know. Just work it out on the piano or on the guitar.

**Cavett:** But then do you tape it, or what preserves it?

**Harrison:** Sometimes, sometimes put it on tape but usually you can remember it in your head, if you don't. I wrote the words down and remember the tune in my head.

**Cavett:** Do you wish you had studied composition?

**Harrison:** No.

**Cavett:** Don't need it.

**Harrison:** Well, maybe, maybe it would help somewhere. I probably wouldn't have to pay a copyist.

**Cavett:** But you don't miss it?

**Harrison:** No, no.

**Cavett:** It would just help.

**Harrison:** Because it's not really sort of music you know. It's like, uh—I mean, there's a difference between people who write music, and classical things, and big arrangements, to the sort of thing I do. It's just really, it's very simple.

**Cavett:** And the other guys, most of the melodies were John's or Paul's that were done on the album?

**Harrison:** Yeah. That was funny when John was on [*the program*]. Every time you had a commercial break and then came back, part twenty, and they'd keep playing Paul's songs.

**Cavett:** Put our guests at ease, I guess is what we do. They always talk about you as the real musician of the group, and if you haven't studied music, what do they mean by that? You're more serious about music?

**Harrison:** I don't know. It's probably because I didn't smile so much.

[*Laughter.*]

**Cavett:** To be a real musician you have to be sour, I suppose.

**Harrison:** Yeah.

**Cavett:** OK. There was also the theory that you attracted more girls by being the quiet one, in the same sense that a guy at a party who sits in the corner will have the girl come over and say, "Awww, what's the matter?" This was not a calculated philosophy on your part . . . ?

**Harrison:** It's just a dirty rumor.

**Cavett:** Was it?

**Harrison:** Just a rumor, yeah. I think Paul used to get them all, with his, you know. [*Shimmies shoulders and grins at camera; audience laughs.*]

**Cavett:** Do nerves hit you badly?

**Harrison:** Oh, yeah, terrible. Sometimes I sit down right before the show and try and figure out what it is inside that starts all this tension.

**Cavett:** Where is it coming from?

**Harrison:** I don't know, I have no idea, otherwise I could control it.

**Cavett:** They used to say that's a way to get rid of tension is if you can try to sit down and think exactly where it is, is it in your stomach or what gives you that wave . . .

**Harrison:** No, it comes from everywhere all at the same time. That's the problem. That's the problem, it's sort of abstracts and unknowns, the way nerves act upon you.

**Cavett:** Does any kind of meditation help before . . . ?

**Harrison:** Yes, but that's a sort of different thing to this. I mean you can't . . . you can meditate and get peaceful but then the moment they say, "*The Dick Cavett Show!*" [*snaps and laughs*] . . . and then there you are again. [*Writhes with mock stress; audience laughs.*]

**Cavett:** Does this happen when you're watching the show, or just when you're . . . ?

**Harrison:** Yeah. Yes, it does. Just *thinking* about it.

**Cavett:** I didn't know it, but I'm giving you the beginnings of an ulcer.

**Harrison:** Yes.

**Cavett:** So you wouldn't use meditation as a tool to calm you down as a most important thing. I think that's why some people go into it, though. They say, "I've tried everything, I take tablets, I . . ."

**Harrison:** I mean, maybe I'm more calm now than I would have been a few years ago, I don't know. But there's still something about the idea of this, [*turns to look into camera*] you know, Big Brother and all them people tuned in, "OK, what's he gonna say. . ." [*Indistinct, possibly censored.*]

[*Laughter.*]

**Harrison:** And so, you know, you don't— [*Notices prompt screen.*] Awww, we have to take a station break.

**Cavett:** And what? And what else?

**Harrison:** And sell some more oranges . . .

**Cavett:** No, read the whole thing.

**Harrison:** And we'll be back!

**Cavett:** That's the important part.

---

**Cavett:** "Tomorrow night my guest will be Danny Kaye." That was Jack Benny, could you tell that? Could you tell that I was doing Jack Benny?

**Harrison:** No. Who's Jack Benny? We don't have a Jack Benny in England.

**Cavett:** You're kidding? When Jack Benny goes to the . . . they throw themselves at Jack Benny.

**Harrison:** Do they?

**Cavett:** Oh yeah, he goes to the Palladium and people just tear the place apart.

**Harrison:** Really?

**Cavett:** Oh yeah. Jack Benny.

**Harrison:** Fancy that.

**Cavett:** Yeah. You'll learn a lot here with me. We have a piece of film here, and I'm anxious to see it because I didn't get to go to that concert [*referring to the Bangladesh concert —Ed.*], but I heard all about it. [*Audience cheers.*] They're really ahead of us. It's supposed to be one of the best things ever done of this kind, and one of the most successful charity things of this kind, that anybody ever put together. Did you get the idea just sitting alone one day, or how did it come to you?

**Harrison:** Um, it came, really it was Ravi Shankar's idea. He wanted to do something like this, and he was talking to me and telling me about his concern for the thing and asking me if I had any suggestions and then after half an hour he talked me into being on the show and so once I decided I was going to go onto the show then that was it. I just had to try and get a band together and set up, and I organized the things, with a little help from my friends, at Madison Square Garden. And that's it, it just snowballed and the whole thing was thought of and planned and executed all within about four weeks.

**Cavett:** It raised an enormous amount of money. The thing that always bothered me was how do you know that the victims of the problems in India and Pakistan will get the money that you raise at a thing like that? Where does it go once it goes into the Madison Square Garden box office, then? How does it get to the people that you see starving?

**Harrison:** Well, because this concert was done with such short time for preparation, also because so many of these concerts were rip-offs, we wanted to ensure that we could do the concert and nobody would think that we were keeping the money ourselves. So with such a short time there's only like three weeks by the time we'd more or less decided the concert was going on, and then we set the date for Madison Square Garden, which was the only available day that we had, so we decided the best thing would be to give the money, and say out front that, this money is going to such and such a charity.

And then we checked different things out, we were going to give it to the Red Cross, this was the first idea—that we give the money to the American Red Cross who in turn could give it to the Indian Red Cross— but then we heard so many different stories about the Red Cross, and how there's, you know, hurricanes hit someplace in America, and they just take care of the whites, and all the blacks are there and they're not taking care of them. You hear so many different stories about things.

**Cavett:** I hadn't heard that.

**Harrison:** We heard so many stories about all different organizations. In the end, we had to really say what we're going to give the money to. So we said we'll give the money to UNICEF, and they have to say to us exactly what they need, and they can come to us and say we need this and this and this, and then we'll sign the check and let them buy the things they need. So the concert made $250,000, which actually is really very small in terms of the amount of money we're going to make from the record.

**Cavett:** The record and probably the film.

**Harrison:** But the record—for the record, I'm hoping when we realize some of the money, which should be around January, if the record comes out at all this year. That's another problem we're having—a slight problem with the record company. But if the record does come out early December, by mid-January we should have realized quite a lot of money, a few million dollars. At that time Ravi was going to be in India, so I was going to go out there and get the money into India, and then I'll take it there myself because I don't want the money to get lost. It's taken three or four months' work to do it. I don't want the money to end up in somebody's pocket.

[*Applause.*]

**Cavett:** I haven't seen this bit of film, but I know this is the concert that people saw pictures of in the magazines. Bob Dylan showed up as a surprise, at least to the audience.

**Harrison:** It was a surprise to me too.

**Cavett:** Was it really a surprise, yeah?

**Harrison:** Yes.

**Cavett:** Let's take a look at this from that night at Madison Square Garden.

---

**Cavett:** Will you do that kind of thing again do you think? It seems like a very good idea.

**Harrison:** Yeah, maybe, maybe. I thought . . . you see it's difficult, not all musicians are rich enough through record sales or such like, to be able to donate their services all the time, so I figured a good way to do it would be, maybe, two concerts in each town, like, similar to Madison

Square. The first show we keep the money and the second show we give the money to the charity, and that way we can feed the starving musicians, and the second we can feed the people. I think that sounds fair.

**Cavett:** I mean, they criticize rock groups for being overcommercialized on the one hand, and yet members of them are supposedly socially conscious on the other hand, so it seems like this is a wonderful way of combining those two things if you can draw a lot of money, ridiculous sums by the average person's reckoning. Then why not to do it this way? There must be loopholes, there must be other problems. Are there?

**Harrison:** I don't think so.

**Cavett:** Is the government suspicious of anything that is passed on, because you say there have been rip-off concerts.

**Harrison:** Yeah. I think if you take, sort of, precautions, which is really when we said we'd give the money to UNICEF, the concert. That was really a precaution, you know, because too many things could have gone wrong, and it would have been terrible to have done the concert and for it to turn out really bad. So many concerts turn out bad, like, I think the Stones' did, you know, and people getting killed. It's really bad. So, it's very important I think for something to come out really good, that feels good, and the people—that actually *does* something, you know.

**Cavett:** Glad it turned out so well. Another one of those little messages. We'll be back, right after this one.

---

**Cavett:** A Stratolounger LoBack—the living room chair that's got everything: looks, superb styling, marvelous comfort. [*To Harrison.*] No, this isn't one, actually. Don't try to go back in this one—this is not a Stratolounger.

We were talking during the break, and George said the Red Cross shouldn't get too upset. He said he had heard bad things about all organizations, and good things and it just became very hard to know which is which, and that's one of the things that makes it hard to do this. So the Red Cross should not feel particularly singled out. Right?

**Harrison:** Right. I mean, that's just what I heard. I've heard things about everybody. I heard a lot about you.

**Cavett:** It's only a ninety-minute show, we won't have time to go into that . . . what have you heard?

**Harrison:** Whatever you try to do, you know somebody would say don't give it to the Red Cross, give it to them . . . so you'd say, "Okay, we'll give it to them." And then somebody will say, "Don't give it to them, they're terrible." Every move you make . . .

In the end, I just think, well, maybe we shouldn't do anything. Really, that's the easiest thing would just to be sit at home and not try and do anything for anybody. It's funny because that's the situation. You know, you can create some money, and then you got the problem of who to give it to. If you can give it to somebody then you have to worry about if they're going to get it. And it's the same with the record, all these musicians came, some of them flew thousands of miles, didn't get paid for anything, they came and did the show all out of the kindness of their hearts.

Then I spent a month with Phil Spector, produced the record in a studio until like seven in the morning, making this record, getting the package together, and we get that ready and we give it to the record company and then they say, "Now, how much are we going to make?" "No, you don't make anything, we make it. It's for the refugees." They don't want to do it for cost—we want them to do it for what it costs to manufacture it.

Actually we've paid the costs so far. Our company has paid for all the boxes, millions of boxes and things, books that go with it, and then we give it to them on a plate, and they want more money, and it's really not on . . . you know. It's really unfair.

**Cavett:** What about Apple?

**Harrison:** Well, Apple, that's our company, we've paid, so far, all the costs to make the record, to make the box, make the package, all the expense involved in the show, and then Capitol, who Apple has a contract with to distribute, they just have a distribution deal. So we're giving it to them saying, "Aren't you lucky. You're the company who's going to distribute this wonderful record." They say, "No, no, we want this money. That's not enough. We want that . . . " Because they lost so much bread, you know, they just really lost and they kicked all the staff out, fired everybody, brought in a new guy who was working in England, he was really from India, good old Bhaskar Menon. And Bhaskar happens to be from India and I thought really, at first, he was really into the whole idea of it. But you know, it's just been held up. This record should have been out a month ago really, but now we still haven't solved the problem.

**Cavett:** It will come out though.

**Harrison:** We got Dylan. Dylan is CBS, and, you know, they're cool about it. We got Shelter and Elektra and all different record companies have said, "Okay, right. Put it out." And the problem is with our distributor.

**Cavett:** You'll get it out though?

**Harrison:** We'll get it out. I'll just put it out you know, put it out with CBS and let . . . you know, Bhaskar will have to sue me. Bhaskar Menon. We're going to play the "Sue Me, Sue You Blues."

**Cavett:** That's right Bhaskar, sue *him*.

**Harrison:** Sue me, Bhaskar.

**Cavett:** Let me ask you . . .

**Harrison:** [*Bleeped comment.*] . . . Bleep!

**Cavett:** George! Uh, [*chuckles*] television in America isn't as mature as it is in England. You can't say certain things.

**Harrison:** No. It's very good in England. I can't watch TV in America, to tell you the truth. It's such a load of rubbish.

**Cavett:** Really?

**Harrison:** Yeah. Terrible. Not *The Dick Cavett Show*, of course.

**Cavett:** Oh, uh, I wondered.

**Harrison:** It just drives you crazy, the commercials, you just get into something and it's, "Sorry, now another word from . . ." and, "Another word from . . ." and in the end they just put commercials on all the time.

**Cavett:** Yeah, but you have commercials too, over on your side of the pond.

**Harrison:** Yeah, but it's really done good you know, it's really done good. They show maybe—if it's a thirty-minute show they'll have the commercial at the beginning, and then the show will start, and after fifteen minutes or so it will end. And it will say, "End of Part 1," *ding*, and then it goes into the commercial, and then the commercials end, and then it says, "Part 2." Here it just goes *ching, ching, ching*, from one into the next. You don't know if it's a commercial or if it's the show.

[*Laughter and applause.*]

**Cavett:** Let's say there are a lot of commercials. I'll give you that. I have a serious question I want to ask you, and I have a feeling we're going to get interrupted before I get to, but I meant to get into this with John and with you . . .

**Harrison:** Have you ever seen *Monty Python's Flying Circus*?

**Cavett:** Yes, yes. They're good.

**Harrison:** You'll want to get that on in America, it's really good.

**Cavett:** I thought of trying to get some of that and showing it.

**Harrison:** Try and get it, it's really good.

**Cavett:** Can I get to my serious question?

**Harrison:** Yeah.

**Cavett:** You have this tremendous influence, and when you were together, you had this gigantic influence on the young people, right? And everybody knows that the Beatles went through a drug phase. Did it ever occur to you, or did you ever stop and think of it this way, that the fact that this was known, and the fact that you were the Beatles, might have caused thousands of kids to go into drug problems that might not have otherwise?

**Harrison:** Uh, well . . . [*Audience boos.*] No, no, let him ask the question, let him ask the question.

**Cavett:** Shut up, will you?

**Harrison:** First of all, when we took the notorious wonder drug LSD, it was—we didn't know we were having it. John and I had this drug and it was given . . . we were having dinner with our dentist . . . and he put it in our coffee and never told us. And we'd never heard of it. I mean, it's a good job we hadn't heard of it because there's been so much paranoia created around the drug, the people now if they take it they're already on a bad trip before they start. Whereas for us we didn't know anything, we were so naïve, and so we had it and we went out to a club and it was incredible, it was really incredible.

So a couple of years later Paul had the drug too, and the TV people in England came and they said, "So you've had this wonder drug LSD?" And he's saying look—you know, the question you asked me about the responsibility for everybody else, Paul said to the TV people, "Look, I'm not saying if I had the drug. It's you. If you're going to ask me if I've had it, I'm going to say yes because I've had it, I'm not going to lie." They said, "Well have you had LSD?" And before they asked he said, "It's your responsibility because if you're going to ask me and I'm going to say yes, and you're going to put it on the TV saying, 'Yes we've had LSD . . . '"

So really it was their fault, so they asked the question and Paul said yes and then put it on and said, "Oh, they've had LSD!" And then the world goes crazy.

**Cavett:** Yeah . . . I just wondered if you have to stop and think about . . . you used the word responsibility, which always sounds so hokey when your school teacher says, "You have a tremendous responsibility." Did you ever take that kind of thing seriously and think, "Gee, we gotta watch ourselves because if we do this other people will do that."

**Harrison:** Yeah, we always had to watch ourselves. Because if we weren't watching ourselves there was somebody else out there who was, and there was always reporters who would follow us around on tour, and always try and break into our room, catching us doing something, something maybe that we shouldn't have been doing, and the whole thing is that people want other people to do nasty things because they feed off it and then they write, "Aha! They're doing nasty thing."

It's like in a newspaper in England. I met David Frost the other day . . . can I say David Frost, or do you bleep it out?

**Cavett:** [*Smiles.*] Once.

**Harrison:** Okay. I bumped into him in a hotel and he said, "Hey, to really bring you down, here's a copy of the *News of the World.*" He had just come from England, and he brought this paper and this big story on the front saying . . .

**Cavett:** That's a scandal sheet in England.

**Harrison:** Yeah. But a big story saying about this group called the Marmalade, how they had orgies with their teenage fans and all this sort of thing. But the whole idea of these reporters going out for months and months scraping around, you know, lifting up the pavement, trying to see what rubbish there is to write about. And then they write about it as if they're saints and as if everybody isn't doing it. So I don't know where the responsibility . . . I mean maybe you should just stay home and never say anything. That's definitely the easiest.

**Cavett:** Why do people do things just because famous people do them is another question. I've never been able to figure out exactly. Anyway . . .

**Harrison:** On with the show.

**Cavett:** . . . here's a happy thought for the holidays, from Singer.

---

**Cavett:** We have a few minutes here. Let me ask you one other thing George—do you have any thoughts on why hard drugs and rock stars have become synonymous? I mean, you could see if you had a life like Bessie Smith or Billie Holiday or something like that, what they went through. If I were them I suppose I would take anything that was available. But I mean, most of the people in rock haven't had that dismal, grinding, horrible kind of life. Is it in any way a way of emulating those other people who were like those . . . [*Indistinct.*]

**Harrison:** A lot of pop people go through a hell of a lot you know. Just say in one year, they see so much and they go through so many different things that they either just want to get high . . . I mean, basically it starts with people who just want to get high, you know, like people drink. That's a big problem people get, have a drink like suppose after the show; maybe you have a drink, just, again, a little high. So musicians, you know, either drink a little bit, maybe they smoke a bit, and then they want to get a bit high, and they're sort of really looking for something, and it's the same with all those Bessie Smiths and all those people. Because the world is such a hard place to try and make it in. They're all just like buffers, all those drugs and things. And I suppose if they get on top of you, they get next to you, and then you can't stop it. I don't know, the hard things . . .

**Cavett:** That's why I wonder, like heroin, why that? Certainly, hardly anybody has been through thing like those people I mentioned, the Judy Hollidays, and Bessie [*stumbles over words*] . . . aww, hell. The Billie Holidays. A life like that I can see—the really violent hard drugs, I *suppose*, because anything might be better than what they're going through. But unless you get to the point where you can say, "I'm just in the fires of hell all day . . . all day and night," why . . . the ones who've killed themselves, your colleagues, why heroin?

**Harrison:** That seems to be the big one. I don't . . . I'm really unqualified to talk about heroin, because I've never taken it and I really don't intend to. You know, I'm sure it's probably just the best high, that's what it's down to, it's the one that gets them the highest the quickest. But it just happens to kill you faster as well. I mean, they all sort of kill you in one way or another, and there's very few people who seem to be able to experience something like heroin and then get away from it. Because it just gets in the system and they become dependent on it. I don't know. It's sad you know, it's really sad, because they're all looking for some deep love or something like that, and they miss it. It's much better to try and not take any drugs you know. If you can get straight . . . really straight, then in a way it's much higher. I mean I'm not really qualified to talk about that either. I'm in the middle, you know.

**Cavett:** Indian music and drugs don't mix, as I understand it.

**Harrison:** No, there's been a big . . . there was a problem. You know the Indian music really got popular during that '66, '67, the psychedelic period, and I think from that most people have started to associate it with drugs because the hippies, apart from the classical people who used to go and watch the music anyway, like the hippie people at that time were the ones who caught onto a new music. And it just happens that most of them were either smoking pot or something, and since then, I don't know, maybe Ravi will be able to explain how the two got caught up together. But it's really a problem; it's a problem for Ravi, because he's trying to do this . . . he's spent years and years of real discipline in life in order to play this music and then people think he must have taken dope to play that good. It's a terrible thing you know, and it's completely the opposite. The audiences are really misunderstanding what the whole thing is about.

**Cavett:** Maybe we can talk about that . . . if we don't go now, we won't have time. We have a message from our local stations, and we'll have time. He'll play and then he'll talk.

---

**Cavett:** This is Ravi Shankar, this is George Harrison. Before you came out George was saying . . . I don't know if you could hear it back there because you were sitting in place, that people often think that there must be an intimate connection between Indian music and drugs maybe because of the bizarre sound and to play that way, or to appreciate it at least, there should be a drug connection.

**Harrison:** Just watch who you're calling bizarre, Dick.

**Ravi Shankar:** Yes, I have difficulty with the word bizarre.

**Cavett:** I meant b-a-z-a-a-r. No, wait a minute—there's no way I can get out of it. To Western ears, the unusual sound might suggest some sort of chemical intoxication.

**Shankar:** No, I don't think, it doesn't suggest anything. It has been somehow established from the very beginning, and I'm not blaming George, but you know somehow because of him, the sitar became really popular with the young people and among many rock groups. And it was because of the association of those rock groups you see, and people took it for granted from the very beginning that it's something like rock music, see. And then there happened to be people like Timothy Leary and Allen Ginsberg who somehow also established that Indian music is associated with drugs and things like that, so it's all connected and that's why you see some of his films when they show any scene with an orgy or some . . .you know . . .

**Cavett:** Pot party.

**Shankar:** . . . pot party, you hear this bizarre sound of sitar. Which is bizarre because . . .

**Cavett:** To the Western ear.

**Shankar:** But that's really bizarre, because the sound you hear is not the real sound of the sitar. It's somehow played badly, some low-string sitar with electronic . . .

**Cavett:** But I think you'd have to have an unusually clear mind to be able to do the seventeen parts of the instrument, that you have to be thinking of all at once.

**Shankar:** That's true. That's why I request my listeners to be in a clear mind, because I like to put them . . . make them high.

**Cavett:** Yourself.

**Shankar:** Yes, and I feel rather cheated if they are already high.

**Cavett:** What goes on at these raga classes of yours?

**Shankar:** Well, see, actually, our music is taught from person to person, like, from, the guru teaches his disciple. It's a very personal thing. It's like . . .

**Cavett:** *Sisya?* What is the name for the student?

**Shankar:** *Sisya.*

**Cavett:** *Sisya,* there's the guru and the *sisya.*

**Shankar:** Oh, you know that.

**Cavett:** Well, two words is . . . I'm going fast.

**Shankar:** So that's the personal . . . but we are trying to also establish these classes and taught, as much as possible, in the modern manner.

**Cavett:** Whereas an actual guru only had one *sisya* probably, at one time, you . . . can you work with several at once . . . because of the shortage of gurus?

**Shankar:** [*Laughs.*] Well, it can happen, but it is best when it is more personal, you know. It depends on the *sisya* as well, how serious he is, and if he's learning just for, you know, not really very seriously . . . but . . .

**Cavett:** We have a piece of film that was taken at one of your classes. Let's take a look at that, and that will give us a better idea of what goes on there.

[*Clip of rhythm workshop plays.*]

**Cavett:** The second the film came on, Mr. Shankar said, "That's wrong." What did you mean?

**Shankar:** This was not actually a class, this was—George was also there— this was Esalen [*Institute*] in Big Sur. It was kind of a semiclass, but not actually a class of sitar.

**Cavett:** Yes, I misrepresented that. We'll be right back after this message from our local stations.

---

**Cavett:** I should have mentioned we got that piece of film from a long film, called *Raga*, which does show you working with students. And George said that it was really interesting to see several sitar players trying to play the same pieces—the same passage, I assume, over and . . . is *Raga* around now, where anybody can see it?

**Shankar:** Yes, yes, it has been released today.

**Cavett:** As we sit here. Are you performing anywhere in the U.S. now?

**Shankar:** I have a few concertos with the symphony orchestra. The next one is in Detroit, would be on the third, and one in Kalamazoo on the seventh. And Friday—this Friday—in Carnegie Hall, that's a sitar recital.

**Cavett:** How do we get George to perform again someday?

**Harrison:** Perform what?

**Cavett:** You'll be appearing in public . . . ? Oh, perform, the act of music.

**Harrison:** Oh, well that's easy.

**Cavett:** When you get everything arranged, would you ever consider . . .

**Harrison:** If I ever get a minute free, I may just do that. I'm too busy working.

**Cavett:** What's keeping you too busy?

**Harrison:** All this editing films, and . . . you know, since June, I've really had very little time. See, we did that concert, then we did the mixing of the record, then we did the film . . . editing the film, and that's still going on now. Like this morning I was down, just stuck in a room, looking at bits of footage.

**Cavett:** Everybody ends up editing film, whatever else they started out as, they all end up editing film.

**Harrison:** Yes.

**Cavett:** Have you noticed that? One of those conversation stoppers. Every time I call on someone, they're busy, uh . . .

**Harrison:** . . . editing film.

**Cavett:** We didn't have time to see the Indian dance clip, which I wish we had seen. [*To Shankar.*] Come back sometime and we'll take a look at that and talk about that some more.

Does it ever bother you that the sitar, which is a, in a sense, sacred instrument, is carted around and appears in all sorts of commercial concerts?

**Shankar:** It can, but sitar mainly is a classical instrument, just like the place of the violin in the Western classical music. But it can be used for, played in semi-classical music, as well as pop music, and in the film music.

**Cavett:** It would be bad taste, say, to play "Turkey in the Straw" on a sitar, I suppose. I saw you carrying it down the stairs, and you were carrying it so carefully; do you live constantly in the fear of the sound of a sitar dropping down a flight of stairs?

**Shankar:** Yes, I have to carry it all the time like a baby. I have to buy a ticket for it all the time, on a plane.

[*Laughter.*]

**Cavett:** You do? You carry it on a seat beside you on the plane, with a safety belt on it?

**Shankar:** And always the hostess asks what it is, so I always tell them it's a dead body so they keep away.

**Cavett:** Oh! We have a message, we'll be back.

———————

**Cavett:** I know that neither of you likes to hustle things, so I'll just point out that the Bangladesh Concert is on record, and so is your concerto record with Andre Previn, and *Raga* is also . . . there's a soundtrack album. This time has really flown.

**Harrison:** You're going to hold them up, are you?

**Cavett:** Oh. Oh! [*Harrison holds up LPs.*] Can you get a good shot of those?

**Harrison:** Good-shot *Raga*—at your record stores now . . .

**Cavett:** After what you said about the Lennons, well I'll . . .

**Harrison:** I learned a lot of things from the Lennons.

[*Laughter.*]

**Cavett:** I wish we had more time—good night!

# CONVERSATION WITH GEORGE HARRISON, SRI PRABHUPADA, AND ISKCON MEMBERS

**July 22, 1973 | Conversation Transcript**

In the middle of summer 1973, Harrison had much to be thankful for. *The Concert for Bangladesh* album had won a Grammy award. In line with his intention of using his name and music to serve those in need, he had established The Material World Charitable Trust. His latest album—*Living in the Material World*—had topped the US chart and was number two in the United Kingdom.

On a personal level, he and his wife Pattie were separated, each exploring other possibilities. But this was also the year when Harrison's relationship with Sri Prabhupada kicked into high gear: in February Harrison bought and donated a manor—formerly known as Piggott's Manor—to ISKCON, to serve as their new home in the United Kingdom. Dubbed Bhaktivedanta Manor, it still stands as one of the most enduring symbols of Prabhupada's life work and of Harrison's generosity. That July Harrison attended a dinner and discussion with Prabhupada and his disciples. The evening was recorded and transcribed; an excerpt follows, with food and gratitude flowing in abundance. —Ed.

**Sri Prabhupada:** Hare Krishna. [*Laughs.*] *Jaya.* First when I entered this room, I said, "All glories to George Harrison." [*Laughs.*] Yes. You have given us this shelter, and Krishna will give you shelter at His lotus feet. We shall pray always like that. Yes.

**George Harrison:** Well, maybe in the future this will—

**Prabhupada:** Why future? In this life.

**Harrison:** No, I mean in the future in this life, the future. Or maybe . . .

**Prabhupada:** Oh, yes. No, you will be . . . Krishna is favoring you. You are sincere, and Krishna has already favored you. So just intelligently utilize your favorable condition. Then everything will go on right.

**Harrison:** Well, everything feels so exciting at the moment, what's happening. The future is just going to be overwhelming.

**Prabhupada:** Now, take first of all *prasadam*.

**Revatinandana:** This is sour cream. I hear you like with your samosa some sour cream.

**Shyamasundar Das:** Revatinandana fixed you a feast.

**Prabhupada:** You take. You take.

**Shyamasundar:** They are bringing for us.

**Revatinandana:** They're bringing more.

**Prabhupada:** They are bringing.

**Shyamasundar:** They're bringing some more.

**Prabhupada:** Hmm. Nice. [*Takes* prasadam.]

**Revatinandana:** Is it all right? Really? He just taught me yesterday how to perfect these, and I tried to do it.

**Harrison:** Samosa? [*Takes* prasadam.] Mukunda, when the next person comes, do you think he'd send some tissues . . . ?

**Prabhupada:** We have prepared a cookbook, Hare Krishna. Have you seen it?

**Harrison:** I just got one. It's the . . . is that the same thing? It's like a photostat.

**Shyamasundar:** Oh, no. This is a . . . there's two cookbooks.

**Revatinandana:** I just wrote one also. [*Laughs.*] He's got one of those.

**Shyamasundar:** He's got one of those. Printed up in New York.

**Prabhupada:** Krishna is enjoying with His friends.

**Harrison:** Yeah? So it's full instructions on how I can . . .

**Shyamasundar:** Yes.

**Harrison:** Great. Fantastic.

**Srutikirti:** And it tells you where to buy it, I mean, the whole works. Pictures. How to offer it. Everything's there.

[*All take* prasadam.]

**Prabhupada:** Take one more samosa. Eh? You have got?

**Harrison:** Yes, there's so much here. Next year you'll be able to have the food from . . . grown in the garden. You won't even have to go to . . .

**Prabhupada:** Where?

**Srutikirti:** From our garden here, he says we'll be able to grow.

**Shyamasundar:** Next year we will have.

**Prabhupada:** You have spoken about these doll stalls?

**Shyamasundar:** Also we're going to make up displays like this of, you know, of dolls, china dolls of Krishna and His friends and all their pastimes, put them in display cases around on the grounds, so people, when they walk around, they won't just see trees; they'll see Krishna doing something.

**Harrison:** Another way of doing that, it's fantastic.

**Prabhupada:** Vegetable is very nice. Vegetable.

**Revatinandana:** You made it like this in Los Angeles once about four years ago, and I remembered a little bit how to make it.

**Harrison:** You know, the idea in Europe in the Catholic countries, if you go in Spain and Portugal, you drive along and they have like a little wooden frame like this and then with tiles, and all it is, is tiles. But the tiles show like saints and different things. Did you see those tiles I had made with Krishna, with the mantra?

**Shyamasundar:** Yes.

**Harrison:** So, things like that. And here you can get very simple, you know, and just have them glazed and put the tiles together.

**Shyamasundar:** Hmm. Yes. That's also a good idea. George suggested also that we print up these pictures like this in the postcards.

**Harrison:** And birthday cards, Christmas cards, all sort of cards.

**Prabhupada:** Oh, yes. Very good idea.

**Shyamasundar:** Because people are tired of seeing these old postcards of . . .

**Harrison:** Now there's lots of new postcards, but this . . . you know, it's much better now, but there's still no Krishna postcards.

**Prabhupada:** What is that?

**Malati:** Popadams?

**Prabhupada:** Eh?

**Malati:** Poppers?

**Prabhupada:** Oh, popper. That's nice.

**Malati:** Unfortunately we have no coal, so they are cooked in the ghee.

**Prabhupada:** Eh?

**Malati:** We did it in ghee because there was no coal.

**Harrison:** This is great. *Khicuri? Khicuri?*

**Prabhupada:** What is that *khicuri*? No, not *khicuri*. This is very good.

**Harrison:** It's like potatoes and dal?

**Prabhupada:** No, cauliflower.

**Revatinandana:** Potatoes and cauliflower.

**Prabhupada:** Cauliflower, yes.

**Harrison:** Cauliflower. It's very nice.

**Prabhupada:** Yes, it's very nice. He is good cook.

**Revatinandana:** That's because I like to eat too much. I am so attached to eating *prasadam*.

**Prabhupada:** Krishna consciousness so nice. Eat nicely, sing nicely, dance nicely, and go to Krishna. I was thinking, before starting this movement, that people they are starting so many dry movement. And my movement is so nice—chanting, dancing and eating. Why it will not be accepted?

**Shyamasundar:** It seems that nowadays, especially young people, they are looking in music to listen, to find some instruction in the music they hear on the radio. They get some instruction from the music.

**Prabhupada:** Yes.

**Revatinandana:** Usually from the music they get the instruction to go to hell.

**Harrison:** Yeah. Well, I think that's only the thing, you know, *Nada, Nada Brahma*, the sound. Just the idea of a thing. Musically, there's just the sound in music. Well, it's transcendental. It bypasses your intellect, and you can feel, even if you don't understand.

**Shyamasundar:** That's good.

**Prabhupada:** Hmm?

**Shyamasundar:** We were just talking about sound vibration, how it bypasses the intellect and is actually appreciated by the spirit.

**Prabhupada:** So Mukunda, why you are sitting without eating? You come here.

**Mukunda:** No, I have already eaten.

**Prabhupada:** Oh. You can come.

**Malati:** How can you [*indistinct*]?

**Shyamasundar:** Once you said that the origin of everything is sound vibration.

**Prabhupada:** Yes, yes.

**Shyamasundar:** How is that . . .

**Prabhupada:** Sky. Sky is first creation. So the symptom of sky is sound. Just like . . . [*Hits something.*] This is beating the sky and the sound is produced.

**Shyamasundar:** Oh, because the sound travels through sky?

**Prabhupada:** Yes. Sound is . . . there is sky. The proof is the sound.

**Shyamasundar:** But the sound was before the sky?

**Prabhupada:** No. After the sky.

**Shyamasundar:** After the sky.

**Prabhupada:** And from sound, air is produced. And from air, electricity, fire.

**Shyamasundar:** Fire.

**Prabhupada:** Hmm. And from fire, water. And from water, earth. This is this creation of five elements. In physics they teach sound and light. Is it not?

**Revatinandana:** Also gravitation, they teach about that.

**Prabhupada:** Malati, if you give more *singara* to George.

**Malati:** What?

**Prabhupada:** *Singara.*

**Malati:** Revatinandana Maharaja has prepared.

**Shyamasundar:** No, bring more.

**Malati:** Oh, bring more.

**Harrison:** Really, I've got such a lot. Thank you.

**Prabhupada:** You are young man. You can eat.

**Harrison:** This is great, this dish. Did you make this one?

**Revatinandana:** Can you take a little more of it?

**Harrison:** Ah, no, let me . . . I'd rather finish it all first. But what do you call that?

**Revatinandana:** You might not see it. Taste that purple preparation and see if you like that, the cherry chutney.

**Prabhupada:** Yes, you will get appetite. Chutney is meant . . .

**Harrison:** Actually, I was saving that for pudding later. I eat all the savory things, and then finish off with the sweet.

**Shyamasundar:** It increases the appetite. This is not sweet. It's a chutney.

**Revatinandana:** It's a pretty sweet chutney. It's not too hot chutney. It's cherries.

**Harrison:** It tastes like good plum jam. But is this just your own creation? This . . .

**Revatinandana:** No, Prabhupada himself cooked that once in Los Angeles, and I learned at that time. That was four years ago.

**Harrison:** Does it have a name? What would you call this one?

**Prabhupada:** Which one?

**Shyamasundar:** Potatoes and cauliflower?

**Harrison:** Potatoes and cauliflower.

**Revatinandana:** It's in the cookbook that I wrote.

**Prabhupada:** This is called, in Bengal it is called *koliya*.

**Harrison:** *Koliya.*

**Revatinandana:** Just like the same name as the serpent?

**Prabhupada:** No, it is Muhammadan name. Actually, this preparation the Muhammadans make with meat. What is that? No, not meat. [*Laughter.*] It has come out very nice, tasteful.

**Harrison:** Did you give David Wynne some *prasadam*?

**Shyamasundar:** Yeah.

**Harrison:** Did he like it?

**Shyamasundar:** Oh, yeah.

**Harrison:** That's . . . I mean, in the end that's what will catch everybody. Even if that's all that gets them is the food. It's going to get them.

**Shyamasundar:** In Portobello Road we have a stall, you know, one of those street stalls.

**Prabhupada:** Bring one day your wife also.

**Shyamasundar:** We distribute *prasadam* all day long, free.

**Prabhupada:** One day bring your wife. She is very nice girl.

**Harrison:** Okay, next time I come.

**Prabhupada:** Yes.

**Harrison:** Also, Donovan wants to come.

**Shyamasundar:** Oh, that's nice.

**Prabhupada:** Who is it?

**Harrison:** But I wanted to come once, you know, first on my own.

**Shyamasundar:** A friend of George's.

**Revatinandana:** He's another singer from . . . quite popular.

**Shyamasundar:** He's reading Bhagavad Gita, isn't he?

**Harrison:** I gave it to him for Christmas.

# PRESS CONFERENCE

**October 23, 1974 | Los Angeles**

At first glance, 1974 promised to be another big year for Harrison. In May he formed his own record company, Dark Horse Records, in partnership with the A&M label. Dark Horse immediately released albums by Ravi Shankar and the British rock duo Splinter. In July he announced his first full-on, fifty-date tour as a headlining act, supported by Shankar and keyboardist Billy Preston, and in October, as his band rehearsed and got ready to hit the road, he held a rare press conference. Given the crisp and short answers below, one can imagine the energy of the event: a roomful of reporters shouting out their questions from left, right, and center, bouncing between all topics, as Harrison deftly smacks back his replies like a Wimbledon pro at the net.

Predictably, the questions focused on the Beatles—including the inevitable reunion queries—as it did on present projects. In his answers, one can tell he was neither a fan of *Rolling Stone* magazine, nor the recent hit Beatles-inspired musical *John, Paul, George, Ringo . . . and Bert*.

Sadly the throat cold Harrison mentions in the conference would not go away by the time of the tour, leaving him with a raspy singing voice and causing overall exhaustion as he served as tour director, master of ceremonies, and headline artist on the two-month run of concerts. The tour met with harsh criticism, especially from *Rolling Stone*. On a more positive note, during the rehearsal period for the tour in Los Angeles, Harrison met Olivia Trinidad Arias, then working at A&M Records. Their romance was just starting to blossom as he answered one question saying that divorcing Pattie Boyd would be "silly as marriage." Harrison and Arias would fall in love, have a son, and marry.

The following transcription of Harrison's 1974 press conference is synthesized from the accounts of two culture reporters in attendance: Andy McConnell for the UK's *Sounds* magazine, a pop-rock music weekly established in 1970, and Anne Moore for the *Valley Advocate*, a liberal arts and politics weekly based in Northampton, Massachusetts. McConnell and Moore joined dozens of journalists who crowded into the Champagne Room of the Beverly Wilshire Hotel in Los Angeles. —Ed.

**Reporter:** Why, after all these years, have you decided to return to the States?

**George Harrison:** I've been back here many times. This is the first time I've been back to work. It's the first time I've had an H-1 visa since '71.

**Reporter:** What are the reasons for not having an H-1?

**Harrison:** I had the same problem as John Lennon. I was busted for marijuana back in '67 by Sergeant Pilcher.

**Reporter:** Did you have a hard time convincing the people to give you a visa?

**Harrison:** It takes a long time, you know. A lot depends on Washington and how busy they are, and they've been pretty busy lately. We applied for it months ago. It's come through fine, but once the tour's over I've got to get back.

**Reporter:** What are your feelings about the upcoming tour?

**Harrison:** I think if I had more time I'd be panic-stricken, but I don't even have time to worry about it.

**Reporter:** What kind of songs will you be doing on the tour?

**Harrison:** Couple of old tunes and a lot of new ones. The old tunes seem to have got slightly different arrangements. I'm gonna do "My Sweet Lord" and "Give Me Love," but slightly different variations of them. They should be much more loose.

**Reporter:** Are the concerts going to be planned like Bangladesh?

**Harrison:** They're going to have some format inasmuch as there's a certain amount of time you have to play in. We have to have a format so we can get everybody on to do a decent amount of music, and get off in time to let the second house in.

**Reporter:** Are you going to be doing any solo acoustical tunes when it's just you on stage?

**Harrison:** I hope not. I'd like to do some acoustical tunes, but I still like a little backbeat.

**Reporter:** Will Ravi open the show?

**Harrison:** No, I'll be opening the show, but it's definitely not going to be a Bangladesh Mark II, if that's what people are thinking.

**Reporter:** Will you be playing Britain and Europe?

**Harrison:** I'd like to. I tried to squeeze a concert in just before Christmas although all the halls were booked out. The feeling within the band is that we should do a gig in London. They're saying, "Let's do 12 dates, let's tour England, let's tour Europe." I want to go to Japan. I want to go everywhere. This year there's too much for me to do and not enough time to do it in.

**Reporter:** Is there a paradox between your spiritualism and the atmosphere when you're touring?

**Harrison:** It is difficult, yeah. It's good practice in a way, to be, as they say, in the world but not of the world. You can go to the Himalayas and miss it completely. Yet you can be stuck in the middle of New York and be very spiritual. I noticed some places like New York bring out a certain thing in myself while I found in places like Switzerland there were a lot of uptight people because they're living in all this beauty; there's no urgency in trying to find the beauty in themselves. If you're stuck in somewhere like New York you have to look within yourself; otherwise you go crackers.

**Reporter:** Do you have any anxieties as the tour approaches?

**Harrison:** The main one is that I've lost my voice, I mean to a degree. It's getting a bit rough and gravely. There's a good chance the first few concerts I'm gonna come out playing instrumentals. [*Laughs*]

**Reporter:** Would you welcome people coming up and jamming with you on the dates?

**Harrison:** Well, it depends. If somebody goes jumping up jamming, I'd like to know what we're going to do. I hardly know the tunes myself. The wrong people always seem to want to jump up and jam with you. . . .

**Reporter:** Is your guitar playing sharper?

**Harrison:** Not particularly, no. It will be after this tour and during it. One of the reasons for doing it was because I was turning into a lawyer or an accountant. I wanted to try and get back to being a musician.

**Reporter:** Do you have an album in the can?

**Harrison:** Almost. I have a few things to do on it.

**Reporter:** Who plays on it?

**Harrison:** Some of the basic tracks I did last November. I had [*Jim*] Keltner, Ringo, Gary Wright, Klaus [*Voormann*]. Some of the tracks I did this year with Willie Weeks, Andy Newark, Tommy Scott: the people in the band on tour with me.

**Reporter:** What's the album entitled?

**Harrison:** *Dark Horse.*

**Reporter:** Why was there such a gap between this album and *Living In The Material World*?

**Harrison:** I've been busy working. I was busy being deposed. I've been doing some tracks of my own, did the Splinter album, finished up Ravi's album, been to India for two months, organized the music festival from India; I've done a million things.

**Reporter:** Why don't you grant personal interviews?

**Harrison:** There's nothing to say, really. I'm a musician, not a talker. If you get my album it's like *Peyton Place*, I mean it'll tell you exactly what I've been doing.

**Reporter:** When will it be released?

**Harrison:** When I've finished it.

**Reporter:** What are your hopes for your Dark Horse Records? Do you see it becoming very large?

**Harrison:** No, no! I don't want it to turn into a Kinney [*A successful company built on parking garages and lots, and corporate owner of Warner Bros., Atlantic, and Elektra record labels at the time. —Ed.*]. I'd like it to be decently small.

**Reporter:** What artists do you hope to get on it?

**Harrison:** I don't hope to get any in particular. To tell you the truth, I've been here just over a week, and if I signed all the people who gave me tapes, I'd be bigger than RCA and Kinney put together, but fortunately I don't have time to listen to them all.

**Reporter:** Do you pay much attention to what the critics say?

**Harrison:** I cancelled all my newspapers five years ago, so I don't really know what people say. If I do see a review of an album I'll read it, although it doesn't make too much difference what they say, because I am what I am whether they like it or not.

**Reporter:** Are you still amazed at how much the Beatles still mean to people today?

**Harrison:** Not really. It's nice. I realize the Beatles did fill a space in the '60s, and all the people the Beatles mean anything to have grown up. It's like anything; if you grow up with something you get attached to it. One of the problems in our lives is that we get attached to things. I can understand that the Beatles did nice things and it's appreciated that people still like them.

The problem comes when they want to live in the past, when they want to hold on to something. People are afraid of change.

**Reporter:** Have you seen the play?

**Harrison:** You mean *John, George, Harry, Ringo, Fred, Bert and Stigwood*? That's been going on there, but I haven't had a chance to see it yet. I hear conflicting reports. Some people say that it's lousy and they're in tears because they say Brian Epstein is lousy; others say it's fantastic, Brian comes off like an angel. I'll have to see it when I get a day off.

**Reporter:** Are you involved in any serious negotiations to get the Beatles back together for one night?

**Harrison:** No, you've been reading *Rolling Stone*.

**Reporter:** What did you think of that article?

**Harrison:** I thought that the $15 million for one shot . . . after reading that I was a bit disappointed at Bill Graham saying he could make us $4 million, especially when CSN&Y [Crosby, Stills, Nash, and Young] made $8. I'm sure we could make more than that. The point is, it's all a fantasy, the idea of putting the Beatles back together again. If we ever do that, the reason will be that we are all broke. There's more chance that we'll do it because we're broke than because . . . and even then . . . to play with the Beatles . . . I mean, I'd rather have Willie Weeks on bass than Paul McCartney. That's the truth, with all respect to Paul.

The Beatles was like being in a box—we got to that point. It's taken me years to be able to play with other musicians. Because we were so isolated it becomes very difficult playing the same tunes day in, day out. Since I made *All Things Must Pass*, it's just so nice for me to be able to play with other musicians. I don't think the Beatles were that good. I think they're fine, you know.

Ringo's got the best backbeat I've ever heard. There's him and Levon Helm from the Band are the best drummers I've ever heard. They don't play technically, no drum solos, just play. Ringo plays a great backbeat, twenty-four hours a day. He hates drum solos. Paul is a fine bass player . . . but he's a bit overpowering at times. John's gone through all of his scene, but he's like me, he's come back around. To tell the truth, I'd join a band with John Lennon any day, but I couldn't join a band with Paul McCartney, but it's nothing personal. It's just from a musical point of view.

**Reporter:** Allen Klein [*former Beatles business manager*] is suing the Beatles for $30 million. Does that mean you have to put out more albums?

**Harrison:** To tell the truth, there's a whole lot of money that's been held in receivership since Paul McCartney sued us. Actually, it's fortunate that he did sue us, because while the money is in receivership nobody can spend it. There's a lot of million dollars in the Beatles partnership, and we either give it to the lawyers or we give it to the Inland Revenue.

**Reporter:** How did you choose the musicians in your own band?

**Harrison:** I didn't really choose them . . . so many things in my life I don't really do; I just feel like an instrument. I knew I was doing a tour and I knew I had to have a band, but I didn't want to commit myself to anybody, I just let things roll on. I only met Andy Newmark and Willie Weeks a few months ago. If I hadn't met them, I wouldn't have a rhythm section, but I believe the Lord provides me or you or all of us; if you believe that, he provides you with whatever you need.

**Reporter:** What is your relationship with John and Paul?

**Harrison:** It's very good, actually. I haven't seen John because he's been in the States, although I've spoken to him over the phone. He seems like he's in great shape. I just met Paul again and everybody's really friendly, but that doesn't mean we're going to form a band.

**Reporter:** Let me change the subject . . . I'm writing for women's pages, and you are married. May I ask you, does your wife cook for you, and do you have any food you enjoy eating?

**Harrison:** First of all, I don't have a wife anymore. Anyway, even when I did, she only used to cook sometimes. I learned to cook myself. I cook vegetarian Indian food, although I like other food as well. I don't eat fish. I don't eat chicken. I don't eat meat; that's why I'm so pale and thin.

**Reporter:** Are you getting a divorce?

**Harrison:** No, that's as silly as marriage.

**Reporter:** Did you make any musical rebuttal to "Layla"?

**Harrison:** Pardon?! How do you mean, musical . . . what rebuttal! That sounds nasty. Eric Clapton's been a close friend for years. I'm very happy about it, I'm still very friendly with him.

**Reporter:** Seriously? How can you be happy about it?

**Harrison:** Because he's great. I'd rather she was with him than with some dope.

**Reporter:** George, do you still meditate? And if so, what kind do you practice?

**Harrison:** That's too difficult a question to answer. There's a state of consciousness which is the goal of everybody. It's really an awareness. I haven't sat down in the morning and meditated like that for some time. At the same time, I constantly think of The Lord in one fashion or another. The main thing for us all is to try and find him within all of us.

**Reporter:** What's your attitude on drugs now?

**Harrison:** Drugs? Got any? What drugs? Aspirin? What are you talking about? What do you define as drugs? Whiskey? I don't want to advocate them because it's so hard to get into America.

**Reporter:** What do you consider to be the crowning glory so far in your musical career?

**Harrison:** As a musician? I don't think I've got any yet. As an individual, just being able to sit here today and be relatively sane. That's probably the biggest accomplishment to date.

**Reporter:** Who are some of the contemporary artists that you admire most?

**Harrison:** Smokey Robinson, I'm madly in love with Smokey Robinson. There's so many of them. I like Dicky Betts. I think Ry Cooder is sensational.

**Reporter:** What about Stones?

**Harrison:** Yeah, the Stones, you know, they're fine, you know, nice. I like the Stones. Variety's the spice of life.

**Reporter:** Can you see a time when you'll give up being a musician?

**Harrison:** I can see a time when I'd like to give up this kind of madness, but I'd never stop music. Everything's based on music.

# RADIO INTERVIEW

**Dave Herman | April 19 and 20, 1975 | WNEW-FM**

*Extra Texture (Read All About It)*—as the album title suggests—was Harrison's wry comment on the critical disparagement that came his way at the end of 1974 and early '75. It was the harshest he had experienced in his career. He was disappointed and exhausted, and the outpouring of music he created in Los Angeles in '75 yielded an album that was at times moody and, surprisingly, free of an overtly spiritual focus. "This Guitar (Can't Keep from Crying)" was obviously self-referential, a promise from the man who wrote "While My Guitar Gently Weeps" to carry on.

Ironically, from 1975 and into '76, as Harrison dealt with his dismay at the dissolution of the spirit of the '60s and cultural sense of unity, the efforts to get the Beatles to reunite reached a fever pitch. A million-dollar offer from Sid Bernstein—who produced their first New York City concert at Carnegie Hall—was upped to $10 million by the promoter Bill Sargent, whose specialty was closed-circuit broadcast events like boxing matches, historic reenactments, and a to-the-death battle between a diver and a shark. In spring '76 Sargent raised the ante to $30 million, then $50 million—a staggering amount for the day, enough to land the story on the cover of *People* magazine that April and inspire Lorne Michaels, the Canadian comedian who had created NBC's *Saturday Night Live*, to step into the fray and make his own offer to the Beatles. On April 24, 1976, he appeared on the program at the start of its second season and displayed a cashier's check for . . . $3,000. "You divide it any way you want," Michaels said as part of his pitch. "If you want to give Ringo less that's up to you. I'd rather not get involved." Much laughter and comment ensued, raising the show's profile and adding to its reputation for irreverence.

Six months later, *SNL* announced a rare double bill—George Harrison with Paul Simon—and millions tuned in. The show cold-opened with a memorable example of Harrison's penchant at laughing at himself: a faux negotiation backstage with Michaels that shows him bristling at receiving but a fourth of the $3,000. "It's pretty chintzy," he says to the producer, who answers: "I tell you what, I know there's another $250 available, uh . . . for the opening, for the person who says, 'Live from New York, it's Saturday night.'" Harrison, still miffed, pauses and then turns to the camera. With a smile, he delivers the show's signature line. Cue more laughter and applause.

In some ways the world was learning how best to handle the legends of the counterculture: as figures worthy of respect and not over-reverence—as people. On FM radio, a new breed of rock deejays was speaking to the heroes of the '60s on a more human level. Dave Herman, one of New York City's leading on-air hosts, interviewed Harrison in Los Angeles while he was in the midst of recording *Extra Texture*. Their conversation was recorded over two days, and later broadcast on multiple stations across the country when the album was released. Harrison was comfortable and candid, sharing everything from his earliest childhood exposure to American culture to his disillusionment with the dwindling "Love Generation" zeitgeist. The interview was popular enough to be released as a bootleg album, *A Conversation with George Harrison (Hear All About It)*. —Ed.

**Dave Herman:** Hello. I'm Dave Herman and this is a conversation with George Harrison. We met with George at his Los Angeles home on a sunny California weekend. We found him cheerful, pleasant, warm and friendly and, in a sense, eager to talk. We began our conversation by asking him about his early years as a child in Liverpool and about the people who influenced him personally and musically.

**George Harrison:** It's pretty vague thinking of musical things. I mean I can remember names like "Bonar Colleano" and things like that. [*Laughs.*]

**Herman:** Who?

**Harrison:** Bonar Colleano [*an American film and stage actor who worked exclusively in the UK in the 1950s and '60s. —Ed.*]. I don't know. I mean I just remember hearing things. I remember being younger and I'd sing at parties, you know, if my mother took me to a party I'd end up singing. I don't know if that was, you know, even then I was full of ego, or if I just liked being the laughing stock of the party. But whatever it was, there was always something going on there.

But you know, it was ... Liverpool was ... I was born just at the end of the war, and it's hard for Americans to imagine that anybody, say, in England or Europe can know it easily. It's like you can still go in Liverpool today, and you'll find like a row of houses and then just one earlier that's just leveled were they had a direct hit from a bomb. So I grew up in *that* atmosphere of, you know, just broken-down houses and, you know, there was a lot of just feeling leftover from the war.

It was pretty stark in the north of England, you know, it was nothing much going on there until, for me, until say around the time I was thirteen, which was the first thing I got into was ... there was this guy, I keep talking about this guy called Slim Whitman who was an American.

**Herman:** Didn't he do a record, "Whispering," or didn't he play a little slide guitar thing ... ?

**Harrison:** Well yeah, he was like a country singer, but nobody seems to have heard of him, or very few people in the states, but he was big in England. He used to top the bill on the big theater circuit.

**Herman:** Didn't he do like, [*sings*] "Whispering, da da ...."?

**Harrison:** [*Sings.*] "Oh Rosemarie, I love you ...." And he did "Indian Love Call." So he was just a guy playing a guitar. I remember that was the first time I felt like playing the guitar. But then what happened in England was they had what they called "trad jazz," traditional jazz, which was really just the English version of Dixieland and that type of thing. But there was something that came out of that.

Like in England there was a band called Chris Barber's Jazz Band. They had upright bass and banjo and clarinets, that type of thing. So out of this band came the banjo player Lonnie Donegan, and he was into ... it was really bluegrass and what is like, Hank Williams, or country blues type of thing. So he started this thing which they call "skiffle," because, you know, Lonnie Donegan had a number one hit in America with "Rock Island Line."

So he started a thing which enabled all the kids, really ... they could just buy a guitar for thirty dollars, less—my first guitar cost three pound ten, which is, I don't know, fifteen dollars. And with a guitar, acoustic guitar, and then a bass made out of a tea chest with a broom pole and a piece of string, and a washboard—you know a washboard with thimbles? And so he had the whole skiffle thing, so the skiffle craze came and lots of people got guitars, went into that, and then that died out. But the ones who hung on . . . then came the rock 'n' roll thing with, you know, Buddy Holly and Little Richard and all that.

So I suppose the '60s rock groups, particularly in England anyway, were the ones who had initially started out say, in the late '50s skiffle craze. But then we all got a bit . . . the ones who stuck with it got guitars, electric guitars, and drums, got rid of the washboard and the tea chest bass, got proper drums and electric bass.

**Herman:** You've always kind of exhibited a very fine wit, a sarcasm if you will. Does that also go back to childhood? Were you kinda the class wise guy with teachers and things? I think I recall reading somewhere where you had made a deal with some teachers when you were in school.

**Harrison:** I wasn't . . . I don't think I was funny then. I didn't like school, you know? This is, say, the grammar school, the high school period up until seventeen, from say being twelve, thirteen, to seventeen. I never liked that because it was very . . .

I mean, it's so different to, like, the American school thing. I went to school where Paul McCartney went. It was an old Victorian building, and it was all that old English sort of attitude. It was *cold* and very serious and for the first time going in that school, it was very serious. You know, you had to do your maths and algebra and Latin and German, and you had to do all these things, and it was no fun anymore, you know? I just used to sit at the back, drawing pictures of guitars. I was not there really, you know? But I wasn't particularly funny at that period.

But there is a thing from Liverpool they say you got . . . a lot of the people in Liverpool are, or the north of England, are quite funny. But then you have to be in order to live there, you know, because it's . . . I remember once saying to Billy Preston, "Have you ever been to Liverpool?" He says, "Hey man, there's ten Liverpools in every state." [*Laughs*] It's like that. Liverpool is not . . . it's a good place to come *from*, they say, but not to actually *be*, particularly.

**Herman:** You said that Lonnie Donegan and the skiffle music started and you were already into your teens and there's no sense going over the whole story about how the Beatles came together, I'm not going to ask you all about that. But what I would like to find out from you is how you were feeling as a person, as a man, when you first started to realize that something very big was happening, that it wasn't . . . in other words—let me ask you this first, what was your idea of what it would be to be successful when the Beatles were first getting started? What were you hoping for yourself?

**Harrison:** I don't know. I mean that . . . I remember before the Beatles got going, this is when were just still at school, I used to have flashes like going to sleep at night, I'd just have flashes of speed boats and motorcars and all things which you get when you're famous and rich. And when we formed the band and we started just being semi-professional, there was something about us, which could be ego, or cockiness, or whatever, but I think we were too naive to even realize anything like that at that time. There was something . . . *in* us, and I don't know what it is. Karma . . . I call it karma—It's something, again, to do with what you were before. But we always felt as though we're going to be successful.

**Herman:** But did—what you were feeling . . .

**Harrison:** So really it was just a matter then of pursuing that and just keeping on playing. So we were just enjoying, really. That's all. We enjoyed just working as a band because there was nothing else we wanted to do. We really got off on that, and we were very happy when we could make, you know, five pound a week each. And then when we started making forty pound a week each, you know, we were ecstatic. And then we were on our way. We just wanted to make a record because we were still cocky enough to feel that all we needed was to make a record and we'd be okay. I mean, it was like blind faith.

**Herman:** But was there ever a point where you felt that the success just seemed to almost be getting out of control, where it was difficult to deal with?

**Harrison:** Yeah, that was that period. I mean it was then when it got out of control, it I suppose contributed to us going into sort of semi-retirement because it just became too difficult. And one of the things was, that whole Beatlemania in the sixties, I think even though at first we all got off on it, I think the world, or the pop or music world, got off on it either more than we did or as much as we did. But then they carried it too far, you know? Where it was cute for the policeman to have bullets in his ears, and there are pictures of everybody screaming, and for the Pope to wear a Beatle wig.

And it got to the point where the Beatles became like an excuse for everybody to freak out. You know, they'd say, "Oh well the Beatles are in town, it's Beatlemania" . . . so everybody would go around smashing shop windows and turning motorcars over because of Beatlemania.

**Herman:** Well, how did these kind of things make you feel?

**Harrison:** Well they made us feel, like, isolated, because, first of all, we never saw much of what was going on; we were always trapped in a room. And it was fun at first thinking of how much attention was being given to us, but it got very boring, it got tiring because we just became the recipients of all that madness.

**Herman:** Now that it's seven or eight years later, I guess you've had time to reflect on all of that. And do you have any explanation of what that phenomenon really was? I mean people have called the Beatle phenomenon the biggest cultural change of the century and that it had an influence on the world that goes far beyond music and entertainment. But now you've had so long to reflect on that, what do you think it actually was that caused all of that? I mean it was just music.

**Harrison:** I've no idea, I have no idea. You know, the only thing I can think of is . . . and even then, I really would prefer these days to avoid this type of dialogue, but it's the whole idea of, say, how come Tchaikovsky when he's three can play the piano better than Liberace can when he's fifty? How come one kid at eight can do mathematics better than an IBM computer? You know, there's people like that where all . . . what we are now is really the effect of whatever we'd been in the past.

And, you know, I do, through this Hinduism, believe in reincarnation and all that. So, what I believe basically, simply, is we all live from birth to death. We all create a lot of action, which is action-reaction, they call karma, and it's like that. It's like credit and debit. It's just like an account. At death you . . . death is actually your physical body packs in, but we keep going and at some period later we take another body and we try again. But at that point of birth, even somebody born today, is not just something totally new.

Because all those scriptures tell us anyway that there is never a time when we weren't, and there won't ever be a time when we're not. It does get heavy philosophical . . . but that's what the Lord teaches in all . . . in every scripture that we, it's only . . . the physical body is the thing which goes through the changes and which is impermanent. So actually, everyone that's alive is, in some way, born into a position or a situation or a country or a time which is the direct result of their previous actions and their reactions.

**Herman:** Do you feel at all that you've ever been in touch with any of your past lives, any way through clairvoyance or déjà vu experiences? Do you have any idea of where you might have been and of what time you might have been before?

**Harrison:** No, no idea at all. But I do feel something . . . it's like learning that knowledge, sometimes you don't have to have certain experiences to learn something. Sometimes you just . . . something triggers something else off. And you somehow intuitively, you just *know* something. I don't know, I believe that's because of whatever happened in the past.

I've got no idea of . . . I wouldn't go that far to say, "I was this in my past life," or anything. I don't even know if in a past life, if it was two hours before . . . if I died two hours before I got born in this life, or if it was a thousand years before. I've got no idea. But I do believe in karma and rebirth, which go hand in hand, that whole thing of action, reaction, life and death, they're just the same really. Life and death are the same.

Somebody said what's the cause of death, is birth. Everybody is worrying about dying, but in order not to die you just don't have to get born because the moment you're born, you're automatically going to die because birth and death go hand in hand. So does action-reaction, karma and rebirth.

So I just believe . . . this is getting pretty far out to say how come the Beatles did that . . . I don't know, all I can put it down to is that whatever it was, the chemistry of four people being born in that period, based upon whatever we'd been in our past, in that place, that time, with everybody else, it's relative. I believe it's like you meet people in your life, I think a lot of your friends are people who were your friends in other lives. And I think people who . . . if you hate somebody, I'm sure you're going to keep coming through life after life hating. It'll be the same people. You know, because—

**Herman:** Until you learn to love them.

**Harrison:** Sure. So, I don't know, it's magic. It's only the same as how Tchaikovsky can play the piano, and how this kid who is smart at doing that, it's all down to karma, somehow.

**Herman:** Anyway, it would be safe to assume from what you're saying that you feel good about yourself and—

**Harrison:** I know, it's the art of dying. All things must pass.

**Herman:** Okay. The art of dying.

**Harrison:** There comes a time when all of us must leave here, and there'll come a time when most of us return here.

**Herman:** Well maybe we can leave the subject of the Beatles by saying that you obviously feel good about what that contribution was, what your contribution was as one of the Beatles, to *whatever* that was.

**Harrison:** Yeah, I think generally speaking it was a good, positive . . . I'd say really all we did was pick up on the music of all the people, Chuck Berrys and Buddy Hollys and all those, with whatever influences we'd received by being born in that situation in Liverpool, and somehow translated it with our own personalities, or the individuality of the four of us, translated it into . . . without knowing actually . . . into something which a wider variety of people could communicate with, or could relate to.

**Herman:** Do you consider yourself a Hindu? Do you label yourself as a Hindu?

**Harrison:** Well, you know, on a simple level of talking about religions and Buddhists, and this and that and the other, I mean there was a period, like the '60s, when everybody freaked out on acid and everything and everybody started getting into this and that and the other. And I read a bunch of different things, but I was very attracted to Hinduism. But then, one of the things that Hinduism teaches is that all religions are . . . there is a truth which underlies all religions.

So, yeah, I'm a Hindu actually at heart, I'm a Hindu, but all that means is that I can relate more to the teachings in the Gita than I can in the Bible, but that's no putdown of the Bible; it's just that from a Christian point of view they always taught us how it was *painful* and how you have . . . the crucifixion and the whole thing, whereas from the Hindu point of view, it's all playful, Krishna as the name of the Lord.

I think the most simple way of putting it is that, brought up as Catholic until I was about twelve or thirteen, I went to church, I was taken to church, and I was taken to communion and all that sort of thing. So, I was young and maybe I misinterpreted it, but what I felt was pain, fear, and that type of thing, as opposed to the thing I've found from the Indian point of view, which was—it's playful, it's to enjoy, it's to try and enjoy the moments. But that is not to say that you have disregard for the past or the future, but to actually be conscious of being here now.

And the play, it's like Shakespeare said, "The world is the stage, the people are the players," and to realize that is like . . . It's not . . . To feel that the whole of your life is actually just a play could make people commit suicide, make you feel there's no end, no aim. But actually to see it from a positive point of view is then to be pleased to be playing the part that you're playing, because that's all we're doing. I'm playing the part of ex-Beatle George, you're playing the part of Dave interviewing me, and we're all playing. . . . You know what I mean? But to enjoy it as opposed to see it as a dead end.

And that's what the Hinduism is like, because Krishna plays. It's—the whole thing is a play. He acts out his incarnation in order to show people how to play.

**Herman:** Well, we do exercise free choice, and you have chosen to do with your life what you're doing with your life, to express yourself through your music, and to try to tell other people . . .

**Harrison:** To a degree, but I don't *really* choose, you know? This is the funny thing. It's like, to say, in some respects, my life, to be me, is . . . I'm not sure if it was a blessing or a curse, you see, because, the blessing is that you're rich and famous and all this looks rosy. But on the other hand, behind the scenes, to know that what then you expect of yourself by knowing what you know through being what you've been, that's the thing of learning and knowledge. And then, of what others expect of you and then all the millions of situations you get involved with by being that person. This goes for like anybody who goes through a similar sort of situation. Then in some respects it's a pain in the neck.

**Herman:** Is it sometimes quite lonely?

**Harrison:** Sure, sometimes it is. Sometimes it's just hard. You'd just like to be anonymous. Sometimes I'd just like to be invisible, even now after ten or whatever, twelve years, of that. I still find I can't even go out. If I want to go out and watch somebody singing at the Roxy or something, I go in there and it's like the club tilts over. I become part of the show. And that's amazing after all that time. Sometimes it's nice to be invisible and just go out and just be nobody.

**Herman:** And I guess the realization that you can't even if you decided to ever walk away from it, that's *it*, and it's going to always be that.

**Harrison:** Yeah. So that is the point where it's not exactly your choice. In a way, you know, there's a lot of things that—I think most people get into things in their lives either by what they think is their choice, or by just happening to fall into a situation. But I think even if you think you choose a certain role that there's a lot of other things which—you know, subtle things—which get you involved into that. And in some ways, I don't see any way for me, you know, just to get out of that situation.

It's not like the choice of being able to be this or be something else, it's not that simple, because then you have a lot of other involvements. And again, karma is, action-reaction, there's a lot of other situations which are all hanging upon . . . this is resting upon that, which is resting upon something else. You know? It's like you build a house and you put the first bricks down, and then you build it up to the second floor and decide you want to take the bottom bricks away. You have to, like, consider the overall situation.

**Herman:** A friend of mine once said to me that of all of the creative forms, of all of the ways that people express themselves, music is something very special and very different because it's the only art form which does not exist in space, but it exists in time. He said that dance or acting or painting or sculpture, you need a physical place, you need a thing, you have to watch it or look at it or read it. But music is the only thing that exists only in time. You need nothing but being able to hear, and you hear music and it's just there.

**Harrison:** Yeah. In a way, I think film is the same. I have always, for the last few years anyway, felt film and music can really enhance each other to get a point out. Because again, film can exist the same way. Like music can exist as long as you've got ears and a machine and a record or a tape to play it, you can play it in an airplane or in a basement, or in the country. You can play it this week, next week. It's the same with film too. If you have a monitoring machine and a videotape, you know. It's like that, in a way that can be developed.

But music I think . . . what I feel is that our physical bodies, and this is all related again to what we're saying, that we get born into a body in order to . . . the goal is actually to get full knowledge. So we gain our knowledge through our experiences. In order to have experience, we take a body which has the senses, so we have smell and taste and touch and sight and hearing.

So then, if you take all the senses in a body, maybe different people have developed different senses better, maybe somebody's got a finer sense of touch than somebody else, but I think generally speaking, apart from people who are deaf, sound is . . . I mean, sound is so important you don't realize. Just walk down the street. It's like the sound of tires screeching can make you, even unconsciously, stop yourself stepping in the road. It's like that. This is why I feel like when you get down to somebody like Stevie Wonder, his sense of hearing is so *fine*, it's so sensational, maybe because he doesn't have the distraction of sight.

So in some respects I think sound is so subtle and so much can happen in sound, and again it's personal, you can make a song, put a record out, and take a million people and let them all hear that song. But they'll all hear it in their own way because once you put it there, they are free to interpret it through their own ears, which swings at, hangs a lot on what they have been through to get to that position in space where they can sit and listen to that.

You know, that's the great thing about music is that people . . . it becomes personal. Even though it's a mass media, you can make a record and put it out for whoever wants it. Once the people who do want it get it, it becomes so personal to them.

**Herman:** But the musician has to deal with a very real, cold, and calculating business—the music business—where records aren't called "records," but they're called "product," where they're merchandised and packaged and marketed like soap and underarm deodorants. Do you think this can change at all? Do you think that there is any way that a musician can operate more freely?

I mean now you're not only a musician, you're also a music executive. You have your own record company, Dark Horse Records, which we'll be talking about in a bit, but what do you think the musician's role in the world is? How do you think he can best be catered to and nurtured and made to grow, taking into consideration what the business is?

**Harrison:** It's very complicated because there's musicians who don't have that problem that say, I may have, which is by being in the record industry as an executive, there's . . . see there's like musicians, if I get musicians to play on a song with me, they're just interested in trying to do their best for the song, trying to play it right, and all this.

Whereas I'm at the . . . and just recently, over the last year or so, I've become so aware of program planners, and it's terrible. I tell you, it's *awful* when as a musician you're trying to make a record and you're trying to make it . . . you know, a song, I would never stop making a song as long as it feels it should be. But at the back of my mind, I'm always thinking of some guy is going to be saying well if you can edit it down to three minutes, because the program, they won't put it on the radio.

So now I find, as I record a tune and as I go and listen to it back, as I was still working on it, I'm automatically pressing the timer to see if it's three-minutes-thirty because if it isn't there's not much chance they're going to play it on the radio, you know?

**Herman:** Basically you're talking about singles and Top 40 radio?

**Harrison:** Yeah, talking about that one. But there is a point where, and especially when it's on the coldest level of the record business, when they say, "Well, we think the tune is pretty good but if we're going to edit it down." Then people start chopping . . . it's like butchers, they just take out the chopping block and they chop out a piece to make it shorter, with no consideration for . . .

You see, sometimes—because, also I'm not only in the record executive thing and a musician, but I'm a songwriter too. So as a songwriter I think of music as . . . you know, whether it has an intro, some tunes you can come right in and some tunes need an intro to establish a certain mood before you start singing, and that leads to this piece, into the second verse or whatever, you have a middle bit if, you have a middle there, but you know the song . . . I like tunes that resolve, that go somewhere and resolve.

So in all of that as a songwriter, sometimes you're locked into a certain length of time just by trying to get the story of it. It's like say, trying to tell a story that really needs to be told in ten minutes but OK, just tell it in two. Well, you may be able to, but you may have to sacrifice a lot of the minor details which contributed to how nice the story actually was in the end.

**Herman:** I always liken the editing of an album track that might be seven minutes to a single, which might be three minutes and ten seconds, to like taking a Picasso and saying, "Well, look, we've got to get it in an eight by ten frame. So we'll just take the painting and we'll slice it down like that and put it in a frame."

**Harrison:** Just cut the nose off. That's much better.

**Herman:** George told us how Dark Horse Records evolved for him from his association with Apple Records.

**Harrison:** We just wanted out of that group therapy that was called Apple. I mean, we just wanted to be free as individuals. But at that time, I was still involved with making records for Apple.

**Herman:** Jackie Lomax.

**Harrison:** Well, I did that a long time before. But I just started making this album of Ravi's—*Shankar Family & Friends*—a ballet, and that was . . . I was just really into that and enjoying that. It was so nice . . . and I was thinking that at Apple they sort of . . . nobody wants to do anything. I mean I don't blame John and Paul, [*they*] really didn't want to know about that. They just wanted . . . let's just chop it up into four pieces, and let's get out of here. But at the same time, I was involved. I was committed to certain things. And a little bit later that band, Splinter.

So I found that I was still going along the same lines as I had been with Apple—that is, doing my own records, and then doing a few other people. So I had the decision to make because Apple didn't have much future left, based upon the way John and Paul, what they had indicated. And there was some talk with Ringo and I—what we were planning to do at that time is, if John and Paul didn't really want to know about Apple, we were just going to try and get the rights to take over Apple Records. And then we just put a new logo and new management, bring in a couple of new people, and keep going. And so that sort of thing couldn't happen because of the settlement, you know, it was all business. The legality is that—it was just like a hold on it. It was just sort of stuck in a limbo.

**Herman:** So you couldn't put Ravi's album and Splinter's album on Apple?

**Harrison:** No, because they . . . in fact, if you go back now to . . . there hasn't been one other artist, other than the individual Beatles, put out on Apple since that split with Clive [*Epstein, Brian's brother*]. In fact, Apple folded up, actually, Apple as a record label, other than the Beatles individually appearing on the Apple logo. And also that we'd establish

Apple label much quicker if we put the Beatles on Apple too. So we did the deal with EMI for that. So we went on Apple and Apple went on EMI, in actual fact. So, since then we are still on Apple, EMI, up until I think it's next January—January of '76.

**Herman:** And then you will perhaps record for your own label?

**Harrison:** Yeah, there is a good chance that I would do that because it's only like . . . you know, even with Apple, there is no point in us forming a label called Apple and then we all go on RCA. [*Herman laughs.*] It seems logical. It seems a logical thing, but, although, at this point in time I'm still . . . in fact, this new album I'm making now will still be on Apple label, distributed by Capitol.

**Herman:** And Ringo now has a label, Ring O' Records. But Ringo will have to also record for Apple at least until next January if I understand you right?

**Harrison:** Right. Although there's another point is that the contract that we had with EMI originally, that Brian Epstein made before he died, was, it had . . . I think they call it a product requirement clause, that says that you have to give them a certain amount of product. But we actually fulfilled that clause after the Beatle *White Album*, which was like '67. You remember the double white . . . ?

**Herman:** Who could forget it?

**Harrison:** Well that album . . . from then on, we didn't really owe them anything, but obviously we're not going to stay out of the record [*business*] . . . what we found out, we thought it was like we had to give them so many tunes. Or it was a seven-year contract, I think. So we thought once we had given them the tunes we were out. And what happened was that we found out . . . we gave them the tunes by '67, but it just meant we didn't have to give them anything else, but if we *did* anything else then it was automatically with EMI.

So, therefore, it means that for the last five years, none of us had to ever make a record ever again. We didn't owe to our contract to do any more records. But if we do anything else, it still goes on that label until

'76, January. So, Ringo wouldn't have to do another record, I don't have to do . . . you know, nobody *has* to.

**Herman:** I see.

**Harrison:** It's just that that's what we do.

**Herman:** You make records. Let's talk about what your plans are for Dark Horse records. So far two albums have been released, the beautiful *Shankar Family & Friends* album, and *Splinter*, which is another very beautiful album. I think so far you're two for two, at least in the quality. They're very fine records, in my opinion. Tell me who Splinter are or what Splinter is, whatever is grammatically correct, where they come from, and what you have planned for them.

**Harrison:** Yeah, they were two guys from the same part of England as the Animals came from, you know, Eric Burdon, that place around Newcastle, which is right up northeast of England, near Scotland. They're called Jordies, and they came from there. They were both in a band which broke up, and that's why they called themselves Splinter—there's just two guys.

And I met them through this movie, *Little Malcolm*. Somehow I got involved with a movie. There's this actor called John Hurt, who was in *A Man for All Seasons* and *10 Rillington Place*, he is quite a well-known actor. He's a friend of mine who I'd seen play the part of Little Malcolm in a stage play called *Little Malcolm and His Struggle Against the Eunuchs*.

So I'd known him for years, and I was always trying to talk him into doing this as a film. And incidentally they tried to make this into a movie two or three times before. Anyway, [when] I got through [with] Apple . . . we started to produce this movie . . . we made the movie, which was about '73. Late '73 they started the movie. And there was one sequence in the film where he enters an all-night club, and they just wanted two tunes in there by two different acts, which was sort of the way they do in film, they dissolve it to create the scene from night into morning.

And so, these two guys, Splinter, got the part to play in the film. And the song they sang in the film I thought was so nice, that I thought I'd try and make it as a single. And then I heard the rest of their tunes, and

I liked them so much that I decided to produce an album. Because if you did a single it's hardly worth just doing a single, you know? So, I did the album and that became *Splinter*. At that time, Apple had folded up and all this, and I had the decision to either just lease the stuff I produced to a label, or to have my own logo. Really that's the main difference is just a logo, to have your own identification.

For whatever reason, I don't know now, but I decided to have the logo. And so, Splinter is just about to make their second album. In fact, they should have been here in the States to do that last week, but they couldn't get here with work visas. That's why I'm using the studio time to make a new album of my own. We've just signed a new band called Jiva, who are from San Bernardino.

**Herman:** What kind of a band is Jiva? What kind of a sound?

**Harrison:** They're just two guitars, bass and drums—three of them. The two guitar players and the bass player all write their own tunes. They sing separately and together. But they're very up . . . they're a little R&B rock band. Very nice, very positive. That's the great thing about them is they're positive. At this time in world history when there is so much negative and confusion and stuff, they're really . . . they know where they're going and full of love and up, positive, loving awareness, and they're pretty funky too for . . . you know, they're young.

I think this will be the first album they're making with a guy, a producer, called Stewart Levine, who has just done the Minnie Riperton second album. And he's the producer of the Crusaders. That's quite interesting. In fact, they just start tonight to record.

**Herman:** How do you feel about the way things are going in the world and all the chaos, and what is happening? Do you think much about it? I know it is all *maya* and all illusion, but it's still very real to all of us.

**Harrison:** It is very real, very real. I feel . . . I don't know, I think in some ways I have to split it into positive and negative. If you get negative about it, it's in a hell of a state. The world is in a *mess*, really. And it seems to have gotten more of a mess the last four or five years with all this . . . I mean, the wars are going on just as usual, there's just as many wars as usual. There's the whole thing that happened with the fuel crisis, the energy crisis.

And then also we passed out of that '60s period, where there was something that happened in the '60s which brought the flower power and the hippies and the whole Love Generation. This is what kills me now, is when I see these people who supposedly, a few years ago, loved me and I'm supposed to love them. And I see them, they're just dropping apart at the seams with hate. I'm talking about *Rolling Stone*, actually, talking about Jann Wenner.

But this is the thing though, God, we all came through so much in the '60s, and we all wanted so much to create something positive, something good. It's hard to . . . when we come out into the '70s, we find it's hard to go on. A lot of these people were only part-time hippies or part-time lovers. The badness of the world, or in them, caught up on them too soon, and you find that they'll just turn around and they all start stabbing each other in the back.

It's like, we all need to support each other in many ways in order to exist. For example, just the other day I heard that the guy from Badfinger, you know Badfinger? Who was on Apple Records—"Day After Day" [*Pete Ham*]. The guy who wrote the big Harry Nilsson tune, "Without You"—he hanged himself! So, he's hanged himself because he can't go on, you know? Can't go on. So that's not made easier by people who were supposedly your brothers.

**Herman:** Why do you think so many people take such delight in taking a man who had achieved some kind of fame or notoriety or acceptance in the world, and this is not only true with you, but I'm talking about the so-called critics and people who write about people who are doing things. Why do people take such delight in taking people and dissecting them so viciously? What do you suppose that phenomena [*sic*] is?

**Harrison:** Frustration. I think it's frustration, is a reason why . . . I don't know, maybe a lot has to do with the stars, the planets, I mean like *those* stars. I don't know. Because sometimes I've seen that type of thing happen in the past—well, it happened to me before, as a part of the Beatles. We went through a thing of going up and up and up, and part of the up is by people, that people contribute to your success by writing things about you. By getting behind you, you know?

And a lot of the time, because they want to just go out and do that on their own . . . like, initially, you try and promote yourself and the record company and the press agents and that sort of thing. But say in the Beatles' case, once it starts rolling along, people just get behind it and write good things and then it gets up to a point where so much has been said, and then they decide to take it from a different point of view and decide to . . . write about your faults.

**Herman:** Kind of somebody getting their own ego off by saying, "Well, I'll be the one to knock at everybody who's saying such wonderful things.

**Harrison:** Yea. That type of thing happened with Beatles, particularly when we went through Apple and all that situation. And then everybody came down on us, and all kinds of things happened. We all got busted and stuff, and we went through bad press. And then you get good press and you get bad press, good, bad, good, bad, good, bad. And it's just . . . I don't know, the thing . . . I see it happen to all kinds of people.

The thing that bothers me is if it comes from different directions, it's okay. But when it seems to come from one basic source, then it bothers me because it seems to get more of a personal thing than just an actual point of view.

**Herman:** By one source do you mean kind of the rock press?

**Harrison:** Well, yeah. Because, I mean, I've seen them do things to people, like, for an example . . .

**Herman:** Bob Dylan?

**Harrison:** Yeah. They tried to kill Bob a few times. Also, the whole thing that split the Cream actually. You know, the band the Cream? It was something they said in *Rolling Stone* just sort of depressed Eric, I know, to such a point where he just thought . . . "just get out of this."

**Herman:** Fortunately it doesn't seem to have an effect on people. All the bad press in the world does not really destroy an artist of great stature and great talent. It hasn't destroyed anybody, not Dylan, not Eric and not you, not anyone.

**Harrison:** Yeah. Because you either have to agree completely with them and commit suicide, or take them with a pinch of hate, salt . . . [*Laughter.*] You know, really, just—because I could read criticisms of myself and if I'm in a decent mood, I'll think, "Well that's unfair that is . . . maybe that's fair." But if you get depressed you start agreeing with them. If you start agreeing with them, then you just go do yourself in. But I wouldn't do that because enough things happen to prove that it's not exactly how they see it.

I mean one situation with the rock press, for example, was one guy who came to write an article because he disagreed with another article that had been written in his paper. And so, he said, "I've seen seven of these concerts, and I disagree, and I want to write it from my point of view." Then his article came out and it was not really good at all. And I thought, well, he's just . . . he was just cheating me, just to get in to talk to me.

But then he just wrote a letter to me and sent what he wrote and to compare that to what they printed. He just said, you know, "They just cut out any favorable references to the music, or to the response from the audience." It made me feel, "Oh, forget it. They're just trying to nail me now," and that's it, that's all it is.

In fact, I think that's one reason I went on that tour with all those people, to do something which was, you know, not done every week. The whole idea of having such a whole different bunch of people, and different attitudes, and different types of music, and just a broader type of show was because it's *boring* just going on and on and on, pretending that we're all happy.

**Herman:** You can't boogie every night.

**Harrison:** You know, yeah. But people think you go down to Madison Square, wherever, we go down and the Who's on this week, this week it's him, next week it's somebody else, somebody else, and there's a million different record companies and artists and bands. And, you know, a lot of the time the music is fine, a lot of the time . . .

How many people, the audience, who's like your audience now, or the audience of Madison Square Garden, who are the same people, and you come back and how many times did you really enjoy that show? Or you were just there because you were with a chick who wanted to see it, or you're a chick who was with a guy who wanted to see it, or you just went because it was something to do, you know? I don't know. It gets pretty tedious. You know?

I don't like to just become part of something which is like Monday, Tuesday, Wednesday, Thursday . . . something which just is repetitious. And suddenly we find we're all old and we're all dying and what did we do? We just got caught in a rut.

**Herman:** Don't you think what happened in those late '60s, that great feeling of optimism did, in one way, light the world and change consciousness and raise awareness in a subtle way that the world will never be the same again?

**Harrison:** Definitely, definitely. And that's the thing. Maybe the thing that disappointed me was there might have been a million people who showed signs of being that, and now in the '70s, out of the million, there may only be a hundred left. The thing that's sad is what happened to the other 990,000?

**Herman:** Is there anybody, in particular, in music or out of music, men or women, that you really admire greatly as people, as human beings, and what they're doing in the world?

**Harrison:** Yeah, yeah. In music, well, it breaks down into . . . I mean there's people who have a sort of a more worldly consciousness, and that's why I've always been with Ravi Shankar because he's bringing, particularly in the west, something obscure and creating an audience. And through his audience then he is giving them something extra which . . . that's something which the people who appreciate that can get into. It's a whole other train of thought that comes from the music.

In simpler terms, there's people, I like people who just convey in their music some sort of sincerity. I'm a big fan of Smokey Robinson just because musically he is so sweet, he makes you feel nice, he makes me feel *good*, whereas a lot of music I listen to, which is popular music, just makes me uptight. Even if I'm not really listening too close to it, it's just the sound of it and the whole thing, and the repetition, the boring sort of repetition of how it's played. . . .

I always have been a fan of Dylan's, and I think I always will be, because, I don't know, somehow Dylan has always managed to upstage everybody. You know? When it comes down to being aware of . . . and also, of being able to put into words . . . I mean you can feel and see a lot of things, but when it comes down to writing a tune, and being able to communicate it through words, I mean he is very good at being able to put words down.

**Herman:** I think you're one of the few people, one of maybe three people, who have ever collaborated with him on a song. Just you, and I think Rick Danko did, and I think Jamie Robertson did, but that's about all.

**Harrison:** Yeah. And then what he wrote is so simple: "All I have is yours, all you see is mine, and I'm glad to hold you in my arms; I'd have you any time."

I find now, like the '70s seems to . . . there's a lot of people who are just forced into being so much more individual. And that's where I'd put me, and people like Eric Clapton. If you hear his new album, I think it's so sweet, and he is one of the people who can play every guitar lick that all them people who are still playing while he was playing, when he was in the Cream, they're still doing it now. You know what I mean?

But he, in a way, is more out on a limb too with his music. But for my money, it's better than he has ever been. It's sweeter, warmer, but it's more personal to him, now. And maybe that's why I like it better because it's . . . you know, it's just richer because he is showing more of how he feels.

But there's a lot of us from the '60s, who came up in the '60s, and there I put John Lennon there as well, you know. Like *Walls and Bridges*, that album, in particular, where we were the people who came up through . . . we battled our way up through the '60s and became something. And then in the '70s, there's a whole multitude of other people who are just battling their way through and being really successful and all that.

But that situation has forced all of us into more . . . going inside ourselves more. You know? It's like say that this new album of mine, all I want is to be able to sing the tunes I have, and to do them as warm and as simple as possible. That's really . . . and I think by that in itself, again, it puts you into that position of . . . I don't see my music anymore as being Top 20, somehow. I just played you one track before. . . .

**Herman:** Does that matter to you anymore?

**Harrison:** No. It matters more to me that I can simply sing it better, play it better and, with less orchestration, get over more feeling. Because again it gets down to say . . . of the million people, if there's only hundred left out of the million who were supposedly the potential Love Generation, if there's only hundred left, it's again . . .

**Herman:** You'll make your music for them. . . .

**Harrison:** If the ten people out of the hundred prefer it as it is now, then it makes me valid, otherwise, you know, it's down to a suicide. [*Laughter.*]

**Herman:** Do you think the time might come when you'll get tired or bored with writing songs and making records?

**Harrison:** Well, not really. Not tired, not really. I don't always do it. I write tunes . . . like I never wrote a tune, actually, for about six months, up until last Saturday, I sat down and decided I better get some tunes together, and I just got into the mood of it and wrote or finished nine tunes and wrote a couple of new tunes. So, I don't always do it.

But it is nice because, like you were saying earlier, music somehow is a way . . . you know, I can talk to you for hours, but if I just sang you one tune it will somehow get to you easier, quicker.

**Herman:** You did that before when you played me those tunes.

**Harrison:** So that's . . . in some respects, it's better to be able to communicate without so many words. You can say just a few simple words and put it in such a way that it gets over, such a better point than talking for days.

**Herman:** In closing, there will be not ten people and not a hundred people who will hear this but many thousands of people who have a genuine and a real affection for you listening and maybe there is something you'd like to say to them?

**Harrison:** Yeah, good. Thank you. God bless anybody who has . . . given us a smile. Anytime I'd rather have a smile than a . . . bite in the back.

# THE GEORGE HARRISON INTERVIEW

**Mitchell Glazer | February 1977 |** *Crawdaddy*

Mitch Glazer is best known as a screenwriter and film producer of consequence; *Scrooged* (1988), *Great Expectations* (1998), *The Recruit* (2003), and a number of television productions have all profited from his creative flair. Back in the 1970s, two years after graduating New York University, he was plying his craft as a music journalist, writing for *Rolling Stone* and *Crawdaddy*. On November '76, the latter publication assigned him an interview with Harrison, and off to Los Angeles he flew. Harrison was set to release the first album on his Dark Horse label—*Thirty Three & 1/3*—with the single "Crackerbox Palace."

"That George Harrison interview was one of the joys of my professional life," says Glazer today, adding:

George was everything I had imagined: honest, humble, spiritual, funny and incredibly generous and patient with a 24 year-old, massive Beatles/George fan. I spent a week with him in LA and then Boston and finally at his appearance with Paul Simon on *Saturday Night Live* in New York City. The access was crazy and every second a delight. He literally answered everything and anything I asked him. He told me that his answer to my question—"Why would you have Eric Clapton play lead on your song called 'While My Guitar Gently Weeps' when you are George Harrison the world's most well-known guitarist?"—was the very first time he'd ever addressed that mystery.

When I arrived at LAX to do the interview, I was expecting a PR person might meet me and give me a lift to my hotel. I walk towards the curb and it's *George Harrison* sitting there, alone, waiting behind the wheel of a vintage Mercedes sedan. George drove me into town. And that is how it started . . . I've since spoken with George's amazing widow Olivia who remembered my week with George well. I witnessed their beautiful, early, falling-in-love days. It was a magical time for them, and a week I'll never forget.

The conversation finds Harrison remarkably comfortable and open. It helped that, in addition to a youthful degree of guilelessness, Glazer was fully acquainted with the details of the Beatles and Harrison's own history and that he had a grasp of Vedic mythology and Krishna consciousness. Time was on his side as well: Harrison's answers suggest he was now comfortable enough to discuss Beatlemania and his post-Beatles battles, such as the copyright infringement lawsuit claiming "My Sweet Lord" had lifted its structure and sound from the Chiffons' "He's So Fine."

"This transformation has come in the face of a staggering torrent of difficulties," Glazer wrote in the introduction to his piece for *Crawdaddy*, published in February '77. "The well-intentioned yet financially convulsed *Concert for Bangladesh*; marital conflicts/separation; two lawsuits (one dropped, one lost); a couple of somber, noncommercial albums and a label change . . . but he has returned triumphant, turning one lawsuit loss into a hit single, creating his most positive/productive album since *All Things Must Pass* over a half-decade ago."

The text below is comprised of all of Glazer's conversation with Harrison but does not include the writer's framing commentary in order to more closely fit the format of this collection. Worth quoting, however, is Glazer's description of riding shotgun as Harrison drove him through the canyons: "George spins the radio dial searching for his album. He hits on an ELO song and says quietly, 'sounds like a Beatles tune. I guess it's a compliment, really.' The Beatles are safely distant—a known quantity, at any rate. That's when past and present, when worlds collide. 'Be here now,' he teases when I lock into the past—his past and my own." —Ed.

*I grew up in Miami and saw you live on the* Ed Sullivan Show *with Mitzi Gaynor* [both break into laughter] *doing this whole dance number in a really low-cut dress and some guy sitting on top of a flagpole, and everybody just wanted to see the band. Ed kept teasing, putting another act in. Then, when you finally played, we couldn't hear, anyhow, which was the saddest thing about it.*

It was so long ago; it was '64, about 12 years. Seems a long time.

*Were you nervous before the show?*

The Sullivan show was funny because I didn't attend the rehearsal, I was sick somehow on the flight over on the first trip to the States. The band did a long rehearsal for the sound people, they kept going into the control room and checking out the sound. And finally when they got a balance between the instruments and the vocals, they marked on the boards by the control and then everybody broke for lunch. Then we came back to tape the show and the cleaners had been 'round and polished all the marks off the board. It was sort of a bit tacky in those days, with the sound. People would put amplifiers off the side of the stage so it didn't spoil the shot, you know.

*I just always wondered if you felt the pressure. I was nervous watching it.*

Oh, yeah, we did, but we knew we'd had sufficient success in Europe and Britain to have a bit of confidence. And we really needed a hell of a lot of confidence for the States because it was just such an important place. I mean, nobody'd ever made it—you know, no British acts—apart from the odd singer like Lonnie Donnegan.

But Ed Sullivan was, you know, everybody had told us how he was really big. But again, we were pretty naive to certain things so that helped at the time. I remember them asking us, did we know who Walter Cronkite was. And I said, "I dunno, isn't he somebody on the television?" You know, things like that were good because they all had fun—the people asking questions and the press; us being naive and not seeming to care about that sort of thing.

*Was there ever a tendency to still act naive after you wised up?*

I dunno, but by that time, you know, we'd got into that whole sort of routine that we used to have, you know, at press conferences. A lot of it was just nervous energy. You know, just for jokes and stuff which everybody seemed to like. That was one of the big helps for the Beatles at the time: If anybody dried up in the press conferences there was always somebody else there with a smart answer. There was always a good balance, so nobody could every really quite nail us.

The Sullivan show was just the climax to the Beatles' whole America thing. In retrospect it probably wouldn't have mattered what we'd have done on the Sullivan show, it was like already established by the previous press that had gone before. But that was a long time ago. We'll get over the question "Are the Beatles getting together again?"

*I won't even ask you.*

Because the answer is just like going back to school again, really. The four of us are so tied up with our own lives, and it's been eight years since we split, and time goes so fast. It's not beyond the bounds of possibility, but we'd have to want to do it for the music's sake first. We wouldn't stick together because somebody had put an ad in the paper putting us on the spot.

*Somebody in New York is saying the Beatles are getting back together to wrestle a Great White Shark in Australia.*

That was the other guy, Sargent. He was gonna try and do the Beatles show and then try and do the other one with somebody fighting a shark. I thought, "If he fights the shark, the winner of the competition can be the promoter."

*It seemed that all four of you were locked into something larger than its parts.*

It was. But none of us really thought about leaving until '67 or '68, which was after we stopped touring. I know the first time for me, which was the most depressing, was during "The White Album." It was a problem making a double album because it takes such a long time.

*Why did you make a double?*

I think it was because there were so many songs. But it was the period that had started a bit negative. It was a bit difficult and we got through it and it was fine. We finally got through the album and everybody was pleased because the tracks were good. Then I worked on an album with Jackie Lomax, on an Apple record, and I spent a long time in the States and I had such a good time working with all these different musicians and different people. Then I hung out at Woodstock for Thanksgiving and, you know, I felt really good at the time. I got back to England for Christmas and then on January the first we were to start on the thing which turned into *Let It Be*. And straightaway again, it was just weird vibes. You know, I found I was starting to be able to enjoy being a musician, but the moment I got back to the Beatles, it was just too difficult. There were too many limitations based upon our being together for so long. Everybody was sort of pigeonholed. It was frustrating.

The problem was that John and Paul had written songs for so long it was difficult. First of all because they had such a lot of tunes and they automatically thought that theirs should be the priority, so for me I'd always have to wait through ten of their songs before they'd even listen to one of mine. That was why *All Things Must Pass* had so many songs, because it was like you know, I'd been constipated. I had a little encouragement from time to time, but it was *a very little*. It was like they were doing me a favor. I didn't have much confidence in writing songs because of that. Because they never said, "Yeah, that's a good song." When we got into things like "Guitar Gently Weeps," we recorded it one night and there was such a lack of enthusiasm. So I went home really disappointed because I knew the song was good.

The next day I brought Eric Clapton with me. He was really nervous. I was saying: "Just come and play on the session, then I can sing and play acoustic guitar." Because what happened when Eric was there [Harrison is stressing his words, relating this anecdote confidentially] on that day and later on when Billy Preston—I pulled in Billy Preston on *Let It Be*—it helped because the others would have to control themselves a bit more, John and Paul mainly, because they had to, you know, act more handsomely. Eric was very nervous saying, "No, what will they say?" And I was saying, "Fuck 'em, that's my song." You know, he was the first [non-Beatle] person who'd ever played on anything.

*It must have been terrifying . . .*

. . . and it was a good date. Paul would always help along when you'd done his ten songs, then when he got 'round to doing one of my songs, he would help. It was silly. It was very selfish, actually. Sometimes Paul would make us do these really fruity songs. I mean, my God, "Maxwell's Silver Hammer" was so fruity. After a while we did a good job on it, but when Paul got an idea or an arrangement in his head . . . but Paul's really writing for a 14-year-old audience now anyhow. I missed his last tour, unfortunately.

*"Guitar Gently Weeps" was such a personal song, I'd always wondered why Eric was there.*

Well, I'd been through this sitar thing—I'd played sitar for three years. And I'd just listened to classical Indian music and practiced sitar—except for when we played dates, studio dates, and then I'd get the guitar out and just play, you know, learn a part and play for the record. But I'd really lost a lot of interest in the guitar. I remember I came from California and I shot this piece of film for the film on Ravi's [Shankar] life called *Raga* and I was carrying a sitar. And we stopped in New York and checked in a hotel and Jimi Hendrix and Eric Clapton were both at the same hotel and that was the last time I really played the sitar like that. We used to hang out such a lot at that period, and Eric gave me a fantastic Les Paul guitar, which is the one he plays on that date. So it worked out well. I like the idea of other musicians contributing.

I helped Eric write "Badge," you know. Each of them had to come up with a song for that *Goodbye Cream* album and Eric didn't have his written. We were working across from each other and I was writing the lyrics down and we came to the middle part so I wrote "bridge." Eric read it upside down and cracked up laughing. "What's 'badge'?" he said. After that Ringo walked in drunk and gave us that line about the swans living in the park.

*I always thought that, although it went unstated, your contributions guided the band's direction: Beatles '65, the country influence or the Indian influence.*

Well, Ringo, as well, you know. We all gave as much as we could. The thing was, Paul and John wrote all the songs in the beginning. And they did write great songs, which made it more difficult to break in or get some action on the songwriting thing. But, you know, we all did contribute such a lot to the Beatles. There was a period of time when people thought, "Ringo doesn't play the drums"—I don't know what they thought of me—but they tended to think it was John and Paul for a period of time.

I helped out such a lot in all the arrangements. There were a lot of tracks, though, where I played bass. Paul played lead guitar on "Taxman" and he played guitar—a good part—on "Drive My Car."

*You played bass?*

No. I didn't play. We laid the track because what Paul would do, if he'd written a song, he'd learn all the parts for Paul and then come to the studio and say (sometimes he was very difficult): "Do this." He'd never give you the opportunity to come out with something. But on "Drive My Car" I just played the line, which is really like a lick off "Respect," you know, the Otis Redding version—*duum-da-da-da-da-da-da-dum*. And I played that line on the guitar and Paul laid that with me on bass. We laid the track down like that. We played the lead part later on top of it. There were a lot of things: Like on a couple of dates Paul wasn't on it at all or John wasn't on it at all or I wasn't on it at all. Probably only about five tunes altogether, where one of us might not have been on.

*Which of the Beatles albums do you still listen to?*

I liked when we got into *Rubber Soul, Revolver*—each album had something good about it and progressed. There were albums which weren't any good as far as I was concerned, like *Yellow Submarine*. We put all the songs together into an album form—I'm talking about the English albums now, because the States we found later that for every two albums we had, they'd made three because we put fourteen tracks on an album, and we'd also have singles that weren't included on albums in those days. They'd put the singles—take off a bunch of tracks, change all the running order and then they'd make new packages like *Yesterday and Today*, just awful packages.

*That entire era was so productive; did it seem that way to you?*

Yeah, it was good, it was enjoyable. We'd get into doing harmonies and this and that. Because in the early days we were only working on four-track tapes. So what we'd do would be work out most of the basic track on one track, get all the balance and everything set, all the instruments. Then we'd do the vocals or say, overdub. If there was guitar, lines would come in on the second verse and piano on the middle eight with shakers and tambourines. We'd line up and get all the sounds right and do it in a take and then do all the vocal harmonies over.

Those old records weren't really stereo. They were mono records and they were rechanneled. Some of the stereo is terrible because you've got the backing on one side. In fact, when we did the first two albums—at least the first album—which was *Please Please Me*, we did straight onto a two-track machine. So there wasn't any stereo as such, it was just the voices on one track and the backing on the other. *Sgt. Pepper* was only a four-track.

*It's hard to believe.*

Yup. Well, we had an orchestra on a separate four-track machine in "Day in the Life." We tried to sync them up, I remember; they kept going out of sync in playback so we had to remix it.

*Was the rest of the band difficult when you started getting into Indian music?*

Not really. They weren't really as interested. When I'd first met Ravi, he played a private concert just at my house and he came with Alla Rakha, and John and Ringo came to that. I know Ringo just didn't want to know about the tabla because it just seemed so far out to him . . .

*. . . he couldn't relate to it . . . ?*

. . . well, he could relate to it as a percussion instrument, as drums, but how Rakha actually played it he couldn't figure that out at all. But they liked it; they knew there was something great about it, but they weren't into it as I was. Then they all went to India and had those experiences in India, too, which you know, for anybody who goes to India, I think straightaway you can relate much more to Indian music, because it makes so much more sense having been there.

———

*Was it intimidating to you to start out at age 17 or 18 and be younger than the others?*

No, there are nine months between me and Paul; nine months between Paul and John. In the early days, when I was still at school, I was really small, I sort of grew in height when we were away in Hamburg. A few years before that, when I was still at school, we did a few parties at night—just silly things—John, Paul and I, and there were a couple of other people who kept coming and going. John was in school, the College of Art, which was adjoining our school. Paul and I would sneak out of our school and go into his place, which was a bit more free, you know—ours was still in school uniforms—and we could smoke in his place and do all that. I think he did feel a bit embarrassed about that because I was so *tiny*—I only looked about ten years old, but in Hamburg . . . We were living right in the middle of *St. Pauli*, which is right in the middle of the *Reeperbahn* district in Hamburg, all the clubowners were like gangsters and . . . everybody in the nightclubs, all the waiters had tear-gas guns, truncheons, knuckle-dusters—they were a heavy crew. Everybody around that district were homosexuals, transvestites, pimps and hookers [*breaks into a laugh*], you know, being in the middle of *that* when I was 17!

It was good fun, you know, but when we moved into the second club we were becoming so popular with the crowd of regulars, that we never got in any problems with all these gangster sort of people. They never tried to beat us up, because they knew, you know, the Beatles. And you know, they'd say *die pedels, die pedels*, whatever little kids' terminology would be for it. That's German for prick. They'd say, *die pedels.*

*The whole image of the Beatles got cleaned up and smoothed over which is always attributed to Brian [Epstein].*

In the Hamburg days we had to play so long and really rock it up and leap about and foam at the mouth and do whatever. We missed the whole period; in England Cliff Richards and the Shadows became the big thing. They all had matching ties and handkerchiefs and gray suits. But we were still doing Gene Vincent, Bo Diddley, you know, Ray Charles things. So when we got back to England that was the big thing. They didn't know us in Liverpool and there was a gig at the town hall, or something, at a dance. There was an advertisement in the newspaper saying "Direct From Hamburg" and so many people really dug the band and they were coming up to us and saying, "Oh, you speak good English!"

But a year or so after that, when Brian Epstein came on the scene, he said, "You should smarten up because nobody wants to know you"—TV producers or record producers or whatever. We just looked too scruffy. In Germany they had a lot of leather stuff, like black leather trousers and jackets and cowboy boots.

*Do you miss that Hamburg in your music?*

I just had such a good time just playing, you know. That's what I miss. Even when we sold records and started doing a lot of tours, it was a bit of a drag because we'd go on the road and we'd play the same tunes to different people and then we'd drop a few and add news ones all the time, but basically it was the same old tunes. It got stale. I felt stale, you know because you play the same riffs *da-da-da-ding-ding-dow*, you know, "Twist and Shout" and things. By the time you came off the road, been touring the world, I'd just want to not particularly . . .

*. . . look at an instrument . . .*

. . . yeah, for a while, and so we did get very stale and that's a period when—I was saying about being into the sitar—I got really friendly with Eric, and all the kids were playing *guitars*. I'd felt as though I'd missed so many years out.

*You mean like Hendrix and Cream and that whole era?*

Yeah, and all the young kids coming up were all playing go good and I hadn't been involved with it for so long, both being in the Beatles, just playing the same old tunes, and playing Indian music. So I felt a long way behind, that was one reason why I had all the instruments. I suddenly realized "I don't like these guitars" and Eric gave me this Les Paul which really got me back into it because it sounded so funky. That was one of the reasons I started playing slide, you know, because I felt so far behind in playing hot licks. With slide I didn't have any instruction, I just got one and started playing.

*Did you feel self-conscious about your guitar playing?*

I just had to force myself back. A lot of it was just confidence.

*That was the fault of being in a band . . .*

. . . that was stagnating.

*John said that the best Beatles music happened before you ever cut a record.*

. . . mmmh, well, yes, I think some of the best stuff we did was when we stopped touring and spent a lot of time in the studio. You know, we lived in a studio, really. A lot of the things which were innovations as far as recording went—I think that was some of the best music. But as far as playing live, I agree with what John says about the old days. We were really rocking. We had fun, you know, we really had fun.

*Since you've gone solo your signature, musically, is different from that now. Like when you did "Wah-Wah" . . .*

. . . That was the song—when I left during the *Let It Be* movie, there's a scene where Paul and I are having an argument . . .

. . . and we're trying to cover it up. Then the next scene I'm not there and Yoko's just screaming, doing her screeching number. Well, that's where I'd left, and I went home and wrote "Wah Wah." It'd given me a wah-wah, like I had such a headache with that whole argument, it was such a headache. . . .

*When did you actually meet Eric for the first time?*

We were in Hammersmith Odeon, and the Yardbirds were sort of supporting a group on the bill, and I just met him then but really didn't get to know him. Met him again when the [*Lovin'*] Spoonful were at the Marquee and John and I went down and were just sort of hanging about backstage with them. We were going down to their hotel, I can remember just seeing Eric: "I know him, I'm sure I know this guy and he seems like, you know, really lonely." I remember we went out and got in the car and went off to Sebastian's hotel and I remembered thinking, "We should've invited that guy 'cause I'm sure we know him from somewhere and he just seemed, like, lonely."

And then a couple of years, maybe a year or so later, the Bee Gees, the Cream, were involved with Brian Epstein originally, so I started meeting Eric and hanging out with him then at Brian Epstein's house. We sort of went out quite a bit with Brian for dinner and stuff, and then the whole Cream thing started happening. Through that period he played "Guitar Gently Weeps" and after that he just escaped out of London because some cop was after him, and he bought a house just a bit further out in the country from where I was and we used to hang out.

"Savoy Truffle," on the White Album, was written for Eric. He's got this real sweet-tooth and he'd just had his mouth worked on. His dentist said he was through with candy. So as a tribute I wrote, "You'll have to have them all pulled out after the Savoy Truffle." The truffle was some kind of sweet, just like all the rest: cream tangerine, ginger sling—just candy, to tease Eric.

*I remember him saying he was dedicating "Layla" to some mysterious woman. Did you know what was happening?*

Well, yeah, sort of. I mean, you know, the thing with . . . is with Eric, over the years, and, you know, we both [George and Pattie Harrison] loved Eric—still do—and there were a few funny things. I pulled his chick once. That's happened, and now you'd think he was trying to get his own back on me [*laughing*]. But much later, when all that thing was going on, when I split from Pattie, you know . . .

Pattie and he got together after we'd really split and actually, we'd been splitting up for years. That was a funny thing, you know, I thought that was the best thing to do, for us to split, and we should've just done it much sooner. But I didn't have any problem about it; Eric had the problem. Every time I'd go and see him and stuff, he'd be really hung up about it, and I was saying: "Fuck it, man, don't be apologizing," and he didn't believe me. I was saying, "I don't care."

*You said* All Things Must Pass *was like an explosion for you.*

Yuh. I had a lot from during the Beatles time and I was writing all the time, and I wrote a few while I was making the album as well.

*Which was your favorite—"My Sweet Lord"?*

No, not particularly. I like different songs for different reasons. I like the first song that was on the album, "I'd Have You Any Time," and particularly the recording of it. Because Derek and the Dominoes played on most of those tracks and it was a really nice experience making that album, because I was really a bit paranoid, musically. Having this whole thing with the Beatles had left me really paranoid. I remember having those people in the studio and thinking, "God these songs are so fruity! I can't think of which song to do." Slowly I realized, "We can do this one" and I'd play it to them and they'd say, "Wow, yeah! Great song!" And I'd say: "Really? Do you really like it?" I realized that it was okay, that they were sick of playing all that other stuff. It's great to have a tune, and I liked that song, "I'd Have You Any Time" because of Bob [Dylan].

I was with Bob and he'd gone through his broken neck period and was being very quiet, and he'd didn't have much confidence, anyhow—that's the feeling I got with him in Woodstock. He hardly said a word for a couple of days. Anyway, we finally got the guitars out and it loosened things up a bit. It was really a nice time with all his kids around and we were just playing. It was near Thanksgiving. He sang me that song and he was, like, very nervous and shy, and he said, "What do you think about this song?" And I'd felt very strongly about Bob when I'd been in India years before—the only record I took with me along with all my Indian records was *Blonde on Blonde.* I felt somehow very close to him, or something, you know, because he was so great, so heavy, and so observant about everything. And yet to find him later very nervous and with no confidence. . . .

But the thing that he said on *Blonde on Blonde* about what price you have to pay to get out of going through all these things twice—"Oh, mama, can this really be the end." . . . So, I was thinking, "There is a way out of it all, really, in the end." He sang at Woodstock that song, "Love is all you need [*singing*]/makes the world go round/Love and only love can't be denied/No matter what you think about it/You're just not going to be able to live without it/Take a tip from one who's tried." And I thought, "Isn't it great, because I know people are going to think, 'Shit, what's Dylan doing?'" But as far as I was concerned, it was great for him to realize his own peace; and it meant something. You know, he'd always been so hard . . . and I thought, "a lot of people are not going to like this." But I think it's fantastic because Bob has obviously had the experience. I was saying to him, "You write incredible lyrics," and he was saying, "How do you write those tunes?" So I was just showing him chords like crazy. *Chords*. Because he tended just to play a lot of basic chords and move a capo up and down. And I was saying, "Come on, write me some words," and he was scribbling words down. And it just killed me because he'd been doing all these sensational lyrics and he wrote: "All you have is yours/All you see is mine/And I'm glad to hold you in my arms/I'd have you any time." The idea of Dylan writing something like . . . so very simple.

*Did you get any feedback from John or Ringo or anybody, saying "Congratulations"?*

I remember John was really negative at the time, but I was away and he came 'round to my house and there was a friend of mine living there who was a friend of John's. John just saw the album cover and said, "He must be fucking bad, putting three records out. And look at the picture on the front, he looks like an asthmatic Leon Russell." There was a lot of negativity going down. You know . . . Ringo played on almost the whole album. I don't care about that. Fuck it, we've been through the thing. I felt that whatever happened, whether it was a flop or a success, I was gonna go on my own just to have a bit of peace of mind.

*So you weren't apprehensive about how it would go over?*

No. Not at all. I felt it was good music, whether people bought it or not. I was concerned that the musicians who played on it were concerned. It was good.

*By the time it was finished, you were confident that it was good?*

Even before I started I knew I was gonna make a good album because I had so many songs and I had so much energy. For me to do my own album after all that—it was joyous. Dream of dreams.

*Let's move ahead. On the new album I've never been able to figure out whether you're talking about Krishna or a woman.*

That's good—I like that. I think individual love is just a little of universal love. The ultimate love, the universal love or the love of God, is a basic goal; each one of us must manifest our individual love, manifest the divinity which is in us. All individual love between one person loving another or loving this, that or the other, is all small parts or small examples of that one universal love. It's all God; I mean if you can handle the word—God.

Ultimately the love can become so big that we can love the whole of creation instead of "I love this but I don't like that." Singing to the Lord or an individual is, in a way, the same. I've done that consciously in some songs.

*I always thought Hindu mythology was fascinating like Greek mythology . . .*

The mythology part was one thing I could never figure out, and it took me a long time to be able to realize—just like when they talk about Jesus Christ, I think of him as an historical thing. The same thing with Krishna. Krishna actually was in a body as a person, and the whole thing with the mythology which makes it complicated was, if he's God, what's he doing fighting on a battlefield? It took me ages to try and figure that out and, again, it was [*Paramahansa*] Yogananda's spiritual interpretation of *Bhagavad Gita* that made me realize what it was. Our idea of Krishna and Arjuna on the battlefield in the chariot. So this was the point—that we're in these bodies, which is like a kind of chariot, and we're going through this incarnation, this life, which is kind of a battlefield. The senses of the body, the five senses, are the horses pulling the chariot, and we have to get control over the chariot by getting control over the reins.

And Arjuna in the end says, "Please Krishna, you drive the chariot." Because unless we bring Christ or Krishna or Buddha or whichever of our spiritual guides or guru, what's called a sat-guru . . . we can go so far on our own, but without divine guidance or without being established in some sort of god consciousness, then we're going to crash our chariot and we're going to turn over and we're going to get killed in the battlefield. That's why we say "*Hare Krishna, Hare Krishna,*" asking Krishna to come and take over the chariot. It's beautiful you know, because it works. In a way, Christ will help drive your chariot, or whoever the guru would be.

These people with shaved heads and saffron robes and bowing down to Krishna—in the West it may appear strange to people because of their ignorance of what it's about. On that count I think Prabhupada has done amazingly well, because in spite of people's ignorance and the barriers of ridicule that have been put up against them, they've set up so many temples and saved so many people from being drug addicts and what-have-you, just from the clutches of the battlefield. It's a fantastic thing and it should be encouraged, and it's only people's ignorance that puts it down.

*You see Prabhupada as a friend?*

He is a friend, he is my master who I have great respect for. It's just like if you want to learn how to ski, you go to somebody who'll teach you how to ski. You have to accept that instructor's word to be final if you want to get anywhere, otherwise you don't have it. I accept Prabhupada as qualified to teach people about Krishna. I felt in a way, it's something that is in you consciousness or in your heart, I don't have to dress in saffron robes and shave my head to be in a spiritually involved way of thinking. I've had a lot of interest in different ways and one of the things I never liked was the whole bit in the late '60s when everyone started getting into it. One thing I really disliked was this "My guru's better than your guru"—it's like kids on the street: "My dad's better than your dad." The point is that there is only one God, he's got millions of names, but there's only one God. All Maharishi ever gave me was good advice and he gave me the technique of meditation, which is really wonderful.

*They say he was a . . .*

Well, you know, John went through a negative thing more so than I did with Maharishi. I can see now much clearer what happened, and there was still just a lot of ignorance that went down. Maharishi was fantastic and

I admire him like Prabhupada for being able, in spite of all the ridicule, to just keep on going. And there's more people now—especially in the United States—who are all doing it, and in the '60s, they were laughing at us saying it was stupid. All of these people have influenced me and I've tried to get the best out of all of them without getting spiritual indigestion.

*I've always wondered about the individual practice of various sects. Krishna Consciousness devotees get up at 4:00 a.m. so they won't have wet dreams.*

[*Laughing*] Well, that's not the point. The point is they get up at four in the morning because, first of all, sleep they call the "little death." It would be great if we only needed four or five hours' sleep a night. The thing is that when you realize that every soul is potentially divine—the goal is to manifest the divinity. People may frown on that, may think it's ridiculous, but every one of us should become—is—a potential Christ, and should become Christ-conscious. To become fully realized—like masters. And the moment that you realize we're potentially divine, there's no time to lose. Prabhupada probably sleeps an hour or two a day. These yogis don't need sleep at all, they don't need food; they're living on the divine energy. We call it the Cosmic Energy, *prana*.

*What about your albums like* Living in the Material World, *the whole concept of* maya, *it's so ironic that you got caught up in it.*

Oh, yeah. I'm living in it. But people interpret it to mean, money, cars, that sort of thing—although those are part of the material world. The material world is like the physical world, as opposed to the spiritual. For me, living in the material world just meant being in this physical body with all the things that go along with it.

*The litigation involved in the Concert for Bangladesh, didn't that depress you?*

Yeah, that is sure enough to make you go crazy and commit suicide. The whole thing of being Beatles, it was very heavy on us four, it was like some people wrote saying, in those days, "Well, the problem with the Beatles is that when we were all growing up they were just tooling 'round the world in limousines." Actually, it was the reverse. We were forced to grow up much faster. And what they call growing up was actually just being stuck in a rut while we were transcending layer upon layer. So the heaviness of just the things we've been through and are still going though, we either use it or rise above it or it pulls you down. For me, it's like it made me have to call upon the inner me for the strength in order to rise above it because that is part of the *maya*. Whereas if you just cop out, it doesn't do anybody any good.

*Have you ever seen that as an ultimate possibility?*

Yeah, I can see that, quite easily disappear in another five or six years. But, I dunno, when it gets to that point we'll have to see—it's something which is growing all the time. The demand for my own realization. It is priority to go 'round being a rock 'n roll star? That's what I'm saying, there's no time to lose, really, and there's gonna have to be a point where I've got to drag myself away and try and fulfill whatever I can.

*You get to a point where being a rock star is almost a deviation.*

It is, in many ways. Since I got involved with it in the '60s, I've been heavily into it and then at times come right back out of it. There are a lot of people in the business that I love, friends, you know, who are really great but who don't have any desire for knowledge or realization. It's good to boogie once in a while, but when you boogie all your life away it's just a waste of a life and of what we've been given. I have to pull myself back out of that *maya*. Unfortunately, I don't have much to relate to the friends who just boogie all the time. It's very difficult. I can get high like the rest of them, but it's actually low. The more dope you take the lower you get, really. Having done that, I can say that from experience. Whatever it is you just need more, and the more you take the worse you get.

*In the temples I've been to . . .*

. . . women look after the kids, they cook and serve all the food . . .

*. . . and even more so, there's no sex unless there's marriage and even then it's only for procreative purposes, right?*

Yuh.

*Abstinence is a part of almost every major religion when you get right down to it.*

When you get really into it, yeah.

*Is it something you can live with?*

Well, it's something—we have to do what we can do. The main thing is we can make an effort, you know. I think that's what really counts. What you feel in you heart and what effort you can put into it, counts. I think if you do something and you don't really like doing it, then you're a hypocrite about it. In a way, we all have desires; we must learn either to fulfill the desires or terminate the desires. If you can do it by being celibate and it's easy to handle, it's okay. You can either lose certain desires you had when you were younger or the thing that you have to watch, particularly the sex and things like drugs, too, the problem is, you can go, "Oh, well I'll just have a bit and then I'll be fulfilled." But it doesn't work that way. First, you have a bit and then you want more and you want more and more.

*Is it impossible to balance that when you're in a relationship to please the woman you're with, and your own spiritual inclination?*

Yes, I think it can. If I'm reading what you're saying, you've been reading those interviews with Eric Clapton saying about my ex-wife, Pattie, that we hadn't—I brought it up, I don't mind being personal—because I was always meditating. The point is to have a balance between inner life and the external. Again, with relationships with people, it never works if one person is into it and the other isn't; it's difficult on both sides. Usually if a fellow's on smack his girlfriend either has to leave him or get in on it; it's like that.

*Did the pressures of being on the road bring you to Krishna?*

You either go crackers and commit suicide, or you try and use every incident in order to realize something and attach yourself more strongly to an inner strength.

*Is that what you were looking for in '66 and '67?*

For me, it was like a flash. The first time I had acid it just opened up something in my head that was inside of me and I realized a lot of things.

I didn't learn them, because I already knew them, but that happened to be the key that opened the door to reveal them. From the moment I had that, I wanted to have it all the time—these thoughts about the yogis and the Himalayas, and Ravi's music.

*Were you religious when you were growing up?*

I wasn't really, although, when I got into meditation, I'd been having sort of experiences like when I was a kid. I used to always see things. [*He chuckles.*] At night I'd be half in between awake and asleep, and I'd have like what used to be called nightmares.

I used to have an experience when I was a kid which used to frighten me. I realized in meditation that I had the same experience and it's something to do with always feeling tiny. There was always this thing which I later related to the *mantra*, and this feeling would just go with it. I'd feel really tiny and at the same time I'd feel I was a whole thing as well. It was feeling like two different things at the same time. And this little thing, with this feeling that would vibrate right through me, would start off rolling around and it would start getting bigger and bigger and faster and faster and faster [*his voice races*] until it was going like so far and getting so fast that it was mind-boggling and I'd come out of it really scared.

I used to get that experience a lot when we were doing *Abbey Road*, recording. I'd go into this big empty studio and get into a sound box inside of it and do my meditation inside of there and I had a couple of indications of that same experience, which I realized was what I had when I was a kid.

# RADIO INTERVIEW WITH GEORGE HARRISON AND MICHAEL JACKSON

David "Kid" Jensen | February 9, 1979 | *Roundtable*, BBC Radio 1

While searching out topics for a radio documentary program in 2018, Richard Latto of Radio Solent—a southern-based BBC service broadcasting to Southampton, Hampshire, and the Isle of Wight—made a tantalizing discovery online: a recording of a 1979 BBC program that featured George Harrison and Michael Jackson discussing music of the day. The audio quality was exceedingly poor, and the ensuing search in BBC archives turned up only a short excerpt of what had been a ninety-minute broadcast.

Undeterred, Latto reached out to the ever-active community of Beatles fans. "I put the word out on the collectors' circuit," he says, "and a chap called Richard White came forward with a cassette recording of the entire broadcast." With almost the full interview in hand and after some audio doctoring, they secured the participation of deejay David "Kid" Jensen, who had led the original 1979 discussion, and produced a radio documentary that aired on the fortieth anniversary of the rare and special moment.

Much of the conversation followed the program's theme—musicians commenting on present-day releases: Harrison and Jackson opined on recent singles by Foreigner, the Blues Brothers, Dave Edmunds, Nicolette Larson, and others. Some Jensen chose because of their relevance to his guests: drummer Lenny White's version of the Beatles' "Lady Madonna" had just come out, while Jackson himself had previously covered Bill Wither's "Ain't No Sunshine."

Harrison and Jackson have much in common: musical tastes, a sense of service in their music, and parallel experiences proving their own songwriting skills while in groups that didn't necessarily value them. It's intriguing to hear how deferential Jackson is to Harrison ("Could you ask George first what I think about it, please?" he says at one point) and yet how determined he is to explain the sincere message of the film *The Wiz* (still to arrive in the United Kingdom at the time). It's equally revealing how Harrison picks up on Jackson's idea of music-as-message, and ends the conversation speaking about that as a priority of their craft.

That Harrison popped into a London BBC radio studio on a Friday evening was of little surprise; it was a forty-minute drive from his home. Jackson, living in Los Angeles then, was the less likely guest, but he and his brothers were in town promoting their *Destiny* album, and would play the Rainbow Theater that weekend. The interview catches Jackson on the verge of his career breakthrough; later that year, *Off the Wall* would establish him as a songwriter and solo artist. His follow-up, *Thriller*, would launch him to a level of celebrity and mania-producing popularity only a handful of artists—such as the Beatles—had ever experienced. —Ed.

**David Jensen:** I have a very special *Roundtable* tonight, too, because I have two very distinguished people in the world of popular music. Michael Jackson, welcome for the first time to the *Roundtable*.

**Michael Jackson:** How are you?

**Jensen:** I'm doing good. I saw you of course on *Top of the Pops* last night; I was *with* you on *Top of the Pops* last night. [*Jackson laughs.*] You're in the midst of a big world tour now, right?

**Jackson:** That's true. We're doing a lot of different things in Switzerland and Paris.

**Jensen:** How far into the tour are you?

**Jackson:** We just started, actually. We're two weeks into it.

**Jensen:** And you're all geared up—you've got to pace yourself for something like that I would imagine.

**Jackson:** Yes, we've been so busy. We had rehearsal the other day.

**Jensen:** I'm going to find out about some of the things that you've been doing. I'm glad you were able to make it along to the program. And in terms of global popularity, I suppose the Jacksons are only eclipsed by my next guest's old band. George Harrison, welcome.

**George Harrison:** Good evening, Kid. Hi. How are you doing?

**Jensen:** I'm pretty good. And you have had a busy time too because you've just flown in from . . . ?

**Harrison:** Rio. [*Sings lyric from "Flying Down to Rio."*] "Rio by the sea-o. The only star for me-o, oh me-o." [*Jackson laughs.*]

**Jensen:** Were you doing anything musical down in Rio or was it a proper holiday?

**Harrison:** I sort of used the excuse of going to see the Brazilian Grand Prix to have a look at Brazil, or a part of Brazil, because I've never been to South America before. In fact, none of the Fab Four have ever been there, which I found out when I arrived because it's a bit of mania down there. But it's a wonderful place.

**Jensen:** I'd love to go there. A country I . . . one day I will go there. Well, you're both on the program; there is so much to talk about, and we'll do that and also play as many of the new releases as we can between now and eight o'clock. It's the *Roundtable* and our first record up tonight is from Foreigner, who enjoy great success in America. In fact, this current record is number twenty in the charts over there. It's called "Blue Morning, Blue Day."

[*Plays song.*]

**Jensen:** "Blue Morning, Blue Day." That's Foreigner and that's a new single release over here for them on blue vinyl . . . not just on blue vinyl but it's sort of a picture disc as well. And Michael Jackson, I'll go to you first and ask your reaction to that?

**Jackson:** I like the guitars on that. It's very strong in the beginning. I love the guitars on the . . . the one you played of him when the . . .

**Jensen:** George.

**Jackson:** . . . yeah, on Dark [*Horse*] Records, I liked that a lot, really. I think it gets your attention in the beginning.

**Jensen:** Right. Actually, it's strange that Michael should talk about guitar work in that because the guitarist is Mick Jones who was the guitarist in a band I saw you with in New York television a few years ago called Wonderwheel. . . .

**Harrison:** Right, that's right. In fact, Mick Jones, I'm pleased for him that this band is a success because we first met him in '64 in Paris in the Olympia and he was the musical director for Sylvie Vartan and what's his name, Johnny . . .

**Jensen:** Johnny Hallyday.

**Harrison:** Johnny Hallyday. And at that time Mick was, like, conducting the band and playing guitar. And he was with Gary Wright also in, apart from Wonderwheel, in Spooky Tooth. I thought the record was . . .

**Jackson:** [*Laughs.*] Spooky Tooth.

**Harrison:** . . . very pleasant and he is a great guitar player.

**Jackson:** Yeah, I like that, too.

**Jensen:** The thing about Wonderwheel was it was a band and . . . I had never seen of you or your former pals talk about . . . still friends of yours presumably, the Beatles . . . talk about other bands, but seeing you on television in New York with Wonderwheel, you obviously were very keen on them. Whatever became of them?

**Harrison:** Well actually, Wonderwheel was sort of in between Spooky Tooth splitting up and then getting back together again. So, Gary Wright formed Wonderwheel, and then part of that band . . . well, they split Wonderwheel and then they got back the singer from Spooky Tooth with Mick Jones and Gary Wright and I forget the drummer's name. But they re-formed Spooky Tooth for a couple of records, and then Gary Wright went his own way, made a solo album, which you know, *Dream Weaver.*

**Jensen:** That's right. And he's appeared on a record with you of course.

**Harrison:** Yeah. And Mick Jones, I don't know what happened to him up until they made the first Foreigner album, which was a huge success.

**Jensen:** In America. Strangely enough they've never really happened here. But I think that is the record to do it for them. This is Nicolette Larson, and this is a new single on Warner Brothers. It's a Neil Young song called "Lotta Love."

[*Plays song.*]

**Jensen:** Nicolette Larson. And in America, that's number ten. It's just been released over here on Warner Brother Records, and "Lotta Love." And George Harrison, you expressed interest in that record before the program.

**Harrison:** Yeah, I think she's very nice. She looks nice too. [*Jackson laughs.*] She sings good. And the production is really good—Ted Templeman, one of those producers. I'd be interested to know who played the sax on here. It sounds a bit like Tommy Scott. But I think if Stan [*Cornyn*] and Reg [*Barnes*], the Warner Brothers, promote that, it should be a big hit.

**Jensen:** [*Laughs.*] Were you familiar with that song before or just Nicolette Larson?

**Harrison:** Just Nicolette Larson, yeah. Actually, my Mrs. did play it to me this afternoon—coincidence. So, she likes it too.

**Jensen:** She's a session singer. Not your Mrs. but Nicolette Larson.

**Harrison:** Oh yeah. I've never met her before; I've never really heard much about her until this album.

**Jensen:** What about you, Michael?

**Jackson:** I like it a lot. I've heard it lots of times in the States.

**Jensen:** I guess so, yeah, right.

**Jackson:** Of course . . . and I think it has a beautiful melody, especially the punch line, [*sings*] "It takes a lotta love." That thing. I think it's nice.

**Harrison:** Very familiar tune.

**Jensen:** Melody is obviously these days a very important part . . .

**Jackson:** *Very.*

**Jensen:** . . . of your music. I notice that the last couple of things that have been released have had a very strong melody line, that it was not maybe so obvious in the earlier records that you released.

**Jackson:** Uh, that's true for the *singles* but for the other stuff, I mean it's different. I mean I think melodies are always important, I mean especially like some of the old Beatle things, I mean I think the melodies are beautiful. I mean that's what I think makes them stay around so long.

**Harrison:** Yeah, that's why I like melodies too . . .

**Jackson:** Really?

**Harrison:** . . . the thing that put me off a lot of pop music is the way you can't distinguish what the tune is supposed to be.

**Jackson:** That's right.

**Harrison:** Actually, I disagree. I think the Jacksons have a lot of melodies. I remember the first big hit that I ever heard was . . .

**Jensen:** "I Want You Back"?

**Harrison:** No. What was that one? Where it had a fantastic bass line . . . I'll remember the title later.

**Jensen:** "The Love You Save," maybe? "ABC"?

**Jackson:** Probably.

**Jensen:** Something like that . . .

**Harrison:** No. I forgot it. Anyway. But it sounded a bit . . .

**Jackson:** Yeah, that's really important, the melody. I mean if you just hum "Here Comes the Sun" or "[*The*] Fool on the Hill," I mean the melody is so pretty you don't . . . I mean the lyrics are beautiful too, but you don't really need it.

**Jensen:** [*To Harrison.*] Those are both songs of yours, are they not?

**Harrison:** Not "Fool on the Hill." That was Paul's song. The other one is mine.

**Jensen:** And you were mentioning that, from an album that's coming out soon, the "Blow Away" single is taken from a new album called *George Harrison*. You've got a song on it, a cousin to "Here Comes the Sun."

**Harrison:** Oh yeah. Yeah. "Here Comes the Moon." [*Jackson laughs.*] I saw it . . . I mean it was the circumstance. I was in a particularly great place when I saw the moon coming up and I thought, "Wow, you know, all this, *and* here comes the moon!" And then I thought, "No, I couldn't write a song called that, they'll kill me." But as it happened, I wrote the song and it turned out really nice, so it stands up in its own right. And any other songwriters around, they have had ten years to write "Here Comes the Moon" after "Here Comes the Sun," but nobody else wrote it, I might as well do it meself.

**Jensen:** Is it a pretty song like "Here Comes the Sun?"

**Harrison:** Yeah, it is. In fact, it's a very peaceful song. And the problem with mixing it was I kept falling asleep, by the time it gets to the end it's put me into a dream world.

**Jensen:** Well it's obviously a track that we look forward to hearing from this new album, which should be out . . . soon?

**Harrison:** Soon. I don't recall which day, twenty-third I think, for my birthday.

**Jensen:** Ahhh! Here's the record I've been looking forward to playing on the program most of all, from Van Morrison; it's going to be my record of the week next week, he's been a hero of mine for a long time. On the Warner Brother[s] label, this is called "Natalia."

[*Plays song.*]

**Jensen:** Van Morrison and that's his single release called "Natalia" on the Warner Brother[s] label. And as I said, that's my record of the week next week. And Michael, I'll go to you first and get your reaction on hearing that.

**Jackson:** Well, what I tell you about each record, I try to be as truthful as possible. In each song, there's always something I like about each one. I loved the melody of the rhythm track on that. [*Sings rhythmic hook.*] "Doo-dah, dun-dah, din-dah." And they do that all through the track—I think it's pretty.

**Jensen:** OK. George?

**Harrison:** Yeah, I agree. The backing sort of is OK. I think Van Morrison is a great singer, but the song I thought was a bit predictable, you know it wasn't a very strong song, and that's about all I can say. It's a well-made record but a very predictable *tune*.

**Jensen:** Of course, Van's band Them were around at the same time as the Beatles were playing back in the early part of the '60s, and I'm wondering if you ever had any kind of relationship with . . .

**Harrison:** No, I met Van Morrison more so when he was with the Band, you know, hanging out with Robbie Robertson and the Band, and he sang a lot on their albums at different times. But I think he's a great singer, but I just didn't really think the song was that strong.

**Jensen:** OK . . . I loved it! [*Laughs.*] I want to talk about your forthcoming album if I can, now, George, because it's been a while since you've recorded an album; 1976 was the last time an album was released here and that was *Thirty Three & 1/3*. And so, I should ask you what you've been doing in the intervening period—first, in musical terms.

**Harrison:** Well, in music terms I sort of skived for 1977. I went on strike. I just went to the races, actually, and, um—

**Jensen:** Car races?

**Harrison:** Yeah, to the motor racing. I was just really getting a bit fed up with the music business to tell you the truth. I mean it has been a long time being in it and, you know, I just felt like a break. So I took 1977 away from music, and I didn't actually write a tune during that year. I just sort of forgot all about music, went to the races, and then at the end of '77 I thought, "God, I better start doing something." I heard all these stories about people drying up, you know, so I thought, "Well, maybe I'll write a tune, see if I can just write a tune." And I wrote "Blow Away." It was a miserable day, pouring with rain, and we were having a few leaks in the roof of the house and all that sort of stuff.

**Jensen:** Whereabouts was this?

**Harrison:** At home, here in England.

**Jensen:** England is your home?

**Harrison:** I live here, yeah. I live here all the time. People seem to think I live in America . . .

**Jackson:** Yeah. [*Laughs.*]

**Harrison:** . . . but I live here. So, I wrote that song and to tell you the truth, I was a bit embarrassed by it. It seemed like it was so catchy, and it seemed like . . . I was a bit embarrassed to play it to anybody. You know, I thought, "God, is it too obvious?"

**Jensen:** It's funny because I remember reading that when John and Paul were writing songs for the Beatles and all that output, it was a while before you worked up, sort of, courage to present your songs in that concept.

**Harrison:** Well . . .

**Jensen:** Was that for the same reason?

**Harrison:** No, no. They wrote right from . . . during school, you know, when we were at school, they wrote a load of tunes, which were not really that good—well a couple of them . . . I think one of them we recorded on the *Let It Be* album, "One After 909." That one they wrote when we must have been about fifteen years old, sixteen. So they had a bit of a head start.

But because they did write such good tunes and the Beatles took off, it made it more difficult for me as a songwriter because the starting point had to be a bit . . . I mean if there's already so many good tunes, then I have to try and write better. So, I think the first tune I wrote was 1963, as an experiment to see if I could write a tune. It was called "Don't Bother Me," a grumpy song. [*Laughs with Jackson.*] It, actually, it was all right for the first tune, but then it was really a matter of practice. The more you do, the more easy it becomes, you know.

**Jensen:** So here you are at the stage today where, obviously, you're doing your own solo albums. Michael, I'm going to talk to you about *your* album, which is doing well, the *Destiny* album, after we hear another record, which is going to be some rock and roll from Dave Edmunds, who guested on the program last week. This is "A1 on the Jukebox."

[*Plays song.*]

**Jensen:** Two weeks ago he was in the studio with Charlie Gillett talking about other folks' records, and I know he listens to the program—Dave Edmunds, good evening. That's "A1 on the Jukebox" which is taken from the album *Tracks on Wax 4*. And, like Nick Lowe—who produces Dave

Edmund's songs—his songs have some sort of familiarity about them. It reminds me of other things somehow.

**Harrison:** Yeah, I agree, I like Dave Edmunds. But that song reminds me straight off, I've never heard it before, but it's . . . [*sings*] "I waa-aant you to tell me how you walked out on me." You know, the Everly Brothers, "Walk Right Back," speeded up a bit, except for the bridge, different bridge. [*Jackson laughs.*] But it's a pretty pleasant record though all the same. It's nice.

**Jensen:** Rock and roll, I would imagine, played an important part in your early days.

**Harrison:** Yeah, I think so.

**Jensen:** Did you have any heroes that are still with you today?

**Harrison:** Yeah, I must admit that the stuff I liked back in the late '50s, early '60s is still the music I like the most now. You know, Eddie Cochran, Buddy Holly, Little Richard, Larry Williams, you know, those sort of things.

**Jensen:** Timeless.

**Harrison:** Yeah.

**Jensen:** What about you, Michael Jackson?

**Jackson:** As far as the record or . . . ?

**Jensen:** Rock and roll, generally speaking.

**Jackson:** Um . . . just about the same people he said. Chuck Berry and Buddy Holly and Little Richard and all those kinds of . . .

**Jensen:** You recorded a song, "Rockin' Robin," but you never really got into . . . recorded a rock and roll number, as such, have you?

**Jackson:** Umm. Yeah. On our new album, *Destiny*, there is one. I mean, it's kind of disco-y but rock and roll, it kicks off, it's called "All Night Dancing."

**Jensen:** The new album, you're kind of pleased with I would imagine because you've actually produced and wrote all the songs on the album.

There's one song that you didn't have a 100% hand in recording but most of the album you had. This was a first time for you, wasn't it?

**Jackson:** Yes, right.

**Jensen:** Why this album and not before?

**Jackson:** Because it's kind of difficult to get people to believe in you, you know. You have to tell them, "I want to *do* it for once." And some people believe in you, some don't, and finally they give you the chance, and they see what you can do, and then they let you do it.

**Jensen:** So you're confident in it just going on from here, I suppose, and doing your own stuff.

**Jackson:** Mmm-hmmm. [*To Harrison.*] Let me ask you a question. Did you guys always write your own stuff, I mean, from the beginning?

**Harrison:** Yeah, well John and Paul wrote right from before we ever made records.

**Jackson:** How did you ever manage that?

**Harrison:** I don't know, they were clever little fellas. [*Laughter.*] We did record . . . you know the first two albums, we recorded about half of the albums were other people's songs. Like we did a lot of cover versions of . . . like we did "Twist and Shout" . . .

**Jackson:** Oh, yeah!

**Harrison:** . . . by the Isley Brothers.

**Jensen:** "Matchbox," "Slow Down."

**Harrison:** "Matchbox." We did all kinds of . . . and some more obscure tunes, we did "Money" too. . . .

**Jensen:** "Dizzy Miss Lizzy"?

**Harrison:** Yeah, yeah sure, we did a lot of other people's songs in the early days.

**Jackson:** Hmmm.

**Jensen:** That's right. But it's amazing the way that your careers have gone and you've lasted, both of you, through so many, many years. And

Michael, you particularly overcame the initial kind of teenage hysteria and have really established yourself in other areas where you do cabaret rooms and you fill concert halls and things like that, where people will listen and not just scream all the time.

**Jackson:** Thank you. I mean I'm thankful that there's so many different things that I want to do and being able to do it is important.

**Jensen:** Good. Dave Edmunds, I like the record "A1 on the Jukebox," by the way, we almost forgot about that. [*Laughs with Jackson.*] What about you, Michael?

**Jackson:** I like the story. I do. It seems like oh, rock and roll, kinda. I mean, it reminded me of an old tune when it first kicked off, the style of the music. [*Sings the rhythm beat.*] I like the story, though. But why did he end it with "I'm nowhere?" I noticed.

**Harrison:** No, he's saying he's A1 on the jukebox, but it's nowhere on the charts, which is a good story.

**Jackson:** [*Sings.*] ". . .and I'm nowhere . . ."

**Harrison:** It's like nowhere on the charts, I think he said?

**Jensen:** Yeah, yeah, that's right.

**Harrison:** It's like a sort of country-western type idea, that sort of . . .

**Jackson:** Yeah.

**Jensen:** There is a certain amount of truth in that, of course, whereby a jukebox in America, they have their own charts because jukeboxes, you see songs in jukeboxes for years and years, the same songs keep coming.

**Harrison:** Yeah, it's a good idea for a lyric. Sometimes to write a song is . . . if you get a good idea, then you're off and running, you can't . . . you can sit there for hours and it's the initial idea. So that as a song is a good idea.

**Jensen:** It's seven o'clock; it's *Roundtable* with George Harrison and Michael Jackson, and here's Jimmy Lindsay, "Ain't No Sunshine" . . .

[*Plays song.*]

**Jensen:** Jimmy Lindsay, guy who covered the Commodore's record "Easy" a couple of years ago, and that didn't happen in the charts for him. That's on the GEM Records label which is a new record label to me. A Bill Withers composition which you, Michael Jackson, took into the charts here in 1972. So it'll be interesting to hear what you think of that reggae-fied version of the song.

**Jackson:** Uh, it kind of turned—George was mentioning this too—it kind of turned into reggae in the middle of it, at first it wasn't. Personally, I always liked the original version better than anyone's. The one that Bill Withers did, I think that's the most special one of all. But this one is nice—I like the saxophone, the sax is good. What is the guy's name again?

**Jensen:** Jimmy—Jimmy Lindsay. I can't tell you very much about him because I don't know much about him. George?

**Harrison:** Yeah, I don't know anything about Jimmy Lindsay either, but I think the song "Ain't No Sunshine" is a fantastic tune and again, I prefer the Bill Withers version. In fact, it's very seldom that there's a cover version that's usually better. I mean there *are* cases, but not that often. I prefer the Bill Withers version. But incidentally, I liked the way it started out much more, and when it turned into reggae, I sort of lost a bit of interest, although it's a pleasant record . . .

**Jensen:** This gets us into the field of reggae because I wanted to ask you both your thoughts on reggae. For the last couple of years music critics and some others have said, "Well, this will be the year of reggae" . . .

**Jackson:** Yeah . . .

**Jensen:** . . . "there will be much more reggae-dominated music in the charts." It's meant a lot more in Britain through the years, I think, than America.

**Jackson:** Bob Marley was a big influence, especially in the States, for reggae. I think . . . did he write, yeah, he wrote "I Shot the Sheriff" and then he made another version of it in reggae, and ever since then, I mean, we've been into it. Peter Tosh . . .

**Jensen:** Yeah.

**Jackson:** He—him and Mick Jagger did [*indistinct*] . . . it's happening in the States too. I like it.

**Jensen:** What about you George, does reggae ever appeal to you?

**Harrison:** Yeah, yeah. I like reggae. In fact, the first time I saw Bob Marley I was so impressed with his band and the show, I went back . . . I mean I stayed for the second show, and I went back the next night and saw him again, so . . . Bob Marley in particular, because, apart from the musical thing—I mean, it's sort of hypnotical [*sic*]—apart from that, I just liked the way he looked and the way he moved, sort of like he was in a dream. I don't know why. [*Laughter.*]

**Jensen:** I remember a few years ago Paul McCartney talking and saying that reggae, he was very, very interested in reggae, and said that it was a much more difficult form of music to play.

**Harrison:** It *is*. It's incredible—it's like, well, like Lord Buckley said, "It's just like a jitterbug, it's so simple it evades me." It is. It's like the hardest thing really to play *right*. I decided a few years ago that the way it must have evolved—or the way it could have evolved—was that, they were probably copying rock 'n' roll, or copying the music of the '60s, like we were, like a lot of the stuff we did, we were trying to do like other people but we could never do it right, and it turned into something else. And I think that's how reggae—they were sort of doing their version of what they thought everybody else was doing, and it turned into reggae.

**Jensen:** There's "fun reggae," and I suppose you could say there's "heavy reggae," from the point of view of lyrics, that's used as a base off of political and social statements these days. Tell me, are you ever consciously influenced these days by reggae or any sort of other ethnic style?

**Harrison:** Well, I've tried a couple of times—I must say, not too serious—but I've tried to make a tune into like a reggae feel—"Crackerbox Palace." But like I say, it's harder than it appears, you know? And the one thing I like about it is the drum sound they always get, like the high [*vocalizes timbale-like fill*] *ta-tang-tang!* The tom-toms . . . fantastic.

**Jensen:** Anything else that you discovered that we may not know about? What about down in South America?

**Harrison:** Oh, down in South America, I don't know about that. "Mull of Kintyre" [*by Wings, written by Paul McCartney —Ed.*] was a huge hit . . . in Brazil . . . [*Laughs.*]

**Jensen:** [*Laughs.*] I can't imagine that.

**Harrison:** . . . but if I had had more time I would have stayed for the Carnival and I would have been able to tell you more about it, but I'm not too hip to Brazilian music except, you know, the mambo and all that sort of stuff.

**Jensen:** There's a great Brazilian musician you must hear sometime if you haven't—Jorge Ben.

**Harrison:** Well actually, just before I left last night—or whichever night, the other night—I asked the record company, and they gave me a couple of big bags full of Brazilian records, so I'll do my homework on them.

**Jensen:** [*Laughs.*] OK. I'm going to play a couple of tracks from the new Eddie Money album—the album is entitled *Life for the Taking*. It's a new release over here on CBS and this is the title . . .

[*Plays songs.*]

**Jensen:** The new album called *Life for the Taking*, which [*Radio 1 deejay*] Andy Peebles previewed along with Eddie Money last week. Don't forget Andy Peebles will be on Radio 1 tonight at eight o'clock till ten minutes before ten o'clock. Two tracks from that album *Life for the Taking*, the title, and that one, which I liked a lot, "Maureen." George, and you were saying that Money is perhaps not his real name. . . .

**Harrison:** Oh, just that a friend of mine told me he was called Eddie Mahoney [*Jackson laughs.*] and they took out the "h" and called him Eddie Money. It's a good name, it's a better name, "Eddie Money." In fact, I've watched him on TV in the States just because of his name. You gotta check this guy out, and incidentally, I would say, watching him on TV I enjoyed him a lot. He just looks good and I like his sort of attitude. But of the two tracks I was not very impressed by "Life for the Taking"—that song didn't grab me at all, and the second song, this one "Maureen," I liked much more.

But again, it's not the sort of record, personally, that I would play over and over again.

**Jensen:** Currently in the country, Eddie Money will be appearing here in London for his last dates in the UK this weekend, before he comes back again Sunday. What about you Michael?

**Jackson:** I felt the same way. [*Laughs.*]

**Jensen:** Exactly the same way about that?

**Jackson:** Yeah.

**Jensen:** OK. Maybe I could ask you, then, if you can think—it might be a difficult question—when you find time to listen to other people's record, who you like to listen to these days?

**Harrison:** Uh, me? Well, I must say, out of the popular music thing, I still like probably most of all, is Ry Cooder. And I think he's quite popular in Europe, but he's . . .

**Jensen:** Cultish.

**Harrison:** Yeah, he is sort of cultish. But I like him. I think he's the best guitar player, and I like the way he draws his . . . like he never writes his own songs, but he always draws from crazy material and gets songs which, in a way, the sound's always very personal kind of music, although he never writes the tunes. I like . . . you know I still, I'm a big fan of Bob Dylan's, you know. I like Eric Clapton, those sort of people still, a lot. But my favorite music still, and I think it's always going to be, classical Indian music.

**Jensen:** Still?

**Harrison:** Yeah.

**Jensen:** I want to talk to you about your association with Indian in a little while. What about you Michael, records of other people's songs?

**Jackson:** Ummm, I like all kinds of music, but as far as popular music, like he said, I like Stevie Wonder. . . .

**Jensen:** Who incidentally has an album out here in a couple of weeks' time. . . .

**Harrison:** Really?

**Jackson:** A new one?

**Jensen:** Yeah, *The Secret Life* . . .

**Jackson:** . . . *Secret Life of Plants*, yeah. I heard some of that, it's so good.

**Jensen:** It's supposed to be very different from other things, but it's from the movie, and he's also got another album coming out before the end of the year, so there'll be two Stevie Wonder albums before the end of this year.

**Harrison:** What is this one, a film soundtrack?

**Jensen:** Yeah, I don't know much about the film, but one of his associates I talked to . . .

**Harrison:** [*To Jackson.*] We'll have to try and get our records out quick before he comes out. [*Laughs.*] He's good, isn't he?

**Jensen:** Eddie Money is . . . getting back to Eddie Money, you were talking about his live performance. Again, maybe I should talk about live performances—George, you appeared onstage in Guilford recently I understand with . . .

**Harrison:** Oh, you heard? [*Laughter.*] Well, with Eric, yeah. Eric was doing a concert tour—Clapton—and he, it was the last show in the tour and they always go a bit silly on the last show, so I was there with Elton watching the show, and before you know what happens, they've just put a guitar around your neck and they shove you out, and it's been so long now with that sort of thing, it's easy just to go on. It was good fun really, it was great.

**Jensen:** Are you planning to do any tours to promote or to play songs from the forthcoming album?

**Harrison:** With a band? I don't know. At the moment I don't have any sort of band, I don't really have the plan to do that, although there's a part of me which would like to do some concerts. I don't know, maybe I will do that later. But the only problem being, though, that the time it takes to get a band together and rehearse, it's pointless just going and doing a couple of dates. You might as well do a world tour and at this point in my life I don't really feel like touring the world, you know. . . .

**Jensen:** Because you've got a family. . . .

**Harrison:** Yeah, I overdosed on that. Yeah, I like to stay home, watch the baby grow, and plant flowers in the garden and have a peaceful life, and that is sort of like going back to the craziness. Also because I don't trust myself, because, at the drop of a hat, I'll *party*, like I did on the last tour. I'd come off the stage so wired up I'd want to boogie all night long, and then I'm wiped out, like, by the end of the first week and ready to drop. Maybe I'll do it and bring a straitjacket and a doctor with me. [*Laughter.*]

**Jensen:** What about you Michael? I mean, you work an awful lot, how do you avoid the kind of pressures that must be socially on you when you come off stage—"Let's go to a party," or "Why don't you come and see me . . .?" What do you do, do you keep a very strict discipline, and you kind of go to bed at the end of each concert, or what?

**Jackson:** That's it—I just go to sleep, just watch TV. [*Laughs.*]

**Harrison:** Take a sleeping pill before the last tune.

**Jackson:** [*Laughs.*] That's it, you said it.

**Jensen:** This is Diana Ross and some more friends of yours, Michael: Diana Ross, Marvin Gaye, Smokey Robinson, and Stevie Wonder—on a new single on Motown called "Pops, We Love You." It's a tribute record to Berry Gordy Sr., and this was recorded just before he died.

[*Plays song.*]

**Jensen:** On Motown, that was Diana Ross, Marvin Gaye, Smokey Robinson, Stevie Wonder. What a line up. "Pops, We Love You." Almost as good as the line up in tonight's *Roundtable*, George Harrison and Michael Jackson. Michael, obviously you know a lot about Motown records. Would they have all been in the studio *together* recording that song, you think?

**Jackson:** Umm . . . I don't think so, no.

**Jensen:** I hadn't heard that record before and it felt pretty good. George?

**Harrison:** Yeah, I like it a lot. I mean the song by any one of them would've been great, but with the four of them it's sensational. I think they were there together, at least, I think Diana Ross and Smokey Robinson were.

**Jackson:** Yeah.

**Harrison:** Because the way she come in with the Smokey a little bit, it would've been a bit hard doing that sort of thing, but contrived, if they weren't both together.

**Jensen:** Well, you arrived on the scene, Michael, through Motown Records, and that's where you found success around the world. And then you left Motown Records, and you're now on Epic Records, here. Tell me about the days with Motown. Are they affectionate days that you remember Motown Records by?

**Jackson:** The early days of Motown are really . . . I mean they're kind of like classical days. I mean, we were so young at the time, I remember everything. We first performed for Berry Gordy at his big estate in Detroit, poolside, and all the Motown stars were there. . . .

**Jensen:** Was it an audition that you did?

**Jackson:** Yeah. [*Laughs.*] All these great artists came down, from the Temps to the Supremes, and they loved our performance. And Diana came over special, made a special thanks. And she congratulated us and told us she wanted to be a special part of our career.

**Jensen:** And of course she was. What songs were you doing? That interests me. Were you doing some old Motown hits, or did you have original things you were performing?

**Jackson:** We were doing some James Brown stuff, some old Motown hits. We were doing "It's Your Thing" by the Isley Brothers.

**Jensen:** How old would you have been then?

**Jackson:** Around seven.

**Jensen:** Seven!

**Jackson:** Yeah.

**Harrison:** Gee.

**Jensen:** Oh, wow.

**Harrison:** That's young, you know?

**Jensen:** Yeah. [*Laughs.*] The thing is that Motown, you think of, as you said, a family thing. And that's that all the artists knew each other really, really well. Was that the case, then?

**Jackson:** That's very true.

**Jensen:** But what happened? Because things obviously were not so good, otherwise you would have left presumably . . . you *wouldn't* have left.

**Jackson:** [*Laughs.*] Right. There were a couple of things in . . . I mean, I hate deals and contracts and all that stuff. I think most artists do. But like I was saying before, we always wanted to write our own material and have our own publishing company and production company, different things like that, and we finally got a chance to do it. We never got that chance on Motown to write our own songs, which we always wanted to do.

**Jensen:** There's maybe a parallel with Apple, I suppose. That was a very family type thing, wasn't it, with everybody? I mean we get the impression that it was in the early days.

**Harrison:** Well, the thing is we always had the freedom to do what we wanted and that's I think the main difference, that Tamla/Motown, you know, up until like Stevie Wonder really turned it around, because up until then everybody was expected to do the same sort of tunes and it was all the same production. It was like an assembly line from Detroit, it was like the motorcars in a way, and they made really good records. But for the artist who wanted to be very individual, I think I could imagine it would be quite hard.

For us it was more of a thing to . . . you know, Apple was just really our own identity sort of thing, away from . . . although we were still with EMI. We wanted to have some other artists on the label, although we were with EMI up until '75 I think. It was like the Foreign Legion. But I think if we'd have had a contract that was shorter, we would have left EMI much sooner, you know, just in order to . . . because we signed with them when we were very young, not seven years old, I mean, we were about four years old. [*Laughter.*] We signed with them until we were about forty-three.

**Jensen:** The Apple days though, as you said, you just brought in talent to expose through your own label. I mean, I associate Mary Hopkins very much with Paul McCartney. I associate, actually, Hot Chocolate with John Lennon because I remember that single, "Give Peace a Chance."

**Harrison:** Right, yeah. Yeah.

**Jensen:** Who do you, which of the artists . . . Jackie Lomax?

**Harrison:** Well yeah, I produced Jackie Lomax's record and I did Billy Preston, Doris Troy, and . . .

**Jensen:** Oh, Doris Troy?

**Harrison:** Yeah. And I did a sort of one-off record with the Krishnas, you know the Krishna Temple?

**Jensen:** Yeah.

**Harrison:** They actually got in the *Top of the Pops*. I got them on *Top of the Pops*; it was great, all there with their shaved heads.

**Jensen:** "Govinda."

**Harrison:** Well, that was the second one, they did the "Hare Krishna Mantra." But I don't know, I think with Jackie Lomax it was . . . he was from the old Liverpool days in a band called the Undertakers, and there was a lot of other friends of ours who were always saying, "Go on, why don't you record Jackie, give him a break."

**Jensen:** And you did. What happened to Apple? Is it a simple story—sort of a fable, somewhere?

**Harrison:** It's the most complicated story ever. It's still there. Apple is more or less just a company that employs lawyers, still. I mean it's like . . . I don't know, we've been trying to dissolve the thing for years, but it's very difficult. It's very complicated. It's like *War and Peace.*

**Jensen:** [*Laughs.*] Okay, we won't get into that but into some more music. Manfred Mann's Earth Band and a Bob Dylan song called "You Angel You," which is out on the Bronze Label as their new single.

[*Plays song.*]

**Jensen:** Manfred Mann's Earth Band. And that was, as I said, a Bob Dylan song called "You Angel You." Well of course, Manfred Mann has chosen other Bob Dylan songs—and Bruce Springsteen songs before—and successfully taken them into the chart. Michael, did that appeal to you at all, that treatment of that song? I don't know if you're familiar with the original version, but what about the song?

**Jackson:** Could you ask George first what I think about it, please? [*Laughs.*]

**Jensen:** George? Yeah well, you . . . you're a friend of Bob Dylan's, why don't you react to that?

**Harrison:** Well yeah, I prefer Bob's version to tell you the truth. But, I mean, that is like a really strong record. To tell you the truth, I've no idea what's a hit and what isn't a hit these days. But that was quite pleasant. But, as I say, I prefer Bob Dylan's version, nothing personal, Manfred.

**Jensen:** Okay. Michael?

**Jackson:** Uhh . . . I could never fall asleep on it because it was so up and out. Um . . . God, I don't know what to say.

**Jensen:** Okay.

**Jackson:** What is the name of it again?

**Jensen:** "You Angel You."

**Jackson:** And the group?

**Jensen:** Manfred Mann's Earth Band.

**Jackson:** I never heard of them before.

**Jensen:** It would be interesting to get Bob Dylan's reaction on this. Actually, I wonder, would he be aware—or would you be aware, in the same kind of category of celebrity-hood, I suppose, of other people recording your songs and taking them into the charts? Do you . . . ?

**Harrison:** Oh yeah, I'm sure once it . . . if it gets a lot of radio play and it does anything in sales, I'm sure he will know about it. That's really nice as a songwriter if somebody else does the songs. Even bad versions, it's nice, just the idea . . . but Bob was probably not impressed because . . . it takes a lot to impress Bob Dylan. [*Laughs.*] But, I mean, everybody has recorded his tunes.

**Jensen:** What about your songs? Is there anybody that's recorded any one of your songs that you're particularly happy with the way they did it?

**Harrison:** Oh yeah. Well, there's quite a few. I've been a big fan, for years, of Smokey Robinson. He did "Something." Actually, when I was writing that song, in my mind I was thinking of Ray Charles singing it. As it happened, the song ended up with over 150 cover versions, but when Ray Charles did it, I was really disappointed, except for the middle, the bridge to it, he sings great. But it was a bit of a corny sort of way he did it. But the one that really made up for all of that was James Brown.

**Jensen:** Oh, I didn't realize . . .

**Harrison:** James Brown did it in 1972, he redid "Think" as a single, and on the B-side he did "Something" which is fantastic. I've got it on my jukebox at home and I mean it is just unbelievable, the way he sings it. And the arrangement is really beautiful.

**Jensen:** Michael, you were going to say something?

**Jackson:** I never . . . you wrote "Something"?

**Harrison:** Oh, yeah.

**Jackson:** Oh, I didn't know that. I was surprised. That's another one of my favorite ones. I thought Lennon and McCartney did that.

**Harrison:** Everybody thinks that.

**Jackson:** They do, don't they. I didn't know you wrote that one. It's beautiful.

**Jensen:** It's twenty-four minutes before eight o'clock, and here is an exciting sound that Paul Gambaccini has been playing on his American charts show on Saturday afternoons, mainly because the Blues Brothers album is number one in America. This single I'm about to play from the album is number sixteen in the charts. And this is their version of a Sam & Dave song from many years ago, "Soul Man."

**Jackson:** Yeah.

[*Plays song.*]

**Jensen:** Blues Brothers and a single from America's number one album called "Soul Man." Actually, the Blues Brothers have other identities and, George, maybe you can tell us a bit about them because you are quite friendly, are you not, with them?

**Harrison:** Yeah. John Belushi and Dan Aykroyd, they do . . . they've been for years on a show called *Saturday Night Live*. And also, John Belushi is Randy Klein, who is the Rutles manager. And Brian Thigh, Dan Aykroyd, was the one who turned down the Rutles. So, I was surprised . . . although Belushi has always been quite famous for his impersonations of Joe Cocker.

**Jackson:** Yeah.

**Harrison:** So he obviously is a potential serious singer too. So, I thought the album was going to be maybe a comedy album but obviously with Duck Dunn and Steve Cropper and Tommy Scott and all those people playing on it, it's good, very good.

**Jensen:** They sound like they mean it.

**Harrison:** Oh yeah, they do, they seem to mean it. I'd like to hear the rest of the album and see if they get into comedy.

**Jensen:** You mentioned the Rutles, and I'd like to obviously come back to that in a moment. But to you Michael, Steve Cropper and Duck Dunn also played on the original hit version of Sam & Dave's "Soul Man," and you expressed delight when the record first went on the turntable. Did you enjoy that version of it?

**Jackson:** Yeah, I like it . . . I liked the *song*. I think the song is so good, but Sam & Dave did it first, I think. And I was reading the credits—I didn't know Isaac Hayes had anything to do with the writing. His name is on it.

**Jensen:** Oh yeah, with David Porter.

**Jackson:** I was surprised. I think the song is great. But, I don't really like the mix of it.

**Jensen:** It's a live recording.

**Jackson:** It's really live? Ahhh.

**Harrison:** Not bad for live.

**Jackson:** See, I was just saying that because my favorite part is the guitar: [*sings answer riff*] *di-diddle-di deh-deh*—and I didn't hear much of it, that was why . . .

**Jensen:** What about those Stax records of the late '60s? I mean disco is very, very big today, but me, in my heart, my favorite dance music will always be Sam & Dave, Eddie Floyd, Carla Thomas, Rufus Thomas, Otis Redding—those sort of records. Do they mean much to you? I always got the impression that Stax as a sort of a label was bigger and better known in this country than really over the entire US.

**Jackson:** Ummm, not really. All those people you named are really great people to us in America too, especially Rufus Thomas and Isaac Hayes and the Staple Singers. I think they're all great.

**Jensen:** What about you, George? You obviously would be aware of the package tour that whisked through here in the late '60s . . .

**Harrison:** The Stax, yeah . . . I liked all the Stax artists, that was good. They always seemed to bind the Stax records together by using Booker T. and the MGs as a backup band, which is a fantastic band, God knows.

**Jensen:** What about the Rutles film—because you were involved—or appeared—in the Rutles film, which has been shown on television a couple of times here, and was very, very popular and successful and the album as well. Where did that all come from? Did you have a hand in the actual concept of it because you're . . .

**Harrison:** No, the concept was Eric Idle's really, although once he got writing, I must admit I did show him a few Beatle films, just so that he could have more material to draw from. But the Rutles—I love the Rutles, you know, just because it was a way of liberating me from that whole thing. You know the Beatles was sort of OK, it was a good thing at the time, but it goes on and on and on, and people get too serious about it, and I think the good thing about comedy, you can make jokes at anything. If you're a satirist, you can joke about anything and get away with it. And so, it was a good way of having a laugh out of the Fab Four, Dirk and Stig and Nasty . . .

**Jensen:** [*Laughs.*] The names! What about the other fellows' reactions, John, Paul, and Ringo. Are you aware what their reaction to that Rutles . . .

**Harrison:** No, but they've never spoken to me since. [*Laughter.*]

**Jensen:** Talking about comedy, I must ask you about your involvement in the forthcoming Monty Python film, which is *Brian of Nazareth*?

**Harrison:** Well yeah, I think it's called *Monty Python's Life of Brian*, although some people think maybe it should be called *Brian of Nazareth*, but it could be called *Monty Python's Life of Brian of Nazareth*.

Well, I got involved with it because . . . well, actually, it probably should say in the beginning of the film: "Bernard Delfont [*chief executive of EMI at the time*] doesn't proudly present *Monty Python's Life of Brian*." I mean I got involved with it when they backed out of the film, EMI, because really, I'm just a Monty Python fan. I wanted to go and see it at the movies so somebody suggested to me maybe I could figure out a way of raising the money for them to make it. That's all really, but it's very funny, and it should be at your local cinema during the summer.

**Jensen:** Could you tell us a little about the plot, is there . . . ?

**Harrison:** Yeah, well, it's really . . . it's nothing to do with Christ, really. What it is, is a guy called Brian who gets born at the same time as Christ in the manger just across the road. And it really just follows his life. And he's, you know, a bit of an idiot really.

**Jensen:** Okay, that's *Monty Python's Life of Brian*.

**Harrison:** It's, yeah, how everybody was into Messiah mania, you know? They mistake all kinds of things as signs and stuff, following Brian around, thinking he's the Messiah.

**Jensen:** Okay, [*laughs*] I look forward that in the summer. A lot of things to ask you. Michael, I'm going to ask you about your motion picture *The Wiz* after we hear something from Cat Stevens. [*Plays station ID.*]

**Jensen:** That wasn't, of course, Cat Stevens, but this is. This was his new single release which is called "Last Love Song." It's from the album *Back to Earth.* [*Plays song.*]

**Jensen:** Cat Stevens and the "Last Love Song," from the album *Back to Earth.* And it's been a long time . . . almost as long as between your last album and your forthcoming album, George, that we've heard from Cat Stevens. And, uh, what did you think of that one?

**Harrison:** Yeah, I like Cat Stevens a lot—actually before, earlier when you asked me who I like, Cat Stevens has been a consistent person that I've enjoyed. I've always liked his voice, he's got a lovely voice, and he always seems to have style, class, you know? Good melodies, good production. And also, I think in his life he's been through a lot of heavy ups and downs, and I don't blame him for taking two years to make a record. [*Laughs.*] You know, I like him a lot.

**Jensen:** An artist I suppose is entitled to breaks and rests . . .

**Harrison:** Yeah, sure. Because people just hear your record, you know, they don't really know what's going on in your life. And I think that Cat Stevens had a lot of heavy things going on his life, and I think it comes across in his music; he's a very emotional sort of singer. I like that a lot.

**Jensen:** Michael . . .

**Jackson:** I feel about the same way. I've always liked his songs, like "Morning Has Broken" and "Moonshadow" . . . his voice is so—you get into it, it's really dramatic, the sound of it.

**Jensen:** It's certainly an *identifiable* sound that he's got.

**Jackson:** Yeah . . .

**Jensen:** It'd be interesting to see if that charts now, because of the singer-songwriter sort of period we went through, of which he was certainly in there, one of the kingpins of that period in the early '70s. It's been a long time coming since we—as I said—we've had an album. And I would like to think that will chart for him, and I would like to think that he'll tour again, because he's magic onstage. He had a bunch of magicians last time I saw him, instead of a support act, you know, going through some magic tricks.

What about your movie, then, Michael, *The Wiz*, which American audiences have been seeing now for the past few months? It's out here very soon. Tell us a little about that film, *The Wiz*, it's based on *The Wizard of Oz*, is it not?

**Jackson:** Yes, it's taken from the play, *The Wiz*. It was all filmed in New York, six months . . . half in the studio, half on location. It's from [*writer*] L. Frank Baum, and Diana Ross plays Dorothy, I play the Scarecrow, Nipsey Russell the Tin Man. It's more of an updated *Wizard of Oz*, I mean . . . like, in the original one the flying monkeys are flying . . . and like, [*enthusiastically*] our flying monkeys are Hells Angels with big glasses, and their bodies are made into the bikes, and . . .

**Jensen:** So a bit of a comedy in many ways . . . ?

**Jackson:** Yeah, it's comedy—and it's serious, and it follows more the original book, what L. Frank Baum was really trying to say. Because he was trying to put across the message in his story—a lot of people call it a children's story, but it's really heavy, it's a heavy thing.

**Jensen:** Can you simplify basically what your conception of that message is?

**Jackson:** Well, what he was saying, like for instance, the Scarecrow who's looking for a brain—he has all the brains in the world, he just don't have the belief in himself to realize it. He's looking for something he has already, and it's, uh, millions of people today—geniuses—walking around, doing the same thing. They just don't have that belief in themselves. And that's what he was trying to say by using the Scarecrow, Tin Man, and Lion. It's like Aesop's fable used animals instead of people.

**Jensen:** It must have been a lot of work dressing up as a . . . scarecrow . . .

**Jackson:** [*Laughs.*] Yes, you know, three hours of makeup every day, for six months . . . just makeup.

**Jensen:** With straw, and all that, it must have been fairly warm! But you're obviously happy with the results.

**Jackson:** Yes.

**Jensen:** I look forward to seeing the film. And of course, the song we're familiar with, "Ease on Down the Road," which came from *The Wiz*.

This is Inner Circle. We mentioned reggae before, and this is a great new release on the Island label from a band that have just moved to this label. This is called "Everything Is Great."
[*Plays song.*]

**Jensen:** That's Inner Circle and a song called "Everything Is Great"—a reggae band who recorded a funky song, and I reckon that's going to go into the charts for them. Michael, did you appreciate the sentiment of the song?

**Jackson:** Yes, I loved the music.

**Jensen:** Good—you look like the sort of guy who enjoys life a lot. I mean, is everything great for you at the moment?

**Jackson:** Yes, very good. I've always been happy with what I'm doing—it's something I love to do.

**Jensen:** George, what about you, you were associated . . . well, let's talk about the record, because I've got so much to talk about . . .

**Harrison:** This record, yeah. Actually, that was Inner Circle? You know, I like the sentiment, everything *is* great if you've got the eyes to see it. It isn't great, actually, if you don't have the eyes to see it, like if you look at England at the moment, it's really down in the dumps. It's *awful*. But it *is* great if you can tune into it and plug into the divine consciousness . . . everybody, "Hare Krishna," and all that.

**Jensen:** Are you still involved with Eastern religion?

**Harrison:** I am, yeah. I mean, it's the sort of thing . . . just, to simplify it, it's just that, like Michael was talking about *The Wiz*, and he was saying the moral to the story is that this guy has actually got everything he needs, it's just he doesn't have confidence in himself. The parallel to that—within all of us—is this divine consciousness that we need to learn how to plug into. And there's the little story of the farmer who lived for years in a little shack and then moved into the city, and he remained in his house in the city in the darkness because he didn't know that, the plug in the wall, he could plug a light in. And so, it's like that, everything *is* great, except, you have to to plug in to realize that.

And so, the sentiment is nice, but I thought the record was just good if you're dancing the disco, but for me it's just a bit of background music.

**Jensen:** We're going to get one more song on, and Lenny White, we had to play this really, being as how you're here, George. Anyway, this is "Lady Madonna."

[*Plays song.*]

**Jensen:** Well, earlier on, George, you mentioned that very often cover versions are not as good as the original versions. You were involved very much, obviously, with the original version of this song.

**Harrison:** Yeah.

**Jensen:** How does Lenny White's version grab you?

**Harrison:** I like it a lot. I think it's fantastic. It's *still* not as good as the original version, though. [*Laughter.*] No, I still prefer the Fab Four's version, but it *is* great, I liked that a lot. But again, it's like, a lot has to do with the song. Sometimes, you know, if you get a good song, whoever does it, it's good. And you can have the best singer and if it's not a good song, it can sound terrible.

**Jensen:** George, thanks very much for being with me here tonight on the *Roundtable*. And I look forward to hearing the fruits of your efforts in the past . . . couple of years, anyway, with the new album.

**Harrison:** Thank you. It's been a pleasure.

**Jensen:** Excellent. Michael, what about your reaction to that record?

**Jackson:** I think it's very good, the way they updated it and made it sound good for today's sound.

**Jensen:** And what about your tour dates? Can we quickly slip those in, in the UK?

**Jackson:** Oh! Uhh . . . I think we're, yeah, we're in Brighton tomorrow, and then we do London twenty-third and the twenty-fourth . . . of February.

**Jensen:** Good luck in your concerts, and I hope we see you both back here again—in action—again, real soon. Thanks very much. Michael Jackson and George Harrison on tonight's *Roundtable*. Well, that's it for me, it's time, eight o'clock, for me to hand over to Andy Peebles and his music. . . .

# A CONVERSATION WITH GEORGE HARRISON

**Mick Brown | April 19, 1979 |** *Rolling Stone*

Despite Harrison's love-hate relationship with *Rolling Stone*, the magazine was one of the most valuable outlets for any rock musician desiring their news and message to be delivered to a widespread American audience—especially if it meant a cover story. The publication employed top, young writers—well informed and well written—and had the budget to make sure the story was well-designed and marketed.

Mick Brown—who has written six books on culture, business, spirituality, and his own life—was still in his twenties when he got the assignment to interview Harrison in 1979. He was an active freelancer at the time, his byline appearing in the *Sunday Times*, *Guardian*, and *Observer* in the United Kingdom, and *Crawdaddy* and *Rolling Stone* in the States. As he mentions in his opener to the interview, he spoke with the Harrison in London immediately after he had met with Paul McCartney, and quickly dispels any hopes that it might lead to a Beatles reunion.

Brown's précis further portrays Harrison in the late '70s as the rock star in repose, ready to take a few gap years to become a father for the first time and explore domesticity (the same thing John Lennon was doing on the other side of the Atlantic.) Harrison still had a few projects on the burner, though. The interview for *Rolling Stone* coincided with the release of the eponymous album *George Harrison*, a burgeoning interest in film (brought on by his involvement with the Monty Python project *Life of Brian* and the television Beatles parody *The Rutles*), and a book about his songs—*I Me Mine*—which would be published a year later as a limited-run leather-bound book (and later available in a more traditional—and affordable—format). —Ed.

Up for the day from his home in Oxfordshire, some 30 miles from London, George Harrison had spent the morning in the recording studio with Paul McCartney. It was not, he hastened to explain, a meeting that presaged any sort of Beatles reunion. ("Fab Four" is the term Harrison prefers, used with an affectionate irony, as if to reduce the implications of the name to a manageable level.) Indeed, it is a sign of the times that even the most stubborn Beatles fans no longer hold it as an article of faith to entertain that particular idea. The old antagonisms attending the breakup of the Beatles in 1970, and the protracted legal wrangles that went on for years afterward, have long been mended, but a musical realignment is as unlikely as Richard Nixon regaining the presidency.

Of all the former Beatles, it is Harrison whose interests have proved to be the most far ranging over the past ten years, from organizing the Concert for Bangla Desh to aiding and abetting Monty Python's Flying Circus. His own musical career has encompassed eight solo albums and just one tour—of America in 1974. Since the release of his last album, *33 1/3*, more than two years ago, Harrison has endeavored to maintain as low a public profile as possible. He married Olivia Arias, his girlfriend of some four years standing, in September 1978, and they have a baby son, Dhani. When he's not at his English country home (the author of "Taxman" brazens out England's punitive taxation rate for the sake of "the countryside and the seasons"), Harrison is often travelling on the international Grand Prix circuit, where he indulges a passion for watching car racing he has held since his childhood days in Liverpool.

Harrison has long been reluctant to give interviews, acquiescing on this occasion only in the interests of discussing his new album, *George Harrison*. But despite his professed disinterest in dialogue with the media, he proved to be a genial and good-humored subject—happy to discuss his music, his personal and professional tribulations of the past few years, the Beatles and more. The interview took place one afternoon in late February, over French cigarettes and cups of tea, in the London office of Warner/Elektra/Asylum Records. We broke off our conversation at one point to watch the early evening TV news broadcast of an interview Harrison had taped earlier that day. In the clip, Harrison was shown pulling up outside the TV studio in his black Porsche and clambering out for an abbreviated discussion about the new album and his reactions to the *Sgt. Pepper's Lonely Hearts Club Band* film, which had opened in London that week. The news item concluded not with a musical extract from the *George Harrison* album but with vintage newsreel footage of the Beatles receiving their Member of the Order of the British Empire awards in June 1965, to the accompaniment of "Help!" Harrison heaved a deep sigh of resignation. All things must pass, perhaps, but after almost ten years George Harrison has come to learn that some things take longer to pass than others. . . .

*When did you actually start work on* George Harrison?

I started working on it midway through April 1978 and finished it at the beginning of October. It's been a bit late coming out because the artwork wasn't ready; then it was a bit late to get it in for Christmas. And then *everybody* and their aunties had one coming out at Christmas, so we decided to take our time over getting everything ready.

*Has it been long in the gestation stage?*

Well, all of 1977 I didn't write a song, I didn't do anything; I was not working at all really, so I decided I'd better start doing something. I'd just turned off from the music business altogether. I *am* a bit out of touch with the other music. There're certain artists that I always like to listen to, but I don't listen a great deal to the radio. I just got out of it—I was "skiving," as the English say. Everybody else doesn't notice, because if your past record's still get played on the radio, people don't notice that you're not really there. But I just got sick of all that. . . .

*Sick of all what?*

Just sick of the whole thing. If you look at the trade papers, everybody's changing companies, and this artist has gone to that label and that artist to this one, and everybody's doing this and that. [*Sighing*] Having been in this business now for so long—it was 1961 when we first made a record, I think, so it's eighteen years now—the novelty's worn off. Really, it comes down to ego. You have to have a big ego in order to keep plodding on being in the public eye. If you want to be popular and famous, you can do it; it's dead easy if you have that ego desire.

But most of my ego desires as far as being famous and successful were fulfilled a long time ago.

I still enjoy writing a tune and enjoy in a way making a record. But I hate that whole thing of when you put it out, you become a part of the overall framework of the business. And I was a bit bored with that. If I write a tune and people think it's nice then that's fine by me; but I hate having to compete and promote the thing. I really don't like promotion. In the Sixties we overdosed on that, and then I consciously went out of my way at the end of the Sixties, early Seventies, to try and be a bit more obscure. What you find is that you have a hit and suddenly everybody's knocking on your door and bugging you again. I enjoy being low profile and having a peaceful sort of life.

So anyway, to answer your original question, it got to be the end of 1977 and I thought, "God, I'd better do something."

*Were you getting bored with yourself, bored with your inactivity?*

I was getting embarrassed because I was going to all these motor races, and everybody was talking to me like George, the ex-Beatle, the musician, asking me if I was making a record and whether I was going to write some songs about racing, and yet musical thoughts were just a million miles away from my mind.

And then what really touched me was meeting Niki Lauda. I have a great respect for him. After that crash he went through in 1976, I felt really bad for him and I was very happy when he didn't die. You have to read about his life, his books and things, to realize what he was put through—people trying to photograph him with his face all scarred, trying to break into his hospital room, all that very unpleasant reporting stuff. I could really relate to that. Anyway, I talked to him once after he had won the world championship again, in 1977 at Watkins Glen, and he was talking about all the bullshit in his business—the politics and the hassles—and he was saying how he just likes to go home and relax and play some nice music. And I thought, "Shit, I'm going to go and write some tunes, because these people are all relating to me as a musician, and yet I'm here just skiving; maybe I can write a song that Niki on his day off may enjoy." So that was it.

The other side of it, too, is that my friends at Warner Bros., who I have a deal with, they never ask, "Why aren't you doing anything?" They always treat me very civil, but at the same time I was thinking, "Well, it's been awhile. . . ." They may start to think, "What are we doin' with this fella?"

*So was the album prompted more by other people's expectations of you, a sense of obligation on your part, rather than an inherent desire to make music again?*

Well, partly perhaps. But once you *do* write a tune, I don't know why, but there is that desire to have it made into a proper record. If I were to die, I'd rather people find a good finished master of my songs than a crummy old demo on a cassette. Maybe originally it was other people's expectations that prompted me, but once I got writing tunes I got my motor ticking over again and it's fun—you get in the studio, you get going and you can enjoy it all over again.

The other thing is that I decided to get somebody to help me produce this record. So I went to Warners in Burbank and spoke to the three staff producers there—Ted Templeman, Lenny Waronker, and Russ Titelman. And I played them some demos of the tunes I'd written and said, "Come on, you guys, give me a clue. Tell me what songs you've liked in the past, what songs you didn't like; give me a few ideas of what you think." And they didn't know what to say. Templeman said he had liked "Deep Blue," the B-side of the "Bangla Desh" single, which is a bit obscure—so I went home and wrote a song, with a similar sort of chord structure to that, "Soft-Hearted Hana." But in the end I decided I'd work with Russ Titelman. He did the first Little Feat album and, with Lenny Waronker, he's co-produced Randy Newman, James Taylor, and Ry Cooder—he's Ry Cooder's brother-in-law, in fact. And he's a nice, easy person to get along with, which is more important than the person's musical taste, because you spend five months together—you've got to like each other a bit. He helped me decide what sort of tunes to use, encouraged me to actually finish certain songs, and helped actually lay the tracks down. It's hard for an artist to be in the booth and in the studio.

*Did you feel that, in that period when you weren't writing and recording, you might have lost a feel for the public ear?*

Yeah, I had that feeling because they'd told me stories about Randy Newman, about how he can't write songs and feels as though he's dried up, then suddenly he's written an album that's successful and now he's writing ten songs a day. So it's just your own problem. When they mentioned that to me, I did think, "Hey, maybe *I* could dry up."

*How much has your inactivity, and your disenchantment with the music business, had to do with the various lawsuits you've had to fight over the past years? For instance, the plagiarism lawsuit over "My Sweet Lord" and "He's So Fine."*

Well, that has been going on for years. It's like a running joke now. The guy who actually wrote "He's So Fine" had died years before, Ronnie Mack. Bright Tunes Music, his publisher, was suing me. So we went through the court case, and in the end the judge said, yes, it is similar, but you're not guilty of stealing the tune. We do think there's been a copyright infringement, though, so get your lawyers together and work out some sort of compensation. But Bright Tunes wouldn't settle for that; they kept trying to bring the case back into court. They even tried to bring it back into court when I did "This Song."

It's difficult to just start writing again after you've been through that. Even now when I put the radio on, every tune I hear sounds like something else. But most of the lawsuits are gone. Now we're gearing up for the next batch.

*There are more to come?*

There's not much more *we* [the Beatles] can be sued for, but we can sue a lot of other people. Being split and diversified over the years has made it difficult to consolidate certain Beatles interests. For example, all those naughty Broadway shows and stupid movies that have been made about the Beatles, using Beatles names and ideas, are all illegal. But because we've been arguing among ourselves all these years, people have had a free-for-all. Now we've gotten to the point where everybody's agreed and we've allocated a company to go out and sue them all. It's terrible, really. People think we're giving all these producers and people permission to do it and that we're making money out of it, but we don't make a nickel. So it's time that should be stopped.

Maybe we should go and do *The Robert Stigwood Story* or something [*laughing*], although I suppose the *Sgt. Pepper* film is all right because they've paid the copyright on the songs and make up their own story line.

*Have you seen the film?*

No. The reports on it were so bad that I didn't want to see it. But maybe it's good. I don't know.

*Do you see it as an insult to the memory?*

No. I just feel sorry for Robert Stigwood, the Bee Gees, and Pete Frampton for doing it, because they had established themselves in their own right as decent artists and suddenly . . . it's like the classic thing of greed. The more you make the more you want to make, until you become so greedy that ultimately you put a foot wrong. And even though Sgt. Pepper is no doubt a financial success, I think it's damaged their images, their careers, and they didn't *need* to do that. It's just like the Beatles trying to do the Rolling Stones. The Rolling Stones can do it better.

*How does it feel to be an object of nostalgia already?*

We've been nostalgia since 1967. It's fine. There was a time when I don't think any of us liked it—that 1968 to 1969 period. But now it's funny. [*Grinning*] It's like being Charlie Chaplin or Laurel and Hardy. But the music still stands up, still sounds very good, a lot of it.

*Apart from films and stage productions done without the Beatles' permission, are you happy with the way the actual Beatles recordings have been repackaged and promoted over the years?*

It doesn't bother me anymore. At first it was pretty crummy. We always had complete artistic control from the outset, and we took great care over running orders, having the right songs in the right places and good sleeves—it was all done with a bit of taste. But straightway they started screwing that up in the States, holding back tracks from albums so that, for every two albums released in Britain, they could release three over three. But still, everything we did continued to be in pretty good taste until the contract expired, and then they started shoving out all these repackages with crummy sleeves and everything. It doesn't bother me as long as they keep paying the royalties.

*Another sub-industry that's grown up in the Beatles' wake is all that personal reminiscence about the band. There seems to be an extraordinary number of people who were either your manager, your road manager, delivered the milk. . . .*

[*Laughing*] Yeah, and the fifth Beatle . . . there're about 10 million fifth Beatles. No, really, that's sickening. All those Beatlefests and things are a terrible rip-off. These people—"the man who gave away the Beatles"— none of them know what they're talking about. It's like Britain has always been hung up talking about the Second World War—even now you turn on the TV and they love to talk about the war. It's like that. The Beatles were in and out of these people's lives in a flash, and yet they're still there fifteen years later talking about the ten minutes we were in their lives, and robbing the money of innocent kids while doing it. It's pathetic. It's immoral; it shouldn't be allowed.

*But the fact that those people can prosper suggests that people still don't want the memory of the Beatles to die. There's an incredible need people still feel to have the Beatles.*

Well, they've got 'em. They've got the films—*Help!*, *A Hard Day's Night*, *Let It Rot*, *Tragical History Tour*. They've got lots and lots of songs they can play forever. But what do they want? Blood? They want us all to die like Elvis Presley? Elvis got stuck in a rut where the only thing he could do was to keep on doing the same old thing, and in the end his health suffered and that was it.

The Beatles fortunately did that hit-and-run. But every year we were Beatling was like twenty years; so although it might only have been five or six years it seemed like eternity. That was enough for me, I don't have any desire to do all that. It might have been fun for everybody else, but we never saw the Beatles. We're the only four people who never got to see us. [*Laughing*] Everybody got on a trip, you see, that was the thing.

We were just four relatively sane people in the middle of madness. People used us an excuse to trip out, and we were the victims of that. That's why they want the Beatles to go on, so they can all get silly again. But they don't have consideration for our well-being when they say, "Let's have the Fab Four again."

*You wouldn't want to go through it again?*

Never. Not in this life or any other life. I mean, a lot of the time it was fantastic, but when it really got into the mania it was a question of either stop or end up dead. We almost got killed in a number of situations—planes catching on fire, people trying to shoot the plane down and riots everywhere we went. It was aging me.

But we had a great time. I think fondly of it all, especially as we've been through all the aftermath of Apple. Everybody's sued each other to their hearts' content, and now we're all good friends.

*Do you see the others often?*

Paul and Ringo I see from time to time. I haven't seen John for a couple of years. I get post cards from him—it sounds like the Rutles [*smiling*], but he keeps in touch with tapping on the table and post cards.

*Why is he so inactive?*

He's probably not. Just because he's not Beatling doesn't mean he's inactive. It's like, for me to do this interview now people can see that I'm talking. But if I'm not doing the interview I'm inactive. But I'm not *really*—I'm at home doing other things, or going places doing various things. . . .

*But John is publicly inactive, not making records.*

Well, I don't blame him. I've found if I take a two-week holiday, by the end of those two weeks, I'm just about ready to enjoy the holiday and I have to get back to work. If you retire or knock off the work, then there's a while of feeling, "Wow, I should be doing something," until you slowly mellow out and think, "Wow, this is good. I don't *have* to be mad all my life. I don't *have* to live in the public eye." And I'm sure that's all he's doing, enjoying his life.

*Fans feel almost cheated when the performer stops performing. . . .*

I know, but that's their own concept. It's a selfish concept to think, "Go out and kill yourself for me. . . ." But I myself would be interested to know whether John still writes tunes and puts them on a cassette, or does he just forget all about music and not touch the guitar. Because that's what I did, all of 1977 I never picked up a guitar, never even thought about it. And I didn't miss it.

*Do you like the music Paul is making now?*

I think it's inoffensive. I've always preferred Paul's good melodies to his screaming rock & roll tunes. The tune I thought was sensational on the *London Town* album was "I'm Carrying," but all the noisy, beaty things I'm not into at all. But then that's not only with Paul's music, that goes right across the board. I'm not a fan of that sort of punky, heavy, tinny stuff. I like a nice melody.

*But the Beatles could turn out a fair rock & roll song in their day.*

Yeah, we used to do all that, but as far as listening to it, I'd rather hear someone like Little Richard or Larry Williams. I never liked all that stuff in the late '60s after Cream had broken up—all those Les Paul guitars screaming and distorting. I like more subtlety—like Ry Cooder and Eric Clapton. Eric is fantastic. He could blow all those people off the stage if he wanted to, but he's more subtle than that. Sometimes it's not what you do, it's what you don't do that counts. And personally I'd rather hear three notes hit really sweet than to hear a whole lot of notes from some guitar player whose ears are so blown out he can't hear the difference between a flat and a sharp.

*It seems as if Paul was the Beatle with whom you were least compatible musically—you've gone on record as saying you wouldn't play with him again.*

Yeah, well now we don't have any problems whatsoever as far as being people is concerned, and it's quite nice to see him. But I don't know about being in a band with him, how that would work out. It's like, we all have our own tunes to do. And my problem was that it would always be very difficult to get in on the act, because Paul was very pushy in that respect. When he succumbed to playing on one of your tunes, he'd always do good. But you'd have to do fifty-nine of Paul's songs before he'd even listen to one of yours. So, in that respect; it would be very difficult to ever play with him. But, you know, we're cool as far as being pals goes.

*Do you miss not playing with a regular band and going on the road?*

No. I don't like going on the road. Sometimes I feel physically very frail. I can feel knackered, really tired, just having to get up early to get an airplane—I can feel ill having to travel. On the road there're all these medicines flying about to help you catch the plane on time, all that sort of stuff. And I'm a sucker for that. I could do myself in.

That was the problem in 1974, when I toured America. I'd done three albums before I went on the road, and I was still trying to finish my own album as we were rehearsing, and also we'd done this other tour in Europe with these classical Indian musicians. By the time it came to going on the road I was already exhausted. With the Beatles we used to do thirty minutes onstage, and we could get it down to twenty-five minutes if we did it fast. We were on and off and "thank you," and back to the hotel. Suddenly to have to be playing two and one-half hours for forty-seven gigs, flying all round, I was wasted.

But I had that choice of canceling the tour and getting everybody uptight, or going through with it. So I decided, "Sod it, it's probably better to do it." But no, I don't miss it at all—being in crummy hotels, eating lousy food, always having to be somewhere else.

*There was a lot of flak about that tour. Did you think the criticisms were justified?*

The flak about the tour was terrible. [*Exasperated*] There're always people who don't like something, but on the average it wasn't a disaster. I wanted it made clear that it was a tour with Ravi Shankar, but Bill Graham wouldn't do that. They tried to make it look like it was just me coming, that sort of trip. But even in the Indian music section there was a part of that, every place we played, where the audiences were up on their feet screaming and shouting their approval.

But the press clippings were unbelievable. By the time I got back to England people were saying, "That's it, you're finished, man." It was the worst thing I'd ever done in my life according to the papers. But really, there were moments of that show that were fantastic. So all the negativity about that was a bit depressing, but [*grinning triumphantly*] I fought my way back to recovery!

*That tour coincided with the formation of your own record label, Dark Horse. You were signing and producing other performers such as Ravi Shankar and Splinter, and seemed very active in promoting other artists' careers.*

Yeah, right, and that was another reason why 1975 wasn't so good . . . why I was so wiped out, and it resulted in me saying, "Sod it, I don't want a record company." I don't mind me being on the label because, all right, I can release an album and it makes some profit, and I don't phone myself in the middle of the night to complain about different things. But artists are never satisfied. They spend maybe $50,000 more than *I'd* spend making an album, then they won't do any interviews or go on the road—whatever you'd organize for them, they'd foul it up. It was just too much bullshit. They think a record company is like a bank that they can go and draw money out of whenever they want. But, nevertheless, there were some good things that came out of it: the Attitudes album, *Good News*, is really good. And I'm happy about the Indian music we did—the Ravi Shankar's *Music Festival From India* and the *Shankar Family & Friends* albums. But generally the record company was too much of a problem.

*Was there a lot of resistance from the other Beatles when you first introduced sitar on the group's albums?*

Not a lot, because at that time it was all experiments and stuff. In fact, I think it was John who really urged me to play sitar on "Norwegian Wood," which was the first time we used it. Now, Paul has just asked me recently whether I'd written any more of those "Indian type of tunes." He suddenly likes them now. But at the time he wouldn't play on them. "Within You, Without You" was just me and some Indian musicians in the studio by ourselves. It sounds a bit dopey now in retrospect, except the sitar solo's good.

*Your interest in Indian music, and particularly, in mysticism and the disciplines of spiritual development has always been the most misunderstood and most derided facet of your life. Do you have any theories as to why that should be?*

It's ignorance. They say ignorance is bliss, but bliss is not ignorance—it's the opposite of that, which is knowledge. And there's a lot of people who have fear. It's like I was saying earlier about all those guys in Liverpool who knew us in the early days and are now running Beatlefests. All of those guys had a good opportunity when the Beatles left Liverpool to leave, too; they could have been running their own TV shows and doing all kinds of things now. But they were like big fish in a little pond. And the fear of failure is a bad thing in life; it stops people from gaining more knowledge or just understanding deeper things. So when somebody presents them with a whole set of ideas they don't understand, fear takes over. The want to destroy it, chop it down. Just like that loony guy in America who claims to go round deprogramming people from Krishna and the Divine Light Mission and that. That's his fear coming out, because if you understand something, you don't have to fear it—there's no panic, no problem.

Basically I feel fortunate to have realized what the goal is in life. There's no point in dying having gone through your life without knowing who you are what you are or what the purpose of life is. And that's all it is. People started getting uptight when I started shooting off my mouth and saying the goal is to manifest love of God—self-realization. I must admit, there was a period when I was trying to tell everybody about it; now, I don't bother unless somebody asks specifically. I still write about it in my songs, but it's less blatant, more hidden now. I'm a very poor example of a spiritual person. I don't really want anything in my life except knowledge, but I'm not a very good practitioner of that.

*Has remarrying and having a child significantly changed your life?*

Yeah, that's been a wonderful thing for me. Everybody who has a baby thinks their child is wonderful, and it is. I'm enjoying it a lot and, again, that's probably why John isn't working. After a long time of waiting, he and Yoko finally had a child and I think he wants to give most of his time to watching the child grow up.

*You met your wife, Olivia, at the end of what seems to have been a pretty low period for you personally—1974.*

Yeah, well after I split up from Pattie [Boyd, Harrison's first wife], I went on a bit of a bender to make up for all the years I'd been married. If you listen to "Simply Shady," on *Dark Horse*, it's all in there—my whole life at that time was a bit like [*laughing*] *Mrs. Dale's Diary* [a now defunct British radio soap opera].

*Were you going down fast?*

Well, I wasn't ready to join Alcoholics Anonymous or anything—I don't think I was that far gone—but I could put back a bottle of brandy occasionally, plus all the other naughty things that fly around. I just went on a binge, went on the road . . . all that sort of thing, until it got to the point where I had no voice and almost no body at times. Then I met Olivia and it all worked out fine. There's a song on the new album, "Dark Sweet Lady": "You came and helped me through, when I'd let go, you came out from the blue, never have known what I'd done without you." That sums it up.

*There are a number of love songs on the album—in fact, it's a very positive record altogether. Is there any one song that you're happiest with, or means more to you than the others?*

I like them all really, but the two I least like are "If You Believe"—I like the sentiment of that, but it's a bit *obvious* as a tune—and "Soft Touch," which is just pleasant but there's nothing special about it, I feel. All the others I like for various reasons. "Blow Away" I like because it's so catchy; in fact, I was a bit embarrassed about it at first, but it turned out good and people seem to like it. That was the first new tune I wrote. I was in the garden and it was pouring down with rain, and I suddenly became aware that I was feeling depressed, being affected by the weather. And it's important to remember that while everything else around you changes, the soul within remains the same; you have to constantly remember that and fight for the right to be happy.

And I like "Faster" because I fulfilled the thing the Formula One motor-racing people kept asking me—to write a song about racing—and I did it in a way I'm happy about because it wasn't just corny. It's easy to write about V-8 engines and *vroom vroom*—that would have been bullshit. But I'm happy with the lyrics because it can be seen to be about one driver specifically or any of them, and if it didn't have the motor-racing noises, it could be about the Fab Four really—the jealousies and things like that.

*Is that the Beatles' life story?*

Exactly, and when people keep asking, "Why don't the Beatles keep on going?" they don't realize that you can kill yourself. Or maybe they do realize that; maybe they want you to. There's a lot of that in motor racing I've seen people say they want somebody they don't like to crash, which is crazy.

*"Not Guilty" is an interesting song, a rebuff to your critics.*

Actually, I wrote that in 1968. It was after we got back from Rishikesh in the Himalayas on the Maharishi trip, and it was for the *White Album*. We recorded it but we didn't get it down right or something. Then I forgot all about it until a year ago, when I found this old demo I'd made in the Sixties. The lyrics are a bit passé—all about upsetting "Apple carts" and stuff—but it's a bit about what was happening at the time. "Not guilty for getting in your way/While you're trying to steal the day"—which was me trying to get a space. "Not guilty/For looking like a freak/Making friends with every Sikh/For leading your astray/On the road to Mandalay"—which is the Maharishi and going to the Himalayas and all that was said about that. I like the tune a lot; it would make a great tune for Peggy Lee or someone.

*Critical reaction to the album in England has been exceptionally good. People have said it's the best since* All Things Must Pass. *Is that your feeling?*

Well, I hope it does as well as *All Things Must Pass*. I think this album is very pleasant. It's like I was saying earlier, when I went and asked the guys at Warner Bros., "You're so smart, tell me what's happening," because I really don't follow the charts and all that anymore. When it came down to it they don't know any more than I do. But I think even without following trends, paying no real attention to what's going on and just writing your own songs, you still have as much chance as if you follow things closely. In fact, you probably have a better chance, because you're less affected by superficial change. It's more likely to be original.

*Do you listen to any current music?*

I listen to Clapton, Elton John, Bob Dylan, those sort of people. I couldn't stand punk rock; it never did anything for me at all.

*Do you feel very estranged from what is happening musically and socially at a grass-roots, youth-culture level?*

Well, musically the punks have been and gone, haven't they, and it all seems to be very musical again. Elvis Costello is very good—very good melodies, good chord changes. I'm pleased about his success, but I never liked those monotone kinds of yelling records.

*Didn't they say the same thing about Larry Williams and Little Richard?*

Yeah, but those guys were inventing something at the time and I don't think punk was inventing anything except negativity. The old rock & roll singers sang fantastically, they had great drummers, great sax players. As far as musicianship goes, the punk bands were just rubbish—no finesse in the drumming, just a lot of noise and nothing.

*Did the lyrical preoccupations of British punk—the way it was addressing itself to contemporary social issues—did that excite or depress you?*

Well, I felt very sorry when the Sex Pistols were on television and one of them was saying "We're educated to go into the factories and work on assembly lines . . ." and that's their future. It *is* awful, and it's especially awful that it should come out of England, because England is continually going through depression; it's a very negative country. Everybody wants everything and nobody wants to do anything for it. But it's a very simple thing; how do you give people money if there is none? The only way you make more money is to work harder. Now that may be all right for me to say because I don't have to work in a factory, but it's true. But out of all that is born the punk thing, so it's understandable. But you don't fight negativity with negativity. You have to overpower hatred with love, not more hatred.

*Could you personally afford not to work again?*

Yes. It's not for the money that I do what I do; it was never for the money really. We hoped we'd make a living out of it when we [the Beatles] were teenagers; we hoped we'd get by [*smiling*], but we weren't doing it for the money. In fact, the moment we realized we *were* doing it for money was just before we stopped touring, because we were getting no pleasure out of it. Then we found out we weren't even getting the money. The Americans were keeping it all, and we were paying so much tax—ninety-five percent or more. So it's never been for the money really, although it can be nice to have some money. I mean, there's nothing worse than standing at a bus stop in the pouring rain, wishing you had a car.

*You've invested in the new Monty Python film,* The Life of Brian.

Well, I'm what they call the executive producer. What happened was that I helped to raise the money for them in order to make the film when the previous backer pulled out. As I'm a Monty Python fan, I wanted to see the movie—I like to go and have a laugh too—and a friend suggested that I try and raise the money. So we just got a loan from a bank. It's a risk I suppose.

I first met Michael Palin and Terry Jones in 1972, I think. I met Eric Idle in 1975, at the California premiere of the *Holy Grail* film. And although that was the first time I'd ever met him, I felt like I'd known them all for years, because I'd watched all the programs and had had them on video-tape. So it only took ten minutes before we were the best of friends.

I think after the Beatles, Monty Python was my favorite thing. It bridged the years when there was nothing really doing, and they were the only ones who could see that everything was a big joke.

*You were involved in the TV production of the Rutles'* All You Need Is Cash *as well. Did Eric consult you on some facts?*

Yes. I slipped him the odd movie here and there that nobody had seen, so he could have more to draw from. I loved the Rutles because in the end the Beatles for the Beatles is just tiresome; it needs to be deflated a bit, and I loved the idea of the Rutles taking that burden off us in a way. Everything can be seen as comedy, and the Fab Four are no exception to that. And there were so many good jokes in it. Belushi as Ron Decline: "You ask me where the money is. I don't know where the money is, but if you want money I'll give it to you," and "You ask me where the money is. You know I was never any good at maths. . . ." [*Laughing*] It was just like Klein. Even Allen Klein himself thought it was just like him. I think he liked it. One thing you can say about Klein is that he's got his good side, too. Even though we've sued each other for years I still like the man.

*How do you spend your time when you're not recording?*

I stay home and dig—not so much with a spade—but I dig the garden, putting trees in. I like gardens; I like the pleasure they give you. It's like a meditation in a way—you can get everything out of your mind groveling in the soil! I spend a lot of time with the wife and the baby.

For the last year, I've been spending a lot of time working on this book of song manuscripts. The idea came from some guy who does these limited-edition books that are leather bound, printed on nice, thick parchment paper—the whole works. He approached Eric Manchester, the Rutles' press officer [alias Derek Taylor, the Beatles' press officer], and asked if I'd be inclined to do a book of my own songs. I'd been meaning to put together as many of the songs I'd written as I could find, just for my own archives, anyway. I've spent a year collecting together all the old songs. Eric Manchester is writing an intro. The problem was to think of a title, but we've called it *I Me Mine*, because it's the old ego problem of "This is *my* book." [*Grinning*] So this is like a little ego detour of mine really.

*It's rather expensive, isn't it?*

Well, the price is about $250, I think. But the original idea was just to do one for myself, for my own interest, and it's just grown a bit from that. It's limited now to 1000 copies, but I don't think anyone will make any money out of it. Each one is handmade, and it's a very expensive sort of thing to do. But we'll probably do a cheaper paperback version as well if anybody's interested.

*You haven't had a major chart success for a while; is it important to you that the new album is a hit?*

Not really. It would be nice, but I'm not into the competitive type of thing with the record business anymore. It would be nice just because there are a lot of records out that sell a lot that are no better—put it that way. Also it would be nice to have a hit because it would make me feel more like doing another one. But if it's not, I won't be in tears or be upset.

*So it's important for your self-esteem?*

No. But the thing is, the general public thinks if you have a hit and you're on the TV and in the papers, then you're more successful than if none of those things are happening. Out of all the ex-Beatles, that is most evident with Paul, because Paul is continually making records, films of himself onstage and more records—keeping in the public eye. And to the public that constitutes success. In the record business that is success. Whereas I choose not to be on TV so much or that much in the public eye, and so therefore my record sales must suffer because there's less exposure.

*But you plan to continue making records?*

Oh, I'll make another couple, I think, before I call it a day.

*You can foresee a time when you will call it a day?*

Oh yeah.

*So you're not going to die for rock & roll?*

[*Emphatic*] Oh no. I'm not going to die for rock & roll. Not at all.

# PART IV
# 1982–1989

# MAGAZINE INTERVIEW

**Mukunda Goswami | September 4, 1982 | *Back to Godhead***

Harrison's relationship with ISKCON continued after the death of Sri Prabhupada in 1977. He remained particularly close with Mukunda Goswami (born Michael Grant) and Shyamasundar Das (Sam Speersta), who had met Prabhubada in 1965 and '67, respectively, and become important members of the organization. Mukunda had been one of Sri's earliest American disciples and helped establish ISKCON's first temple in San Francisco, where Shyamasundar had first encountered the movement. Given their age and cultural upbringing, the pair helped serve as a bridge between ISKCON and the burgeoning rock generation.

The two were also at the forefront of the movement's first forays to England, were present at all meetings between Harrison and Prabhupada, and can be heard singing on *The Radha Krsna Temple* album released by Apple Records in 1971. In the last few days of Harrison's life, both Mukunda and Shyamasundar were at his side, chanting and keeping him company, per Harrison's request.

In various ways, each chose to chronicle this association. In 1980 Harrison brought forth his book *I, Me, Mine*, describing different songs he had written, using each as a means of sharing life experiences and philosophy, including the role that Prabhupada played in his pursuit of god-consciousness. In 2017 and '19 respectively, Shyamasundar published two volumes of *Chasing Rhinos with the Swami*, a spirited, lighthearted take on life inside the Hare Krishna movement, including many stories involving Harrison.

Mukunda, as one of ISKCON's leading spokespersons, interviewed Harrison at Friar Park in 1982. Their conversation ran as a two-part Q and A at the start of '83 in consecutive issues of *Back to Godhead*, a magazine Sri Prabhupada established in 1944 in India as a supplement to his teachings, and which was revived in the '80s in the US. The conversation offers a number of intriguing revelations, including Harrison's views on the power of chanting, the role of music in spiritual enlightenment, and the connection between various religions. –Ed.

**Mukunda Goswami:** Oftentimes you speak of yourself as a plainclothes devotee, a closet *yogi* or "closet Krishna," and millions of people all over the world have been introduced to the chanting by your songs. But what about you? How did you first come in contact with Krsna?

**George Harrison:** Through my visits to India. So by the time the Hare Krsna movement first came to England in 1969, John and I had already gotten ahold of Prabhupada's first album, *Krsna Consciousness*. We had played it a lot and liked it. That was the first time I'd ever heard the chanting of the *maha-mantra*.

**Mukunda:** When Gurudasa, Syamasundara, and I [the Hare Krsna devotees sent from America to open a temple in London] first came to England, you cosigned the lease on our first temple in central London, bought the [*Bhaktivedanta*] Manor for us, and financed the first printing of the book *Krsna*. You hadn't really known us for a very long time at all. Wasn't that a kind of sudden change for you?

**George:** Not really, I always felt at home with Krsna. You see, it was always a part of me. I think it's something that's been with me from my previous birth. Your coming to England and all that was just like another piece of a jigsaw puzzle that was coming together to make a complete picture. It had been slowly fitting together. That's why I responded to you all the way I did when you first came to London. Let's face it. If you're going to have to stand up and be counted, I figured, "I would rather be with these guys than with those other guys over there." It's like that. I mean I'd rather be one of the devotees of God than one of the straight, so-called sane or normal people who just don't understand that man is a spiritual being, that he has a soul. And I felt comfortable with you all, too, kind of like we'd known each other before. It was a pretty natural thing, really.

**Mukunda:** What was it that really got you started on your spiritual journey?

**George:** It wasn't until the experience of the '60s really hit. You know, having been successful and meeting everybody we thought worth meeting and finding out they weren't worth meeting, and having had more hit records than everybody else and having done it bigger than everybody else. It was like reaching the top of a wall and then looking over and seeing that there's so much more on the other side. So I felt it was part of my duty to say, "Oh, okay, maybe you are thinking this is all you need—to be rich and famous—but actually it isn't."

**Mukunda:** George, in your autobiography, *I, Me, Mine*, you said your song "Awaiting on You All" is about *japa yoga*, or chanting *mantras* on beads. You explained that a *mantra* is "mystical energy encased in a sound structure," and that "each *mantra* contains within its vibrations a certain power." But of all *mantras*, you stated that "the *maha-mantra* [the Hare Krsna *mantra*] has been prescribed as the easiest and surest way for attaining Realization in this present age." As a practitioner of *japa yoga*, what realizations have you experienced from chanting?

**George:** Prabhupada told me once that we should just keep chanting all the time, or as much as possible. Once you do that, you realize the benefit. The response that comes from chanting is in the form of bliss, or spiritual happiness, which is a much higher taste than any happiness found here in the material world. That's why I say that the more you do it, the more you don't want to stop, because it feels so nice and peaceful.

**Mukunda:** What is it about the *mantra* that brings about this feeling of peace and happiness?

**George:** The word *Hare* is the word that calls upon the energy that's around the Lord. If you say the *mantra* enough, you build up an identification with God. God's all happiness, all bliss, and by chanting His names we connect with Him. So it's really a process of actually having a realization of God, which all becomes clear with the expanded state of consciousness that develops when you chant. Like I said in the introduction I wrote for Prabhupada's *Krsna* book some years ago, "If there's a God, I want to see Him. It's pointless to believe in something without proof, and Krsna consciousness and meditation are methods where you can actually obtain God perception." You don't get it in five minutes. It's something that takes time, but it works because it's a direct process of attaining God and will help us to have pure consciousness and good perception that is above the normal, everyday state of consciousness.

**Mukunda:** How do you feel after chanting for a long time?

**George:** In the life I lead, I find that I sometimes have opportunities when I can really get going at it, and the more I do it, I find the harder it is to stop, and I don't want to lose the feeling it gives me.

For example, once I chanted the Hare Krishna mantra all the way from France to Portugal, nonstop. I drove for about twenty-three hours and chanted all the way. It gets you feeling a bit invincible. The funny thing was that I didn't even know where I was going. I mean I had bought a map, and I knew basically which way I was aiming, but I couldn't speak French, Spanish, or Portuguese. But none of that seemed to matter. You know, once you get chanting, then things start to happen transcendentally.

**Mukunda:** The *Vedas* inform us that because God is absolute, there is no difference between God the person and His holy name; the name *is* God. When you first started chanting, could you perceive that?

**George:** It takes a certain amount of time and faith to accept or to realize that there is no difference between Him and His name, to get to the point where you're no longer mystified by where He is. You know, like, "Is He around here?" You realize after some time, "Here He is—right here!" It's a matter of practice. So when I say that "I see God," I don't necessarily mean to say that when I chant I'm seeing Krsna in His original form when He came five thousand years ago, dancing across the water, playing His flute. Of course, that would also be nice, and it's quite possible too. When you become real pure by chanting, you can actually see God like that, I mean personally. But no doubt you can feel His presence and know that He's there when you're chanting.

**Mukunda:** Can you think of any incident where you felt God's presence very strongly through chanting?

**George:** Once I was on an airplane that was in an electric storm. It was hit by lightning three times, and a Boeing 707 went over the top of us, missing by inches. I thought the back end of the plane had blown off. I was on my way from Los Angeles to New York to organize the Bangladesh concert. As soon as the plane began bouncing around, I started chanting, Hare Krsna, Hare Krsna, Krsna Krsna, Hare Hare / Hare Rama, Hare Rama, Rama Rama, Hare Hare. The whole thing went on for about an hour and a half or two hours, the plane dropping hundreds of feet and bouncing all over in the storm, all the lights out and all these explosions, and everybody terrified. I ended up with my feet pressed against the seat in front, my seat belt as tight as it could be, gripping on the thing, and yelling Hare Krsna, Hare Krsna, Krsna Krsna, Hare Hare at the top of my voice. I know for me, the difference between making it and not making it was actually chanting the *mantra*. Peter Sellers also swore that chanting Hare Krsna saved him from a plane crash once.

**Mukunda:** Did any of the other Beatles chant?

**George:** Before meeting Prabhupada and all of you, I had bought that album Prabhupada did in New York [Krishna Consciousness, *Happening Records, 1966*], and John and I listened to it. I remember we sang it for days, John and I, with ukulele banjos, sailing through the Greek Islands chanting Hare Krsna. Like six hours we sang, because we couldn't stop once we got going. As soon as we stopped, it was like the lights went out. It went on to the point where our jaws were aching, singing the mantra over and over and over and over and over. We felt exalted; it was a very happy time for us.

**Mukunda:** Although John never made Hare Krsna a big part of his life, he echoed the philosophy of Krsna consciousness in a hit song he wrote, "Instant Karma."

Now what's the difference between chanting Hare Krsna and meditation?

**George:** It's really the same sort of thing as meditation, but I think it has a quicker effect. I mean, even if you put your beads down, you can still say the *mantra* or sing it without actually keeping track on your beads. One of the main differences between silent meditation and chanting is that silent meditation is rather dependent on concentration, but when you chant, it's more of a direct connection with God.

Chanting Hare Krsna is a type of meditation that can be practiced even if the mind is in turbulence. You can even be doing it and other things at the same time. That's what's so nice. In my life there's been many times the *mantra* brought things around. It keeps me in tune with reality, and the more you sit in one place and chant, the more incense you offer to Krsna in the same room, the more you purify the vibration, the more you can achieve what you're trying to do, which is just trying to remember God, God, God, God, God, as often as possible. And if you're talking to Him with the *mantra*, it certainly helps.

**Mukunda:** What else helps you to fix your mind on God?

**George:** Well, just having as many things around me that will remind me of Him, like incense and pictures. Just the other day I was looking at a small picture on the wall of my studio of you, Gurudasa, and Syamasundara, and just seeing all the old devotees made me think of Krsna. I guess that's the business of devotees—to make you think of God.

**Mukunda:** How often do you chant?

**George:** Whenever I get a chance.

**Mukunda:** Once you asked Srila Prabhupada about a particular verse he quoted from the *Vedas*, in which it's said that when one chants the holy name of Krsna, Krsna dances on the tongue and one wishes one had thousands of ears and thousands of mouths with which to better appreciate the holy names of God.

**George:** Yes. I think he was talking about the realization that there is no difference between Him standing before you and His being present in His name. That's the real beauty of chanting–you directly connect with God. I have no doubt that by saying Krsna over and over again, He can come and dance on the tongue. The main thing, though, is to keep in touch with God.

**Mukunda:** So your habit is generally to use the beads when you chant?

**George:** Oh, yeah. I have my beads. I remember when I first got them, they were just big knobby globs of wood, but now I'm very glad to say that they're smooth from chanting a lot.

**Mukunda:** Do you generally keep them in the bag when you chant?

**George:** Yes. I find it's very good to be touching them. It keeps another one of the senses fixed on God. Beads really help in that respect. You know, the frustrating thing about it was in the beginning there was a period when I was heavy into chanting and I had my hand in my bead bag all the time. And I got so tired of people asking me, "Did you hurt your hand, break it or something?" In the end I used to say, "Yeah. Yeah. I had an accident," because it was easier than explaining everything. Using the beads also helps me to release a lot of nervous energy.

**Mukunda:** Some people say that if everyone on the planet chanted Hare Krsna, they wouldn't be able to keep their minds on what they were doing. In other words, if everyone started chanting, some people ask if the whole world wouldn't just grind to a halt. They wonder if people would stop working in factories, for example.

**George:** No. Chanting doesn't stop you from being creative or productive. It actually helps you concentrate. I think this would make a great sketch for television: imagine all the workers on the Ford assembly line in Detroit, all of them chanting Hare Krsna Hare Krsna while bolting on the wheels. Now that would be wonderful. It might help out the auto industry, and probably there would be more decent cars too.

**Mukunda:** We've talked a lot about *japa,* or personalized chanting, which most chanters engage in. But there's another type, called *kirtana,* when one chants congregationally, in a temple or on the streets with a group of devotees. *Kirtana* generally gives a more supercharged effect, like recharging one's spiritual batteries, and it gives others a chance to hear the holy names and become purified.

Actually, I was with Srila Prabhupada when he first began the group chanting in Tompkins Square Park on New York's Lower East Side in 1966.

**George:** Yes, going to a temple or chanting with a group of other people—the vibration is that much stronger. Of course, for some people it's easy just to start chanting on their beads in the middle of a crowd, while other people are more comfortable chanting in the temple. But part of Krsna consciousness is trying to tune in all the senses of all the people: to experience God through all the senses, not just by experiencing Him on Sunday, through your knees by kneeling on some hard wooden kneeler in the church. But if you visit a temple, you can see pictures of God, you can see the Deity form of the Lord, and you can just hear Him by listening to yourself and others say the *mantra*. It's just a way of realizing that all the senses can be applied toward perceiving God, and it makes it that much more appealing, seeing the pictures, hearing the mantra, smelling the incense, flowers, and so on. That's the nice thing about your movement. It incorporates everything—chanting, dancing, philosophy, and *prasadam*. The music and dancing is a serious part of the process too. It's not just something to burn off excess energy.

**Mukunda:** We've always seen that when we chant in the streets, people are eager to crowd around and listen. A lot of them tap their feet or dance along.

**George:** It's great, the sound of the *karatalas* [cymbals]. When I hear them from a few blocks away, it's like some magical thing that awakens something in me. Without their really being aware of what's happening, people are being awakened spiritually. Of course, in another sense, in a higher sense, the *kirtana* is always going on, whether we're hearing it or not.

Now, all over the place in Western cities, the *sankirtana* party has become a common sight. I love to see these *sankirtana* parties, because I love the whole idea of the devotees mixing it up with everybody, giving everybody a chance to remember. I wrote in the Krsna book introduction, "Everybody is looking for Krsna. Some don't realize that they are, but they are. Krsna is God . . . and by chanting His Holy Names, the devotee quickly develops God-consciousness."

**Mukunda:** You know, Srila Prabhupada often said that after a large number of temples were established, most people would simply begin to take up the chanting of Hare Krsna within their own homes, and we're seeing more and more that this is what's happening. Our worldwide congregation is very large—in the millions. The chanting on the streets, the books, and the temples are there to give people a start, to introduce them to the process.

**George:** I think it's better that it is spreading into the homes now. There are a lot of "closet Krsnas," you know. There's a lot of people out there who are just waiting, and if it's not today, it will be tomorrow or next week or next year.

Back in the '60s, whatever we were all getting into, we tended to broadcast it as loud as we could. I had had certain realizations and went through a period where I was so thrilled about my discoveries and realizations that I wanted to shout and tell it to everybody. But there's a time to shout it out and a time not to shout it out. A lot of people went underground with their spiritual life in the '70s, but they're out there in little nooks and crannies and in the countryside, people who look and dress straight, insurance salesmen types, but they're really meditators and chanters, closet devotees.

Prabhupada's movement is doing pretty well. It's growing like wildfire really. How long it will take until we get to a Golden Age where everybody's perfectly in tune with God's will, I don't know; but because of Prabhupada, Krsna consciousness has certainly spread more in the last sixteen years than it has since the 16th century, since the time of Lord Caitanya. The *mantra* has spread more quickly and the movement's gotten bigger and bigger. It would be great if everyone chanted. Everybody would benefit by doing it. No matter how much money you've got, it doesn't necessarily make you happy. You have to find your happiness with the problems you have, not worry too much about them, and chant Hare Krsna, Hare Krsna, Krsna Krsna, Hare Hare.

**Mukunda:** In 1969 you produced a single called "The Hare Krsna Mantra," which eventually became a hit in many countries. That tune later became a cut on the Radha-Krsna Temple album, which you also produced on the Apple label and was distributed in America by Capitol Records. A lot of people in the recording business were surprised by this, your producing songs for, and singing with the Hare Krsnas. Why did you do it?

**George:** Well, it's just all a part of service, isn't it? Spiritual service, in order to try to spread the *mantra* all over the world. Also, to try and give the devotees a wider base and a bigger foothold in England and everywhere else.

**Mukunda:** How did the success of this record of Hare Krsna devotees chanting compare with some of the rock musicians you were producing at the time like Jackie Lomax, Splinter, and Billy Preston?

**George:** It was a different thing. Nothing to do with that really. There was much more reason to it. There was less commercial potential in it, but it was much more satisfying to do, knowing the possibilities that it was going to create, the connotations it would have just by doing a three-and-a-half-minute *mantra*. That was more fun really than trying to make a pop hit record. It was the feeling of trying to utilize your skills or job to make it into some spiritual service to Krsna.

**Mukunda:** When Apple, the recording company, called a press conference to promote the record, the media seemed to be shocked to hear you speak about the soul and God being so important.

**George:** I felt it was important to try and be precise, to tell them and let them know. You know, to come out of the closet and really tell them. Because once you realize something, then you can't pretend you don't know it any more.

I figured this is the space age, with airplanes and everything. If everyone can go around the world on their holidays, there's no reason why a mantra can't go a few miles as well. So the idea was to try to spiritually infiltrate society, so to speak. After I got Apple Records committed to you and the record released, and after our big promotion, we saw it was going to become a hit. And one of the greatest things, one of the greatest thrills of my life, actually, was seeing you all on BBC's *Top of the Pops*. I couldn't believe it. It's pretty hard to get on that program, because they only put you on if you come into the Top 20. It was just like a breath of fresh air. My strategy was to keep it to a three-and-a-half-minute version of the *mantra* so they'd play it on the radio, and it worked. I did the harmonium and guitar track for that record at Abbey Road studios before one of the Beatles' sessions and then overdubbed a bass part. I remember Paul McCartney and his wife, Linda, arrived at the studio and enjoyed the *mantra*.

It still sounds like quite a good recording, even after all these years. It was the greatest fun of all, really, to see Krsna on *Top of the Pops*.

**Mukunda:** Shortly after its release, John Lennon told me that they played it at the intermission right before Bob Dylan did the Isle of Wight concert in the summer of '69.

**George:** They played it while they were getting the stage set up for Bob. It was great. Besides, it was a catchy tune, and the people didn't have to know what it meant in order to enjoy it. I felt very good when I first heard it was doing well.

**Mukunda:** How did you feel about the record technically, the voices?

**George:** Yamuna, the lead singer, has a naturally good voice. I liked the way she sang with conviction, and she sang like she'd been singing it a lot before.

You know, I used to sing the *mantra* long before I met any of the devotees or long before I met Prabhupada, because I had his first record then for at least two years. When you're open to something it's like being a beacon, and you attract it. From the first time I heard the chanting, it was like a door opened somewhere in my subconscious, maybe from some previous life.

**Mukunda:** In the lyrics to that song "Awaiting on You All," from the *All Things Must Pass* album, you come right out front and tell people that they can be free from living in the material world by chanting the names of God. What made you do it? What kind of feedback did you get?

**George:** At that time, nobody was committed to that type of music in the pop world. There was, I felt, a real need for that, so rather than sitting and waiting for somebody else, I decided to do it myself. A lot of times we think, "Well, I agree with you, but I'm not going to actually stand up and be counted. Too risky." Everybody is always trying to keep themselves covered, stay commercial, so I thought, Just do it. Nobody else is, and I'm sick of all these young people just boogeying around, wasting their lives, you know. Also, I felt that there were a lot of people out there who would be reached. I still get letters from people saying, "I have been in the Krsna temple for three years, and I would have never known about Krsna unless you recorded the *All Things Must Pass* album." So I know, by the Lord's grace, I am a small part in the cosmic play.

---

**Mukunda:** From the very start, you always felt comfortable around the devotees?

**George:** The first time I met Syamasundara, I liked him. He was my pal. I'd read about Prabhupada coming from India to Boston on the back of his record, and I knew that Syamasundara and all of you were in my age group, and that the only difference, really, was that you'd already joined and I hadn't. I was in a rock band, but I didn't have any fear, because I had seen *dhotis*, your robes, and the saffron color and shaved heads in India. Krsna consciousness was especially good for me because I didn't get the feeling that I'd have to shave my head, move into a temple, and do it full time. So it was a spiritual thing that just fit in with my life-style. I could still be a musician, but I just changed my consciousness, that's all.

Actually, it gives me pleasure, the idea that I was fortunate enough to be able to help at that time. All those songs with spiritual themes are like little plugs, "My Sweet Lord" and the others. And now I know that people are much more respectful and accepting when it comes to seeing the devotees in the streets and all that. It's no longer like something that's coming from left field.

And I've given a lot of Prabhupada's books to many people, and whether I ever hear from them again or not, it's good to know that they've gotten them, and if they read them, their lives may be changed.

**Mukunda:** When you come across people who are spiritually inclined but don't have much knowledge, what kind of advice do you give them?

**George:** I try to tell them my little bit, what my experience is, and give them a choice of things to read and a choice of places to go—like you know, "Go to the temple, try chanting."

**Mukunda:** In the "Ballad of John and Yoko," John and Yoko rapped the media for the way it can foster a false image of you and perpetuate it. It's taken a lot of time and effort to get them to understand that we are a genuine religion, with scriptures that predate the New Testament by three thousand years.

**George:** The media is to blame for *everything*, for all the misconceptions about the movement, but in a sense it didn't really matter if they said something good or bad, because Krsna consciousness always seemed to transcend that barrier anyway. The fact that the media was letting people know about Krsna was good in itself.

**Mukunda:** Srila Prabhupada always trained us to stick to our principles. He said that the worst thing we could ever do would be to make some sort of compromise or to dilute the philosophy for the sake of cheap popularity. Although many swamis and yogis had come from India to the West, Prabhupada was the only one with the purity and devotion to establish India's ancient Krsna conscious philosophy around the world on its own terms—not watered down, but as it is.

**George:** That's right. He was a perfect example of what he preached.

**Mukunda:** How did you feel about financing the first printing of the *Krsna* book and writing the introduction?

**George:** I just felt like it was part of my job, you know. Wherever I go in the world, when I see devotees, I always say "Hare Krsna!" to them, and they're always pleased to see me. It's a nice relationship. Whether they really know me personally or not, they feel they know me. And they do, really.

**Mukunda:** At lunch today we spoke a little about *prasadam*, vegetarian foods that have been spiritualized by being offered to Krsna in the temple. A lot of people have come to Krsna consciousness through *prasadam*. I mean, this process is the only kind of *yoga* that you can actually practice by eating.

**George:** Well, we should try to see God in everything, so it helps so much having the food to taste. Let's face it, if God is in everything, why shouldn't you taste Him when you eat? I think that *prasadam* is a very important thing. Krsna is God, so He's absolute: His name, His form, *prasadam*, it's all Him. They say the way to a man's heart is through his stomach, so if you can get to a man's spirit soul by eating, and it works, why not do it?

There's nothing better than having been chanting and dancing, or just sitting and talking philosophy, and then suddenly the devotees bring out the *prasadam*. It's a blessing from Krsna, and it's spiritually important. The idea is that *prasadam*'s the sacrament the Christians talk about, only instead of being just a wafer, it's a whole feast, really, and the taste is so nice—it's out of this world. And *prasadam*'s a good little hook in this age of commercialism. When people want something extra, or they need to have something special, *prasadam* will hook them in there. It's undoubtedly done a great deal toward getting a lot more people involved in spiritual life. *Prasadam* breaks down prejudices, too, because they think, "Oh, well, yes, I wouldn't mind a drink of whatever or a bite of that." Then they ask, "What's this?" and "Oh, well, it's *prasadam*." And they get to learn another aspect of Krsna consciousness. Then they say, "It actually tastes quite nice. Have you got another plateful?" I've seen that happen with lots of people, especially older people I've seen at your temples. Maybe they were a little prejudiced, but the next thing you know, they're in love with *prasadam*, and eventually they walk out of the temple thinking, "They're not so bad after all."

**Mukunda:** The Vedic literatures reveal that *prasadam* conveys spiritual realization, just as chanting does, but in a less obvious or conspicuous way. You make spiritual advancement just by eating it.

**George:** I'd say from my experience that it definitely works. I've always enjoyed *prasadam* much more when I've been at the temple, or when I've actually been sitting with Prabhupada, than when somebody's brought it to me. Sometimes you can sit there with *prasadam* and find that three or four hours have gone by and you didn't even know it. *Prasadam* really helped me a lot, because you start to realize "Now I'm tasting Krsna."

You're conscious suddenly of another aspect of God, understanding that He's this little *samosa*. It's all just a matter of tuning into the spiritual, and *prasadam*'s a very real part of it all.

**Mukunda:** We've served about 150 million plates of *prasadam* so far at the free feasts around the world, what to speak of our restaurants.

**George:** You ought to have it up outside on billboards like those hamburger places do. You know, like "150 million served." I think it's great. It's a pity you don't have restaurants or temples on all the main streets of every little town and village like those hamburger and fried chicken places. You should put them out of business.

**Mukunda:** You've been to our London restaurant, Healthy, Wealthy, and Wise?

**George:** Lots of times. It's good to have these and other restaurants around, where plainclothes devotees serve the food. People slowly realize, "This is one of the best places I've been," and they keep coming back. Then maybe they pick up a little bit of the literature or a pamphlet there and say, "Oh, hey, that was run by the Hare Krsnas." I think there's a lot of value to that kind of more subtle approach. Healthy, Wealthy, and Wise has proper foods, good, balanced stuff, and it's fresh. Even more important, it's made with an attitude of devotion, which means a lot. When you know someone has begrudgingly cooked something, it doesn't taste as nice as when someone has done it to try and please God, to offer it to Him first. Just that in itself makes all the food taste so much nicer.

**Mukunda:** You've been a vegetarian for years, George. Have you had any difficulties maintaining it?

**George:** No. Actually, I wised up and made sure I had *dal* bean soup or something every day. Actually, lentils are one of the cheapest things, but they give you A-1 protein. People are simply screwing up when they go out and buy beef steak, which is killing them with cancer and heart troubles. The stuff costs a fortune too. You could feed a thousand people with lentil soup for the cost of half a dozen filets. Does that make sense?

**Mukunda:** George, you and John Lennon met Srila Prabhupada together when he stayed at John's home, in September of 1969.

**George:** Yes, but when I met him at first, I underestimated him. I didn't realize it then, but I see now that because of him, the *mantra* has spread so far in the last sixteen years, more than it had in the last five centuries. Now that's pretty amazing, because he was getting older and older, yet he was writing his books all the time. I realized later on that he was much more incredible than what you could see on the surface.

**Mukunda:** What about him stands out the most in your mind?

**George:** The thing that always stays is his saying, "I am the servant of the servant of the servant." I like that. A lot of people say, "I'm it. I'm the divine incarnation. I'm here and let me hip you." You know what I mean? But Prabhupada was never like that. I liked Prabhupada's humbleness. I always liked his humility and his simplicity. The servant of the servant of the servant is really what it is, you know. None of us are God, just His servants. He just made me feel so comfortable. I always felt very relaxed with him, and I felt more like a friend. I felt that he was a good friend. Even though he was at the time seventy-nine years old, working practically all through the night, day after day, with very little sleep, he still didn't come through to me as though he was a very highly educated intellectual being, because he had a sort of childlike simplicity. Which is great, fantastic. Even though he was the greatest Sanskrit scholar and saint, I appreciated the fact that he never made me feel uncomfortable. In fact, he always went out of his way to make me feel comfortable. I always thought of him as sort of a lovely friend, really, and now he's still a lovely friend.

**Mukunda:** In one of his books, Prabhupada said that your sincere service was better than some people who had delved more deeply into Krsna consciousness but could not maintain that level of commitment. How did you feel about this?

**George:** Very wonderful, really. I mean it really gave me hope, because as they say, even one moment in the company of a divine person, Krsna's pure devotee, can help a tremendous amount.

And if I didn't get feedback from Prabhupada on my songs about Krsna or the philosophy, I'd get it from the devotees. That's all the encouragement I needed really. It just seemed that anything spiritual I did, either through songs, or helping with publishing the books, or whatever, really pleased him. The song I wrote, "Living in the Material World," as I wrote in *I, Me, Mine*, was influenced by Srila Prabhupada. He's the one who explained to me how we're not these physical bodies. We just happen to be in them.

That was the thing about Prabhupada, you see. He didn't just talk about loving Krsna and getting out of this place, but he was the perfect example. He talked about always chanting, and he was always chanting. I think that that in itself was perhaps the most encouraging thing for me. It was enough to make me try harder, to be just a little bit better. He was a perfect example of everything he preached.

Srila Prabhupada has already had an amazing effect on the world. There's no way of measuring it. One day I just realized, "God, this man is amazing!" He would sit up all night translating Sanskrit into English, putting in glossaries to make sure everyone understands it, and yet he never came off as someone above you. He always had that childlike simplicity, and what's most amazing is the fact that he did all this translating in such a relatively short time—just a few years. And without having anything more than his own Krsna consciousness, he rounded up all these thousands of devotees, set the whole movement in motion, which became something so strong that it went on even after he left. And it's still escalating even now at an incredible rate. It will go on and on from the knowledge he gave. It can only grow and grow. The more people wake up spiritually, the more they'll begin to realize the depth of what Prabhupada was saying—how much he gave.

**Mukunda:** Did you know that complete sets of Prabhupada's books are in all the major colleges and universities in the world, including Harvard, Yale, Princeton, Oxford, Cambridge, and the Sorbonne?

**George:** They should be! His contribution has obviously been enormous from the literary point of view, because he's brought the Supreme Person, Krsna, more into focus. A lot of scholars and writers know the Gita, but only on an intellectual level. Even when they write "Krsna said . . ," they don't do it with the *bhakti* or love required. That's the secret, you know—Krsna is actually a person who is the Lord and who will also appear there in that book when there is that love, that *bhakti*. You can't understand the first thing about God unless you love Him. These big so-called Vedic scholars—they don't love Krsna, so they can't understand Him and give Him to us. But Prabhupada was different.

**Mukunda:** The Vedic literatures predicted that after the advent of Lord Caitanya five hundred years ago, there would be a Golden Age of ten thousand years, when the chanting of the holy names of God would completely nullify all the degradations of the modern age, and real spiritual peace would come to this planet.

**George:** Well, Prabhupada's definitely affected the world in an absolute way. What he was giving us was the highest literature, the highest knowledge. I mean there just isn't anything higher.

**Mukunda:** A lot of people, when they just get started in spiritual life, worship God as impersonal. What's the difference between worshiping Krsna, or God, in His personal form and worshiping His impersonal nature as energy or light?

**George:** It's like the difference between hanging out with a computer or hanging out with a person. Like I said earlier, "If there is a God, I want to see Him," not only His energy or His light, but Him.

**Mukunda:** What do you think is the goal of human life?

**George:** Each individual has to burn out his own *karma* and escape from the chains of *maya*, reincarnation, and all that. The best thing anyone can give to humanity is God consciousness. Then you can really give them something. But first you have to concentrate on your own spiritual advancement; so in a sense we have to become selfish to become selfless.

**Mukunda:** What about trying to solve the problems of life without employing the spiritual process?

**George:** Life is like a piece of string with a lot of knots tied in it. The knots are the karma you're born with from all your past lives, and the object of human life is to try and undo all those knots. That's what chanting and meditation in God consciousness can do. Otherwise you simply tie another ten knots each time you try to undo one knot. That's how *karma* works. I mean, we're now the results of our past actions, and in the future we'll be the results of the actions we're performing now. A little understanding of "As you sow, so shall you reap" is important, because then you can't blame the condition you're in on anyone else. You know that it's by your own actions you're able to get more in a mess or out of one. It's your own actions that relieve or bind you.

**Mukunda:** I don't think it's possible to calculate just how many people were turned on to Krsna consciousness by your song "My Sweet Lord." Why did you feel you wanted to put Hare Krsna on the album at all? Wouldn't "Hallelujah" alone have been good enough?

**George:** Well, first of all "Hallelujah" is a joyous expression the Christians have, but "Hare Krsna" has a mystical side to it. It's more than just glorifying God; it's asking to become His servant. And because of the way the *mantra* is put together, with the mystic spiritual energy contained in those syllables, it's much closer to God than the way Christianity currently seems to be representing Him. Although Christ in my mind is an absolute *yogi*, I think many Christian teachers today are misrepresenting Christ. They're supposed to be representing Jesus, but they're not doing it very well. They're letting him down very badly, and that's a big turn off.

My idea in "My Sweet Lord," because it sounded like a "pop song," was to sneak up on them a bit. The point was to have the people not offended by "Hallelujah," and by the time it gets to "Hare Krsna," they're already hooked, and their foot's tapping, and they're already singing along "Hallelujah," to kind of lull them into a sense of false security. And then suddenly it turns into "Hare Krsna," and they will be singing that before they know what's happened, and they will think, "Hey, I thought I wasn't supposed to like Hare Krsna!"

People write to me even now asking what style that was. Ten years later they're still trying to figure out what the words mean. It was just a little trick really. And it didn't offend. For some reason I never got any offensive feedback from Christians who said "We like it up to a point, but what's all this about Hare Krsna?"

Hallelujah may have originally been some mantric thing that got watered down, but I'm not sure what it really means. The Greek word for Christ is Kristos, which is, let's face it, Krsna, and Kristos is the same name actually.

**Mukunda:** What would you say is the difference between the Christian view of God, and Krsna as represented in the *Bhagavad-gita*?

**George:** When I first came to this house it was occupied by nuns. I brought in this poster of Visnu [a four-armed form of Krsna]. You just see His head and shoulders and His four arms holding a conch shell and various other symbols, and it has a big *om* written above it. He has a nice aura around Him. I left it by the fireplace and went out into the garden. When we came back in the house, they all pounced on me, saying, "Who is that? What is it?" as if it were some pagan god. So I said, "Well, if God is unlimited, then He can appear in any form, whichever way He likes to appear. That's one way. He's called Visnu."

It sort of freaked them out a bit, but the point is, why should God be limited? Even if you get Him as Krsna, He is not limited to that picture of Krsna. He can be the baby form, He can be Govinda and manifest in so many other well-known forms. You can see Krsna as a little boy, which is how I like to see Krsna. It's a joyful relationship. But there's this morbid side to the way many represent Christianity today, where you don't smile, because it's too serious, and you can't expect to see God—that kind of stuff. If there is God, we must see Him, and I don't believe in the idea you find in most churches, where they say, "No, you're not going to see Him. He's way up above you. Just believe what we tell you and shut up."

**Mukunda:** Anyone who's sincere about making spiritual advancement can usually see the value of chanting, whatever his religion may be. I mean if that person was really trying to be God conscious and trying to chant sincerely.

**George:** That's right. It's a matter of being open. Anyone who's open can do it. You just have to be open and not prejudiced. You just have to try it. There's no loss, you know. But the intellectuals will always have problems, because they always need to know. They're often the most spiritually bankrupt people, because they never let go; they don't understand the meaning of "transcending the intellect." But an ordinary person's more willing to say, "Okay. Let me try it and see if it works." Chanting Hare Krsna can make a person a better Christian, too.

**Mukunda:** When you were in Vrndavana, India, where Lord Krsna appeared, and you saw thousands of people chanting Hare Krsna, did it strengthen your faith in the idea of chanting to see a whole city living Hare Krsna?

**George:** Yeah, it fortifies you. It definitely helps. It's fantastic to be in a place where the whole town is doing it. And I also had the idea that they were all knocked out at the idea of seeing some white person chanting on beads. Vrndavana is one of the holiest cities in India. Everyone, everywhere, chants Hare Krsna. It was my most fantastic experience.

**Mukunda:** You wrote in your book: "Most of the world is fooling about, especially the people who think they control the world and the community. The presidents, the politicians, the military, etc., are all jerking about, acting as if they are Lord over their own domains. That's basically Problem One on the planet."

**George:** That's right. Unless you're doing some kind of God conscious thing and you know that He's the one who's really in charge, you're just building up a lot of *karma* and not really helping yourself or anybody else. There's a point in me where it's beyond sad, seeing the state of the world today. It's so screwed up. It's terrible, and it will be getting worse and worse. More concrete everywhere, more pollution, more radioactivity. There's no wilderness left, no pure air. They're chopping the forests down. They're polluting all the oceans. In one sense, I'm pessimistic about the future of the planet. These big guys don't realize for everything they do, there's a reaction. You have to pay. That's *karma*.

**Mukunda:** Do you think there's any hope?

**George:** Yes. One by one, everybody's got to escape *maya*. Everybody has to burn out his *karma* and escape reincarnation and all that. Stop thinking that if Britain or America or Russia or the West or whatever becomes superior, then we'll beat them, and then we'll all have a rest and live happily ever after. That doesn't work. The best thing you can give is God consciousness. Manifest your own divinity first. The truth is there. It's right within us all. Understand what you are. If people would just wake up to what's real, there would be no misery in the world. I guess chanting's a pretty good place to start.

**Mukunda:** Thanks so much, George.

**George:** All right. Hare Krsna!

# UNPUBLISHED INTERVIEW

**Charles Bermant | September 17, 1987 | Interview Transcript**

The interview below is more a typical Q and A than loose conversation, and yet it is filled with details and attitude, catching Harrison at the height of the MTV era: a point when many survivors of the '60s were dismayed by the widespread commercialization of all the '60s once stood for. The counterculture had become absorbed into mainstream; what was once irreverent and revolutionary was now a means of selling sportswear and sodas.

Charlie Bermant, whose writing has focused on culture, new media, and computer technology, feels his moment with Harrison could have been handled better, and still cringes to think he answered "no" when he was offered a bit of Beatles information no one knew. "Stupid, stupid, stupid. The answer was reflective," Bermant now says, but he had a reason. "I didn't want to invade his privacy." He describes how the interview happened:

> I drove down to LA from San Francisco, arriving at the Burbank office at around 1 pm. I sat in a room for three hours or so. There was a tape I could listen to of the unreleased *Cloud Nine* album, which the surly PR lady told me that I could not record. She also told me there would be nothing personal, no autographs. I said "of course not" and kept my copy of Harrison's book hidden. After several hours she led me to an office, introduced me to George and left the room. It was not a particularly good interview. I was extremely nervous and read from my list of questions. He was open and answered each one honestly and completely. He let me end the interview. When it was over, I bolted out of the building, got in the car and headed up 101. I put the tape in the dash. I was up a few highway exits when I realized I'd forgotten to thank the PR lady.

It's a solid interview nonetheless. Bermant's questions were spot on for the time: digging into the story behind *Cloud Nine*—Harrison's first album in five years, produced by Electric Light Orchestra's Jeff Lynne—and focusing on the different ways the Beatles were being co-opted at the time, including the 1982 two-hour documentary *The Compleat Beatles*, which had not been received well critically, and the use of "Revolution" in an '87 Nike Air advertising campaign.

Bermant ended up crafting reports from this discussion for a number of newspapers in major cities, including Toronto, New Orleans, St. Louis, Cleveland, San Diego, Portland, Honolulu, San Jose, and eventually the New York Times Syndicate—all edited differently, with different perspectives. What follows is the complete, unedited transcript of their conversation.

"So the piece went around the world in various versions," Bermant says. "I'm still ambivalent today, pissed that I blew an opportunity while proud that I was able to sustain a conversation with a Beatle. For years after, I'd relive the moment, realizing I could have asked him anything." —Ed.

**Charles Bermant:** How did you pick this time to reemerge?

**George Harrison:** I wanted to have a little break away from it. I still continued writing and putting songs on tape—I never really stopped doing that. I never put out a record; I had a chance to get away from it for a bit, then I felt much better about the idea of doing it, and then it was a question of finding someone I could work with. I'm the past. It's handy to have someone to bounce ideas off of—I really miss that part of being in a group, where you can come up with all of your own ideas, and you have other people's, ideas and they all mix together, and they become even a different idea. Here, the whole burden isn't on just myself. I decided it was time to make a new album, but this time I was going to make it with some other producer.

**Bermant:** Are they intimidated by you?

**Harrison:** No, I just don't really know that many record producers. So I thought, "Who would be good? Someone I really admire and someone who would respect me and my past, and not try to turn me into something I'm not." I thought of Jeff Lynne of the Electric Light Orchestra, he'd be fun, if I only knew him. . . .

**Bermant:** You'd never met?

**Harrison:** I'd never met him. He's a very private person, Jeff. He's one person who I don't think has done interviews, or television, or anything. He's just very private. Anyway, I got a message to him through Dave Edmunds that I'd like to meet him. And I met Jeff, and over period of eighteen months I got to know him and suggested that I'm going to make a record and just sounded him out. And he said he'd help, but he never committed himself. So last November I finally said that's it, I'm going to make a record, at least get some musicians over, and so he said OK, and we worked from January straight through until August.

**Bermant:** But you used pretty much the same musicians.

**Harrison:** When I think of who I want to play drums on a track I think of Jim Keltner—I know Jim so well, he's such a great drummer, and at the same time Ringo, because Ringo, I don't have to tell him what I want, he'll just listen to the tune and he'll play like Ringo. So same goes for guitar solos—that should be Eric on that one. So there's a lot of my same old friends. The added influence of Jeff helping to produce worked well indeed; he has a good structural sense of songs, he's a composer and a guitarist himself, a lot of similarities.

**Bermant:** Were you talking to other producers at the same time?

**Harrison:** No, I was just trying to think of who, if I had my choice of the people I could think of, and he was the one person I came up with.

**Bermant:** You haven't been idle, musically. How did you pick these songs?

**Harrison:** I had a lot of demos. I played them to Jeff; he picked them out. I asked him to write me a song, too. Since I've been not making albums, I've done a lot of other people's songs. Just as demos, some old tunes, I do a quick version. I like the idea of singing somebody else's songs.

**Bermant:** Such as?

**Harrison:** Dylan's "Every Grain of Sand," a great song. I did a version of that, a couple of other Dylan songs, writing other crazy songs. He wrote me a song, we wrote a couple together, and the song that they're putting out as a single is one that neither of us wrote, from the very early 1960s, called "I've Got My Mind Set on You."

**Bermant:** Which sounds like nothing you've ever done.

**Harrison:** It's true, that came about because Jim Keltner just started playing that drum pattern, and the song seemed to fit right on there. . . . Does this bother you?

**Bermant:** I'm just surprised you're still smoking.

**Harrison:** Well, off and on. You know, something like this, it's, ah, on.

**Bermant:** You've recently been a filmmaker, and now you're making your first video. What can we expect?

**Harrison:** We haven't made the video. We're not making it until next Wednesday.

**Bermant:** What do you have in mind?

**Harrison:** We're still just talking about it. It's a bit early for that.

**Bermant:** Next week?

**Harrison:** That's it. It's silly, isn't it? We'll finalize what's going to happen. It's difficult to make a video that doesn't look like all of the other videos. Occasionally, there's a really nice one. Like that Dire Straits or Peter Gabriel. But you can't say, "Oh, I'm going to make one like Peter Gabriel," because he's already done that. This video isn't going to be me making a movie. Maybe later when we start doing different singles off of the album, then maybe I'll work more along those lines. I've just finished the record, mixing it, all the artwork and mastering it, and then it's like, "Make a video. . . ." So this video, Gary Weis is making the video. I knew him from the Rutles. Gary has a real good sense of humor, he's done the *Saturday Night Live* stuff as well. It's how to present it so it's funny, but at the same time the song isn't particularly a comedy song. Neither was "You Can Call Me Al," but they gave it a comical flavor.

**Bermant:** So you want to make people laugh.

**Harrison:** Well. I'd like it to not look like the same old videos that just keep coming. At the same time, with the limited time span I'm pretty much in the hands of Gary. It's up to him to do it really good.

**Bermant:** What makes you laugh?

**Harrison:** A lot of things. I've always liked comedy. Back when I was a kid, I liked *The Goon Show*, I was a big fan of Peter Sellers, and later on I was a good friend of his. I liked Peter a lot. I loved Monty Python, I couldn't explain how much I liked it. The rut that television gets into, and people's lives, Python just blew all that away by making fun of everything. Right down to the style of television we've been watching. The result is that I got to know some of them, and we made the *Life of Brian* and *Time Bandits* and a couple of films with Michael Palin, so that kind of stuff makes me laugh.

**Bermant:** *The Rutles* is probably the best Beatles movie.

**Harrison:** I think so.

**Bermant:** *The Compleat Beatles* was horrible.

**Harrison:** *The Compleat Beatles* is like taking all the footage they can scrounge and then trying to do a serious thing. The great thing about *The Rutles* is that, even though it was a parody, it was the nicest thing about the Beatles. It was done with love even though it was a send-up. And because of Eric Idle being a friend of mine, it gave him access to things that any other potential Beatle filmmaker wouldn't have. I showed him footage that was obscure, like when we first came into NYC, in the back of a limousine, and Paul's listening to a radio and a guy is saying, ". . . the Beatles are going to be here at the station to read their poetry." And that isn't a famous bit of footage. So in *The Rutles*, you see them, and he's listening to the radio, and the disk jockey, and "the Rutles are coming to talk about their trousers." And also, just the detail, where they got exactly what sort of suits we were wearing on that day, even at Shea Stadium, little marshal's badges, the Rutles even had the psychedelic guitars—it had a good eye for detail. At the same time, it sent up documentaries, the style and those boring questions that they ask.

**Bermant:** If I had read every Beatles book and seen every documentary, in a general sense, what would I have missed?

**Harrison:** Do you want me to tell you something nobody else knows?

**Bermant:** No.

**Harrison:** A lot of the stuff in the books are [sic] wrong. A lot of them are written out of malice, or from people with axes to grind for one reason or another. And they've perverted certain things for their own gain. Not many are actually factual and honest. There is a saying in the old house that I have, it's in Latin, translated it says, "Those who tell all they have to tell tell more than they know." So you probably know more about the Beatles from reading those books than there actually was.

**Bermant:** What would those people who look so closely miss?

**Harrison:** Well, there's that expression, you don't see the forest for the trees. Basically, the Beatles phenomenon was bigger than life. The reality was that we were just four people as much caught up in what was happening at that period of time as anybody else.

**Bermant:** Have you listened to the Beatles CDs?

**Harrison:** I did buy a CD player when they issued them, yeah. I listened to some of them. I still prefer the old versions, how I remember them on vinyl. There's a lot of stuff that you can hear now that's good. In some cases, there's a lot of stuff that you shouldn't hear so loudly, that's somehow come out in the mix. On *Sgt. Pepper* I keep hearing this horrible-sounding tambourine that leaps out of the right speaker. It was obviously in the original mix, but it was never that loud.

**Bermant:** There are still thirty or so songs not on CD. How would you make them available?

**Harrison:** Well, it's none of our business anymore; when our contract expired, we lost any control we had over the Beatles product.

**Bermant:** How would you like to see it done?

**Harrison:** I suppose if you took all the songs you could put them order in sequence of years as they were recorded, then as the technology advanced and our technique progressed, then you'd hear them in proper order. Or you could put all the singles on one, or the B-sides on another.

**Bermant:** Does Michael Jackson own your songs as well?

**Harrison:** He owns some of mine, up to the *White Album*.

**Bermant:** How did "Revolution" end up on a sneaker commercial?

**Harrison:** From what I understand, they were just going to use the song, rerecord it with Julian Lennon, but Yoko got really pissed off at that idea because I don't think she likes Julian, and she insisted that it be the Beatles version. She has no right to insist that because there's a conflict of interest—it's in the Beatles' and Apple's interest not to have our records touted about on TV commercials, otherwise all the songs we made could be advertising everything from hot dogs to ladies' brassieres. We never took advertising. We could have done our Coca-Cola commercials, just like everybody else. We tried to have a little discretion, keep a little taste; that's what we felt. The four of us tried to keep our songs in running orders on the records, we tried to make good records, we tried to do something as quality and something to be proud of. When it's out of our hands, it's like we're made into prostitutes.

**Bermant:** Capitol's new tapes ruin the running order of your old albums.

**Harrison:** This is the problem of not having any control anymore. It's unfortunate. We should have been able to retain the control. That's the way it all went.

**Bermant:** Derek Taylor said you crave your own space and have a long memory.

**Harrison:** Most people need their own space. I still have it, even though occasions like this when I do an album I come out and say hello to people. I couldn't live in a house full of journalist and have them ask me questions all the time. What was the other question?

**Bermant:** Memory.

**Harrison:** Ah, the memory. Sort of more in the past, a lot of brain cells are missing now. Sometimes you don't want to remember things, sometimes you can't, and sometimes they just pop out there.

**Bermant:** Is there any unreleased Beatles stuff aside from the *Sessions* album?

**Harrison:** Not that I know of. When we made records, everything we made came out. The only things that didn't come out were things that weren't supposed to be recorded. Like if we were rehearsing and they were just rolling the tape. But people want to scrape the bottom of the barrel for anything.

**Bermant:** What's next for you?

**Harrison:** It'll be pretty much the same. My film company is jogging along; we have a lot of projects. It's the sort of company that doesn't seem to make a lot of blockbuster movies; they seem to be the sort of films that nobody else wants to make. But it still doesn't mean that they shouldn't be made. The only thing that I would like to accomplish is perfect peace in a spiritual sense, to be able to consciously leave my body at will.

# MAGAZINE INTERVIEW

Anthony DeCurtis | August 27 or 28, 1987 | Interview Transcript

In late summer of 1987, a lot was going on. Harrison was back with a new album. *Cloud Nine* was his eleventh title to date; it featured a generous helping of new, well-crafted songs, the support of famous and familiar sidemen (Eric Clapton, Gary Wright, Elton John, Ringo Starr, and Jim Keltner), and production by Jeff Lynne, leader of the Electric Light Orchestra. Warner Bros., distributor of Harrison's Dark Horse label, was excited, certain that *Cloud Nine* would yield multiple hits (which it did) and be critically welcomed (which it was). Harrison had been off the scene for five years, his longest hiatus to date, and the promotional machine behind his return was in high gear.

That same year, *Rolling Stone* marked its twentieth year of publishing with an expanded issue, sending their lead writers to interview legends who could help remember '67: Mick Jagger, Bob Dylan, Jack Nicholson, Paul McCartney, Tom Wolfe, and others, including Harrison. Anthony DeCurtis, an editor at *RS*, spoke with Harrison twice that summer, once for the anniversary issue and again for an article covering his new projects. Their first conversation took place at Friar Park and focused on the past twenty years. Harrison offered a few familiar stories, and one of the clearest explanations of his ongoing choice to avoid taking a band on the road:

> There was one thing that sticks in my mind. On one of the concerts, I think it was in Long Beach [California], instead of leaving right after the show, I waited until the audience had gone. I was just hanging around the stadium, and I watched them bulldozing. They had a bulldozer in the middle—you know, the festival seating situation, where everybody's standing up—and they were bulldozing all the rubble left by the audience.

There were *mountains* of empty bottles of gin and bourbon and tequila and brassieres and shoes and coats and trash. I mean it was *unbelievable*.

DeCurtis's second interview with Harrison in '87 took place in Los Angeles in the offices of Warner Bros. and focused on more recent matters, including an unusually comprehensive overview of his spiritual associations since meeting the Maharishi in 1967. The full, unedited transcript of that conversation is below; when published in *Rolling Stone*, DeCurtis helped set the scene with the following.

. . . If Harrison's legendary stature has sparked the mood of exhilaration, it's also charged the undercurrent of tension. The video interview being filmed is not for MTV— it's a promotional clip for the annual Warner/Elektra/Atlantic (WEA) sales convention in Miami. Featuring segments with a host of premier Warner Bros. acts, the video is intended to "get the troops up, raise the level of morale, motivate the salespeople for the fourth quarter," according to Adam Somers, the vice-president of creative services at Warner Bros., who is coordinating the filming.

To achieve those all-important ends—the holiday season is crucial to the bottom line throughout the record industry—Warner Bros. has recruited fast-talking NBC West Coast sportscaster Fred Roggin and conceived a quasi-comical baseball theme to link the artists' skits. In the year of the lively ball and corked bats, that theme is, What is Warner Bros. Records putting into its vinyl to give the company so many big "hits"? Get it? Perhaps you do, but Harrison—being British and all—doesn't. Still, because of the priority the label is placing on *Cloud Nine*, Harrison's spot is to be the "culmination" of the tape, according to Somers.

—Ed.

**George Harrison:** . . . They all mean well, it's just that they're trying to cater to the staff here. They're all into baseball. I can understand what they're trying to do, but it just doesn't mean anything to me.

**Anthony DeCurtis:** Right. [*Laughs.*] Yeah, right.

**Harrison:** [*Sighs deeply.*] Phew!

**DeCurtis:** Well, I was struck by one thing that you mentioned there, and that you also brought up when we were in England, and that is that you described after getting in touch with Jeff and talking about working with him, you mentioned sort of *convincing* him . . . and then in England you had mentioned a certain sort of reluctance that he had . . .

**Harrison:** Well it wasn't really—he wasn't reluctant, it's just that, in my mind, I had already decided that it would be good to have some positive help . . . [*indistinct*] . . . on the production side.

**DeCurtis:** Let me say, incidentally, I thought the record came out sounding great.

**Harrison:** Did you?

**DeCurtis:** Yeah, I just heard it last night. It sounds wonderful. It really did seem to be a kind of collaboration, or just infusing some ideas—I think the two of you just worked really well together.

**Harrison:** I think so too. It wasn't—whatever you were just saying. I don't really know a lot of people in the record production situation. . . . I felt that I had to have somebody who—I don't know if I'm going over things we talked about in the other conversation. . . .

**DeCurtis:** No, don't worry about it, don't worry about that.

**Harrison:** I had to have somebody who I respected and who I felt had a legitimate input and, likewise, somebody who was aware of my past and wasn't just going to crowd me out, or turn me into some sort of thing that I wasn't. That's all. So when I thought of Jeff, I hadn't ever met him. I thought, just from his records, he would be really good if we sort of got on together. So it was really a question of, first of all, finding somebody to get in touch with him, and then meeting with him without saying, "Well look, right down the line—[*indistinct, audio interference*]—try and make a record, and *you're* it." I didn't want to frighten the fellow away.

But that was in the back of my mind, but at the same time, even if it hadn't worked out the way it has, I was still looking forward to meeting him anyway just to hang out, because he's been such a big thing in . . . well, I know in America too, but like in British music of the '70s. And yet, he was always mysterious, you know, even in the films I've seen of ELO onstage, he's very mysterious. There's not too much you know about him.

So anyway, that story worked out well—Dave Edmunds knew him, and I mentioned it to Dave, and Dave mentioned to Jeff that I would like to meet him. He came down and then we had dinner and I got his phone number, saying give us a call sometime, and waited, and then I thought, "Well, I'm going to make the move just in case he doesn't mind the idea of hanging out. You know, he may be shy or if he isn't, and he just doesn't want to know—you know, give him a chance to tell me to piss off." [*Indistinct.*] . . . Every so often we just got together, just really [*to*] have dinner and just have a laugh and a drink.

Then he visited my studio a couple of times while I was involved with that soundtrack album—well it wasn't really—not the soundtrack of the movie . . .

**DeCurtis:** The soundtrack?

**Harrison:** It wasn't an album, sorry, it was the soundtrack to *Shanghai Surprise*. I was busy all the year of 1986, like probably April through to August. And, in fact, we did a track on that.

**DeCurtis:** Oh, really?

**Harrison:** There was a song which was just in a nightclub—it was supposed to be the 1920s or early '30s—and I wrote two songs for that club scene: one which was a vocal on it, and I based it on like a Cab Calloway idea, and the other one was just to make this same period, but it was an instrumental, which was called "Zig Zag"—and that was the name of the club in the movie. So Jeff actually played—we sort of cowrote that together one night, so, you know, that was a little prelude to the songs that we wrote later for this album.

So anyway, we got on good together and that was it. We started the album, and we never really talked about "okay, will you be the producer or the coproducer?" He'd said, "Sure, I'll help out, I don't mind helping you out," and it was just on that basis. And it's been like that all the time, even though we've gone through all these months of doing it. But he has become, obviously, the producer, or coproducer with me. And not only that but, what you just said, it fits together so well in all kinds of things. He's a guitarist, he's a songwriter, and he's had his success . . .

**DeCurtis:** Is that the two of you playing on the title track on *Cloud Nine*?

**Harrison:** On *Cloud Nine* it's me and Eric Clapton. But it just seemed to work well, and Jeff is smart enough to know his mind, and I think all the things that he's put into it—which is a lot, but—it's not crowded out. I think it's a good blend between the two of us and our vocals—the backing voices that we did I thought were great, because it doesn't really sound like anybody, it sounds a bit like him and a bit like me, or like somebody different.

**DeCurtis:** Right. There's a real nice texture.

**Harrison:** So I was very pleased because there's a lot of situations [*that*] happen where you think it's good to work with somebody and after a few weeks you're at each other's throats, and you find you've got nothing in common and you hate each other's music. [*DeCurtis laughs.*] And I'm glad to say that didn't happen.

**DeCurtis:** Now, had you gotten to the point that—now I know that, obviously, you're very active in doing stuff with your movie company and you mentioned certain disillusionments about the music industry—but were you at a point where you really began to get itchy to make a record? Or was it something that you kind of felt, "Well, if the right situation and the right people come along, fine. But if not I'm not going to worry about it." . . . ?

**Harrison:** Yeah, that was the situation. When I did my last album, *Gone Troppo*, at that period I felt that I had done so many things in the past, and I didn't feel, you know, I never really spent time promoting that record, and I didn't really give the record company much help, put it that way. But at the same time, the record business was going, it seemed—from the way I could see it—to be going through all these strange things that had happened since . . .

You remember the big fuel crisis [*of 1973*]? The bottom dropped out of the economy and that affected all kinds of businesses, the record business included. And they were firing a lot of staff and they were trimming down all the artists they had, and there was a general confusion that seemed to be going on. And it was like the program planners for the radio stations seemed to be having more control, the disc jockeys were just mouthpieces. And I think I mentioned to you, which I think you already put in the paper, about the fact that somebody said to me on a survey, "How do you get a hit record . . . ?"

**DeCurtis:** Unbelievable! It's funny, so many people have mentioned that. Could you imagine somebody saying that to *you*? It's just unthinkable.

**Harrison:** That kind of thing got me a bit pissed off. In fact, there was one point, on the album before *Troppo*, which is called *Somewhere in England*, I wrote this song which was a bit of an attack on that situation, which was called "Blood from a Clone." [*Quotes lyrics.*]

> They say they like it, but now in the market
> It may not go well because it's too laid back
> It needs some oom-pa-pa, nothing like Frank Zappa
> Not New Wave, they don't play that crap
> Try beating your head on a brick wall [*DeCurtis laughs.*]
> Hard like a stone
> Don't have time for music
> They want the blood from a clone

That's how I felt and that was good to get that off my chest. But by that time, I'd not made a record for a few years.

I was relaxed and cool about everything, and I was just doing all these other things. It's not as if I was out of work or anything like some people who have to just keep doing the one thing. I was always in the studio over that time, writing songs and just putting them down on demos, just having fun.

**DeCurtis:** You had a twenty-four-track studio, right?

**Harrison:** Yeah. Incidentally, the only reason . . . I wasn't sure how to handle that situation when you came out to Henley. But you must have noticed I took you to the lodge, partially because the house is so weird.

**DeCurtis:** I swear when I saw it through the trees . . . I had seen a million pictures of it, but somehow when we met there, I was focusing so much on the interview that I'd kind of forgotten where we were going.

And just as you were driving me up, I saw it through the trees and it just was like, "Oh, right!"

**Harrison:** And I thought I don't normally do interviews at home because it's such a distraction, this big gothic . . .

**DeCurtis:** I understand, and also, you know, it's your house! I mean, I can understand. . . .

**Harrison:** Well, *that's* okay, I always make people welcome to my house. It's just that you can't help but say, "Wow, what's *this*, and why, and what's *that* say"—all these Latin inscriptions and carvings. So, I just thought it [*the lodge*] is less of a distraction.

**DeCurtis:** Well, you know, I really appreciated, incidentally, the kind of focus that you gave that interview because I have this picture book with pictures of both houses in it that I've been showing people at the magazine. First of all, that place is a very comfortable place to do it, and I really liked the idea that we sat down and just *did* it and really just focused right in. I think that that really made the thing have a sort of concentration, rather than wandering through . . .

**Harrison:** The other one is like Disneyland—you need tickets and coupons, and I'll show you this bit.

**DeCurtis:** Right. And it's perfect for that kind of idea we had for that interview, of looking back and all this stuff.

**Harrison:** To get back into this, here . . . there's a twenty-four-track studio in the house. Originally when it was put in it was only sixteen-track, and it's been updated a bit, slowly over the years. So that's where we made the record, and incidentally where I made all my records except for . . . well, all the ones after 1972, except for one album I did at A&M because I was stuck in LA at the time, in 1975.

Anyway . . . so when I'm not really doing record sessions, I still go in there, if I want to write a tune or just record for the fun of it somebody else's tune. I do that occasionally with the drum machine and do it quick, you know, just for the amusement. So I've always been active in the studio and through that period. Plus, the fact that we did have the film company going, plenty of stuff to do there, and there's always been one or two other things that've cropped up, like, for instance, that Carl Perkins TV show and now this Prince's Trust, and little things like that.

**DeCurtis:** The Palomino [*laughs*] . . . [*the club in North Hollywood where Harrison famously jammed the previous February with Bob Dylan, John Fogerty, Taj Mahal, and others —Ed.*]

**Harrison:** I've never really been *retired*. When I say that kind of thing to people, "Oh, I'm retired," [*it's*] just like a "Don't Bother Me" kind of thing. I don't think you ever retire.

**DeCurtis:** One of the things about it, in mentioning that, you've always been a person who's taken such care to keep a private life, to maintain that kind of thing. Does it feel sort of strange to be back in the record company office, sitting down, interviews, tapings? All this business?

**Harrison:** Not really, not really. I feel it's like, sort of, say, somebody who is a fireman, or something, and he doesn't sit around in his fireman suit all of his life. But when he goes to work he puts it on and he goes and gets on his fire engine. It's sort of like that. Once I've done all this bit, I'll walk away and I'm still . . . I mean it's only the moment I'm in Warner Brothers office, or, somebody comes up to me and says, "Hey, will you sign this record," or something, that I'm conscious of being an ex-Beatle and being George Harrison. I don't live my life thinking that I'm this sort of . . . *pop* person. And so I think, now even more so, it's just much easier for me to talk to people. I just talk to them like one human to another. And although that's all superimposed on top of my being, all this past and present, but I just walk away from these interviews and just carry on as if nothing happened.

**DeCurtis:** Mm-hm. [*Laughs.*] It sort of seems like, say, on like "Devil's Radio," there's a feeling of media as something that manipulates things, or that seizes on inessentials and stuff like that. Is that something that you feel real deeply, from a personal standpoint? Or something that you just think is true, and that you've observed?

**Harrison:** Well I've observed it, that kind of "Devil's Radio" stuff. I've *been* it—to a degree. I may still be that. But I haven't consciously thought about it as much since I wrote this song. The song came about because I passed a little church that had a billboard outside. This is in a little country town in England, and they had a billboard on the side of the church saying, GOSSIP: THE DEVIL'S RADIO. DON'T BE A BROADCASTER.

**DeCurtis:** [*Laughs.*] That's great.

**Harrison:** And then I was just thinking, "Yeah, you know" . . . because everybody is doing that, phoning each other up and saying, [*adopts Monty Python-esque matron voice*] "Oh yes, you know, I saw such and such the other day" . . . And, "Oh no, you know, you wouldn't believe it but she's having another baby," and "Oh, they're splitting up and having a divorce" . . . You know, and all this, that, and things that happen that feed back through gossip.

I've always kept away from that a bit because, with my past, I've tended to be one of the people being gossiped about. Although I've had my share of "Oh no, have you seen that guy with his . . ." whatever.

It was just a good vehicle to write a rock 'n' roll song and to say— and to just point out that that's what's happening, because it is such a negative thing that happens. It's such a waste of time and it clouds our lives, and it is like the song says, "It's like a weed, it spreads," and it chokes goodness just by being superimposed upon the top of the truth. It's like a rumor . . .

**DeCurtis:** What about doing "When We Was Fab"? Did you have that song in mind as something you were definitely going to do? Or is that something that just kind of came up when you started working with Jeff?

**Harrison:** Well, during the period in '86—that is to say the period after I had finished that movie that I had done the score to—I went on a trip. I went to Australia, and Jeff Lynne happened to be in Los Angeles at the time, and I said to him, "Look, I'm going to Australia for a bit just to fool about and maybe go to the Grand Prix," because they have the Adelaide Grand Prix in the end of October, early November . . . And I said, "Why don't you come? You'll enjoy it." I just suggested that to him.

So he came down there, and we went to the races and did all that. And then one night, we were going for dinner at somebody's house, and I had this little guitar that somebody had loaned me, and as Jeff, I was waiting for him to get ready, I thought—I don't know why—I just thought that I'd like to write a song like that period, and the first thought I had was . . . I could hear Ringo in my head going, "One! Two!" [*Vocalizes drumming sounds.*] *Dicka-dun, dicka-dun, dicka-dun, dicka-dun . . .*

**DeCurtis:** Oh, yeah, the drums were just amazing.

**Harrison:** I think I was thinking of "Glass Onion." But later, when I checked that song, he doesn't actually do that. He just goes, *duh-dah, duh-dah*, without all these chords, but—

Anyway, that's where it started in my head. I started off the chords, and straight away I got about halfway through the chord sequence for the verse and the string bust, and anyway, then Jeff got ready. We went down to this person's house and there was a piano there. So straight away—I didn't want to lose this, so we got on the piano, started trying to find the chords there on the piano and progress it, and then Jeff got there and joined in on it, and it turned into that verse, the tune. Although, what became the vocal on the top was still a bit vague, it was more just the chords and little bits of melodies that were happening with the bass line on the piano.

We got a cassette and put it on it, just so we would remember it. Later, during the sessions—or just before we started the sessions to do the drum tracks—we started to try and recall that song, and see what was there with it. At that point, I had been writing another song, or trying to, and what is now the bridge of "[*When We Was*] Fab" was this other song I was writing. So that just seemed to fit in okay. We did the basic drum tracks and we did that one, although it was very vague at that time on the chord changes that we wrote.

**DeCurtis:** Is that Ringo playing on that track?

**Harrison:** Yeah. We quickly worked that out before we laid the track down—I got that bridge, and then Jeff figured out all them chords, like where it goes, ". . . take you away," and there's a lot of chord changes there. We laid the drum track down with the piano, I think, and guitar, and I made it later with these sort of sixteen or seventeen tracks that we'd done.

And then we started work on what I thought were . . . would make a good, varied album. And at the same time, the ones that turned out best with the drum tracks—because, you know, there were some songs that will eventually turn out fine but they just didn't come out as good on that day as the ones we chose. And "Fab" was one of these eleven. And we always had this one extra song. We started overdubbing on all the others, and then, every so often we'd say, "Let's just check that one out," and then we'd add a few bits, and then we'd go back to the other stuff. And then we'd get that back out and add another few bits. We were keeping it going so that we'd have the choice at the last minute of which song to ditch to have ten tracks on the album.

That one—it sort of was growing and growing . . . because of the basic thing of it being . . . we called it, incidentally, as a working title—we called it "Aussie" because we were in Australia; that song, you know, we wrote in Australia. So we just put a working title of "Aussie . . Fab," so that we could remember that it was like a Fab [*Four*] song. . . . And so the "Fab" bit sort of stuck, you know, right up until we just had to come up with the lyrics. Then after the engineer went home one night—which is what we sort of did with all the songs that we wrote together—we just had a microphone up in the control room. And then the engineer finished, when we'd finished our serious bit, we'd just have a beer, we'd just sort of sing onto the thing, find which words fit it, and you know, just tried to refine it down, and it [*"When We Was Fab"*] turned out like that. It's got complete joke words.

**DeCurtis:** I know, they're great—as a kind of send-up of that whole thing, too. Did you do the sitar part at the end?

**Harrison:** Yeah.

**DeCurtis:** That's fabulous, that's really great. In terms of this whole year, this whole business of looking back . . .

**Harrison:** The "twenty years ago" bit?

**DeCurtis:** Yeah. Is your sense that there's a genuine understanding of that has emerged out of all this? Does it seem to you to be more like nostalgia, or do you get a sense that people are actually learning something—or *re*learning something?

**Harrison:** Well, maybe both. I think, primarily, it's nostalgia. Because the media, not just with the Beatles twenty years ago, but the media *always*, whether it be five years since something or ten years since . . . We've just had ten years since Elvis died, so we've got all Elvis movies, all nice, old clips of him, never seen, put together into a film, on TV. Or whether it's thirty years or forty years since the Battle of Britain, you know. It's history and they like to—it's a good way of having repeats and filling in time in magazines and on radio and television.

But it's also the people—we all have our nostalgia. Like you said, everybody can remember where they were when the Beatles sang "I Want to Hold Your Hand" on the Ed Sullivan Show. Or I remember where I was when President Kennedy was assassinated. It's all part of our history and our nostalgia.

As to how much it means *now*, I think there's a lot of the young kids who, when this resurgence comes about, are starting to go *back* in time and listen and say, "Hey . . ." I mean maybe ten years ago the Beatles were just like nowhere to those real young kids. And now the new generation latch onto them. My boy is nine, and he just *loves* Chuck Berry—all them old mixes.

**DeCurtis:** Oh, that's great. That one's especially great.

**Harrison:** When I did that Prince's Trust, it was the first time . . . because he's *got* to know a bit about the Beatles. I never pushed that on him and say, "Look who I used to be." So this is the first time he ever saw me hold a guitar on a stage in front of people, and I did my two cute songs—"Here Comes the Sun" and "[*While My*] Guitar Gently Weeps"— and he came back after the show and I said, "What did you think?" He said, "You were good dad, you were good. . . . Why didn't you do 'Roll Over Beethoven,' 'Johnny B. Goode,' and 'Rock and Roll Music'?" And I said, "Aww, I'm sorry."

**DeCurtis:** Had he heard that stuff? Had he heard your versions of that stuff? Or did he just know the Chuck Berry stuff?

**Harrison:** No, I think he's heard . . . I've never consciously sat him down and said, "Listen, here's the old Beatle records," but he's picked up on them because when he was about four or five, *Yellow Submarine*—there's an age group that like *Yellow Submarine*. The kids watch, and they watch it every night for like three months, and then they forget about it. And so he knows, then, songs like "[*Hey*] Bulldog," and all those things to do with that. But Chuck Berry . . .

[*Cassette tape side ends; restarts on other side*]

. . . it was Michael J. Fox I think, who was going to be in *Teenage Were-wolf* or something, and they had "Surfing USA" in the film. Now the kids are all into these Michael J. Fox movies, and he sees it on video, and then he's going around the house singing, "Everybody's gone surfing/ Surfing USA." So the wife digs out the Beach Boys records, so suddenly he's getting into the Beach Boys.

**DeCurtis:** Her California roots?

**Harrison:** Right. And then I said to him, Well, you know, that's really good, there. When you want to hear where that came from and it's, "They're really rocking in Boston . . ."

**DeCurtis:** Right, exactly, "Sweet Little Sixteen."

**Harrison:** "Sweet Little Sixteen"—so then I played him "Sweet Little Sixteen," and he just loved it, so then he wanted me to make him a copy of it, so I put on *all* the good . . .

**DeCurtis:** So you made a Chuck Berry tape for him? Oh, wow.

**Harrison:** I made him a Chuck Berry tape, and he takes it to school with his Walkman. So it's good that everything comes from out of another thing.

**DeCurtis:** This nostalgia thing is coming around again too in different contexts as well. What was your feeling about the Nike commercial, "Revolution" business?

**Harrison:** Well, the thing about it is, in a nutshell, there's all these people who have the rights to everything, or who believe they have the rights to it. It's one thing getting publishing to give you a sync license or whatever of each song, which they do all the time, where they make up their own versions and make it into an ad.

But the fact that the *original master* is used . . . I think we ought to have some say in that, seeing as it was our lives. The complication comes from, I think, the fact that Yoko, when she heard they wanted it, she insisted that it was the Beatle version. And then, the further complication is that Yoko, being now [*acting*] as John's estate—in effect, a cause of the Beatles or Apple—and there's this conflict that's happening [*referring to the ongoing lawsuit to dissolve or restructure Apple —Ed.*].

Plus, the fact that we believe that unless it's restrained—the idea of just handing out Beatle records to become commercials—there's going to be a plethora of . . . I mean, there's going to be four or five hundred ads advertising anything, you know what I mean? Sausage rolls, hamburgers . . . And like, the man, whoever wrote the article—I'm not sure if it was *Time* or *Newsweek*—said at the very end, ". . . And yet it just took somebody three minutes to make John Lennon into a jingle writer."

So we have to try and establish the fact that it's not allowed, plus the fact that if Nike is paying money to Capitol Records, Nike ought to know that we don't get a penny of that. We've got to try and ensure that Capitol don't do this, because they have the rights to sell our records or CDs or whatever. They don't have the rights to use the Beatles and the Beatles name in advertising, and so we have to contest that one.

**DeCurtis:** I guess it was the day before I spoke to you, when I interviewed Paul about it, he was just *livid* about the situation, and especially complicated by his having worked with Michael Jackson and stuff like that. . . .

**Harrison:** Well, I think Paul was very upset—and maybe Michael Jackson would understand, himself, as a songwriter—to suddenly have loss of control of your own songs and to be trying to get them back all the time, and then for somebody who is allegedly your pal, going and now being your . . . whatever happened, I'm not that familiar with it.

**DeCurtis:** Well, evidently . . .

**Harrison:** It's understandable.

**DeCurtis:** Oh, I completely agree. It's also, I think . . . one other point that he made at that time was that he goes, "We were offered everything." He goes, "We could have done any ad—Coca Cola, or Disney, or *all* of them. . . ."

**Harrison:** Absolutely. I mean, the history of the Beatles was we tried to be *tasteful* with our records and with ourselves. And we avoided . . . we could have made millions of extra dollars just to have done all that in the past. But we thought no, it *belittles* the image, or our songs, or whatever.

**DeCurtis:** Well, particularly in that instance, too, a song that had some sort of real context when it came out to be in an ad, was really a little . . .

**Harrison:** As the man said, "Money doesn't speak, it swears."

**DeCurtis:** Yeah, right, exactly.

**Harrison:** Some people seem to do anything for money. They don't have any moral feelings at all.

**DeCurtis:** On your album, the "Wreck of the Hesperus," where you say, "I feel more like Big Bill Broonzy," and all that, are you sort of making fun of perceptions of you, again, as this person retired, in the big house, and sort of removed. . . .

**Harrison:** Well, I don't know if people actually think along the lines of, "Oh well they're all getting old or he's getting old," and like that, but some part of [*the*] time, I've thought that people must be thinking [*something*], because as you do get old yourself it doesn't go exactly unnoticed.

It's just really a funny song. When I started to write the song, I just opened my mouth and it came out, "I'm not the wreck of the Hesperus, I feel more like the Wall of China," and I just continued along that theme. Except to when it gets to the middle eight, and then suddenly I go into a vicious attack on the press! [*Laughter.*]

**DeCurtis:** That's another thing—I remember when I was with you in London and we were talking about the punk thing, I was wondering if that was something that you observed and just didn't like, or if you felt personally indicted by it. Because I always felt like the Beatles were somehow spared, that there were other people that sort of stood as their marks. You guys never seemed to come up in that way, you know? But I was wondering if you felt it or experienced it differently, either in one instance with the press or the other instance with this punk thing, that somehow you or the Beatles or your past was being dismissed or held up for ridicule?

**Harrison:** I think the Beatles were, in many ways. We were loved for one period at a time, and then they hated us, and then they loved us, and then they hated us. And in the history of the Beatles, we went from being the cute, lovable mop tops into being these horrible, weird hippies, and back out of it again. And the press, you know what they tend to do is, you get so big—and not just for the Beatles, they do it all the time, I mean, with anybody; they're doing it in England just last year with this best cricketer that Britain has ever had, this guy [Ian] Botham.

And they put so much praise on you that the only thing left to do is then start knocking you down. So we've been through that, and it got to the point where it didn't even matter even if they had a full broadside on us, they still couldn't really knock us down.

I don't know about what you said about the punk thing. I'm sure some of the punks did have the attitude that everything that went before was just a lot of rubbish. The punk thing I was completely out of it; I was just *gardening* through that period. I just kept my head down, and I'd just see what was going on a bit, but it didn't exactly impress me either musically or as a way of expressing yourself. You're not going to get much joy *ever*, if you just go around kicking people in the teeth or spitting on them. There's a much more subtle way of getting things to your own liking, you know, if that's what they were about: to try and change the situation. But I suppose that's a lot to do with the unemployment and that stuff . . . again, because of that period with unemployment and oil. I think the oil business has a lot to answer to, you know, the way it affected everybody's lives around the world. It was in the '70s wasn't it, when it started happening.

**DeCurtis:** I was wondering if your ideas about touring have altered since the record was done? If your thinking had changed at all, or if you're still thinking that you probably wouldn't?

**Harrison:** Well, put it this way, to jump on the Carl Perkins Show [*the televised concert* Blue Suede Shoes: A Rockabilly Session *broadcast on October 21, 1985, which also featured Eric Clapton, Ringo Starr, Dave Edmunds, and others —Ed.*] with a good bunch of people, doing songs which we all know, is one thing. Same with, say, going on and singing two or three tunes on Prince's Trust with a good backup band who know the tunes.

But to do a tour is hard work. You've got to get your band, find who's going to work for the band, rehearse them, get all these sounds together, the lighting and all the crew, and set up all these dates, and it's such a big—it's like . . . what do they call it, in the army. It's an *invasion*. It's like that, really.

**DeCurtis:** Right, mobilizing or something.

**Harrison:** And so, you can't just do that for a couple of gigs. It's just not justified, I think, three or four gigs with that amount of effort.

So then it means you're on the road, then, for six months—"Oh, well we might as well go to Japan and Australia, and all that." And that . . . I don't know. I'd enjoy moments of it. If you could do that and edit [*together*] all the good bits that I really liked out of it and get back the energy that was spent on the times where we were suffering in some crummy motel someplace, you know?

I do have a feeling that it's much easier as a youth, as a teenager or in your early years. But I'm a forty-four-year-old person now. The ego doesn't really need to have all these people shouting at me or waving at me. But the thrill of being in a band, I've enjoyed that in the past, and I look forward to still doing that occasionally. But to just set up a tour because I made an album, I'm a bit dubious to that, there. I think I'd need a bit more time to figure out, maybe, possibly, to do something with a few friends who are also famous, and make a band like that, so I wouldn't have to do a two-and-a-half-hour show on my own. Maybe I can be in a band that's on for a couple of hours, but I could do one section within that. That would suit me. But again, I'm not sure if I want to go to every little town across the country.

**DeCurtis:** And do five shows a week or something.

**Harrison:** Mm.

**DeCurtis:** One thing, again, that Paul said, at the time that I was talking with him, he was trying to pull together a band and he was thinking about touring, and one thing he was saying—he said, "You know, I never really fully appreciated it or understood it, but with the Beatles it always seemed like we were able to fall in very quickly, that we would start something up, and we'd find a way to make it work." He said it's very difficult to find people to do that with all the time in that way, and he seemed to feel that having gone through the experience, [*it*] made him look back and understand and appreciate that. Did you feel that?

**Harrison:** Well that's true, because we were a little unit on our own, and we grew up together, and we played all our apprenticeship through Liverpool and Germany and all that, working all those clubs and places. So by the time we were out doing the Madison Square Gardens—or, it was actually Shea Stadium and those sort of places—although it was still this little tiny band, we completely understood each other. And if we did change in our recording approaches, that change took place also in our live shows, until it got to the point where we stopped touring.

That, really, is what I was trying to say about working on this album and having Jeff Lynne. It was more, for me, like now I'm back in a group, because we share responsibilities and we share ideas, and ideas snowball off of each other. And, you know, it's just a much nicer thing than having to go on your own or having to find a band who you think is going to . . . and put all that together and be the one person who fronts it all. I don't know if that's the kind of thing that Paul meant. It is—it's tough.

**DeCurtis:** In the course of making the record, did a kind of core band emerge that were on virtually all the tracks?

**Harrison:** Yeah. I always had in mind that when I did this record, I would like to have these proper drummers, and more or less do it like I did it in the late '60s, early '70s, which is to say [Jim] Keltner and Ringo. Those two are perfect. Jim is a very great session drummer, and he's always kept ahead of or up to the technology, so Jim could just as well sit down on his drum kit and play whatever you need. At the same time, if you want to have a machine play it, Jim can play that machine like nobody else, *and* make it sound like real drums. I mean, he's called the "Stenographer of Soul."

**DeCurtis:** [*Laughs.*] That's great.

**Harrison:** Ringo, on the other hand, is like, I feel, myself with the guitar. I don't play it that often, I don't practice—I use it as a tool to write tunes or to make recordings. Ringo may not play the drums from one year to the next, but when he picks up his sticks and gets his drum skins tightened right, he'll just *rock*, and play just like he played in those days. Like "Fab" for instance, those little fills are pure Ringo. . . .

**DeCurtis:** I know! His style—I mean, your style as a player too, I think, are so recognizable. They're real distinct—like the way that you would think of somebody's voice being distinct. There's a real personal expression to it that is marked by the two of you.

**Harrison:** So the basis of the album is to get it so it sounds like a band, and although it's recorded now, it still has a feel of how the records used to be before all these MIDI-ed things and drum machines and all that kind of stuff. Because personally, although there's many records that are really good like that, it's not my favorite sound. I still prefer all the old stuff.

**DeCurtis:** Oh, when you were saying about your son liking the sound of those Chuck Berry records, again—not to sound like a Luddite or something because obviously people can get real hip sounds now and they're good—but still, there's something to that *roomy* kind of sound that those records have that are [*sic*] just incredible.

**Harrison:** I think it's gone crazy really, with what people can do these days. They just switch on a machine, an emulator, and they hit a button and they've got a huge orchestra. But it's not *really* . . . Although it is a real orchestra sample, it's still not the same as having string players in the studio. It lacks that human feel. Like in the early '60s, when we got a Mellotron—OK, we used it on "Strawberry Fields," and basically that was the one. But once you used it and everybody else gets them, you can pick them out a mile [*away*], and they're already finished. Like in the early '70s, it was string ensemble synthesizers, and everybody had these strings playing block chords, which are really horrible sounding. It may be good, the first person who ever happens to get a hold of it and use it, OK. But once the masses get it, it's dead and gone. And I think that's the same with all this MIDI, DX7 stuff.

Everything's become so dependent on sampled sounds. I don't mind sampled sounds, but rather than find one that's already in there [*referring to synthesizer presets and the like —Ed.*]—and this is a great thing about Jeff. Say we wanted to sample a snare drum sound, and this is something Keltner pointed out as well. This is the difference between the "now" kind of consciousness where you get this drum sound, put it in your machine, and then you save it onto your disc. This is what Jim and all these engineers and millions of people will do.

With Jeff, he just gets a good drum sound, say a specific snare drum sound, and he'll use that. And then, he doesn't have Keltner saying to him, "You mean you don't have a disc drive on your drum machine? What happens when you want to use it again?" He said, "I don't use it again, I'll make another one." And I like that idea, I like that approach. Everything, then, is . . .

**DeCurtis:** Fresh.

**Harrison:** Fresh, yeah. Otherwise, you've got people who now are just copying sounds off everybody else's records, and it becomes like . . . washing-up liquid [*indistinct*].

**DeCurtis:** How active have you been with the film company while you've been immersed in making your record? How does your involvement there evolve when you're doing something like this?

**Harrison:** Now the company is rolling along really well. We've got a lot of competent people in the company, and I can choose whether I want to go in and do stuff every day and go to the shoots and go to the edits and go to the sessions to overdub the music. Or I can just stay completely away and wait until they've got a rough cut of the film and then go down and make my comments about it, you know, "I think that bit doesn't work" or whatever, or just, "That's quite nice." I can be as much in or out of as

I like. So during the making of this album I just went down to the studio a couple of times really to see the director [*Jack Clayton*] making this film with Bob Hoskins and Maggie Smith; this is a new one. It's just been . . .

**DeCurtis:** Oh really? What's it called?

**Harrison:** It's called *The Lonely Passion of Judith Hearne.* It's a sort of serious film set in Dublin in about the '50s, I think, and it's a lot to do with her loneliness through the Catholicism thing, the *fear* of God and all that. It's two great actors, and it's a pure performance sort of film, what you would call maybe an "art film." And so I will just visit the set—and it's nice to see the sets and the technicians and all that, so I'm not totally out of touch. There's other people from HandMade Films who are always there, but again because I'm so involved with it that I think it's good when they get to see me too, and know that I *am* and [*I'm*] not totally out of it.

This film that's doing rather well in America at the moment called *Withnail*—

**DeCurtis:** Oh, God! I haven't seen it yet. My girlfriend went to see it last week, and she just loved it.

**Harrison:** Well, that film was just completed around the time we started working on the record. And I went out there to comment about the edits, and then I was in Los Angeles when they had the first showing to our distributors. I'll attend whatever I can, but if I'm doing something else that will take priority. As I said, there's good people in there now. We get so many scripts now. I hate reading scripts, but what I'll do is send them into the office; various people in the office will read the scripts, and if a couple of them happen to like it, then they'll Xerox it and give them back out. Everybody will get a copy, and at that point I'll read it if they are keen on it.

Ray Cooper, who plays drums on one track and percussion on the other, he works full time at HandMade Films. So again, he's my eyes and ears in that. I'm actually more in touch with day-to-day procedure than I would be if Ray wasn't there. And also, being an artist, a musician . . . Because I think there's a good balance there between the business side and the artist side, and I think that's what helps this company being owned by a businessman and a musician. And, for me, Ray does a great job in there. For the directors and the actors, it's nice for them to know that it's not just this faceless money coming . . .

**DeCurtis:** Yeah, investor, or something. All the films that you've made and that you've been talking about have a particular kind of character. *Shanghai Surprise* is sort of like . . .

**Harrison:** The joker in the pack . . .

**DeCurtis:** [*Laughs.*] Kind of, yeah. What was it that you were hoping would happen there?

**Harrison:** Well, sometimes projects come along which are already packaged. Most of the stuff we do, or say fifty percent of what we do, we get involved in the very early stage when maybe there's a first draft screenplay. And if it's interesting we'll go with the writer of the screenplay [*and*] develop that to a point where it's given the approval to go ahead, and then they start . . .

**DeCurtis:** It was an interesting point you made, incidentally, when we were in England; you were talking about doing the work up front. . . .

**Harrison:** Right. So, there's all this preproduction work, which, like— we've still got some films which have been in the works for three or four years, and they're still hoping to see the light of day, maybe next year. So, basically, say fifty percent will come to us and be developed within the company with the writer, or writer-director, and pick up the actors who's [*sic*] going to be in it down the line, and it gets made.

Then, with a lot of other films, somebody will come to us with the screenplay, the director, and maybe even some of the cast—or the producer and the director. And then it's a matter of, again, whether we think it would work. Like for instance, *Mona Lisa*—Neil Jordan, who wrote that screenplay.

**DeCurtis:** Actually, I met him one time when I was doing a story on U2, because he did a video with them. He's a real nice guy.

**Harrison:** Yeah, very good, very talented. He'd already been to HandMade Films a year before we took it on, and, uh—

[*Door opens; muffled voice of assistant speaking.*]

**DeCurtis:** OK, we'll wrap in about fifteen minutes?

**Assistant:** OK . . .

**DeCurtis:** Is that OK with you, George?

**Harrison:** Yeah—oh, [*to assistant*] what happened about the photographer?

**Assistant:** [*Indistinct.*]

**Harrison:** He's here?

**Assistant:** He's here.

**Harrison:** Oh good. Thanks, that's great.

**Assistant:** Oh yeah, he was here all the time . . .

**Harrison:** Because they kept saying they wanted . . . Oh, I did meet him when I came in, but they kept saying they wanted me to go to Hollywood, or somewhere, for the picture?

**Assistant:** Well, he thought we weren't going to have enough room to do it here . . .

**Harrison:** Do you mind if we just stop for a moment, while I [*indistinct*] . . .

**DeCurtis:** Oh, go right ahead.

[*Tape stops; restarts.*]

**DeCurtis:** You were saying about Neil Jordan.

**Harrison:** Right. He came into HandMade with *Mona Lisa* a year before we did it, but, at that point, the decision that our company made was that it was too expensive. We have to watch our budgets and how expensive things are, because that's a large reason for why we've been able to keep going, because we've made low-budget movies, basically, anyway. So it was considered too expensive, and I think he took that film all over the place, and nobody wanted to do it. And then he came back to us and we sat down, and somebody in the office worked out with Neil certain cuts in the screenplay, and then we got a lower budget and we agreed to do it.

And I think even after that that the film came in under budget as well. That kind of thing happens—where it's a total package. He'd already got Bob Hoskins lined up for it. So really, it just comes into our company and we set it in motion.

Same thing was with *Shanghai Surprise*. The director and the producer already had it [*together*], and it was talked about whether to do it or not. And they started, they thought, well, if it was done in a certain way it may be quite interesting, and then somebody thought [*of*] the idea of Madonna being in it, I don't know who, and the producer reckoned he knew Sean Penn because he'd done other films with him. At that time, it seemed, well, maybe if that kind of thing happened with Madonna, it may be worth doing. And it got to about one day away from being scrapped—I thought *forget it*—and then we got a call saying, "Oh, Madonna is going to be in this film!" So, the decision was made by [*HandMade partner*] Denis O'Brien, "OK, well, I think let's do it."

But it was the first time we had ever been involved with companies from Hollywood and . . . it was also the first film that had such a big budget. Anyway, the rest, really, is history—with all the stuff that went down, during it and around it. The film really was doomed even before it was finished being made, largely by the press that had preceded it. Again, if that film had come in our early years of HandMade Films, it probably would have broke us, but as we got ourselves to a position where we could sell our movies anyway, and we had deals for them, we got back the cost of the film just in our deals. So, we didn't go bankrupt. . . . Lucky, really.

**DeCurtis:** [*Laughs.*] Really, it kind of seemed like such an odd—

**Harrison:** But it taught us—it taught us a lesson.

**DeCurtis:** I'm sure it did! You've been so successful both commercially and artistically with the other kinds of things that you've done, it just does [*seem like*] this odd one in the pack. . . .

**Harrison:** Yeah, although when I look at that film, I'd just love to be left alone with that film for a couple of months, and it could be the most hysterical thing ever. [*DeCurtis laughs.*] If you wanted to totally make it into like a cult joke movie, it could be—because it did have some good moments to it, but there were so many things about it which were just ridiculous. . . . Anyway, that's a thing of the past.

**DeCurtis:** Let me ask you one other thing—and I'll try to ask this in a way that doesn't make it sound as banal as it's going to, or trying to trivialize a complex thing—but I think one of the things that you're known for and that's been a real part of you are [*sic*] your spiritual beliefs and that whole component of things. Where is that now? I mean, if you could say, you know, "This is what I think about, or how that's all sort of shaken out for me."

**Harrison:** Well, it's still very much there. But I think to just sum it up, it's probably when I was younger and with the aftereffects of the LSD, that sort of . . . opened up something inside me—1966, I'm going back to—it made this flood of other thoughts and situations came [*sic*] into my head, which led me into India with yogis. I just *had* to know about the yogis, the Himalayas, and then this Indian music, that whole bit.

Well, at that time, it was very much my desire to *find out* what it was—and it still is, although I have found out a lot and gone through the period of questioning and being answered, and I think I've got to the point where there isn't anything, really, that I need to know. The only thing I need is to develop my experience that I got from all of that, and have more, deeper experiences. And likewise, in those early days, everything was . . . all this energy was *going*, and the hippie thing and everybody was saying, "Hey man, listen to *this*, and listen to *that*," and the Beatles were watched with microscopes, as it says in the song: "the microscopes that magnified the tears, studied warts and all."

But as I got a bit older and whatever, the time that's elapsed, it's like [*what*] somebody I read once said: "Be like the wise ant that goes through the grains of sand and picks out the grains of sugar." And, I think, I have no regrets of hanging out with Maharishi Mahesh Yogi, because he gave me the vehicle by which I can just close my eyes and then go into a deep peace.

I had spent a lot of time with some other people in India who were just obscure, like Ravi Shankar's spiritual master, who he had. He died a long time ago now, but I had the pleasure of meeting him and the pleasure of meeting this guy called Sathya Sai Baba, who is a brilliant Indian yogi.

**DeCurtis:** Could you spell that?

**Harrison:** It's spelled S-A-T-Y-A, "Satya," and then "Sai," S-A-I, dash, "Baba," B-A-B-A. And he's very well known around the world, but he never travels out of India. People go to see him. He's reputed to do miracles and all this kind of stuff and, actually, I've experienced it. He did one right in front of my eyes.

**DeCurtis:** What happened?

**Harrison:** Well, a very, very simple thing. I mean, he just does things to make people *realize* or believe in him, but he materializes this stuff called *vibhuti*. It's like, V-I-B-H-U-T-I, I think it's spelled. What *vibhuti* is, is like the ash—you know, when you burn incense or something like that, it leaves this gray ash with a sort of sweet smell. Well, he just materializes that. It's sort of symbolic—fire was always symbolic, and ash, as a purification process.

I first heard about him in the early '60s, in India, when one of his devotees had a photograph of him on the wall, and this stuff called *vibhuti* started forming all over the picture."

**DeCurtis:** Oh, wow.

**Harrison:** And I went to the place and saw it myself, and it was just all over . . . [*Indistinct.*] He was reputed to be the reincarnation of this other saint, who was called Sai Baba [*of Shirdi*], and he's also said he would come back again, after this incarnation, called Prema Sai.

You can believe this if you like or not, but to me, just his *singing*—because I was present at one of these outdoor—it's called *bhajan*, B-H-A-J-A-N, which are the devotional songs that [*indistinct*] sing—and he is a great singer. And his control over the crowd, and the way he walked through that crowd—he just was *gliding*. He's such a very small man, real stocky, well built, *little*, and he's got that famous big afro hairstyle. And he came and he did this thing in front of me; he just put his hand out—he doesn't have any sleeves, like short, very short sleeves—and just put his hand in my hand, he just waved his hand about like that and put his fingers on there, and this *vibhuti* just came out of his fingertips.

**DeCurtis:** Wild . . .

**Harrison:** Now, I saw that. There's [*sic*] all kinds of other stories about him, but that really isn't the important thing. What he's doing is teaching in hospitals and universities and he's trying to educate children in the old spiritual way, and he's doing a fantastic job. I had the pleasure to meet him.

I spent a lot of time with the guru who started the [*indistinct*] Radha Krishna temple—a lot of the time with him, he's called A.C. Bhaktivedanta Swami [*also known as Sri Prabhupada —Ed.*]. And he was a *great* old man. He was really very, very pure. He organized all these things and accumulated millions of devotees, but he was very simple. All he'd ever do, he'd just sit there and hold conversation. He knew, in Sanskrit, the Bhagavad Gita and the Upanishads and the Vedas. He knew them all word for word and understood what they meant. He was a great man, and I think, like somebody has said, just a *moment* in the company of a divine person is a great benefit.

And I believe that, but it's how to know who is and who isn't. It's having discretion. The first yogi that I ever read, who really influenced me, was called Vivekananda—he was the very first Swami who came to America, to the West, in the late 1800s. And Vivekananda's name means—*vivek* means discretion, and *ananda* means bliss, so "blissful discretion." I think I noticed something about what Keith Richards said: "I'm pleased I'm the only one to never have kissed Maharishi's feet. . . ." Well, I never kissed Maharishi's feet, but it was certainly a pleasure to be with him at that time.

Again, it's all part of the process of going through the sand and looking for the grains of sugar. And so, to end all that up, to try and resolve that, is that, maybe in my youth I was more exuberant about it. Now, I have more experience of it, and it's inside of me. I don't talk about it that much.

**DeCurtis:** When you would meet them what would you say? Was it very casual, or was it, like, "What does life mean?" Or was it just more like, you know, "This is what I'm thinking about?" or "what do you think about that?"

**Harrison:** You can either just go meditate with them, or with Maharishi, whom we spent quite a lot of time with, he just became, like, your mate, just some guy who had a certain amount of knowledge that he could pass onto you of how to get rid of stress and strain. Basically, that is one of the things he was teaching: how to help people with their day-to-day stress and strain.

And with Maharishi, we talked to him about everything really. I remember once saying to him, in the early stages, feeling this guilt for having the material possessions. I was saying, "Well, we've got all these motorcars and stuff, what do you think about that?" I mean, a lot of conversations were like one person to another and they're just a lot of fun really, and he'd just laugh. He'd say, [*adopts a higher-pitched voice*] "Hee hee *hee*, you should have *two* motorcars; if one breaks down you've got another one and you can still go where you're going!"

What I realized over the years is that it's not *what* you own, it's how *attached to it* you are. And I think the danger is when you become attached obsessively to each other, even to your own body, or to your wealth, your motorcars, your fame and your fortune. It's to be *unattached* to it, but you still can *experience* it. It's all part of life's experience.

And so, now it's just more and more subtle with me, and I keep it more to myself. Like Christ said somewhere in the Bible, "If you're going to pray, go in a cupboard quietly on your own, but don't do it on the street corner." I mean, I see these people—I thought [*just*] from England—and I read these pieces about all these holy rollers who got arrested and whatever. But I come back to L.A. and switch the TV on, and they're *still* on there, those idiots. Some guy called O.C. Jaggers [*Harrison seems to be referring to Orval Lee Jaggers —Ed.*] talking about the "golden altar." And he keeps reading the same bit out of this passage from the Bible and saying, [*adopts a droning voice*] "And God said, 'If you love me, if you have a have a golden altar, you're going to make it.'" You know, and it's, like, *completely* missing any sort of mystical or subtle point out of what's going on.

**DeCurtis:** There's like no spirituality to that stuff *at all*. Nothing at all.

**Harrison:** Just like people didn't like maybe Maharishi or whatever, and the reason why I'm not with him now or I'm not with the Krishna temple now, I still respect them for what they're doing and for what I got from them. But all these kind [*sic*] of organizations, they're too busy shouting about stuff, or they get too entangled. It's the same with . . . "Christianity," as they call it, or Roman . . . you know, the Catholics. [*When*] I was born, my mother was a Catholic, my father wasn't. I was sort of brought up for about ten years as a Catholic. I look at that stuff now and I think, "What is going on?"

You just take a look at that book called *In God's Name* by David Yallop [*1984*], it's called, and you find out about all this stuff that's going on in the Catholic Church, where they launder all the money from the Mafia and the drug money. And this guy who's been hiding out, the Pope's roadie, he's from Chicago, Archbishop Marcinkus; now they've been waiting for three or four years, trying to get him out of Vatican City to question him about the million, billion dollars, the missing billion dollars, and the death of [*Ambrosiano Overseas bank chairman Roberto*] Calvi and [*Mafia-connected financier Michele*] Sindona, you know, and all those people. It's horrendous. And yet the Pope is out there kissing the ground and waving. He's out, like . . . a promo . . .

**DeCurtis:** . . . in the popemobile . . .

**Harrison:** [*Adopts a stern, jaded voice.*] "OK, look, we've gotta . . . they're getting a bit heavy with us about all these murders. Get a new pope, get him out there, wave a bit, and see if we can distract them." But I'd like to ask the Pope, "What do you think Christ meant when he said, 'Let thine eye be single' and 'thy body full of light.'" What the hell does he think that means? You know, it just annoys me.

The only God we need is within ourselves. It's handy if we can crawl through the grains of sand—or the . . . mountains of garbage—and find some little bit of truth or a guide, somebody who can help us to reach within ourselves and find what *is* within ourselves.

[*Tape ends.*]

# MAGAZINE INTERVIEW

**Elaine Dutka | August 25, 1987 | Interview Transcript**

Harrison did not do many interviews on his film-world experience. The handful he did focused on HandMade Films, the company he created in 1978, partnering with his business manager Denis O'Brien. It was initially set up to fund the controversial *Life of Brian*, the Monty Python comedy EMI Films had abandoned. The success of that relatively low-budget film financed another rescue: the critically acclaimed *The Long Good Friday* (1980), actor Bob Hoskins's cinematic breakthrough, which was followed by Terry Gilliam's *Time Bandits* the year after.

Subsequent films such as 1986's noir-ish crime drama *Mona Lisa* and the quirky *Withnail and I* a year later further bolstered the HandMade brand. In an era when British cinema was dominated by polished Merchant Ivory period pieces, HandMade served up edgy, offbeat fare no one else would touch. By 1987, the upstart company had left its mark, receiving the *London Evening Standard* award for contribution to the nation's film industry.

In August of that year, Harrison sat down with Elaine Dutka, *Time* magazine's West Coast Show Business Correspondent who went on to cover film and the arts for the *Los Angeles Times* and *National Public Radio*. She was on assignment for the highly regarded movie and culture publication *Film Comment*. The two of them met in the Burbank, California offices of Warner Bros. Records, Harrison's label at the time. Sporting a black bomber jacket with "eros" and "erotica" embroidered on the front, the forty-five-year-old, in a candid, hour-long interview, addressed topics ranging from his risky leap into the movie business to the challenge of carving out a post-Beatles life. (The following Q-and-A expands the published interview, incorporating new material from the transcript.)

The conversation came at a good time for Harrison. The "Krishnas," as he called them, were his anchor. He and his second wife, Olivia, were raising their nine-year-old son Dhani. *Cloud Nine*, his first solo album in six years, had just been certified platinum.

"After years of financial, legal, and personal battles, he seemed balanced and serene," recalls Dutka. "It was remarkable that any of the remaining ex-Beatles had any brain cells left or a sense of humor, he conceded . . . and that his battle with cigarettes was ongoing." Harrison admitted he didn't like reading scripts and, though he was on top of the movie operation, bristled at the notion of an office job. His goal was to make movies he liked with people he liked in a no-frills, artist-friendly setting. It was O'Brien who caught the entrepreneurial "bug," he said, the desire to make it big. The $17 million *Shanghai Surprise* (1986), starring the tempestuous honeymooners Madonna and Sean Penn, had proven to be a disastrous detour—a bite into Hollywood's poisonous apple. While increasing the number of films in production made it easier to land distribution deals, O'Brien's ambition put the company in a financial bind and diluted the quality of its offerings.

"Even in '87, Harrison had misgivings," Dutka observes. "He hoped O'Brien wouldn't turn out to be a 'madman' and bankrupt him, he told me—only half in jest."

But that's what happened. Because O'Brien didn't put his name on the bank loans as promised, Harrison soaked up the flops alone. Personally betrayed and short on cash, he sued his partner and, in 1996, won a grueling legal battle. HandMade Films was another victim. Sold to Canada's Paragon Entertainment in the mid-'90s, it never recaptured its luster. By then, Harrison had turned his back on movie-making—a relic of his past. —Ed.

**Elaine Dutka:** You costarred in three films as a Beatle. Now you've surfaced on the other side of the camera. How did it happen?

**George Harrison:** Purely by accident. An English company had backed out of the Monty Python film *Life of Brian* in pre-production. And the guys, friends of mine, asked me whether I could think of a way to help them get the film made. I asked Denis O'Brien, who had been my business manager since the end of '73. After thinking about it for a week, he came back and suggested that *we* produce it.

I let out a laugh because one of my favorite films is *The Producers*, and here we were about to become Bialystock and Bloom. Neither of us had any previous thought of going into the movie business, though Denis had a taste of it managing Peter Sellers and negotiating some of the later *Pink Panther* films. It was a bit risky, I guess, totally stepping out of line for me, but, as a big fan of Monty Python, my main motive was to see the film get made.

**Dutka:** When did you realize this was going to be more than a one-shot venture?

**Harrison:** Denis got a bug for it. And the Pythons, as individuals, were all writing scripts. Terry Gilliam presented us with this brilliant idea, which turned into *Time Bandits*. Michael Palin had done a BBC-TV series, *Ripping Yarns*, a series of 30-minute films, and I once mentioned to him that, if he ever wanted to write a big *Ripping Yarn*, it would be just great. So he did. He also made *A Private Function*, an hysterical little Alan Bennett film that did really well in England. I don't know why it didn't take off in the US. Maybe we should rerelease it now. Anyhow, one thing led to another, and our films just kept happening.

**Dutka:** After spending your life as a performer, does it feel strange to be wearing another hat?

**Harrison:** In a way. When I was acting, there was always the feeling that the artists were the clever ones who do everything—and then there were these horrible people who put the money up and don't know anything. Everyone subscribed to that old Hollywood myth that executive producers hate everything and chop everything up after you've done it. When they'd walk into a studio, it would be, "Look out, lads, here comes 'The Money,'" with everybody cringing at those fat cats. So it is sort of funny being a simple musician who's now a producer or—inverted commas— "The Money." I can see it from both sides. It's nice to let people have as much artistic freedom as possible, but I'm the one who has to pay back the bank. If they want total freedom, they have to get their own money and make their own films. It has to be a give-and-take. But I think we're quite reasonable.

**Dutka:** Does film now take precedence over music in your professional life?

**Harrison:** Fortunately, I haven't had to choose. Last year I spent most of my time doing the record [*Cloud Nine*]. Once I committed to it, I went into the studio and spent all the time needed to get it done. HandMade Films now has a good, competent staff of about 35 people who seem to know what they're doing. If filmmaking becomes a chore for me, I don't want to do it. I can choose how involved I want to be, or I can step back away from it and separate. That way, I can enjoy it more.

Going out and making business deals isn't me. If I had to, I'd soon want to get rid of the entire company. Denis is the business person. He does that. I know all the projects we're working on and who's doing them, and I don't have to be there. I'm not looking for an office job. I just pop in on films a couple times to see how things are going. I never intended to be [*legendary film producer*] David Puttnam.

**Dutka:** Three films: *The Missionary, The Lonely Passion of Judith Hearne, Bellman and True*. All very different from each other, on the face of it. Is there a common thread?

**Harrison:** With the exception of *Shanghai Surprise*, which was a big disaster—and the only expensive "Hollywood"-kind-of-attitude project we got involved with—all of our films seem to be films nobody else will do. No one would go near *Life of Brian*. *The Long Good Friday* was a pickup that had been shelved by the owners. It was the same company, by the way, that had turned down *Life of Brian*. They wanted to cut it and put it on television, while we put it out in the form that the producers, actors, and director had visualized. It's a great little British gangster movie. Critics said they hadn't seen a performance as good since Edward G. Robinson. And it was true. Bob Hoskins was fabulous.

**Dutka:** If Denis O'Brien handles most of the business affairs, do you take primary responsibility for the creative end?

**Harrison:** There are so many scripts coming in now. And, personally, I hate reading them. But a guy on staff named Ray Cooper serves as my ears. He's also a musician, a percussion-and-drums player for Elton John, and I know I can rely on his being sensitive to the artistic side of things. There's always a conflict between the "business," what people see as the brutal business aspect, and the "artistic" side. Since I've been an "artist"—make sure you put that in inverted commas—and have Ray there all the time, it eases the problem a bit. If a couple of people on the staff all happen to like the same screenplay, then copies go out and everybody reads them and decides whether we'll do it or not. I suppose

Denis and I have the final say, but it's rather a committee system. It takes a number of people to like a script before the red light turns to amber.

**Dutka:** Are you happy, on the whole, with the direction the company is taking?

**Harrison:** There are certain things I don't like that always crop up into films. I hate all the violence. I don't mind a few explosions for a laugh, or when it's "integral to the story." But the whole *Rambo* situation, with films where people just want to see others getting their heads blown off, I hate that. What we've released isn't necessarily a reflection of the films I've liked best, of course.

It's a funny business. Some films we've developed for three, four, five years have still not seen the light of day. We'd set them up and the director would drop out. Then, when a new director the actors approve of is lined up, one of the stars has got to go and make his other movie. By the time we replace him, another guy is gone. That kind of situation you learn to live with. And then there are films like *Powwow Highway*, in post-production right now, that go "Number One with a Bullet." It came through my mailbox just a couple of months ago, and we're making it straightaway. Like I said, funny business.

**Dutka:** Is it getting any easier these days?

**Harrison:** Somewhat. With the first batch of films we made we had our own money absolutely on the line—all the bank loans—and it was very hard for Denis to get distribution deals. We may have even finished a movie only to find we couldn't line up a distributor. Now we've got a little bit of charisma going for the company, enough success for people to think, "Well maybe they are serious," and a lot of people who've worked on HandMade Films who've had an enjoyable time. All that has slowly built to the point where, on a business level, it's become slightly easier for Denis, and it's made us want to do more movies.

From my point of view, expanding our production schedule is much riskier. But from his perspective, it's easier to do a deal with someone to distribute ten movies than one. Much harder to do separate deals for each movie. We're also able to get good directors and good actors now because our reputation is getting better all the time. Still, it's sort of frightening when you start a movie and you see all the people you're employing. It's quite a big responsibility. If I was to think about that, I'd panic. I wouldn't want to be involved. I have a sort of kamikaze side to me that is optimistic, and in some ways I have to trust Denis's business sense and hope he's not going to bankrupt me.

**Dutka:** At this point, are you still putting your own money on the line?

**Harrison:** I do put quite a lot into every film. But not like when we started with *Time Bandits* and *Life of Brian*. For our first film, we put our office building, my house, and all our bank accounts—like a pawn shop—into the hands of the bank that was going to loan us the money. It was lucky the film paid off. We paid back the loan and put anything left over into the next one. Out of fifteen films, we've had only three failures—four if you count *Shanghai*. But *Shanghai* was a failure only from an artistic point of view. We didn't lose any money since enough time has elapsed for us to be able to negotiate a more secure kind of deal upfront.

**Dutka:** With more than $50 million invested in production right now, HandMade has, obviously, turned the corner. Just how solid are you?

**Harrison:** We're OK. Though, with all this money tied up, the cash flow does get a bit shaky. It's a matter of timing, being able to avoid getting caught short. A few of our films brought us back more than we expected, which helped us to pay off the flops. Things have been handled well on the business side, managed on a shoestring. We're very penny-pinching, in a way, trying to adopt a sensible approach—not many free limos. And we try to edit the scripts so that we're not shooting footage that's going to end up on the floor. If we continue on our current path, we're poised to make a few dollars somewhere down the road.

**Dutka:** Why have other British film production companies had such a hard time managing to keep their heads above water?

**Harrison:** Basically, because it's hard to get the money. Goldcrest was the big one over here. But all you need is one film like *Revolution* to go that much over budget and fail, and it sort of wipes you out. We were fortunate that the deal Denis set up for *Shanghai Surprise* made sure that it didn't do us in. My understanding is that the cost of the film was covered in all the distribution deals. Once we delivered the film, we got back enough money to cover the budget so, even if the film was a flop, we were OK. If that happened to us back in 1980 or '81, we probably would have gone the same way as most of the others.

**Dutka:** With a budget of more than $15 million and a temperamental, high-profile husband-and-wife team, *Shanghai Surprise* was a tremendous departure for you, financially and aesthetically. Why did you give it a go?

**Harrison:** I was dubious from the first. I get afraid by things like that. And a lot of others at HandMade didn't want to make that film. Denis, himself, was just a couple of days away from just shelving the whole thing when suddenly the producer informed us that Madonna and Sean had agreed to be in it. At that time, it sounded like a good idea. But when we went ahead with it, it proved to be very painful for most of the people involved—the technicians as much as anyone, because of the attitudes of the actors. It was like "Springtime for Hitler" in *The Producers*: we got the wrong actors, the wrong producer, the wrong director. Where . . . did . . . we . . . go . . . right? It wasn't easy, but I was determined not to let it get me depressed.

**Dutka:** Cannon Films suffered a similar fate when it paid Stallone $12 million for *Over the Top*.

**Harrison:** Sure. We have to keep tabs on our budgets and not get carried away thinking we're big shots. Many companies, with some success behind them, move into big, posh, air-conditioned offices that all interconnect with private bathrooms. You see them swarming around in these limousines. It's "Sod's Law": Even if we made hundreds of millions of dollars, once we moved out of our tiny, overcrowded office in London and got into the Big Time, I'm sure the bottom would fall out. The answer is to be humble. That's it. Be humble. It would be nice, I suppose, from a staff point of view, to have a bit more space—our own viewing theaters, cutting rooms, and sound studios. But for me, as an ex-Beatle, I'm not into that trip of being a big shot. I peaked early. I got all that out of my system in the '60s.

**Dutka:** Part of Disney's current success is due to the stable of actors it has signed in what some see as a return to the old studio system. Are you making a conscious effort to do the same?

**Harrison:** It's not an out-and-out strategic move, though we have worked with the same people a number of times. Bob Hoskins, of course, is one of them. He was the main reason *Mona Lisa* was so successful.

We said, "He's done good for us. We've all enjoyed him. Let's let him direct his own film." We take a little chance here and there, calculated risks, not only because he's good but because he's a joy to be with. His charm is that no matter how famous and popular he is, he's so straight and down-to-earth. He makes the Seans and Madonnas look ridiculous. We've also had the pleasure of working with Michael Caine, Sean Connery—"name people" who go about doing their roles. They're not as complicated. They're very professional.

**Dutka:** Were you involved in the music end of things?

**Harrison:** I got really involved with the musical end of *Shanghai*. That was another reason why it was personally sad for me. I'd plugged so much of my own time into it. I worked with a guy who scored movies before, Michael Kamen, who'd done *Brazil* with Terry Gilliam. I worked with him because it's too much for me to take on. I'm not going to write millions of violin parts, conducting orchestras. That's not my idea of having fun. He'd do that kind of stuff, and I'd put in some funny little things that appeared. I also did a couple of songs for *Water* and one for *Time Bandits*.

**Dutka:** Your first American productions, *Five Corners*, will be released in January, and the majority of your current projects bear the US stamp. Is this part of a larger effort to get a foothold over here?

**Harrison:** That isn't my idea, but I think it could be Denis's; he's interested in broadening the base. I, personally, would not like to see HandMade Films turn into an American company in New York or Los Angeles. I like it being in a nice little office in England. When we named the company, it was going to be called British HandMade Films, but for some reason the government registrar or whoever's responsible for company names wouldn't let us call it "British." I think you have to have lost millions and millions of pounds before they let you call it "British"—British Leyland, British Rail. Other than that, I can't see why they'd turn us down. I like to have American actors and directors. We're not closed to anything, really. But I wouldn't like us to become some big, swanky American company. At that point, I'd probably bail out.

**Dutka:** But aren't Denis O'Brien's instincts on target? Isn't the American market as important to the film business as it is to the recording industry?

**Harrison:** Of course. To really make it, you have to have some success in America—in film and in records. You can sell all you like in England and France and Switzerland. But you need a big response in the American market to pay the bills, to pay back the money and make the thing work. The turning point for our company came in the last year or two, when some of the films we made strictly as low-budget projects got accepted in America. *Mona Lisa* was one. *Withnail and I* was another—which came as something of a shock. I really enjoy the film, personally, but thought there wasn't a snowball's chance of the American people getting this kind of humor. The jokes seem very English to me. I'm glad to say I was wrong about that.

We've always been told that Americans want things to happen, Crash! Bang! Wallop!, and want a film to be paced quickly. You get so terrified when there's actually dialogue going on and people have to use their brains and listen. We've tried to give people credit for wanting to see a film with some kind of plot, dialogue, depth, and were pleasantly surprised that there are Americans who don't mind working a bit—particularly given all the competition these days. Someone told me that 170 films were released between last August and Christmas in America alone. A few years ago, you could put a film in a theater in the U.S. and let it build on word-of-mouth. Now if you put a film out on Friday and it hasn't grossed a certain amount of money by Saturday night, it's gone. It's ruthless—even more ruthless than the record business.

**Dutka:** What projects have you got in the works?

**Harrison:** We have a comedy called *How to Get Ahead in Advertising*, about a fellow who wakes up with this great boil on his head and it sort of takes on its own personality. We're going to do Stephen Berkoff's *Kvetch*. We have great hopes for *TVP*, a film with David Stewart of the Eurythmics, who also conceived it. It's about a little planet in outer space where everything has gone under from too much machinery. It's like a little children's thing, brilliant ideas in which the characters are actually musical instruments. They all plug into each other and can play together. Basically animation, but there are some people in it, as well. Because HandMade Films is this warm, little, friendly company, Dave, as a musician, can work better with us. Nicolas Roeg directed *Track 29*, a psychological thriller starring Theresa Russell and Gary Oldman and written by Dennis Potter, who wrote *Pennies from Heaven*. And there's lots more besides that.

**Dutka:** You've upped your U.S. release schedule from two in 1987 to six in '88. Will we be seeing more and more from HandMade films each year?

**Harrison:** I hope not. I don't like to have too much going at the same time. Do you remember those cabaret acts in which people kept all these plates spinning on sticks? They'd start up a couple, add a few more, then have to run back and give the first one a twist. They'd get another couple going, run back to the second and third ones, until they had ten plates all spinning at the same time. The problem is, if you don't watch out, they all go crashing on the floor. I want to be careful not to get too carried away.

**Dutka:** Are you surprised that your baby has grown up so rapidly?

**Harrison:** I am, yes. I just hope that Denis doesn't turn out to be a madman. . . .

**Dutka:** You're worried that he's beginning to spin too many plates?

**Harrison:** Not yet. The logistics of it all make it very difficult to get all those movies going at the same time. These plates you're trying to spin are big, heavy things, you know. It's good that he's going for it in some ways, though. I would have been content just to do *Life of Brian* and *Time*

*Bandits*—much happier just doing comedies. But then, if I was in charge of this company, I don't think it would have gone on as long or gone as far, really. I probably would have encouraged us to have made even crazier films than we've made. I know I wouldn't have been as adventurous in some areas. But at the same time, I don't want to get too adventurous. I like to be safe and sure, you know.

**Dutka:** Any thoughts about the future?

**Harrison:** Someday, I'd like to make a real silly comedy movie full of silly music. I don't really fancy my chances of being a scriptwriter or an actor, but I do have a lot of silly ideas in the back of my head. If we can make enough money so that it doesn't matter if I blow a couple million on my own ideas, I'd like to follow some of them up. Maybe as my last fling, I'll have this huge but very cheap flop with all my mates in it.

**Dutka:** Establishing a post-Beatles existence can't have been easy. How are things going for you these days?

**Harrison:** On behalf of all the remaining ex-Beatles, I can say that the fact that we do have some brain cells left and a sense of humor is quite remarkable. I've had my ups and downs over the years, and now I've sort of leveled out. I'm feeling good. I don't get too carried away or too down about anything. I distance myself from things like the serious business side of the film company, or else I'd crack. I spend plenty of time planting trees, things like that. I have a lot of good friends, good relationships, plenty of laughs. A lot of funny, little diversions that keep things interesting.

**Dutka:** It sounds good. But don't you ever, even for a moment, miss all the excitement, the highs?

**Harrison:** No. Then's then, and now's now. In the late '70s, I just sort of phased myself out of the limelight. And then all the new generations come up. You get older and change your appearance, and they forget what you look like. I suppose, though, with a new record out, that I'm launching myself back into show business for awhile.

**Dutka:** Was that a conflict for you?

**Harrison:** No. I enjoyed making the record, though I don't like to be on TV and do the interviews necessary to promote it. There was a time when I actually hated all that. But now I'm reasonably well balanced about it all and understand in my own mind why I'm doing it. Unfortunately, it will make me a bit "famous" again. I don't really like being famous. I suppose I still am, but I don't really think of myself as a famous person. People will be picking up magazines that will have me in them for a bit—but just for a bit. Then I'll go back to being retired again. Or, at least, putting all this on the back burner. I've managed to find a balance between show business and a kind of peacefulness. It feels very nice.

# ROCK & ROLL HALL
# OF FAME INDUCTION SPEECH

**George Harrison | January 21, 1988 | Speech Transcript**

The Rock & Roll Hall of Fame was only in its third year of inducting musical legends in 1988, and had yet to find a home, when the Beatles were welcomed into its historic ranks—the first non-American act to receive the honor—at a star-studded $10,000-a-table ceremony at New York City's Waldorf Astoria hotel. Others saluted that evening included Bob Dylan, the Beach Boys, the Drifters, and the Supremes, as well as early influencers Woody Guthrie, Leadbelly, and Les Paul. Among the music legends who participated in and/or attended were Little Richard, Bruce Springsteen, Billy Joel, Elton John, Neil Young, and Pete Seeger.

Sadly the rare meeting of the three surviving members of the Fab Four was not to be, as moments before the evening started, McCartney released a statement with his reason for not attending: "After 20 years the Beatles still have some business differences which I had hoped would have been settled by now. Unfortunately, they haven't been, so I would feel like a complete hypocrite waving and smiling at a fake reunion."

Mick Jagger inducted the Beatles with a brief statement about "JohnPaulGeorgeandRingo—the four-headed monster . . ." that described the British music scene of the early '60s, teased at their rivalry with the Rolling Stones, and thanked the group for "their success in America [which] broke down a lot of doors that helped everyone else from England that followed." Following the joviality of Ringo's acceptance speech ("You can sit down, I'm going to be up here for hours...") and preceding the warm sincerity of spoken statements from Yoko Ono and Lennon's two sons—twenty-four-year-old Julian and twelve-year-old Sean—Harrison's declaration of gratitude still comes across as relatively raw, revealing a range of emotions in mere moments: joy, humor, extreme sadness at John's absence, and hints of deep dismay at Paul for not joining his mates, prompting Harrison to use "love" as a truly four-letter word. —Ed.

**Harrison:** Thank you very much. I don't have to say much because I'm the quiet Beatle. [*Laughter; Harrison pauses.*] . . . It is unfortunate Paul's not here because he's the one who had the speech in his pocket . . . [*Laughter.*]

**Starr:** [*Leans in to mic, nods in direction of house band.*] And why didn't they play "Octopus's Garden"?

**Harrison:** We'll talk about that later. [*Laughter; Harrison pauses again, then sighs.*] Anyway, we all know why John can't be here, and I'm sure he would be, and it's hard really to stand here supposedly representing the Beatles. . . . It's what's left I'm afraid. But we all loved him so much, and we all love Paul very much. [*Applause.*]

I suppose, basically, the reason we became a band was all the other people who are in the Hall of Fame already, including Leadbelly— because they actually stole his tunes and turned it into skiffle, and we all became skifflers when we were thirteen. And all of them in there, and all of the people inducted tonight too, they all had great influence on us, and it was for that reason alone we just wanted to get guitars, get in a band, because we didn't have *proper* jobs at the time. [*Laughter.*]

Anyway . . . it sort of turned out fine, [*chuckles*] and it got a bit bigger than any of us expected, and it's certainly wonderful to be here and certainly a thrill. [*Applause.*] And thank you all very much—especially all the rock-and-rollers, and Little Richard, there. It's all his fault, really!

**Starr:** [*Steps to mic, points into audience.*] And don't forget Muhammad Ali! [*Laughter, applause.*]

**Harrison:** We won't forget Muhammad Ali. He picked us up in Miami Beach one day. Anyway, thank you all very much, and on behalf of John, I'm sure he's well covered here with Yoko, Sean, and Julian, and thank you all very much. God bless.

# TELEVISION INTERVIEW

**Ray Martin | February 10, 1988 | *Midday with Ray Martin* (Australia)**

One might not expect a daytime television program to deliver an informed conversation with a music legend, touching upon his history as well as present-day issues with insight. But in early 1988, that's exactly what Ray Martin, the host of Australia's *Midday with Ray Martin*, was able to do—talking to Harrison via satellite, quoting lyrics from his new album *Cloud Nine*, and begging comment on the Beatles' recent induction into the Rock & Roll Hall of Fame.

Though brief, Harrison's discussion with Ray Martin just weeks after his heartfelt speech at the Hall of Fame reveals how he continually leaned into being authentic and gracious, even when speaking of disappointment or personal tragedy. He touches upon his distaste for the use of digital synthesizers and drum machines ("clattery sounds," Harrison calls them) and unflinchingly answers a query about receiving the news of John Lennon's death. Martin ends by apologizing for focusing on McCartney; Harrison's response says it all. —Ed.

**Ray Martin:** . . . This is the first live interview I think he's ever given on Australian television, Mr. George Harrison. [*Applause.*] George, we thank you very much for your time, we appreciate it.

**George Harrison:** Thank you. It's nice to be here.

**Martin:** Can you remember the last time that you were at the top of the charts, as you are at the moment, in Australia?

**Harrison:** No, I haven't got a clue. Probably 1968 or '9, or maybe '70-something, I don't know. You tell me.

**Martin:** We went checking. "All Those Years" was number nine in Australia back in 1981, but "My Sweet Lord" was the last number-one hit that you had in Australia, and that was back in—I hate to say it, but—back in 1970.

**Harrison:** Oh yeah. I remember it well. [*Laughter.*]

**Martin:** Do you feel that old? That's eighteen years ago.

**Harrison:** Yeah. No, I don't feel old at all, actually. I'm getting younger by the minute.

**Martin:** Getting younger and better, right?

**Harrison:** Yeah, yeah.

**Martin:** George, you've spent so much time out of the limelight; why the decision to return?

**Harrison:** Well, it's not really that big a deal actually because, you know, through the years I haven't had a record out. I was still doing film stuff with this company I have called HandMade Films, so I was still very busy. I did soundtracks to movies, and I played on other people's records; I just didn't have my own solo album out. So, you know, it's with the solo album that I got much more higher [*sic*] profile—you know, obviously, here live from Los Angeles. But the decision to do it was really based upon the fact that I felt good about it, and I'd made the decision to work with another producer, and it was just a question of time of finding who would be the right person for me to work with.

**Martin:** With wonderful hindsight now, we can actually say that *Cloud Nine*, the new album, is doing wonderfully well—as I say, with singles number one in Australia, apart from the album selling well—but was there some fear after five years that you hadn't put a single album out that this one could bomb?

**Harrison:** No, not really. I've had so many bombs it doesn't matter anymore. [*Laughter.*]

**Martin:** We have to say, using probably one of your lines anyway, but you did it with a little help from your friends with Ringo, with Jeff Lynne from ELO, with Elton John, with Eric Clapton, et cetera. Did that make it easier for you?

**Harrison:** Yeah, mainly Jeff Lynne, because Jeff was, you know, I spent a lot of time getting to know Jeff, and I thought he'd be ideal to work with. And as it happened it turned out very good, and he's an excellent record producer and also as a songwriter and a performer himself, so the help from the musicians, I've always had help from my friends as musicians, but the main input really that helped me this time was in the production side. Because it's a bit tiring doing everything yourself, you know, and I think the input, which is what I've been missing over the last few albums, I got it with Jeff Lynne.

**Martin:** Who was from Electric Light Orchestra, of course, in the old days, and the sound that was somewhat like the Beatles—but also with Ringo Starr, there. Is it really like riding a bicycle, that you just get back together, and it works?

**Harrison:** It is, actually. With Ringo, there's certain songs with Ringo that, you know, I don't have to tell him what to play, I just play him the song, and he just picks up his sticks, and he just does it, you know.

**Martin:** Listening to the album, though, it sounds like it's got that feeling about it of being a jam session, a bunch of musos get together and just play good music.

**Harrison:** Well, another reason why I like Jeff Lynne was because there's a lot of . . . there's certain things that I don't like about pop music. I'm sure most people don't like everything, but Jeff and I fit in together good, you know, we both have a dislike for certain *clattery* sounds and stuff like that, and I wanted to try and get it so it wasn't so much like a computer record that didn't have any human feel to it, you know? So that's why we did those drum tracks, originally, with a guy called Jim Keltner and with Ringo, and we tried to get it so we had a feel, so it was a bit more like you'd do it in the late '60s or early '70s. But at the same time, these days people are so into computer timing that to have live drumming, you know, that does make it difficult, because people won't accept anything less now than perfect time. So that was the only aspect about having live drumming, you know, that we had to watch out for, but I think we, you know, I think we got the best of both worlds really.

**Martin:** Was it fun, George? One hears the way records are produced these days, and the twenty-four tracks, and overlays, and all sorts of things, and being produced over a matter of month after month—can it be spontaneous fun or was it really just electronic?

**Harrison:** Well, it depends on how you go about it. As I say, I enjoyed this album totally from long before we went in the studio, just writing tunes with Jeff. Actually, the next single that's coming out down there, which is called "When We Was Fab," I wrote it in Australia—at least, I started it with Jeff Lynne, and that was the one song on the album which I think has got the most of the combination of him and myself, you know, together, that we both enjoyed doing that one.

**Martin:** You set it up George, in fact we've got the first time—that video single is released today around the world, and if it's not the first time it's been seen anywhere in the world, it's certainly the first time it's been seen in Australia. Let's have a look at that, and we'll come back and talk with George about the Beatles days.

[*Clip from the "When We Was Fab" music video plays.*]

**Martin:** George, I've got to say that, I guess it should be no surprise that that sounds like the Beatles, but it's a bit *eerie* to me. Is it a bit eerie to you?

**Harrison:** Uh, well, not really, because that's what I set out specifically [*to do:*] to write a tune that brought back all the sounds or some of the sounds, at least, of like that 1967, '68 kind of thing. Actually, you missed the best part on the video there, you know.

**Martin:** [*Laughs.*] Did we?

**Harrison:** You show the end later, you know, when I go through the wall on my bicycle . . . with the tomato ketchup all over me. [*Laughter.*]

**Martin:** Are you more relaxed? I read that you're more relaxed about those years now that you can look back more comfortably now?

**Harrison:** [*Makes a show of shuddering tensely; audience laughs.*]

**Martin:** You're not relaxed?

**Harrison:** Yeah, no, I am. You know, we went through so much, as everybody knows the history of the Beatles by now, you know, I don't have to tell them, but, you know, it was tense at times, you know in the late '60s, and we were hounded a lot, and then we hounded *ourselves* for the ten years following, and it's sort of that space between all those years and all the problems have made it . . . I don't know, I just remember the good things, and I think together—I'm more together, myself, as a person, I enjoy my life really well, and I can just see all the fun side of it, you know; otherwise I couldn't have written a song like that.

**Martin:** And yet we have the Hall of Fame, the reunion of you and Ringo there, and Paul McCartney didn't turn up for that one; he sent a telegram saying that he thought it was a fake reunion and he'd feel like a hypocrite going.

**Harrison:** Well, unfortunately, you know, Paul is a hypocrite sometimes because right before we had that Hall of Fame thing, you know, we'd not been friends for a number of years and we spent a long time really getting to know each other again, and it was so sad really that Paul should use an old business kind of thing and superimpose it on that situation with the Hall of Fame. And it's sad really that he's like that. But it's really sad because we spent a long time this last year and the early part of—well, just the end of the year right before I came away from London, we had lots of dinners and meetings and we were all really on a great course, which we still are in a business sense of solving every problem we ever had, finally, after all these years. And it was just a shame that Paul should use, like, a sort of political sort of situation. Because I think all he's done is miss a great night out, miss meeting Little Richard, and all the old guys, and Dylan. And also, I think it put another nail in his own coffin as far as him as a person because, you know, as Bob Dylan said at the Hall of Fame, "Love and peace is one thing, but we all have to have forgiveness too."

**Martin:** It's hard for Australians, I'm sure, when you think of the Beatles tours to Australia—it's hard for Australia to believe that you three guys who remain don't get on. You were so much a team.

**Harrison:** But we do actually, we do get on. I mean, at this point in time, I'm the closest I've been with Paul now for say the last ten, twelve years, and that's why it seems so silly what he did. But in spite of that I still love him, and it doesn't matter; I'm going to continue my friendship with him regardless of his attitude because I don't have time to screw around anymore, you know.

**Martin:** But you see a lot of Ringo, don't you, obviously?

**Harrison:** I see a lot of Ringo, and I see a lot of some other musicians who are good friends. It's unfortunate because also I know Paul's wife Linda was cursing, she wanted badly to go to that show, and I think Paul did too. Maybe he was badly advised by somebody.

**Martin:** I don't expect you to go into the finances over the details, but is it really a question over $1 million or 100 million? Is that the sort of thing?

**Harrison:** It's not really to do with anything like that. It's a much more subtle thing than that, but, as I say, we've had difficulties with the record company we used to be with, or that the Beatles are still with, and at this point in time we're right on the [edge]—for the first time, really, in ten years—of solving all those problems; now everybody is talking, and it looks like it's all going to be solved. But the personal problem Paul had, which was not actually his problem, it was mine and Ringo['s], because, if you want to know, Paul got extra money off Beatle records that we didn't get when we always agreed that we'd all get it equal. So that was the one thing that we had to do something, in order to make sure that we got equal to Paul. Because of what the history should show, and it was nothing really to do with this settlement we got with EMI, which is great. And as soon as we do that, Paul will be free of any problem he may have of us. But, you know, one way of doing that is working together, and it's unfortunate that he, you know, he's just a sort of a bit foolish, I think.

**Martin:** I didn't think you were down to your last quid. [*Laughter.*]

**Harrison:** [*Chuckles.*] No, I'm not.

**Martin:** Can I ask you, where were you when you heard that John Lennon had been killed?

**Harrison:** I was in bed asleep. You know, it was sort of about—uh, I think 4:00 AM in London time.

**Martin:** When you were told?

**Harrison:** Yeah, that's when I was told. The phone call came through about 4:00 or 5:00 AM.

**Martin:** Can I ask you what the reaction was? You were obviously shocked, but, I mean, could you believe it?

**Harrison:** Well at first, I just thought, "Well, maybe it was just a flesh wound or something," but, you know, it was obvious that it was more serious than that. . . . What does anybody do? I just sort of thought, you know, "You're gone," and went back to sleep again, or tried to.

**Martin:** You have a line in one of the songs on this new album saying that—you say, "I got out of the line of fire."

**Harrison:** No, that's nothing to do with people getting assassinated. It meant, you know, like, *now*. This is sort of the line of fire, me sitting live on a satellite, talking to Australia with you asking me about why Paul didn't show up. That's the kind of "line of fire" I was referring to. [*Laughter.*]

**Martin:** Well—critics have been very good about the album, and what they keep saying—I've read a dozen or so reviews now—and they keep saying that you appear to be laid back, you appear to be relaxed, you appear to be comfortable, you appear to be in fine voice. Are you?

**Harrison:** I appear to be. [*Laughter; Harrison smiles.*]

**Martin:** And are you?

**Harrison:** Yeah, I feel good, you know. I feel fine.

**Martin:** There's a line that you got on one of the other songs which is on the album, you say, "I'm not the wreck of the Hesperus, I feel more like the Wall of China . . . I can rock as good as Gibraltar." You're just getting better as you get older.

**Harrison:** It is, I think it is, definitely, you know. Everything gets easier. I'm less worried about stuff, and I think worries and paranoias and things like that just get in the way, and I seem to have got shut a lot of that out in my system, and consequently I feel better.

As to the performing and singing, being in better voice, I'll tell ya, Jeff Lynne, who coproduced the album with me, has got such a good voice that it made me really want to try hard, you know, to do some decent vocals, and I think they're sort of quite good. Not bad, anyway. I think it's the reason of Jeff being there, you know, during the production that helped me try harder.

**Martin:** I must say, it's a great album. I have it on a cassette in the car and, every time, the more I play it the more I like it.

There is a quote—I won't . . . I know that we've taken our time this afternoon—but there is a quote of you saying that "I have to be more ordinary than ordinary people are." Why do you have to be more ordinary?

**Harrison:** [*Chuckles.*] Well, because, um, people have—we all have concepts of each other, you know? And the concept is, somebody see[s] me on a plane or in the streets or something, and they immediately remember all this Beatle stuff, and they have this concept of me as *that* person. But in reality, I don't go around thinking of myself as "George Harrison the Beatle," or whatever. I do now because I'm on the television, but normally I'm just like you, you know, just like everybody else; I'm just a human, and sometimes you have to, rather than just be ordinary, you have to make an effort to be *more* ordinary, in as much as that they will calm down and try to see that there's actually a person in here [*gestures toward himself*]—other than this big myth about the Beatles. That's all.

**Martin:** Is it good to get your own words down on paper and put them out on records so that your song is there? Is that a therapeutic thing?

**Harrison:** Yeah. I think it's a nice feeling. I think for anybody who writes, you know, whether it be a letter or a postcard or a song or a book, you know, it's nice to be able to get something down and get it out of your system or pass some information onto other people.

**Martin:** George, thank you for your time, it's good to have you back again. The album is *Cloud Nine*, George Harrison's latest, and as we say, there's the release of what will be number one in Australia shortly, the new single. But would you please thank George Harrison for us?

**Harrison:** Thank you, thanks Ray, nice to be on the show.

**Martin:** We thank you, George, very much indeed. I didn't mean to pry with questions about Paul and so on, but we do have such fond memories of the four of you out here.

**Harrison:** Oh, that's okay, that's okay. Are we still on the air?

**Martin:** We are, but, so, let's say nothing else. [*Laughter.*]

**Harrison:** [*Smiles.*] No, that's okay, I don't care. Everything's cool.

# TELEVISION INTERVIEW

Michael Aspel | March 5, 1988 | *Aspel & Company*

George Harrison's memorable encounter with Ringo Starr on one of England's more entertaining talk shows of the 1980s captures an all-too-rare meeting of the two ex-Beatles in full-on "Beatle mode": mocking and interrupting each other, cracking each other up. The actor-turned-television-host Michael Aspel deserves credit for rolling with the free-wheeling spirit of the discussion. He was able to keep up with the nonstop banter, often coming up with a quick retort of his own. As a poignant reminder of how much fun it was to be in the Fab Four in their heyday—something that Harrison explains during the interview in his more settled, adult way—this TV interview is a sheer delight.

*Aspel & Company*, which aired on Saturday evenings in Britain on ITV starting in 1984, was one of the country's more popular sit-down chat programs. Aspel ably handled Q and As with political leaders such as Margaret Thatcher, prime minister at the time, as well as top celebrities of the day, including Arnold Schwarzenegger, Bruce Willis, and Sylvester Stallone (the three together, in fact!). That last show, however, saw the three actors interested only in promoting their joint nightclub venture, Planet Hollywood—an experience that convinced the increasingly disillusioned Aspel to bring *Aspel & Company* to an end. Had there been more encounters like this one with Harrison and Starr, perhaps he would have thought otherwise. —Ed.

**Michael Aspel:** Welcome back. And now it's my pleasure to offer hospitality to a man who hasn't entirely wasted his life: singer, songwriter, author, film producer, keen gardener, and master of understatement—he once said if you're going to be in a rock and roll band you may as well be in the Beatles—ladies and gentlemen, George Harrison. [*Applause as Harrison walks on stage, shakes hands with Aspel.*]

George, it's good to see you. You're back in the charts so you're a happy man.

**George Harrison:** Ah, I don't know if I'm back—I've *been* back, but I don't know if I'm back this week. . . . But, I *am* a happy man.

**Aspel:** Did you feel the time was right to do this?

**Harrison:** Yeah. Well, I didn't really think about it, I just felt . . . "time to make a record," and so I made it, and you know, sometimes things go right and sometimes they don't. This time it went right.

**Aspel:** You're attracting new fans, some of whom, perhaps, who've never heard of the Beatles.

**Harrison:** I think most of them haven't. [*Laughter.*] I met a few people . . . just at Christmas I saw some kids, about eighteen years old, in Los Angeles, and they saw me walk in a shop and they looked at each other and said, "Oh, there's that singer"—which I thought was pretty good.

**Aspel:** Just that singer. [*Laughter.*]

**Harrison:** Yeah, just that singer, you know, who is he?

**Aspel:** You have kept yourself to yourself in recent years. This led to some wild stories about the Howard Hughes of Henley.

**Harrison:** That's right, yeah. Well, it's the silly newspapers. I mean, they're not *all* silly of course, but some of them are very silly, and uh—because I don't go discotheque-ing and things like that where people hang out with their cameras, so they presume that I was Howard Hughes with my big fingernails and Kleenex tissues and that kind of stuff, bottles of urine all around the house, and, uh . . . [*Laughter.*] But I wasn't like that at all. I go out all the time, or a lot of the time, to see friends, have dinner, go to parties. I'm even more normal than, you know, normal people. [*Slight smile; laughter from the audience.*]

**Aspel:** I mentioned gardening; you haven't yet, but to stroll from one end of yours would take about three weeks, wouldn't it? How big is it, actually?

**Harrison:** Not really, no. My garden, you can stroll around it in ten minutes—if you're power walking, which is what I sort of do these days. If you *saunter* it could take half an hour. If you swagger, maybe forty-five minutes. [*Laughter.*]

**Aspel:** You've got lakes as well, haven't you?

**Harrison:** Legs, yeah. I've got legs and arms. . . .

**Aspel:** This is my southern accent. You've got *la-ay-akes.*

**Harrison:** Lakes, well, there's a bit of water, yeah, it sort of flows around; it was built in the Victorian days. It's very nice. It was all covered in soil and broken lavatories from a building site when I bought it.

**Aspel:** Oh, Howard Hughes did have it then, huh? [*Laughter.*] What about your son—who is now nine, I think—is he aware of your glorious past?

**Harrison:** He's become aware now in the last few years. . . . And I didn't really tell him anything about the Beatles because it was so long ago, anyway. I didn't want to burden him with all that. But nevertheless, I think most kids when they get to about four or five, they see *Yellow Submarine*, and then he sort of twigged, and then he came up to me one day and said, "Hey dad, how do you play the piano lick from 'Hey Bulldog'?" I thought, "That's strange, how does he know a song like that?" But it's in *Yellow Submarine.*

**Aspel:** Was he impressed?

**Harrison:** . . . No. [*Laughter.*]

**Aspel:** Has he actually seen you perform?

**Harrison:** Well, if you call it performing. [*Laughs with audience.*] Yeah, he came to the, um . . . I did this show, the Prince's Trust, last July. He came to that show, and I suppose you could call it performing, but after the show I said to him, "What do you think?" and he said, "Eh, you were okay, Dad. But why didn't you do "Rock and Roll Music," and "Sweet Little Sixteen," "Johnny B. Goode"? I said, "Well, actually, that's Chuck Berry." [*Laughter.*]

**Aspel:** He's nine?

**Harrison:** Nine and a half now, yeah. He's really into Chuck Berry, though. . . . As you are too, I saw you on the show with him.

**Aspel:** Yes, didn't have long *enough*, I'm afraid, but a great guy. How long, when you did the Prince's Trust, how long had it been since you had done a live show?

**Harrison:** Uh, last time . . . well, I did one show which I wore this suit for. It's the first time I've worn it since the Carl Perkins show, which was a televised program for HBO. Before that I did a tour in America in 1974, but in England I never performed since the Beatles, which was 1965 or something like that, '66 maybe.

**Aspel:** You could have been very slightly terrified.

**Harrison:** I was, yeah. It felt like I was going to the electric chair. I sat there for hours waiting to go on and very, very nervous.

**Aspel:** But surrounded by old mates.

**Harrison:** Fortunately, yeah. There was a lot of support from the gang, Ringo, and Phil Collins was playing one night, and Eric Clapton, of course, and Elton, and Midge Ure, a lot of people.

**Aspel:** Didn't someone suggest that you should get a sort of oldies group together?

**Harrison:** I think that's sort of an idea that's bubbling about, maybe in Elton's mind, I don't know. It's sort of a good idea because everybody enjoys playing together.

**Aspel:** You could call yourselves "Methuselah." It'd be good for you.

**Harrison:** We could, yeah, yeah. [*Laughs with audience.*]

**Aspel:** Or not, as the case may be. . . . Amazingly, twenty-five years since Beatlemania swept the world. When did you first realize it was happening to you?

**Harrison:** The mania side of it happened, it started happening in, I think, 1963, when we started touring seriously in England, like on the big Moss Empires circuit. And then we did some tours around Europe, and I think it was because of the mania that was happening then that

the Americans caught on and came over, and they did features on us in
*Time* and *Life* and *Newsweek*, so then that sort of set us up for the trip
to the USA in 1964.

**Aspel:** And when did the excitement wear off?

**Harrison:** Well, it sort of wears off and it comes back again. Like just
recently, I feel quite excited to be *alive*, regardless of whether I'm making
a record or promoting my record—[*pauses; looks into the camera*] buy
my album now, right?—you know, quite apart from that. But I think, for
me, the mania got to me in 1966, and around that time I got a bit tired
of what they call "the adulation." I'm still not that keen on that side of
it. It's nice to be popular, it's nice to be loved, but it's not so nice to be
chased around and on the front page of the paper every day of your life
with people climbing over the wall all day long.

**Aspel:** And the endless round, of course, of meeting people, dignitaries, et
cetera.

**Harrison:** Yes, well we did tend to meet most of the dignitaries of the
world.

**Aspel:** Were you bored by all that?

**Harrison:** Well sometimes it was boring, sometimes we'd just make fun
of them. We'd have our own little in-jokes, you know, to get through.

**Aspel:** We noticed that. You did send them up. I mean looking back do
you think that you were cheeky, in a certain sense?

**Harrison:** Oh, we were very cheeky, yeah. We *had* to be really. It's like
a survival kind of thing.

**Aspel:** Your current single harks back to those early days. Are you feeling—apart from being glad to be alive . . .

**Harrison:** Nostalgic?

**Aspel:** Nostalgic.

**Harrison:** Ah, not really, no. I do like, um, like most people, I like the
rock'n'roll years when you see what happened when Cuba attacked
Russia and all that, whatever happened, and you remember that Eddie

Cochran was singing this tune. . . . I like nostalgia in that respect, and I suppose all that "twenty years ago today" stuff that was happening last year, you know, it's nice to be reminded of things that happened, except it reminds you how old you are, which is not so good.

**Aspel:** Let's see the video "When We Was Fab," with, as you say, more than a hint of Sgt. Pepper there.

[*Excerpt from the "When We Was Fab" music video plays.*]

Well, that was made with a little help from your friends, of course, including the one, the only Ringo Starr.

[*Starr enters dramatically to grand applause; walks past Harrison's open hand, shakes Aspel's first, then Harrison's.*]

**Ringo Starr:** [*To Harrison.*] . . . I've met you before.

**Harrison:** Here, take the hot seat. . . .

**Starr:** [*To audience.*] Good evening!

[*Audience calls back "good evening!"*]

**Harrison:** Good evening, Ringo.

**Aspel:** I thought you were dead!

**Starr:** How are you doing, Michael?

**Aspel:** A sharp suit, Ringo.

**Starr:** I hate gardening. [*Laughter.*]

**Aspel:** That's the next question . . .

**Starr:** I love him [*nods toward Harrison*], but I hate gardening.

**Aspel:** You've been doing your own thing as well, of course, but you enjoy a bit of the old nostalgia, don't you?

**Starr:** Oh, I love nostalgia. I think I was nostalgic at birth. [*Laughter.*]

**Harrison:** That's why you got born again.

**Starr:** [*Indistinct.*]

**Harrison:** Oh, sorry . . . [*Chuckles.*]

**Aspel:** Didn't I spot the Sgt. Pepper . . . ?

**Starr:** [*Quietly to Harrison.*] How're you doing?

**Harrison:** [*Back to Starr.*] Didn't we meet on summer cruise?

**Starr:** Yeah.

**Aspel:** I did spot the Sgt. Pepper costume in that video, didn't I?

**Harrison:** That's right, yeah. That quick one. I had a quick one.

**Aspel:** The actual original?

**Harrison:** The original suit. It's a bit tight around the hips now at this moment.

**Aspel:** Have you kept memorabilia?

**Starr:** I keep everything. [*Laughter.*] No, I do, I am a hoarder. And I, you know, I've saved *all* my clothes through the years and I thought, "It always goes 'round, the kids would love this," but the only time they ask me for any clothes is if there's a fancy dress party. You know, they'll have all the hippie stuff on. "Hey, we're going to a fancy dress party, let's ask Dad."

**Aspel:** Would you do me a tremendous favor?

**Starr:** I'm not going to kiss you like [*indistinct*] . . . [*Laughter, as Aspel pulls a face and snaps his fingers in mock disappointment.*] And I'm not going to rub your knees like the other guy!

**Aspel:** Would you . . . [*Ringo grins*] . . .would you take the shades off for a *second*?

**Starr:** Yeah. [*Removes sunglasses for one second.*]

**Aspel:** Oh! There's lovely orbs under there. [*Smattering of applause.*]

**Harrison:** Aww, he's got the bluest eyes in the world. . . . [*Ringo removes sunglasses briefly again, shrugging bashfully.*]

**Aspel:** But they're closed.

**Starr:** [*Puts sunglasses back on.*] Oh, yeah. Well you have to keep them closed, the air gets in them. [*Laughter.*]

**Aspel:** Now, what you haven't kept, of course, the fans have. Were they always desperate for souvenirs?

**Starr:** Uh . . . well, I think we were real lucky. I think the only thing I ever lost in all those days of madnesses was half of my scalp, a shirt, and a gold necklace, which they gave me back in New York. We really weren't beat up too much. *Wales* was the worst place I ever went.

**Aspel:** What were they after?

**Starr:** They were after me head. [*Laughter.*] We had all these policemen, we'd walk down this, like, corridor of policemen, and some hand just came through and just *grabbed* my head! [*Grabs himself by the hair and shakes his head about.*] . . . This child would have *died*!

**Harrison:** Oh, I never went to Wales. I don't remember Wales.

**Starr:** It was before you joined the group. [*Laughter.*]

**Harrison:** Oh. That was Rory Storm and the Hurricanes. [*Chuckles.*]

**Starr:** No, it was you, Georgie. But you were so much younger then.

**Harrison:** Ahhh, I'm older than that now. . . .

**Aspel:** What did they nick of yours, then, George?

**Harrison:** What did they nick of mine? Somebody once broke in my house and nicked a pair of silk pajamas.

**Starr:** That was me. [*Harrison laughs with the audience.*]

**Aspel:** You all four, of course, had your own special followers. How different was a Ringo fan from a George fan, say?

**Starr:** I had the mothers. [*Laughter.*] I had the mothers and the children, always have. George has the mystics, John had the, you know . . . [*Waves hand.*]

**Harrison:** Intellectuals.

**Starr:** Intellectual . . . college . . . attitude, and Paul had the teenies.

**Aspel:** You shared out the human race quite well.

**Starr:** Well that, I feel, was part of our strength, where we were a band that were appealing to children, to grandparents. Like, the Stones where they were mainly on a teenage attitude. How you doing, Mick?

**Aspel:** You were always the down-to-earth one.

**Starr:** [*Seriously.*] That's right. . . . God, you're looking chubby.

**Aspel:** Thank you. [*Smiles, raising a hand to pinch his own cheeks pensively.*]

**George:** Now, now . . .

**Starr:** Oops, sorry, I've got to behave, George is on. [*Laughter.*]

**Aspel:** What did you make of—like I was saying about you being down to earth—what did you make of the Indian episode?

**Starr:** Well, the Indian episode was real interesting. I got two phone calls, one from George and one from John, just, "We're going to Wales"— see, he's always been to Wales, he just doesn't remember—"to meet the Maharishi." So I just got on the train because these guys don't lie to me. So we met him in Wales, and then we all decided to go to this ashram in India. I still thank Maharishi for what he said, but in the end I felt he was telling me stories—but that's my problem.

**Aspel:** In the end, I mean, how long did you actually stick to that course?

**Starr:** Ten days. [*Laughter.*]

**Harrison:** He ran out of beans!

**Ringo:** [*Pushes Harrison's shoulder.*] Aww, I was going to get to that!

**Harrison:** . . . He came all the way up the Himalayas with [*gestures above his head as if carrying a large burden*] big cans of beans!

**Starr:** A suitcase of beans and a suitcase of clothes.

**Harrison:** He didn't like flies and spiders.

**Starr:** [*Throws hands up in mock indignation.*] No, can't stand them. But the interesting part was, you see, I can only eat bland food—[*muttering*] because I was very sick as a child—and so I'd have me, beans and then I was getting fed up with that, and so I said, "You got any eggs?" [*Laughter.*] I usually have eggs in the morning, you know. And so, I caught these guys burying the shells in the ground as if God wouldn't notice. So . . . [*chuckles*] I decided to leave after that. "Oh no, [*looks up as if to heaven, then down as if to hidden egg shells*] He doesn't see those."

**Aspel:** You lived in each other's pockets, didn't you? It was like being a family.

**Starr:** Oh, he's always lived in mine. [*Harrison looks into the camera and shakes his head.*]

**Aspel:** You had family rows.

**Starr:** Yeah, we do, we have terrible rows.

**Aspel:** What was the main cause of your squabbles, in the early days?

**Starr:** Whew . . . I'll leave that one to you, George.

**Harrison:** Oh . . . I don't remember *ever* having any. [*Laughter.*] . . . I don't remember *any* squabbles.

**Starr:** You don't remember anything, do you?

**Harrison:** No. It's an amnesia!

**Aspel:** What about now? What makes you cross with each other now?

**Starr:** Well, the last time we were cross was when George was suin' me. [*Laughter.*] See, what's nice is, he calls me . . .

**Harrison:** That's the last time, fingers crossed.

**Starr:** Yeah . . . he's still cross. The last time he called me he said, "I'm going to sue you." "No, George, don't be so . . ." "No, I'm going to sue you, I don't like what you've done." Because he wrote this song and I had it mixed by somebody else and he didn't like the mix . . . [*Harrison laughs*] so he was going to sue me. I said, "Sue me if you want, but I'll always love you." [*Laughter and "aww"s from the audience.*]

**Aspel:** Speaking of which, you two shared a flat didn't you?

**Starr:** Yes, we did. Yes, we shared a flat.

**Harrison:** Yes, it was on the M1 . . .

**Starr:** Walden House . . .

**Harrison:** I had to get the jack out . . . change the tire . . .

**Starr:** Yeah, it was fabulous . . . we shared a couple of places, actually. When we first came down to London, you know, you're so insecure that we had to live together. We weren't big boys and like, "I'll have my own place. . . ." I [*had*] never left home. Who's going to make the tea and iron your shirts?

**Aspel:** George, what was he like to live with?

**Harrison:** . . . Fabulous. [*Laughter.*] Yeah, I mean, we only ever slept there, we used to always be in the nightclubs really, in those days.

**Starr:** Georgie, you know, all these lines about, "I was never at a discotheque . . ."

**Harrison:** Well, I wasn't.

**Starr:** You had to drag him out of them, you know!

**Harrison:** That was back in '64, '65. No, I stopped going to them around 1967, I think.

**Starr:** I stopped in 1980. [*Laughter.*] . . . Got married, have a wonderful wife, you know.

**Aspel:** But then, you rarely go to bed anyway, to sleep, I mean.

**Starr:** I never go to bed. I'm an insomniac, mainly. [*Chuckles.*] When I'm not an insomniac I sleep. [*Laughter.*]

**Aspel:** Well, that would cure it, I suppose. Let me set the record straight, though, about . . .

**Starr:** This is George. [*Laughter.*]

**Aspel:** [*Gesturing to Ringo's tapping feet.*] He's a drummer.

**Starr:** I can't help it, it happens all the time. Am I making a noise at the moment? [*Harrison looks into the camera and whispers a drum beat while tapping his feet.*] I tap all the time . . . to my heartbeat.

**Aspel:** That's, oh . . . well, it's getting slower. [*Laughter.*]

**Starr:** I can't wait for the coffee. . . . [*Waves arm as if hitting a bass drum.*] *Boom, boom, boom.* Thank you, Lord.

**Aspel:** I hesitate to ask you a serious question but as we're talking about . . .

**Starr:** Well why don't you, Michael? [*Laughter.*]

**Aspel:** I will. Set the record straight about today's situation. The press are keen to imply rifts. How *do* you and Paul get on?

**Starr:** We get on very well.

**Aspel:** George?

**Harrison:** Yeah, no, we do actually, we, I mean . . .

**Starr:** In fact, we love you. [*Leans off-mic toward Harrison.*] Which camera is it, for Chrissake, it's bobbing around. . . . That's it! [*Sincerely to camera.*] We love you.

**Harrison:** For like about ten years, I didn't really . . .

**Starr:** [*Chuckles.*] Ten minutes.

**Harrison:** . . . I didn't really know Paul and never really saw much of him through the last ten or twelve years. But more recently, we've been hanging out and getting to know each other, going for dinner and meeting and having a laugh, and it's absolutely not true what they said in the *News of the World*, last Sunday. Somebody . . . actually, I was in San Remo the day before Paul arrived, and I got a phone call from somebody, the *Daily Mail* phoned up and they said, "George." I said, "No, sorry, George just left," and I pretended I was somebody else, and they said, "There's some people down here who are trying to get this rumor started about you and Paul. . . ." So, I told him that we weren't . . . the reason why we weren't there together was because we didn't even know each other was going to be there anyway, and we all were there on different days. But it's definitely just one of those things that these people sit around and think, "Let's have a fight between George and Paul, now," you know. But actually, I love Paul, he's my mate, and it doesn't matter what they say in the papers, they're not going to get much mileage out of that one.

**Aspel:** What about Yoko?

**Harrison:** Yoko, I'm pleased to say . . . [*looks for camera*] which, where are they?

**Starr:** "Pleased to say . . ."

**Harrison:** [*Chuckles.*] . . . Pleased to say that I had a great time with Yoko in New York . . .

**Starr:** . . . for the first time. [*Laughter.*]

**Harrison:** . . . at the Rock and Roll Hall of Fame, and it was nice to meet her, and . . . fine, yeah. Everything's fine.

**Aspel:** When I—and the rest of us—hear Lennon records, it's still, of course, impossible for us to believe that he's gone. It must be, of course, a *million* times more for you, mustn't it?

**Starr:** Well, you've certainly brought the party down, Michael. [*Laughter.*] . . . It is hard, though, you know? I was stunned on the day, and I still . . .

**Harrison:** Shocked and stunned . . . shocked and stunned.

**Starr:** I mean, I cry easy and just the other day just because we're all sitting here—George and I watched this movie that Yoko is making about John—and I just get emotional. [*Shrilly.*] "Oh, don't show me more!" I do, I do get emotional, so . . . [*more seriously*] I do, I still miss the man, I loved the man, I was close to the man. And he went out just in such a stupid way, you know. . . . And the guy's *famous* now, for God's sake. . . . [*More loudly, as if to the audience.*] What do you think of that?

**Aspel:** That's the cruel irony, of course, you're quite right. How did you hear the news, yourself?

**Starr:** We were in the Bahamas at the time, and my stepdaughter Francesca called, Barbara's daughter, and she said, "There's something on the news about John." I said, "What is it?" "Like a shooting and things like that." "Well, we don't know what it is. . . ." I never ever went to, like, "Good night." And then they called back, and they said, "Yeah, he's . . . [*indistinct*]." So, we just sat around, just devastated, actually. I was just *down.* And so, five o'clock in the morning, I ordered a plane and flew to New York just to see if there was anything you can do, what you *can.* When you get to that position or situation, you know, you just do *something,* and that's what Barbara and I did, because you couldn't have a holiday after that.

**Aspel:** George, how did you hear it?

**Harrison:** I was in bed at the time in England, and, I don't know, the call came through sometime in the morning, four or five in the morning. I didn't take the call, Olivia took the call, and she said John has been shot, and I thought, "Oh, how bad is it?" I just thought maybe a flesh wound or something like that. . . . But they said, "No, that's it, he's dead." So, I didn't know . . . I just went back to sleep, actually, I just, uh . . . maybe it's just a way of getting away from it. I just went to sleep and then waited to see what it said the next morning. And he was still dead the next morning, unfortunately. But I feel . . . not so bad about it, in as much as I have this, you know, unlike Ringo, when I went to Rishikesh in India, I went into meditation and had some experiences, and I got to . . .

**Starr:** I had some good experiences. [*Laughter.*]

**Harrison:** I know you did, and you forget to tell him that.

**Starr:** Well yeah, but he only asked about the eggs.

**Harrison:** So I believe what it says in the scriptures, and in the Bhagavad Gita it says there was never a time when you didn't exist, and there will never be a time when you cease to exist. The only thing that changes is our bodily condition. The soul comes in the body and we go from birth to death and it's—death, how I look at it, is like taking your suit off. You know, the soul is in these three bodies, and one body falls off. And I feel like that. I can feel him around here.

**Starr:** Oh, I've seen him twice.

**Aspel:** Did *he* feel that?

**Starr:** Oh, yeah.

**Aspel:** You've seen him?

**Starr:** Yeah, I felt it one time very strong. I was in a hotel room in LA, and I was real down on whatever was going on; he was in the corner saying, "What are you doing?" I said, "I'm being miserable." He said, "Come on, get it together."

No, I believe like George in that respect—[*mutters*] only we just did the joking bit about the eggs—that we do *continue*, and I do believe in God.

**Aspel:** Did he? What mental state was John in at that time? Do you know?

**Harrison:** I had never seen him for a couple years before that, but I had enough experience, we all did. During the '60s, we had, you know, there was people putting stuff in our coffee which gave us some crazy experiences, and when they stopped doing it, we started putting it in our own coffee for a bit. . . . [*Laughter.*]

**Starr:** [*Pointing into the crowd.*] There's two girls who're wondering what you put in your coffee over there . . .

**Harrison:** But, you know, we had a lot of experiences. I know John was—you know, he knew who he was, that he was a soul that happened to be in this body for this period of time. And, you know, I don't think . . . It's just the method by which you die, you know. I think it's nice if you can consciously leave your body at death as opposed to just some lunatic shooting you on the street or having a plane crash, something like that. I think it's unfortunate the way he went out, but it doesn't *really* matter; he's okay, and life flows on within you and without you. . . .

**Starr:** [*Looking upward.*] How you doing, Johnny?

**Aspel:** Hm. Would anything—

**Starr:** How about you, Michael?

**Aspel:** Well, I was going to ask, would anything have persuaded you—all, that is—to reform the Beatles even for one night, and what kind of offers did you get, anyway?

**Starr:** Well, I think the only time we phoned each other up . . . [*laughs*] because everyone kept trying to get us together, but somebody phoned up, and they offered us just for one gig—and we only used to do twenty-five minutes—they offered us fifty million. . . . [*Laughs with audience.*]

**Aspel:** Dollars?

**Harrison:** Lira.

**Starr:** It could have been in anything—twenty-five quid each! And I just—I do remember, George never called anyone, but I remember calling everyone else, and them calling me, saying, "Well, what do you think? You know, twenty-five minutes . . . buy you a new suit."

**Aspel:** What stopped you, then?

**Starr:** We would never get it together. And we broke up, you know, for all the reasons we know about. To get together . . . I don't really believe in, like, this getting together thing, really. Now, if we got together, it would be George, Paul, and Ringo if we got together; it would not be the Beatles, you know. We'll never do it with Julian because it would then be George, Paul [*stutters*]—what's my name? [*laughter*]—and Julian. You know what I'm saying? I mean, you would never go out there again with that. Well I won't, I don't know about *Georgie*. Would you go out, Georgie, with that name?

**Harrison:** No. It wouldn't be the Beatles. But the thing is, it's not to say that—you know, I mean, Ringo and I hang out occasionally [*strumming motions*] and play some tunes together.

**Starr:** I'm on the album. [*Chuckles with cartoonish glee.*]

**Harrison:** He was on the album, he was on the concert, and Paul does concerts, and, as I say, we're getting to be friendlier with Paul. It's a good chance someday maybe we'll write a tune and play together, but it won't be the Beatles, and if people expect us to be the Beatles, they're going to be disappointed. But you may see three old guys called John, Paul, and Ringo who someday may sing a song together. [*Chuckles.*]

**Starr:** I bet I don't get to sing. [*Laughter.*]

**Aspel:** Ah, but you have other things to offer. I mean, look at . . .

**Starr:** *Oh,* yes Michael, you're telling them now.

**Aspel:** Yes! What about acting? Now, you've—

**Starr:** Acting? I couldn't get a job if I died. [*Laughter.*]

**Aspel:** You've always been a film fan, haven't you?

**Starr:** I love films. I love cameras, as you may have noticed. [*Gestures toward camera; audience laughs.*]

**Aspel:** You've got a lot of new fans, though, with Thomas the Tank Engine.

**Starr:** Oh, I have, it's great, it's great. [*Laughter.*] It's fabulous! I *never* knew it would be so big. In fact, the first time Britt Allcroft—who was the producer of all this—came up, saying, "I'd like you to read these stories about this train," which I never had because I was a Beano man. And I said, "You gotta be crazy, there's Star Wars now and [*indistinct*] years ago, anyway." And so she came back and convinced me, so I said, "Look, I'll just read five of the stories on my own on tape, and you listen to them and see if you still want me." And she did! And then we did Thomas the Train, there's all these little babies screaming again. [*In high-pitched, squawking voice.*] "Ringo! Ringo!" [*Laughter.*] . . . I used to have the mothers, and now I've got the kids!

**Aspel:** [*Solemnly.*] You are of course the . . . the poorest Beatle, aren't you?

**Starr:** I am the poorest Beatle, Michael. That's why I'm on the show! [*Laughs with audience.*]

**Aspel:** That won't do much for your last . . . Well, you're down to your last twenty million now, I think, aren't you?

**Starr:** No, I didn't even make the list. Georgie's got fourteen, so I'm down to, what, twelve.

**Aspel:** Are you a great spender though? I mean, you enjoy it?

**Starr:** Yeah . . . that's why! [*Chuckles.*] I love to spend, that's the only reason to have it. [*Slowly lights cigarette; audience laughs.*]

**Aspel:** What's the biggest waste of money you claim to have done?

**Starr:** Biggest waste?

**Aspel:** Well, the biggest—

**Starr:** I mean, if you call this, [*gestures toward rings on his hands*] like some reality . . .

**Harrison:** [*Quietly.*] Apple.

**Starr:** What?

**Harrison:** *Apple.*

**Starr:** Well, that was *all* of us—you can't blame me for that personally. [*Laughter.*]

**Aspel:** If it had *all* never happened, what would you be doing now?

**Starr:** I'd be a drummer. . . . [*Laughter.*] No, I would. Well, what's funny about that? [*More laughter from the audience; Harrison joins in.*] I mean, I *decided* when I was eighteen, this is my life. You know, just because we *made it*, I don't think . . . I mean, you're asking a weird question, because we don't know what would have happened if it hadn't happened.

**Aspel:** It's all conjecture.

**Starr:** But I just feel that I still would have been playing behind the strippers . . .

**Aspel:** George?

**Starr:** [*Nearly laughing.*] . . . or in front, these days. . . . [*Laughter.*]

**Harrison:** I think I probably would have been a guitar—probably a *better* guitar player than I am now, because . . .

**Starr:** Impossible.

**Harrison:** . . . because, you know, the famous bit sort of made—we ended up just playing the same old stuff for years. But I started playing the guitar when I was about thirteen, and that's the only thing I really wanted to do. I didn't want to be a . . . Thomas the Tank Engine, or . . .

**Starr:** Thanks a lot. [*Laughter.*]

**Harrison:** . . . or a train, a fireman, or anything like that.

**Aspel:** Would you have been happier men if it had not occurred?

**Starr:** Oh, I always feel I was born happy.

**Aspel:** So, happiness . . .

**Starr:** You know, happy, I'm basically happy. I *am* happy.

**Aspel:** And George, you certainly are.

**Starr:** You can tell!

**Harrison:** I'm quite happy, yeah. [*Chuckles with Starr.*] But you can't say, you know. It's all . . . this is our lives, you know. This is the only life I can remember, and I'm happy enough doing it, being up and down, and good and bad, and in the end, I think all of us have come out of it reasonably sane and . . . quite happy.

**Aspel:** The rest of us are happy, and for all of us it's been . . . *fab*. Thank you very much, indeed. Ringo Starr . . . and George Harrison!

**Starr:** . . . and George [*mumbles last name*]!

[*Applause.*]

**Aspel:** And thanks for your company—see you next week. Good night!

# BOOK INTERVIEW

**Dr. Jenny Boyd | April–May 1988 | *It's Not Only Rock 'n' Roll***

Like her older sister Pattie, Jenny Boyd was a model, was married to a rock star—drummer Mick Fleetwood of Fleetwood Mac—and came of age in Swinging London at the height of the '60s. She enjoyed a rare entrée to the heart of the rock scene, exploring spiritual paths and visiting Rishikesh with the Beatles. Singer-songwriter Donovan composed the song "Jennifer Juniper" for her. As she writes in her book *It's Not Only Rock 'n' Roll: Iconic Musicians Reveal the Source of Their Creativity*, growing up "surrounded by talented musicians for over twenty years was inspiring to me." She became a mother of two, later moved to Los Angeles, and in the late '80s set her sights on becoming a doctor of human behavior and working as a psychotherapist. For her dissertation she chose to focus on the nature of creativity, including "information and ideas gathered from 75 interviews that took place between 1987 and 1991." The book based on her research—originally titled *Musicians in Tune*—benefited from the insights and memories that musicians shared candidly with Boyd, a member of their inner circle. (Boyd is currently at work on a second book—her autobiography—*Jennifer Juniper: A Journey Beyond the Muse*.)

Eric Clapton, Joni Mitchell, Keith Richards, Peter Frampton, Graham Nash, Michael McDonald, Mick Fleetwood, Ravi Shankar, and—of course—George Harrison were but a few of the musicians Dr. Boyd spoke with to help craft her dissertation. About her discussion with her former brother-in-law, she says:

George arrived at my house in Sherman Oaks in the afternoon ready for our interview. He was feeling a little hung over but not too bad; he told me he had so much fun the previous evening playing with a new group, the Traveling Wilburys—they had just come up with the name—that it was worth the hangover!!

We sat side-by-side on the sofa in the sitting room, chatting about old times and catching up in general before I pressed Play and began recording. Because many of my questions about creativity verged on the spiritual we were able to go quite deep. I had always had that sort of relationship with him since I was a teenager. It was a very special couple of hours we spent together. Our conversation flowed so well that I hardly had to look at my questions, let alone check the tape player was still running!

Boyd's conversation with Harrison—who is clearly comfortable and generous in his comments on his creative processes—took place in late spring 1988 as the Traveling Wilburys were first gathering steam, readying to record their debut album. —Ed.

## Musical Encouragement in Working Class Families

"Neither of my parents were musicians, but they did have an upright piano in the house, and my dad, who was a merchant seaman, bought a lot of records and a wind-up gramophone from the States. There was always music about the house, and they also liked to dance. My mum was often singing. Since they really appreciated music, they encouraged me. When I was 12, I wanted to buy a friend's guitar, and my mother gave me the 3 pounds and 10 shillings to buy it. My mum really liked the idea of me playing, because Dad was always out working at night or doing shift work.

"There was a friend of my father's who, he remembered, used to play guitar when they were on the ships together. My father had sold his guitar because he needed the money, but this guy had continued playing. So my father called him up and asked him if he would show me a few things. This guy owned a liquor store, and whichever evening of the week he closed the shop, I'd go down there and he would show me how to play the guitar. I'm sure that set a certain pattern in my music, because he taught me all those old songs. He taught me all the chords to what you would call 'dance band music,' and that stayed with me until this day. He was a great help to me, showing me where to put my fingers and how different chords follow each other, just by playing songs, really. In retrospect, I think he had an enormous influence on me."

## Dedicated Hard Work

"I put a lot of time into playing the guitar, learning how to clamp down on those strings while my fingers were hurting and how to change the chords, moving my fingers without the music stopping. I played a lot, even though it was just simple stuff, labouring on until I got it, even if just to play a skiffle tune or 'Peggy Sue.' It was something I didn't think about; I just did it. It was something that I liked. I just liked music and I loved guitars, so it was a labor of love, really.

"When I was 11, we moved from our neighborhood into one of the new housing estates on the outskirts of Liverpool, and just after that, I also moved to the new grammar school. That was a big change in my life, because it was around the time I got my new guitar, and that's the school where Paul McCartney came into my life. There were also other people I met who were guitarists. I would hang out with anybody who had a guitar in those days, either they would come to my house or I would go to theirs. The guitar and music were the first things I was interested in. I didn't like school most of the time; it was much too serious. I didn't have a clue of what I wanted to be. I didn't want to be anything. The only thing that held my interest was music and the guitar and how to get out of getting a proper job. If it hadn't been for the band, I would have just been a bum."

---

## The Collective Unconscious

"I thought it was pretty strange why we made the enormous impact that we did—or have still. It's strange how the chemistry between the four of us made this big thing that went right through the world. There wasn't any country in the world, even the most obscure places, that didn't know about the Beatles—from grandparents to babies. It just blanketed everything, and that amazed me more than anything. We always felt that if we could get the right record contract, we'd be successful. But our tiny little concept of success that we had at the time was nothing compared to what happened. It was just enormous. It does make one think there's more to this than meets the eye."

---

## The Artist as Hero

George Harrison agreed that musicians, with insights drawn from their own experiences, can help those who listen to their music. But he also cautioned, "You have to be very careful, I suppose. In one way, we all have a duty to help each other, to help ourselves and then help each other in whatever way, whether it's just to get through the day. I think it's important to share experiences. For instance, if Dylan hadn't said some of the things he did, nobody else was going to say them. Can you imagine what a world it would be if we didn't have a Bob Dylan? It would be awful. There's that side of it. But then there's the other side, where you can start mistaking your own importance. I think I've been in both of those [positions] at various times. You suddenly think you're more groovy than you are and then usually something happens to slap you down a bit, so it all has to be tempered with discretion."

## A Change in Consciousness

"LSD did unlock something for me, and it released all this stuff. I used to spend time looking at myself in the mirror, and the face kept changing, from looking like a Mongolian and then to a Chinese man. I just kept looking, thinking, 'Who are you?' I think that pot definitely did something for the old ears, like suddenly I could hear more subtle things in the sound. But now I've found it's actually better not to do it while working. I need to be a bit more clear, because my mind is such a scramble at times, and all that does is scramble it more."

## Side Effects of Drug Use

George Harrison told me about a particularly raucous Travelling [sic] Wilburys session that occurred the evening before our interview: "It's like if you have a few beers and you get all excited—like last night. We had great fun and it sounded groovy, but at the same time, the next day you've got a hangover and you're all messed up."

## Conditions Conducive to Creating

Harrison . . . recalled our sojourn in India and the number of people who dashed off to shop and flit about. He found it amusing that at the ashram, through meditation and stillness, they could find everything they needed, yet still they looked elsewhere: "Although we have this divinity, or creativity, within us, it is covered with material energy, and a lot of the time our actions come from a mundane level. There is an expression 'beggars in a goldmine,' and that's what we are. We're like beggars in the goldmine, where everything has really enormous potential and perfection, but we're all so ignorant with the dust of desire on our mirrors. While we were in Rishikesh, I wrote a song called 'Deradune.' I never recorded the song, but it was about seeing people going along the road trying to head for this place called Deradune. Everyone was trying to go there for their day off from the meditation camp. I couldn't see any point in going to this town. I'd gone all the way to Rishikesh to be in meditation and I didn't want to go shopping for eggs in Deradune! The verse of the song said, 'See them move along the road/In search of life divine/Unaware it's all around them/Beggars in a goldmine.'"

---

"I like quietness. I tend to write most of my songs in the night when the world goes to sleep for a bit and everything's quiet."

## Creative Tricks of the Trade

George Harrison told me he needed deadlines to write, but emphasized that creativeness never disappears completely: "I find that, having just finished writing and recording an album, I tend to now work in spurts. At one point I think, 'How do you write a tune?' I have just totally forgotten. But unlike some people who think they've dried up, I don't believe we dry up. Some people are really good at it; they'll set themselves an hour or two every day to go in there and write something. I don't do that. Somebody will say something or I'll see something, and I'll write it down on a piece of paper and later it will come into a tune. But the way I am at the moment I do have to force myself to do it; that's why deadlines are good. I never used to think I could write songs about specific things. I used to just write and the song would be whatever it became. Now somebody will ask me to write a song for a movie, and this is what's happening. I've done a bit of that lately and that's good too. You have to make yourself inspired."

---

### Looking Within

"Meditation is only a means to an end. In order to infuse energy and power and get it flowing through our bodies, we have to meditate. You infuse that energy into your being, and so when you are in activity, it rubs off onto that creatively. To really be in touch with creative energy, you will find that it lies within the stillness."

# HANDMADE FILMS
# TENTH ANNIVERSARY TOAST

George Harrison and Michael Palin | October 1, 1988 | Speech Transcript

A little more than a year after Harrison spoke to *Film Comment*, he gathered with friends and film-world colleagues at Shepperton Film Studios in London to toast the tenth anniversary of HandMade Films. Michael Palin, former Monty Python member and star of a several HandMade films, served as the evening's host, rallying the troops and introducing the man who made HandMade. As the recording of the event makes clear, everyone was enjoying the spirit—and spirits—of the evening, and Harrison's words were brief and jovial. What's also apparent, though, is that—even after ten years in the filmmaking world—Harrison still felt like an interloper. —Ed.

**Michael Palin:** . . . Without HandMade very few of the films that all of us here tonight have made would ever have happened. I ask you to raise your glasses—or contact lenses if you wear them [*laughter*]—and drink a toast to HandMade Films . . . [*with audience*] *HandMade Films*! [*Applause.*]

**George Harrison:** Ladies and gentlemen . . .

**Palin:** Mr. George Harrison! [*Applause.*]

**Harrison:** [*Slightly muffled.*] . . . Really if I had a guitar then I could just say [*strumming motions*] something to you. . . . You know, that'd do me. . . . Anyway, so let's get on with the music. I'll try—I've got my speech here.

Thank you all for coming . . . now, fuck off. [*Laughter.*] Thank God for rock 'n' roll music—anyway. [*Applause.*] Anyway, I love you all, and it's a pleasure to pretend to be in the film business [*laughter*] and this stupid life, the cartoon world we're living in. . . .

But the big[*gest*] thanks of all goes—for me, personally—to Carl Perkins. And Carl has come all this way from Nashville to entertain me—and I don't care about you lot, you know, whether you like it or not; [*laughter*] Carl came here to do it for *me*, you know—and I'd like to thank Carl, after being in show business and being in the film business—just to remind me that . . . it's still much better being a guitar player.

# TELEVISION INTERVIEW

Kurt Loder | October 18, 1988 | MTV News

The Traveling Wilburys—the all-star group spearheaded by Harrison in 1988 that also featured Roy Orbison, Bob Dylan, Tom Petty, and Jeff Lynne—was the kind of project many
top musicians dream of: being part a group that allows each to turn down the magnitude
of their own careers, and to get some fun out of the music again. Yet rarely does such a
collaboration happen free of managerial direction and record label involvement, which can
easily dispel the desired informality and sense of camaraderie. That the Wilburys came
together at all—and the music was actually worthy of the legends involved—is a result of
the unplanned way that it happened.

There's a feel of incredulity on Harrison's part as he relates the Wilbury story—the real
one, not the fictional one Derek Taylor would later invent—to MTV News anchor Kurt Loder
just before their first album was released. By all indications, their conversation constitutes
the first official Traveling Wilburys interview; excerpts were later used in the electronic press
kit (EPK) for the album. To further the conceit of a musical family, Michael Palin (of Monty
Python fame) crafted the album's liner notes, and the Wilburys themselves added to the
pretense in interviews, adopting their respective aliases: Lynne as Otis Wilbury, Orbison as
Lefty Wilbury, Petty as Charlie T. Wilbury, Dylan as Lucky Wilbury, and Harrison as Nelson
Wilbury. They were half brothers all, Charles Truscott Wilbury Sr. their fictional father. Eventually, even HandMade Films began plans to make a film about the family act (which, sadly,
never came to fruition).

It was all done with humor; even the name of the group was a joke. "We'll bury it
in the mix," Harrison would say to Lynne when certain issues happened in the recording
studio. The more gaffes, the more "we'll bury"s would be needed—which later became the

"trembling we'll bury"s. For a former member of a band with a pun-based, inside-joke sort of name, the "Traveling Wilburys" was perfect. —Ed.

**Kurt Loder:** Hi, I'm sitting here with George Harrison—or Nelson Wilbury, I suppose, as you'll be better known soon. George, explain to us the genesis of the Wilburys, if you could.

**George Harrison:** It's one of those things that I think had you tried to plan it, it would never have happened. It just happened by its own accord.

**Loder:** Was it like, one night, you guys were just sitting around?

**Harrison:** It was actually April the fourth, this year—I was asked by my record company to give them an extra song to put on a twelve-inch extended single for Germany and Great Britain. Which—I didn't have any extra tunes recorded at the time, so I just said, "I'll go in tomorrow, go in a studio some place, and I'll just write one and do it then. It's only a C-side." [*Loder laughs.*] They want this extra song.

So I was having dinner with Jeff Lynne, and he was having dinner with Roy Orbison, and I said to Jeff, "Do you feel like coming along?" And he said, "Sure." Roy Orbison said, "Well, if you do something give me a call." I went around to Tom Petty's house to pick up my guitar, which was at his house, and he said, "Oh, I was wondering what I was going to do tomorrow. . . ." And in the meantime, we were with such short notice I didn't know of any studio I could find that quickly. So I called Bob [Dylan] and he said, "Sure, come on over." He's just got a little tape machine in his garage. So we went over, and I just made part of a tune up that morning, and we went to his house. Jeff and I sat in the garden and made up the—finished the tune off. We went in, put it down, wrote the lyrics all together, and mixed it. We did it all—it was all written and done in one day.

**Loder:** How do you write the lyrics all together with, like, five guys in the room? Does that present any difficulties?

**Harrison:** It was five guys in the garden, actually. We were sitting out in the garden. It was really good. I mean, it just happened that I got a piece of paper and a pencil and I said, "Okay, come on. There's all these great writers now, let's have some lyrics!" And everyone was saying, "What's it about? What's it called?" And I just kept [*turns head back and forth as if searching*] looking around for a clue of what it was called. And I saw this cardboard box behind the garage door, and it said "handle with care." I said, "It's called 'Handle with Care.'" [*Pushes up sunglasses; Loder laughs.*] They said, "Yeah, OK, that sounds good."

And then it was easy. Just started, you know, being "beat up and battered around," and somebody else said something else, and that was it. It was written and recorded just on April the fifth.

**Loder:** Was this such a great experience you decided immediately that you'd go ahead and go after an album?

**Harrison:** No, I took it to the record company and said, "Well, there's the extra song for the, um . . . German market." [*Chuckles with Loder.*] And they said, "Oh God, we can't! It's too good to just throw away like that." So, they didn't want to use it.

**Loder:** The Germans wouldn't be happy to hear about that.

**Harrison:** So I just had a hold of this song for a couple of weeks, and I thought I can't think of what to do with it; I can't put it out as a single for me—it's not on my album. So I thought maybe they'd like to do another nine tracks, and I asked the other guys, and they said sure.

So we got together in May, and we did it based on the theory that if we could write one tune and record it in one day then maybe we could write another nine and record them. So we did that. We just got together, and we just sat down, and we wrote a tune; we put it down on tape, wrote another one. And we did it, like, that quick. Then later, Jeff Lynne and myself took the tapes and started overdubbing on it, put bass and drums and various instruments on it, but basically it was all written and done instantly.

**Loder:** Was there any common sound to all this stuff, or do just certain people come out more on certain tracks?

**Harrison:** Yeah, there's—obviously there's tunes that Bob had the most influence on, it sounds like him. And there's a song which we wrote specifically for Roy, which is very much like an old kind of Roy Orbison song. But it's a good—the album, it's not like—we tried to set out to do something that *wasn't* like going and buying an album of mine, or ELO, or Tom Petty, Bob Dylan, or Roy Orbison. We tried to combine everything, and it's worked very well.

**Loder:** What is the—could you describe this music to someone who hasn't heard it? This album?

**Harrison:** Well, I think it's basically . . . it's very "up" music, it's very, very "up." That is to say, it's *danceable*, if you like to dance. [*Loder chuckles.*] But, yeah, it's fun—it's just really good, fun music. It says some funny things, and the sound of it—because we all basically tend to dislike computers, and so—it's very *wooden*. I mean, it's the first band that I can think of that's got five rhythm guitar players.

**Loder:** But Jeff, too, I imagine he'd be adding something in there.

**Harrison:** Yeah, we've added touches here and there, but we've tried to keep it more or less like it was as we wrote it and did it. It's polished off a bit, but not too much.

**Loder:** Is there some story behind the name the Wilburys that you could perhaps let us in on?

**Harrison:** That was last year when Jeff Lynne and myself were doing *Cloud Nine*. And, I don't know, we probably had too many drinks, we were just talking about something, and this came out—the Trembling Wilburys.

**Loder:** The Trembling Wilburys?

**Harrison:** Yeah. Then it turned into the Traveling Wilburys . . . and that was it. It was forgotten about, really, and when we recorded this song I just said to Jeff, "*This is it*, this is the Traveling Wilburys." [*Chuckles with Loder.*]

**Loder:** Is there a storyline in the video you can tell us about? Or, how did the idea come about?

**Harrison:** The story to the video is that there's these five guys singing a song around a microphone, and I don't think you need much more of a story than that. Each person in it has their own story.

# TELEVISION INTERVIEW AUDIO AND TELEVISION PROMO

January 1989 | Interview Transcript, MTV News


The essential idea behind the supergroup that was the Traveling Wilburys was to *not* be a supergroup. Yet, whether or not they were fictional, their immediate success was very, very real. Their first album, *Traveling Wilburys, Vol. 1*, was an international hit and eventually garnered a Grammy. To many critics, it was a refreshing reminder of how a musical project could flourish from a pure, collaborative impulse, rather than from the marketing schemes that typified similar star-studded rock-industry projects. On December 8, 1988, as the Wilburys' debut single "Handle with Care" was taking off, Roy Orbison died, amplifying their story and sales. When the surviving members—George Harrison, Tom Petty, Jeff Lynne, and Bob Dylan—met in Los Angeles a month later to create a video for the album's second single, MTV News stopped by the set.

MTV's news division was little more than a year old at the time, still getting their look and approach together. They sent one of their less seasoned producers to interview the four members of the group about the new video, Orbison's passing, and future plans. The idea was to simply get the answers to a list of questions on video and use excerpts in various news spots on MTV and as teasers for the Wilburys video. The interviewer herself was off camera and her voice would not be heard—which, in the end, was a good thing.

Her nervousness and inability to match the Wilburys' sense of playfulness were parts of the problem. So were a series of technical hiccups at the start and the musicians' obvious frustration with a series of uninformed, poorly articulated questions. There's a general rule of thumb in journalistic situations that the person doing the questioning must pay atten- tion more closely to the conversation than those doing the answering in order to pick up on cues and respond accordingly. That doesn't happen here. (It's also a truism that things are not going well if those being interviewed begin to focus on the interview process itself.)

The transcript below captures the complete interview—a twenty-minute conversation that derails early and never fully recovers. Nonetheless, Harrison sets aside his displeasure to deliver statements more coherent than the questions. The MTV News spot that drew upon the footage from this interview follows and uses—as Dylan predicted—a mere soundbite from the total conversation. —Ed.

[*General laughter; Jeff Lynne, George Harrison, and Tom Petty are clustered together on a small couch and chair. Harrison and Petty smoke cigars, then lean off camera and put them out*]

**Interviewer:** . . . Some people have a thing about, you know, they really don't . . .

**George Harrison:** . . . The *Smoking* Wilburys!

**Interviewer:** I love those shoes so much.

**Harrison:** They're new Wilbury boots that we're going to merchandize. [*Interviewer laughs.*] They're really good aren't they?

**Interviewer:** They're great.

**Harrison:** You know, the best thing about them is they give you *corns* on your toes within five minutes of having them.

**Crew Member:** I'm actually rolling, by the way. . . .

**Interviewer:** Oh, OK.

**Harrison:** Rolling? I'd like to say hi to all those Beatle people out there and thank you for buying our Christmas record, and uh . . .

**Interviewer:** [*To someone on crew*] Are you a happy camper? Are you . . .

**Harrison:** I'd just like . . . are you rolling? You rolling?

**Interviewer:** A compressor kicking in?

**Harrison:** Are you rolling?

**Interviewer:** Where is that compressor . . . [*Indistinct, drowned out by whistling noises.*]

**Harrison:** I'd just like to say that I'm absolutely disgusted with the way they're chopping down the rain forests on this planet to feed hamburgers, to grow hamburgers on.

**Jeff Lynne:** Here, here!

**Interviewer:** OK, we're gonna . . .

**Harrison:** I'm disgusted with it, and you can do all your showbiz nonsense that you like, but the ozone layers and the rain forests is [*sic*] very important. So stop eating hamburgers, get veggie burgers, and let's have some oxygen.
[*Film reel noise, laughter.*]

**Lynne:** Oxygen's all right. . . .

**Interviewer:** [*To crew*] OK, you tell me when you have speed.

**Tom Petty:** [*Whispers*] I think I have speed. . . .

**Interviewer:** OK, now we're rolling.

**Lynne:** [*Whispers to Harrison, laughs.*]

**Petty:** This is serious though. . . .

**Interviewer:** OK, now we're really going to get serious, guys. . . . Let's talk about this video to start off, "End of the Line." What's happening today with you guys chugging away in the train, the whole idea?

**Harrison:** Chugging right along, making a video. Yet another pop video.

**Interviewer:** It's like a continuation of the first?

**Harrison:** Sort of, yes. Now we're on the train, chugging along, doing the next song.

**Interviewer:** Who's idea was this, to make it a continuation?

**Harrison:** Uhhh . . . Jeff's idea.

**Lynne:** Yeah. Well, it's my idea actually. Silly thing. No, it wasn't—it was George's.

**Harrison:** Yeah, I think it was Bob's idea.

**Lynne:** It's a good idea anyway, really, it goes nice with . . .

**Harrison:** Bob can't be with us on this interview because he's outside the door. You know, he can't sort of *get through* the door, so he's decided that we should be spokesmen for him. But he did think of this idea, particularly the idea where we go through the tunnel on the train.

**Lynne:** Yeah, all that . . .

**Interviewer:** Who was directing this video? Is it the same director . . .

**Harrison:** Willy Smax.

**Interviewer:** And that's the same person as before?

**Harrison:** No. Willy did want . . . he's worked with Dave Stewart a lot and done a lot of stuff in England, and he did the "Got My Mind Set on You," he did that one for me. Not the one in chair with the funny hats but the one where the little girl with the nice bun, you know, that one.

**Interviewer:** . . . Falls through the machine. Yes, I do remember that one. [*To crew*] Is that coming through, that typing?

**Crew Member:** That's not a problem . . .

**Harrison:** Hey, Clyde . . . [*Gestures to Warner Bros. Records' VP of product management Clyde Bakkemo, off camera*]

**Interviewer:** [*To crew*] Can you hear it? Do you think we could . . . is there any way we could get that typing to stop?

**Petty:** [*To Bakkemo*] Doing pretty good so far, huh?

**Harrison:** It doesn't matter. People do actually type in, in . . . the world.

**Interviewer:** . . . in video shoots. No, I know. [*Laughs.*] Yeah, right.

[*General discussion among crew.*]

**Harrison:** This is live, we're on the set here. There's people typing, there's people, you know, compressing things. . . .

**Interviewer:** Let's talk about the theme of the video.

**Harrison:** The theme, hmm.

**Interviewer:** [*Laughs.*] Let's get *real* serious, here. No, I mean . . . "End of the Line" . . . uhm.

**Harrison:** . . . Is a very optimistic song, so therefore, we decided, even though Roy died, Roy was an optimist too, and I think I speak [*with mock gravitas*] *for all the Wilburys* when I say that Roy would have liked us to have continued to do the "End of the Line." You know, it's a very optimistic song, and that's really all there is to it.

**Interviewer:** Was there any debate among the four of you as to whether or not you would do another video?

**Harrison:** No, we never talk to each other . . . except in videos, on the videos.

**Lynne:** That's right.

**Interviewer:** You just show up and then . . .

**Harrison:** Yeah, just interviews is the only time we meet and talk.

**Interviewer:** So wait, the decision to come here and do it now, I know it was originally intended to be done in London, correct . . . last week? I mean, obviously that had to change. What made you say let's do it in LA, let's do it now, let's not wait two weeks?

**Harrison:** Because we were all going to be here. Basically, you have to grab the Wilburys when you can.

**Interviewer:** It's kind of hard to grab the Wilburys.

[*Overlapping comments from Wilburys; laughter.*]

**Petty:** . . . the Wilburys!

**Harrison:** . . . very elusive.

**Interviewer:** The Elusive Wilburys.

**Lynne:** That's right.

**Interviewer:** Do you feel like . . . I was told, originally, and now watching you making the video I don't think that's quite accurate, that this is going to be, quote, unquote, "a tribute to Roy." Do you feel like, though there's, in a certain sense, a dedication, I mean, more *inside yourselves*, that this video is a tribute to Roy? Was the choice of this as the second single having to do with that?

**Harrison:** I think whatever song we were doing, we'd do whichever one was going to be the next single. But I mean, I think "a tribute to Roy" is something that you feel to yourself really or to ourselves. We love Roy, and we still do, and he's out there really, his spirit, you know; life flows on within you and without you, and he's around, you know, in his astral body; he'll be . . . he'll be cool.

**Lynne:** I'd like to say that Roy was one of the nicest people I ever met, and he was the best singer ever. It's a real loss to the Wilburys, I might say, and to the world really.

**Interviewer:** What do you think his impact was on music? I mean, all of you really grew up listening to him. You're all one generation behind. . . . George is raising his eyebrow. [*Indistinct.*]

**Harrison:** You know, I was just smiling because I was just thinking that, what Bob said, "They won't use any of this, the lady's [*indistinct*], they'll only use one sentence anyway. . . ."

**Interviewer:** No, I . . .

**Harrison:** . . . I'm just thinking as you go on and elaborate and we talk about a hundred things, and what ends up on the show is: [*muffles voice, adopts a fast-paced television-host tone*] "Here they are, the Wilburys [*indistinct*]. . . ." [*As if a bewildered viewer*] "What was that? Oh, I've missed them."

**Interviewer:** No, we'll make sure that a lot gets used. I think a lot will get used. I'll try anyway.

**Harrison:** No, Roy was just a great singer. He was a fantastic singer, and all of us in that period of time grew up with him, loved his music, and then he sort of disappeared or we all got busy, you know, the world got too busy to notice him, and . . . except for a few people, [*points toward Lynne*] like Jeff, who tracked him down to the end of the earth to say, "Hey you, I want to make a record with you because you're so good."

**Lynne:** Yeah, I did that. I did that. I did sort of do that—*trekked* to see him. It was an expedition, and three years later we finally got to do it.

**Interviewer:** Did you learn anything working with Roy that maybe surprised you? You know like, "Wow, I didn't expect . . ."

**Lynne:** I—well, you know, everybody's got this impression that it was all sad, but he was *so funny*. He was really a funny guy and he laughed a lot and had a great time, and he was a pleasure to hang out with, you know, he was really great fun. And that's like, that was the surprise, really, because I thought he'd be all sad.

**Harrison:** I didn't expect him to know all the words to Monty Python's "Sit on my face/and tell me that you love me . . ." which he did. Also "Immanuel Kant/was a real pissant . . . " and all that. He knew all those things; he knew everything about . . .

**Lynne:** And he recited them regularly. [*Chuckles.*]

**Harrison:** Yeah, he did. He was hysterical really.

**Interviewer:** Tom, how about you? Any surprises?

**Petty:** Roy was just a lovely guy. I don't know if I was surprised by that.

**Harrison:** [*Turns to Petty in mock surprise.*] Oh! [*Laughs.*]

**Interviewer:** You were just surprised by George!

**Petty:** [*Laughs; to Harrison*] You do that so well. . . . It could've been anything.

**Harrison:** I didn't notice you there.

**Petty:** Yeah . . . no, he was just terrific.

**Interviewer:** When you work with people, as you're all working together now, I think you learn things. What are you all learning from each other?

**Harrison:** To go back to being a solo artist.

**Lynne:** Yeah. [*Laughs.*]

**Petty:** There's no future in groups.

**Interviewer:** [*Laughs.*] I see. I wondered that . . .

**Petty:** You don't want to do interviews—you can't get 'em all in.

**Interviewer:** You can't get everybody to do the interviews. [*Laughs.*] OK. Tell me about this song, "End of the Line," you said was very optimistic. There's all these questions about who wrote what on the album, and you can kind of tell because who's singing, but everybody is singing this song.

**Harrison:** You can't tell really. . . .

**Petty:** You can't tell, they're all wrong.

**Harrison:** . . . some of them we said, "OK, we need somebody to sing this one; why don't you do it, because it suited you." So you can't really tell.

**Petty:** Yeah, they don't have it figured out nearly as well as they think they do.

**Interviewer:** So they think they've got it all, but they don't. So tell me about "End of the Line." Who wrote it?

**Lynne:** I think George came up with the first riff of it, the verse, [*to George*] didn't ya?

**Harrison:** Uh yeah. I wrote the "All right" bit under a banyan tree in Hawaii, because I was thinking, "Well, we better try and write one that's like a Bob Dylan song." [*Laughs.*] Wrote that bit, and then we made up the rest later, and everybody wrote the words.

**Interviewer:** So it started like a Bob Dylan song?

**Harrison:** Well, just the [*sings guitar riff*] "ding-dinga-dinga-dinga, ding-dinga-ding." You know, like that.

**Interviewer:** It seems to me like the Traveling Wilburys is really sort of a parody of all of you in a way, too; there are *sort of* Beatle-y songs and *sort of* ELO-y songs, and . . . Is that an accurate—I mean, is that intentional?

**Petty:** A parody?

**Harrison:** Well, we are who we are, really. We are who we are, we do what we do, and, uh . . .

**Lynne:** That's probably why . . . it sounds like that.

**Interviewer:** But, I mean, are you making fun of yourselves a little? It seems like you're taking it a little, like, a step further. It's not just . . .

**Harrison:** It isn't really . . . there's nothing clever about it, really, it's just people who happen to get together because they get on well and made up a few tunes. Obviously, the influences of each individual influence the tunes, but to do it in a way which isn't all stuffy and conceited and try and do it, have fun, not worry about the consequences, and that's really all there is to it. While everybody else is out there all being big shots and all, selling millions of records, and, you know, with their hair permed like us . . . [*Laughs; Petty gets up from chair and exits the camera's view.*] . . . we just wanted to be simple and write a few tunes for a record.

**Lynne:** And sell millions of them.

**Interviewer:** I think Tom's going to juggle. [*Laughs; Petty returns with three apples, hands one each to Lynne and Harrison, sits down and starts eating his.*] I saw three things, I thought maybe . . .

**Lynne:** Why don't you do your trick, Tom?

**Interviewer:** You have a trick?

**Lynne:** He's got a trick like you've never seen.

**Petty:** Nah. You couldn't afford it.

**Interviewer:** Oh, OK. . . . So, well, what about the future of the Wilburys? I mean, obviously, the Wilburys has changed immensely—I mean, you can't—there were five of you, and now there are four of you.

**Harrison:** Yeah, but when it started there wasn't *any*. And we just sort of picked a few up as we, you know, drove down Ventura Boulevard. And there's many Wilburys out there; as some nice man in the New York *Daily News* said, "The best thing about the Wilburys, apart from their album, is that any decent person could be one." So Little Richard and, uh . . . Jerry Lee Lewis, they could be Wilburys. Hall and Oates couldn't.

**Petty:** Or, Jerry Lewis couldn't be in a . . . [*Indistinct.*]

**Harrison:** Keith Richards is a Wilbury, but George Michael isn't. You know, I mean, it's just—that's some writer's attitude about what is a Wilbury. So . . . you know. You can have . . . what was that—good will?

**Petty:** Peace on earth, good Wilbury toward men. [*Harrison chuckles.*]

**Interviewer:** [*Laughs.*] I like that, for Christmas time. So what about the film? I mean there was going to be a Wilburys film, the story of the brothers. . . .

**Harrison:** [*With mock seriousness*] Oh yeah, I was saving that. It's too good to release at this point in time. We're saving it, you know. There's too much interest in it. We want to wait until the interest dies down a bit.

**Interviewer:** And then spring it on everybody.

**Harrison:** Spring it on them when they don't know what's happening.

**Interviewer:** That's great. So obviously there's no problem with the Wilburys sort of coming and going as they please.

**Harrison:** No. In fact, they may even change the name later.

**Interviewer:** And then would they still be brothers?

**Harrison:** Well, if they were the Trembling Wheelbarrows they wouldn't be brothers really; they'd just be sort of things with handles on 'em. [*Laughs.*] It's just a little joke really, it's just a joke, it's just a bit of fun, a lighthearted—something to lighten up show business, which is so serious, and that's all it is. There's nothing to it, really; it's just amazing that it happened, really.

**Interviewer:** Are you having a lot of fun with it? I mean . . . seriously!

**Harrison:** Don't we look like we're having a lot of fun? [*Harrison, Lynne, and Petty strike a pose.*]

**Interviewer:** Yes, you look like you're having a lot of fun. But, you know, you say that about how show business is so serious . . .

**Harrison:** We were having great fun until you came in here with the interview. . . .

**Petty:** Yeah, this interview . . .

**Interviewer:** [*Laughs.*] Thank you very much, George.

**Harrison:** Nothing personal.

**Interviewer:** Oh, right . . . no, I won't take it personally.

**Petty:** We all got a job to do.

**Interviewer:** I'll just go home on my belly. Tom, tell us about the solo album that you're working on.

**Petty:** [*Raises hands as if nonplussed.*] Oh, no, no.

**Interviewer:** Jeff? Production?

**Lynne:** Production? I've been real busy, yeah, doing . . .

**Harrison:** Construction, yeah.

**Lynne:** Construction.

**Petty:** He's building my garage.

**Lynne:** I've just finished his garage, and we're going to record in it.

**Petty:** It's a really nice one.

**Interviewer:** Yeah? Yeah? Well, that's good. And George?

**Harrison:** I'm retiring now. This time probably for good. I mean, I've retired in the past, and I've made my comeback, and now I'm retiring again.

**Interviewer:** But you said you never went away.

**Harrison:** I didn't go away. I just went away from interviews. Planted a few trees. So I think it's time to do that again, now.

**Interviewer:** That's really . . . you're not going to do another solo album?

**Harrison:** Uhh, I don't—not at the moment.

**Interviewer:** What about this—I mean, are you guys going to do a third video, fourth video, a fifth video?

**Harrison:** Oh, it depends, really. Supply and demand, really.

**Interviewer:** If we want it?

**Harrison:** Yeah.

**Interviewer:** I think we want it. Tell me about this blend. The Wilburys, you said, can be anybody, but these brothers here, these Wilburys here, these Trembling Wheelbarrows, what makes it work? I mean, what was it that happened on Ventura Boulevard that made this combination?

**Harrison:** Tom had this really great underwear on, you know, he had these black suspenders and stuff, and we thought, "Hey, we might as well get him in the group. He looks pretty cute."

**Petty:** It's the least I could do.

**Harrison:** Just stuff like that.

**Petty:** Just stuff like underwear and suspenders . . .

**Interviewer:** . . . And having a good time?

**Petty:** And having a good time. [*Takes a bite of apple.*]

**Interviewer:** Can you just keep doing that? I mean, you did say show business is serious, and there are lawyers, and there are managers, and that's the reality of it. . . .

**Petty:** We could go into nylons from here.

**Harrison:** But—we don't wear pantyhose. We hate pantyhose. We like that little bit of skin at the top of the leg.

**Interviewer:** [*Laughs; lights go out.*] Wait, what happened?

[*Videotape stops, then restarts.*]

[*Crew and musicians cross talk.*]

**Harrison:** [*Smoking a cigarette*] Don't have him on, he's . . .

**Interviewer:** No, no, I thought you were going to say that about me, "Don't have her come in. . . ."

**Harrison:** Oh, no.

**Lynne:** No, you're fine.

**Interviewer:** You're on tape, now, you're on tape.

**Petty:** Do they use your questions in the interview? Or will it be like . . .

**Interviewer:** Sometimes they do and sometimes they don't.

**Petty:** It's not going to be that guy with the big hair is it? The blonde-haired . . . he's really an ass.

**Interviewer:** [*Laughs.*] I don't know what you mean. No, I'm too old.

**Harrison:** Anyway, it's very difficult—

**Interviewer:** [*To crew*] Are we speeding?

**Harrison:** —being interviewed when you're busy working, especially when you're so concerned about the world and its problems. Only this morning I saw a fire engine crash into three motorcars on my way to work. . . . Funny, really, isn't it?

**Interviewer:** Did you really?

**Harrison:** Yes.

**Interviewer:** So you were talking about, you know, concerns earlier about the rain forest and stuff like that, and that—do you want to say something, because . . . ?

**Harrison:** Yeah, what I think is that all those people out there, especially the people who are a little bit overweight, should eat *more* hamburgers so we can chop all the rain forests down, put loads of cows there and kill them so they can eat them, and then concrete over everything and make the world wonderful.

**Petty:** Make it one big burger.

**Harrison:** Yeah.

**Interviewer:** One big hamburger from the Traveling Wilburys. OK, if I could get you guys . . . would you be willing to do a generic promo . . .

**Petty:** I'm a Libra.

**Interviewer:** . . . a generic promo saying who you are and that you're introducing your new video, "End of the Line"? "Hi, we're the Traveling Wilburys and coming up next . . ." [*Indistinct.*]

**Harrison, Lynne, and Petty:** [*Intentionally out of sync and faltering*] Hi, we're the Traveling Wilburys, and here's our new video, and it's called "End of the Line."

**Harrison:** It's sort of like the architect sketch. [*Wilburys chuckle.*]

**Interviewer:** How about, "Hi, we're the Traveling Wilburys and coming up next, the Week in Rock"?

[*Harrison, Lynne, and Petty briefly confer amongst themselves.*]

**Petty:** Hi, we're the Traveling Wilburys . . .

**Harrison:** . . . Coming up next . . .

**Lynne:** . . . *The Week in Rock.*

**Petty:** It's really serious.

**Harrison:** The week in rock, yeah . . .

**Petty:** The weakening rock.

**Harrison:** Rock is pretty weak at this point in time.

**Petty:** Coming up next, rock gets weak.

**Lynne:** Weak.

**Petty:** Weak. Weak weak weak.

**Interviewer:** . . . OK, they have to go back to work, right?
[*Cross talk between crew members.*]

**Interviewer:** Oh, yeah. [*Laughs, talks to crew.*]

**Harrison:** Have to make a living you know.
[*Harrison, Lynne, and Petty start removing microphones, standing up.*]

**Interviewer:** Is that that on camera, [*indistinct*]? Yeah, I think it was . . .

**Harrison:** Anyway, Bob says hi. [*Laughter.*]

**Interviewer:** I need you guys to sign this release for me. . . .

## MTV News Report, January 1989

**MTV News Reporter John Norris:** The Traveling Wilburys are in L.A. finishing up a new video for the song "End of the Line"—the clip will start off with the train scene that ended the "Handle with Care" video. It's the first video the group has made since the death of Roy Orbison, but George Harrison—aka Nelson Wilbury—says the video shouldn't be taken as a tribute.

**Harrison:** . . . "A tribute to Roy" is something that you feel to yourself really or to ourselves. We love Roy, and we still do, and he's out there really, his spirit, you know; life flows on within you and without you, and he's around, you know, in his astral body; he'll be . . . he'll be cool.

**Norris:** George getting a little mystical on us once again. . . .

# MAGAZINE INTERVIEW

Mark Rowland | November 27, 1989 | Interview Transcript

By the end of the 1980s, Harrison was, once again, ready for a break. Various projects he had produced, coproduced, or somehow put into motion in the past few years had amounted to his most significant career resurgence. *Cloud Nine*, released in '87, had yielded two big hits and proven his most popular album in years. In '88, the same year the Beatles were inducted into the Rock & Roll Hall of Fame, he had formed the Traveling Wilburys; the once-in-a-lifetime lineup of musical legends had proven to be his most successful partnership since joining the band from Liverpool. And speaking of the Fabs—on November 10, 1989, a *New York Times* headline read: "Beatles and Record Label Reach Pact and End Suit." In effect, the decade-long legal battle between the various Beatles and Capitol-EMI was finally over; fraud and underpayment had been the primary complaints by the band, exacerbated by alleged misuse of their music—such as "Revolution" in the infamous Nike commercial.

The agreement not only delivered a substantial payment to the four litigants, but allowed for fresh, profitable projects to start anew—and there was a *lot* of Beatles music and footage ready to be released to a still-hungry public.

For Harrison the end of '89 represented another bookend: only a few months previously, he satisfied his contract to Warner Bros., delivering a greatest-hits package focusing on his Dark Horse years. Other than a live album in '92, *Best of Dark Horse: 1976–1989* would be the last release he would see during his lifetime. It featured older studio tracks and a new one as well: "Cockamamie Business," his wry comment on the music and film industries.

The *Best Of* album was the reason for an interview with *Musician* magazine's Mark Rowland, who held the title of "Pacific Editor" at the time. His ten-year run at that leading music publication was preceded by freelance writing for *Esquire*, *American Film*, and the *Los Angeles Times* and would lead to a successful career writing and producing for television, specializing in music and sports documentaries including VH1's *Behind the Music* and, currently, TV One's *Unsung* series.

Rowland's lengthy, rambling conversation with Harrison covered much ground beyond the new album: Harrison's self-regard as a guitar player and a songwriter (including comments on specific songs of renown), his Dylan fixation, and the recent Beatles agreement (which Rowland dubbed the "Long and Winding Settlement"). Informed equally on music, film, and current events, Rowland engaged Harrison well. Harrison's words paint him as wonderfully unguarded, as he allowed himself to get heated discussing global crises of the environment, of economic disparity, and of political corruption. One can only imagine what Harrison would have to say today—and at what volume.

The entire, unedited conversation follows, of which Rowland remembers: "I interviewed heroes of popular music, happily at regular intervals in the 1980s and '90s, like Miles Davis at his home in Malibu, Neil Young at Barney's Beanery, Rick James in a posh suite at the Plaza. My interview with Harrison took place in a windowless, grey room at Warner Brothers in Burbank." He adds:

> That's not a complaint. Who among writers or fans wouldn't want the chance to meet George Harrison, any place, any time? And the setting did kind of reveal, or at least reinforce, what most of us figured we knew about George—that this was a guy who met you straight up and without pretense. He was resolutely thoughtful, and often quite funny, even friendly, but with a flint edge in reserve to ward off annoying requests. At one point I clumsily mentioned how Paul and John often talked about their own songs with the Beatles, as a pretext to asking George to do the same. "It gets a bit tedious though, doesn't it?' he snapped. Then he graciously indulged me anyway.

—Ed.

**Mark Rowland:** So, how are you?

**George Harrison:** A bit tired today, but you know, I'm not bad. I'm just going to go and have a rest. I'm looking forward to that.

**Rowland:** Are you going back to England for the holiday?

**Harrison:** No. It's too cold there. [*Laughs.*]

**Rowland:** Good for you. Well, listen, I have a few questions for you, so I'll shoot away.

**Harrison:** Hopefully I have some answers.

**Rowland:** If not just make them up. I've really been enjoying listening to the *Best Of* collection and some of the new songs as well, and one of the lines that always stood out in "Cockamamie Business," [*laughs*] one of many, is right at the end, you know, where you say "I didn't want to be a star, I wanted just to play guitar. . . ."

**Harrison:** Actually, I should have made it sitar. [*Laughter.*]

**Rowland:** I thought, you know, given you had been a star now for a quarter century or so . . .

**Harrison:** I think the word star is a bit of a joke, I use it with a . . . you know, tongue in cheek.

**Rowland:** Have you become more comfortable perhaps with the notion of that?

**Harrison:** Oh, it's been a long time now, isn't it? It's been—since I was in the band playing it's been thirty years, so it's been a long time. You know, I've got used to it. I've never felt that comfortable with people looking at me and stuff, that kind of thing, because, I mean . . . it has its ups and downs. The ups are you may be able to get a table in a restaurant, and the down one is that everybody looks at you and keeps bugging you all through . . .

**Rowland:** All through dinner.

**Harrison:** Yeah. [*Laughter.*]

**Rowland:** But it seemed—I don't know, it seemed that there was some way in which, maybe in the last couple years, having taken the hiatus that you took, from recording, from the music . . .

**Harrison:** I've been trying to retire for twenty years.

**Rowland:** [*Laughs.*] Unsuccessfully, I guess.

**Harrison:** Well, yeah. You know, I had a good break away from the record business before *Cloud Nine*. Although, I was still doing a few things, writing a few tunes and playing on a few things, but . . . and then that album did good for me because, you know, I mean we talked about that story last time, you know, because of the influence of, and the input by Jeff [*Lynne*], who was really what I was looking for, for years—was a friend who can help and give me input and . . . not abuse me, musically. [*Laughter.*]

**Rowland:** He'll respect your own ideas about things.

**Harrison:** Yeah. It's been good.

**Rowland:** I have a question—it's been just about—and I'm sure you've probably been reminded of this a few times already today—but it's been just about twenty years now since the Beatles really had their last recording session. Like everyone else, you know, I think the perspective of what the Beatles really were changes over time, but from being on the inside and being one of them I would imagine that your perspective has really changed and that certain things come to the fore.

**Harrison:** I don't know, I think being in them, I think it's even more difficult to figure them out than maybe just being a casual observer. Really. Because, somehow, I can't separate *any* of it. I can't put it into little . . . you know, like, it goes back to being a schoolboy, really. I met John and Paul when I was in school, and then it goes through all those crazy days of the German stuff and then the recording and the mania, and you know, everything. And then all the history since, everybody trying to dissect them or understand them and talk about them and then have all the generations who keep coming up and discovering them.

Somebody just told me last night their four-year-old boy is into the Beatles, but not with anybody playing them for him; he just sort of somehow found out. So . . . you know, I don't understand it.

**Rowland:** But I guess I didn't mean so much, you know, you trying to analyze why was this what it was, but your own perhaps appreciation of what it might have given you [*indistinct*] . . .

**Harrison:** Once we went through some great times and then we went through some horrible times and once there's so much distance in between then you tend to just remember the good stuff. Basically, I think it was, we just had some good tunes and I think we could have been a really good band if we hadn't have gotten famous. [*Rowland laughs.*]

Musically we were very potential and then—not to say we didn't do good things on our records, but—I think the adulation and the crowds, they forced us into a little box . . .

**Rowland:** . . . Into a room, yeah.

**Harrison:** Into a room on our own, and although we still came up with good stuff, just the playing, the actual thing of performing and being fluid, *fluent* with our instruments, that's what I lost.

**Rowland:** Yeah, I think maybe you feel that most keenly since you really came in as "the guitar player," in a way. But I was thinking about that myself because I had noticed you sort of mentioned that on a couple of occasions in the past.

**Harrison:** Yeah, I feel in a way, you know, I know I'm supposed to be a guitar player, but I don't really feel like one. I pick up the guitar when I want to write a tune, and I play it when I make a record, and I've actually played on a few other people's records, which is really interesting, but I had to do it in my own way. I'm not like somebody, say Eric Clapton—we'll talk about him because he's my friend and I know about him—you know, you say, "Eric, come on over," and he'll plug in his guitar, listen to the thing, and he'll just blow the general thing, play it and be of a certain standard immediately. For me, I have to really figure out what I'm going to do and even learn maybe a part because I'm just not that fluent with it.

**Rowland:** Yeah, but see that's partly, it's your style of really . . . I mean, it seems that part of what your style is, is to really have a very tightly woven kind of pop, constructive part, which I think maybe . . . it seems like, because the "guitar hero" thing came into such vogue in the late '60s, maybe that approach seemed to go out of fashion.

**Harrison:** Well, I'm certainly not a guitar hero. [*Chuckles.*] If you read the lists of great guitar players . . .

**Rowland:** And yet I think that that approach of really coming up with the line, you know, the guitar line, the melody that fits the tune—[*interjection from Harrison, indistinct*]—that's what really kind of stands the test of time a lot. It has. I think it's funny listening to your last record, I hear

Eric playing a lot of parts. In a way—I mean, you recognize him and his tone—but in a way, it's more a reference to a style that you would associate with Beatles '66 than you would with Cream.

**Harrison:** Exactly, yeah. I've been fortunate to have some good friends who are musicians, and I've never been one to try and force myself on everything, you know. I like to have input from other people, and so when I have a song that calls for a kind of Eric Clapton guitar part, I dare say I could practice for an hour or so and do a solo decent enough, but then all I'm ending up doing is denying having the opportunity of having Eric around and hanging out with him for a bit. So I like the input from other people.

You know, I mean, people keep saying about whether to do a tour or something, but the idea of having to go on the stage and try and reproduce everything you've done on your records, the only way I could do that is if I had other people playing, because you play rhythm guitars, and then you play some electric bass, and then you put a solo on the top—you're going to have to have a band that can play it whether I'm there or not. Now I can just come on and, you know, *fit in*.

**Rowland:** I guess what I was trying to refer to before, whereas the fame that the Beatles got at a certain point did change the circumstances so that you didn't continue to play as a band, it seemed that for you what it also did, on the other side, was really create an environment that gave your talents as a songwriter a chance to really kind of come out a lot more.

**Harrison:** Oh, absolutely. Because then the whole game was writing, you know, having your own songs, and after we made our very first album, which was done in a couple of hours—it wasn't the first album in the States, it was *Please Please Me*—after we had done that and Paul and John were really getting into writing songs, I just took a look at them and I thought, "Well, I think I'll get in on this game, I gotta try that." But it was very difficult at that time, and it's still difficult sometimes, to write a decent song. But at that time having *them* as the other people in the group was very difficult, so I started to just write on my own for years and years, because I didn't know how to communicate like that with somebody else. And it was very difficult to write songs that would be good enough.

**Rowland:** Yeah, I would think, on the one hand, it's a great opportunity seeing how they worked, it's great having them as a model. On the other hand, you've got to write songs that are going to approach—or surpass—that standard.

**Harrison:** Yeah, at least being decent on the album.

**Rowland:** So you're saying that actually you did write a lot of songs that just never saw the light of day?

**Harrison:** Not really, no. For the second Beatle album, I wrote—

**Rowland:** "Don't Bother Me."

**Harrison:** Yeah, and that sort of sums up of my state of mind then. [*Rowland laughs.*] I mean, I was involved when they were writing songs. There were a lot of songs that were Lennon/McCartney that actually had other people involved in [*them*], whether it be lyrics, or just structures, or the circumstances. I mean, I know now from writing with friends that when you're all sitting 'round and a song comes out, you know, you have to really think carefully about assigning how many "percent" each person gets, because there's nothing worse than being involved in a situation when you find out that . . . you know, you think, "Wasn't I . . . there?"

**Rowland:** [*Laughs.*] Was there a certain naïveté in that sense with the Beatles? Because, I mean, now *everyone* knows.

**Harrison:** Absolutely. Well, and there was also this thing—because they got together at an early age and they got signed up by this publisher as "Lennon/McCartney"—so consequently, even if, you know—*whoever* wrote it, it was always Lennon/McCartney, even if just John wrote it or just Paul wrote it, or even if I wrote half of it, it was still Lennon/McCartney. Not that I wrote half of it, but I did write bits of things, and you know, I know from my own experience the bits that other people have written in my songs, they always go with a mention. [*Chuckles.*] But I only say that in reference to the fact that I had my one or two songs occasionally, but really, I was involved more.

**Rowland:** Can you give me some examples?

**Harrison:** Well, a good example was crossing the Forth Bridge in Scotland in the back of an Austin Princess when the song which became known as "I Feel Fine" came about, and I'll tell you exactly how that song came about. We were, the three of us, singing "Matchbox" in three-part harmony, and it turned into "I Feel Fine," and the guitar part on it was from Bobby Parker, "Watch Your Step," just a bastardized version of that. So that was a song that I know basically, I was there at the whole of its creation, but it was still a Lennon/McCartney.

**Rowland:** I think a lot of people do appreciate, including people that fiddle around with guitar a little bit, there are a lot of tunes where the guitar break or intro on the pieces is as distinctive as the melody. When I think of "Day Tripper," I think of the guitar part as much as I think of the melody.

**Harrison:** Well on occasion, you know, to be absolutely fair, on occasion something like "Day Tripper," I don't remember exactly about that, but sometimes I will say Paul—if he wrote a song—he could have started by writing the guitar part.

**Rowland:** Oh really, he would do that sometimes?

**Harrison:** Yeah, I admired them. So, you know, it always worked different ways.

**Rowland:** One thing that I kind of wanted to do, and since we're sort of on the subject right now, maybe I can, if you'll allow me. I often see interviews with Paul, and in the past with John, where they'd go over different songs that they wrote.

**Harrison:** It gets a bit tedious though, doesn't it?

**Rowland:** [*Laughs.*] Well, would you indulge me for a few of your own?

**Harrison:** A few. To the best of my memory.

**Rowland:** Okay. And you don't have to give me a whole historical lineup. Maybe we could start with one that's not really brought up that often, which is "Long, Long, Long," from the *White Album.*

**Harrison:** Yeah, that was just a sort of funny little tune I wrote one day, basically. The only thing I suppose that's memorable about it is that I was very hung up on [*Bob Dylan's*] "Sad-Eyed Lady of the Lowlands" at the time. It's got the same chords as "Sad-Eyed Lady of the Lowlands."

**Rowland:** Every now and then I hear . . .

**Harrison:** But "Sad-Eyed Lady" is a much better song. [*Laughter.*]

**Rowland:** A much longer song.

**Harrison:** Oh, yeah.

**Rowland:** Since you mention that, there are times in certain parts of your singing where I'll hear a little Dylan-esque kind of inflection come into your . . . Do you think that that ever happens consciously to you? In your singing, really, I'm thinking about.

**Harrison:** Oh, yeah. . . . It's probably just 'cause my voice is so bad. [*Chuckles.*] You know, out of all the contemporaries of ours, you know, I mean, it goes with the same list of favorites that I've had for years, going from Little Richard and Larry Williams and all that kind of stuff, to the rock 'n' roll Buddy Holly and Eddie Cochran, Carl Perkins, you know, that stuff. And in 1963, Bob Dylan. And Bob, you know, as a songwriter . . . *and* as a singer, I happen to think his voice is great. I love all that sort of madness. And as a person I think somebody who, you know, like he said once, "Time will tell just who has fell, and who's been left behind. . . ." I think being out there, whether you like him or not, he's Bob, and I'm thankful that there's people like that.

So consequently, over the years I've always listened to his music, and I've never tried to imitate. I have just as a joke sometimes. I think, basically, being born in Liverpool, you have this nasal sort of kind of thing.

**Rowland:** Yeah right, you share . . .

**Harrison:** The cold, damp weather of the north.

**Rowland:** You guys share a common nasal passage, is that what you're saying? [*Both chuckle.*]

**Harrison:** Yeah.

**Rowland:** Well, how about "It's All Too Much"?

**Harrison:** . . . That was definitely the psychedelic period. Although, I didn't like what happened to the record. It ended in total madness with all them trumpet players.

**Rowland:** Well, it starts off with such a really biting guitar figure.

**Harrison:** Yeah. The song was basically like one of them naive post-acid things, re-entry songs, sailing around "on the silver suns," and stuff.

**Rowland:** Mm-hm. I remember watching a Frank Sinatra special on television about fifteen years ago, and Frank said that he wanted to pay tribute to one of the great songwriting teams, John Lennon and Paul McCartney, by singing one of the songs from their great songbook, and he proceeded to sing "Something," and I thought in some way that sort of . . .

**Harrison:** Summed me up?

**Rowland:** . . . summed up your peculiar position in the band.

**Harrison:** I know. I met Michael Jackson years ago after the Jackson 5 had split up but before he was as big as he is now, and somewhere I met him in the BBC in London and the disc jockey asked—said something about "Something," and he [*Jackson*] turned around and said, [*imitates Jackson's voice*] "You wrote 'Something'? I thought that was Lennon/McCartney." So he's probably looking through the catalog now, saying, "Well, why didn't I get the rights to that song?" [*Rowland laughs.*] . . . Well, you know, I'm the "Quiet One." [*Chuckles.*]

**Rowland:** In a way, it seemed to me that you really came to the fore on the *Revolver* record because those were, I mean I think that's . . .

**Harrison:** I can't remember. Oh, it was the Indian one, "Love You To" . . .

**Rowland:** . . . and "Taxman." And of course, "I Want to Tell You," which has always been a favorite of mine.

**Harrison:** Yeah, I like that one.

**Rowland:** Do you remember anything about that?

**Harrison:** No, I just remember like the mood of what was happening at that time, and it was a really exciting time because we were young, discovering everything and you know, there was a great, positive reaction to us, musically and socially. And it was a whole bit, and we had sort of these long-distance associations with various other groups through our records, and we knew that they liked you because you'd hear something in their songs. The Byrds and the Rascals, and actually John Sebastian, that kind of thing, and that song "I Want to Tell You." And also there was getting a little bit of political awareness you know, how, you know, the Big Brothers and that had got it all stitched up.

**Rowland:** Right, right. Then it came out a little further on when you did "Piggies." I mean, that was a much more overt statement.

**Harrison:** I don't know where that came from. I remember writing it; I don't remember where the whole idea of "Piggies" . . . because it was before this sort of . . . what would you call it when the police started beating everybody up in the . . . ?

**Rowland:** Right, like the demonstrations in Chicago and in Europe.

**Harrison:** The students in San Francisco and then "pigs" became like a big . . .

**Rowland:** That's right.

**Harrison:** It was a much sort of gentler thing, and it was before that kind of consciousness. It was just an awareness that the big guys up there, they're the ones who are in the stuffed white shirts—"starched white shirts." [*Laughter.*] It was a social comment because it's still the same. Like Phil Collins has that song [*"Another Day in Paradise"*] about people sleeping in the streets, but still everybody else is all tucked away cozy in their big government offices. It's just a portion of the money that's being just *squandered* on ridiculous things like the military. Now with Russia and *glasnost* and communism going away, they're going to have to have a good reason not to give that money to the poor, or to redivert it into helping the planet become safe and unpolluted. Notice how I turned the conversation around. Let's get rid of all the poisons that's going on here.

**Rowland:** Yeah. Well, I think that's so . . . I mean unfortunately, I think that they *will* try to come up with, you know, if it's calling out the military under the pretext of stopping drugs or something like that.

**Harrison:** Well, that's where you could use the army. See, we should have like a big international, I suppose it would be the United Nations Army, who would go around and instead of bullying innocent people, they go around and bully guilty people, you know—like the people who *are* damaging the environment. But you know, then we get into a big political situation where you find that the people who are causing the most damage are the industrialists and the people with all the money.

I've just been involved—in England, there's a similar thing that's in America, that Meryl Streep is doing, you know, with all that poison in our food . . .

**Rowland:** Right, yeah, with Alar.

**Harrison:** . . . for safe food. Alar, it's just been withdrawn by, what is it called . . . Uniroyal.

**Rowland:** Yeah, I thought that was a little suspicious.

**Harrison:** . . . I thought they made *tires*, yeah! At least they withdrew it. Like in England, the ministry of agriculture—they *still* say, "Well, we don't care, we're still using it, it's all right, we think it's all right." And the people who are making it are saying, "You better take it away. It's now proven it's poison."

So I'm involved a bit with that, but there's—everything, you know, on your potatoes and your tomatoes, and everything is *poison*. It's full of poison.

**Rowland:** I know. It's really scary.

**Harrison:** Not to mention the atmosphere we're breathing. But the basic problem there is the agrochemical industries have got a stranglehold on the government, and they're all in cahoots, and they're probably all Freemasons as well. [*Rowland chuckles.*] And that's it. So what we really need is an honest army that goes around busting all them guys. Dow Jones, and all that sort of money business, and Nikkei Dow, and the FTSE Index. They're the people that's ruining this planet, you know—buying, buy, buy, buy, buy, buy. Sell, sell, sell, sell, sell. You know? Really. And this madness that like Reagan and Thatcher together created, where they say, "Everybody is much better off now." Everybody's more in debt, everybody's got two cars, there's more concrete. . . . You know, we're having to sacrifice the planet for the motorcar. *Madness.* That's why I can't practice the guitar anymore. I'm so crazy with what they've done to our planet.

**Rowland:** It seems that there's a part of you that's . . . trying to weigh, in the sense of . . . there's part of you that really likes to remain a private individual, and yet you have a kind of public conscience that wants to drive you and do something with the energy and influence that you might have. Is that so?

**Harrison:** Well, it's true, it does help; if you've got a platform to speak from then you should speak and I think . . . just this morning I saw a program on TV with Olivia Newton-John and somebody else, I didn't catch the name, somebody Bagley . . .

**Rowland:** Ed Begley.

**Harrison:** Yeah, and that's great because now they've got the network TV doing a show trying to make people aware about recycling, and, you know, all that stuff. And in a way, you know, if you're going to have to talk about stuff, you might as well try and help the people on the street level because that's where it's going to be effective. The general public has to go to the supermarket and say, "We're not buying any food that's got poison."

England's got this cockamamie idea called food irradiation, and they take, I mean, they've found things like prawns or shrimp; they come into the country, the Ministry of Agriculture checks them out, and they say, "No, no, this stuff is rotten, we're not having it." It goes back out, they send it to Holland, they nuke it with irradiation, and then they bring it in another port and they check it then, and they say, "Fine, it looks fresh." Instead of getting rid of salmonella, which is now born into the chickens and the eggs, what they're going to do is just irradiate it. To irradiate a chicken, it's the equivalent to having 850 chest X-rays, and they're trying to make that law for our food; instead of cleaning up the food industry, they're just going to smokescreen it. Whitewash over it. And the only way to stop that is have people aware of it—who go to the shops and say, "We're not buying that shit, and we're not having plastic bags, and we're not having . . ." You know, really.

It's a hell of a problem, but . . . without the government [*helping*]. That's what annoys me, it's always the people who start these organizations who raise people's awareness, and the people with the power and the ability to change enormous things very quickly don't want to do it, they want to drag their feet.

**Rowland:** I think especially in recent weeks, with the events in Eastern Europe, you come to see that really only people *are* going to make change; if you invest your trust in politicians, ultimately, you're going to be very disappointed.

**Harrison:** Yeah. But there's always that politician behind the door who's got their guards—like Tiananmen Square—at ready, and it's like they're trying to weigh up now, "Shall we go in there and beat the shit out of them, or is the game up?" . . . That's what's frightening.

**Rowland:** Yeah. I agree with what you said. It's a tribute to popular artists who do this—although, on the other hand, it's sad that it's almost *left* to popular artists to be the only public spokespersons.

**Harrison:** It's the same thing with any of those charities, you know, like going back to Band Aid [*singer-songwriter Bob Geldof's 1984 charity-driven supergroup —Ed.*] and all that kind of stuff. And now there's millions of charities, and it's always musicians or film people who are doing the work that government really is supposed to do. They collect taxes to take care of everybody, but instead they're all off, there, playing their little games with missiles and stuff.

**Rowland:** The irony of when you grew up in the '50s and '60s to be told that rock'n'roll was sort of the devil's music and the music of corruption, and now you see that music figures are really kind of carrying the conscience of the planet.

**Harrison:** And the same people who are complaining about it being devil's music, they're the same people complaining, "Who do these people think they are? They're trying to be *nice* now." It's like you can't win, but it just shows there's a lot of good people out there—and most of them are musicians. [*Both laugh.*]

**Rowland:** I have a question, do you think that, you know, I mean you've had for a long time an awareness of the sort of things you're talking about—a strong kind of moral framework, I would put it—in your songs and a lot of your actions. Do you think that that would have emerged as strongly had it not been that you lived in the crucible of a situation like the Beatles where you got to really experience the excess . . . ?

**Harrison:** Yeah. It might have taken much longer, I think. I mean I think the experience we had in those years—plus certain substances people kept putting in our coffee, you know—just sped up the growth. I don't know. I may just be some sort of thick, sort of . . . miner or something, I don't know, if I hadn't been in a band. But it certainly did heighten the awareness.

**Rowland:** John seemed to write a lot of that into his music early on, but it seemed that you were the one who took it one step further when you actually tried to put it to a kind of practical purpose.

**Harrison:** Well, I found in the '60s, when everybody was all having a great time, we were all sitting around smoking stuff and then thinking of these great ideas, and after a few years I thought, "Wait a minute, nobody is doing anything. Everybody is talking about it, but nobody is *doing* anything." That's why I thought I better change, and then I got involved with all that meditation stuff, and that led me to think, "Well, you know, I can see how risky it was to make a song like 'My Sweet Lord' because you don't want to be like Cliff Richard or Billy Graham." But at the same time, it's like nobody is saying this, everybody is doing that love and peace and happiness, but where do you find that? You're going to find it by getting inside yourself and contacting . . .

**Rowland:** Whoever that is, that you want to call your spiritual leader.

**Harrison:** Yeah. And particularly at that time when we came out of the love and peace, straight into, like, spitting and kicking and all that fear in the '70s, headbanging, and . . .

**Rowland:** But also, I mean, with the Bangladesh concerts, that . . . you actually attempted to put that energy into a concrete, you know . . . which has really become, I think, kind of at least an inspirational model for a lot of the efforts that now have become almost routine.

**Harrison:** Yeah, well it's nice, I mean, I did it just because you have to have a reason. It wasn't just the reason that the people were starving and that the war was going on and that America at that time was giving arms to Pakistan to go and kill the Bengalis. The real thing that tied me to it was my friendship with Ravi Shankar. He being a Bengali, to him it was like so intolerable. To me it was something happening in the newspapers. And the more and more I talked about it with him . . . it was his idea, he was going to do the show anyway. I was just going to introduce it and then plug it into the Beatle concept, of particularly John Lennon's idea, that you might as well make a film *and* a record *and* all that, and get some money going. And it did. Regardless of what people say, it took a long time, but . . . I mean, $11 million doesn't sound much these days . . . you know, but—

[*Warner Bros. President Mo Ostin enters room, greets Harrison and Rowland; a brief discussion about George's schedule follows. Ostin departs.*]

**Harrison:** Mo is great. He's a really . . . real person. Like I'm trying to get him at it with, you know, when they send you records or information, in the mailing room there's like ten tons of paper and packages and cardboard. And I think he could do some good just as far as the record business goes. I know, one thing I learned from this Olivia Newton-John on the telly today, that her new album has got recycled paper.

**Rowland:** So does Ziggy Marley's.

**Harrison:** Now it all sounds like little stuff, but once you get the whole planet doing that, then it's gonna . . . I mean, just these newspapers! I've been in a hotel for like four days, and I've got a stack of newspapers this high. You know they say something like the number of trees for one print of the *New York Times*, probably the Sunday edition, is as big as the United Kingdom. It's madness what's going on.

**Rowland:** That could all be recycled.

**Harrison:** I think they shouldn't need to chop another tree down . . . *ever*.

**Rowland:** Certainly not at least any faster than they grow them.

**Harrison:** And you see what they're doing. They're chopping half of Papua New Guinea down just to make into packing cases for televisions. It's really immoral.

**Rowland:** I quite agree.

**Harrison:** But he's a good sensitive person. [*Rowland makes an indistinct interjection.*] . . . But if I can get them at it, then he can get all the other labels. And I dare say there's probably loads of people in all the other companies anyway already thinking along those lines.

**Rowland:** Yeah, I think more people are thinking about it because we're reaching a crisis stage, and that's usually when people wake up and smell the coffee, so to speak.

**Harrison:** This very eloquent manager we used to have called Allen Klein used to say, "Shit or get off the pot." [*Laughter.*] Stop shitting *and* get off the pot.

**Rowland:** It always seemed that you'd always kind of kept an eye on the more practical business side of things. Is that not so?

**Harrison:** Not true. I once asked Brian Epstein how much money we were getting for a gig, and then after that somebody said, "Oh yeah, *he's* the business people." I hate business. I'm still not into it. I know a lot about it now, but you know, I hate looking at bits of paper and reading all that stuff. Even having to deal with it on that level, it's such a pain and getting in my way of what I want to do. But to actually *do* business is . . .

**Rowland:** Well, it's ironic in a way, then, that you managed to have careers as both a pop star and a film producer.

**Harrison:** Yeah. I think I can operate on a human level; I can get on good with people, and I can get people together, and I can come up with ideas and all that. When it comes down to business, the kind of business I'm in, which is on telephones and lining people up and getting money off of them and talking to banks and signing contracts and lawyers, just that hustle, well, that's why I wrote "Cockamamie Business." It's like, to me, it's all a lot of old cobblers, and I think it's that maniac kind of, you know . . .

Okay, people have to run businesses, and people have to make a living. But there's a point where it gets over the top; it's like greed. It's greed. It's like, "What's the most we can have? What's the most trees we can chop down? What's the most pollution we can put in the atmosphere? What's the most number of roads we can build all over the land and fill it up with people in hatchbacks?"

**Rowland:** Well, it seemed that that was a lot of the thrust to that song, but also kind of throwing up your hands in a way too . . . to say, "Can you believe that this is how we live?"

**Harrison:** That's why I liked that expression. To me it's been a joke word. It's a very American word, and I've heard it over the years, and I just thought it's such a funny word, it's so silly—and yet it's a nice way of saying, "It's *fucking* crazy . . ."

**Rowland:** Yeah it is, without having to be downright insulting. I do want to ask you a few questions, actually, about your film stuff. Do you think that rock and roll has—from your perspective as a film producer perhaps, or maybe just as a fan of films—has had an influence on movies?

**Harrison:** Yeah, I think it's been coming for years in music and film, hasn't it. Music and film, they go together very well. If you make a film you need music on it and since, however many years now, you make music and they stick a film on it whether you like it or not. I think in some cases music and film are part and parcel of the same experience.

**Rowland:** How about in terms of attitude?

**Harrison:** They can all complement each other. It depends on how it's done really. I think in certain areas some things have been good. What I wanted to do someday is to get the music first and then write the movie to go with the music. You know, because as a musician it's very frustrating. And I've got a friend, I know a few people now through having our HandMade Films who score movies. And there's this good friend of mine, Michael Kamen, who has done so many films just since I've known him, and the frustrating thing is they make them, they spend all these millions of dollars making movies and edit it together, and then they present this rough edit to the musician, and they want the music yesterday! And by that time there's no budget left anyway, so they've got a couple of dollars for them to do it. And then you do it, and then they edit it, and the music doesn't fit, and then you have to redo it. And also the idea of—there's already so much good music, in some ways you don't have to write new music.

It's like—Mo Ostin told me this great story about Frank Sinatra where he said, "Frank, when are you going to do another album for us?" Frank said, "When are you going to sell more of the ones I've already made?" [*Laughter.*] I love that! That's perfect.

In that way, I think you can take music that's already there. And I'm not just talking about, you know, like when they use a Ben E. King song for a movie, or a Chuck Berry song, or they'll use "Great Balls of Fire." I mean, there's great music [*indistinct*] . . . there's popular music and classical music and all kinds of ethnic music, which would just make the most incredible soundtrack. That's what I would like to do: put that together and then say, "This piece of music is so brilliant. What would be happening if *this* was on the screen?"

**Rowland:** Yeah. I think that's a great idea.

**Harrison:** I mean, it's a long, weird way around it, and you got to get some good writers to piece together the thing because, let's face it, a movie is still—it's like a pop song, you know. You got to have the intro, the hook, and the catchy thing. And that's all it is, it's like, lay some pipe and a bit of top spin, you know, and then a bit of heat, and a hook, and then get out with a button. [*Laughter.*]

**Rowland:** But it's true, you could tap Fats Waller or something, or Eddie Cochran, you know, and it creates a whole tone. Part of the reason I asked is it seemed to me that the way Richard Lester put together *A Hard Day's Night*, in a way it created the first true rock'n'roll movie, both in terms of the way the movie was cut and the way the humor was. And so much of that seems to kind of have connections with a lot of the work that you've done and what Monty Python has done—that there's a kind of shared irreverence and conception.

**Harrison:** Well, yeah. *A Hard Day's Night* was just, I suppose in retrospect, it was just magic because of the timing—and because we were so rough, and at the same time, Dick Lester being the person to do it. So it was just one of them little packages that wasn't really like these days when they say how are we going to package Batman, we'll get Jack [Nicholson]—it wasn't really like that kind of thing. Like the Wilburys, it just more or less was there, and it just happened itself, and it just happened to be a good combination.

**Rowland:** Right, and that's why it worked. But then it became—because then he went on and did *Petulia*, which really became kind of like the quintessential '60s movie. That movie *Petulia*, do you remember that, with Julie Christie?

**Harrison:** You're talking about Dick? Dick Lester? Yeah, he did the one after . . . I'm not sure if it was after *A Hard Day's Night* or after *Help!*, which he did with Zero Mostel, *A Funny Thing Happened on the Way to the Forum*, and he did a film called *The Knack*, and then he did that one with John.

**Rowland:** *How I Won the War.*

**Harrison:** He's really good, Dick Lester, good sense of humor.

**Rowland:** But was there any sense, when you were involved in that, was there any spark that went off at that time when you were doing those films?

**Harrison:** Oh, yeah. You know that film *Help!* was really . . . we were on the road anyway, and they just got this writer who was from the same place or same area as we were from, a playwright, and he just sort of hung out with us for two days and then went off and wrote it. And then when we came to shoot it, we said, "I'm not saying that. I wouldn't say that." And we just changed it into what we would say. Not in every instance—because I said a word which became like a . . .

you know, people still use it to this day, and it was the dumbest word: "grotty." But that was the scriptwriter wrote that. [*Pretending to sulk.*] I didn't want to say it, but I said it anyway.

**Rowland:** [*Chuckles.*] And now you're stuck with it.

**Harrison:** Well, I'm not stuck with it, but some people are.

**Rowland:** Basically, how did—it sounds like *The Rutles* was really the first thing that you got . . . was that the first project that you became an executive producer [*on*], or . . . ?

**Harrison:** No, I didn't produce *The Rutles*. It was done by Lorne Michaels, from *Saturday Night Live*. I was *in* it, and I actually fed Eric [*Idle*] all the—not all, but *most*—of the information in the old footage so that he could get it historically and get the costumes right. I gave him a lot of input into it. But it was Gary Weis who did the . . .

**Rowland:** The animation . . . or, no, the little short films.

**Harrison:** Well, he directed it with . . . he did that "Got My Mind Set on You" video for me, and the Paul Simon one with Chevy Chase. Well, yeah, he directed with Eric; he did *The Rutles*.

**Rowland:** So what ultimately set in motion your decision to become involved with . . .

**Harrison:** To become a Rutle?

**Rowland:** Yeah. [*Laughs.*]

**Harrison:** Well, my friendship with Eric and those Python fellows. Well actually, he *did* have a TV show called *Rutland Weekend Television*—after Python finished, Eric had his own seasons. The basis of it was, you see, Rutland is a little part of England, but when they drew up these new maps, they forgot about it and they left it off the map. So it's like a joke place: Rutland. So he invented this fictitious television station called Rutland Weekend Television, and the series was very silly, where it was *cheap*, they had no money, no budgets for anything. They'd be trying to do the TV show and the guy would be coming in and try to clean up or take away the props. He did this series, and during the series he thought of this little parody on the Beatles called the Rutles. So they did one song, and that was just so good, and I liked it and was saying, "You should do more of the Rutles," and I'm sure other people did, and Eric just wrote the whole story then.

**Rowland:** To me it's such a wonderful little film because it's so devastating and affectionate at the same time.

**Harrison:** It is. Well, it's the nicest one about the Beatles, I think, compared to some of these other things they've had out, these sort of brainless—what do they call them—docudramas, you know, that are just all based on rumors and all the wrong information.

**Rowland:** Well, plus, those lose the humor and the kind of self-deflating sensibility that really seems so much a part of what was charming, beyond the music of course.

**Harrison:** It has great lines in it. Something about, "Typically, the press got a hold of the wrong end of the stick and started beating about the bush with it." [*Laughter.*] He takes on the press alone. He said, "The rumor became so widespread that eventually even the press found out about it."

**Rowland:** Do you actually look over each . . . I mean, you probably must give a go ahead at some point to each of the projects.

**Harrison:** To some of them, but there was a point where our film company started getting *big*, not big by Hollywood standards but big for us. It was only like a few people when we started out, and then it built up a bit, and it started getting to the point where I tried to pull the plug on it a bit. I mean, it's still going now, but it seemed to me that we were—we started out making things because they either had to be done and nobody else would do them or because it was a certain project that was close to us, through friends of ours or something. Then it got to the point where we got a few more people to help get it going, and then we were starting to make some movies because we had all these people working for us, and I saw that danger and wanted to try and deflate it a little bit. Plus, over the years it's become increasingly difficult to get a small film distributed, or to get it where people, you know, can go and see it.

Some time ago you could put out a film, and it would be a bit of time before it built and got established, and then you'd have some audience. But these days, or even going back five or six years, it was like, if your film doesn't clean up on the first weekend, it's *out*, because there's so much product. This is the frightening thing of the film *and* the music industry. There's too many people, too much product. We had a film which everybody . . . I've never met one person who doesn't think it was a great film.

**Rowland:** *Withnail and I?*

**Harrison:** Not that one. I was going to say this film called *Water*, with Michael Caine. And since, it's been on video and television, and everybody just thinks it's very funny and really nice. But when it came out in the cinema it didn't last long at all, because it was either not promoted right or [*mockingly*] "it didn't make enough money in its first weekend."

**Rowland:** And that's with Michael Caine in it; it's a good movie.

**Harrison:** And Brenda Vaccaro.

**Rowland:** Yeah, geez. But do you think that there is that kind of sensibility in some way of yours that ultimately has run through HandMade films?

**Harrison:** Well, in a way there's a little bit of that, and there's certain films I can relate to more than others, like *Withnail* and *How to Get Ahead*—did you see that?—*How to Get Ahead In Advertising*. You're going to have to wait for the video though. It's written and directed by the same person, Bruce Robinson, and it's the same actor, the guy who played Withnail, [Richard Grant], this guy Bagley in *How to Get Ahead*. It's a very good little film, and it's also—the thing I like about Bruce Robinson is all that stuff we're talking about—the rain forest and Mrs. Thatcher and all that, you know. . . .

**Rowland:** So in a way there is that connection.

**Harrison:** Yeah, absolutely. It doesn't have to be a musical connection or anything, but the people involved. We've got a film coming out in February with Eric Idle [*Nuns on the Run*], which is really nice. It's a very silly film, a funny little film. There's another guy—he's done a few movies that have been shown here—he's called Robbie Coltrane. He's a big Scottish guy. He was in *Mona Lisa*, the one we made—he was Bob Hoskins' friend. I know he's been in two other films just recently, I can't recall the titles. But those two are a couple of nuns. They end up in a nunnery; that's basically what it's about. It's very silly; it's a good laugh. It should be out in February.

**Rowland:** I picked up *Spin* the other day—that magazine, *Spin*—in which Keith Richards, on one hand, compliments you for revitalizing the British film industry . . .

**Harrison:** And knocks me down for something else.

**Rowland:** And in the second sentence . . . yeah, he said he's never been able to take your guitar playing and you've never been able to stand his, and I thought that was interesting.

**Harrison:** I think he's a great rhythm guitar player, Keith. You know, really, I think he's probably one of the best rock'n'roll rhythm guitar players. I don't think he's very good at lead, but he's played . . . this is the thing you see, what I feel about Keith and myself too, it's not a comparison, but in some ways what we do is we *make records*, and the records have some good guitar parts on them, or have some good songs, or good lyrics or whatever, but basically you make records. He's not, to me, like a *guitar player* who that's all he does is go out and play guitar. He writes songs, and he makes records and within that—you know, like, you can't beat a riff to "Satisfaction," you know what I mean?

It's the simple little things like that, and I think he's—you know, I like Keith enormously. I mean, he's great, but you know, I don't think he's an Albert King or a B. B. King or anybody else. But then again, it's adequate for what he does. And you know, the main thing about him is he has the confidence—so even if it's shitty he doesn't care. [*Rowland laughs.*]

I don't rate myself as a guitar player, and I know exactly why I'm not—it's because my life led me to all this other bullshit, and consequently, I didn't want to keep going on the road and playing. At the same time, you can't be everything in life. I'm just thankful I'm still here, and whatever it is I do, you know, that's it.

**Rowland:** Well, now you've got Eric playing on your records, and you write tunes for his, so there's kind of a trade-off, I guess.

**Harrison:** Yeah, everybody . . . you know I'm not trying to be the best guitar player. I don't really care about it. To me you can get the greatest guitar player in the world, and in my eyes, he's *still* nothing compared to the musicians that I really admire, which is the Ravi Shankars and the Bismillah Khans of this world. I've got a record in my bag now of a twelve-year-old South Indian guy playing electric mandolin. He'd blow away *all* them guys in heavy metal bands and the blues and everything, you know, no question about it. And when you've heard other kinds of music, you know, it doesn't impress me really, hearing some guy play all this noisy, fast shit. I'd rather hear Robert Johnson play. Those are the guitar players I like, or Ry Cooder or Segovia. I like *everything*, basically, except noisy, headbanging shit . . . and drum computers, [*Yamaha*] DX7s, and reverb!

**Rowland:** [*Laughs.*] Oh, I think we share a lot of taste and dislikes then.

**Harrison:** You hear . . . let's face it, a sitar is a guitar anyway. It's just a sort of wobbly guitar.

**Rowland:** Right, it's just even *harder* to learn.

**Harrison:** Yeah. They play the blues and jazz and classical and . . . all rolled into one. But sometimes you got to have a bit of background before you can dig how great it is. But you know, I'm not impressed by all these guitar players. I could have become an adequate guitar player, I could learn how to play like B. B. King. He plays the same lick all his life. He plays it very well, but, you know, it's not my goal to try and play this lick that everybody else can play anyway, you know?

**Rowland:** I'm actually surprised that you put down your guitar playing as much as you do, because I guess I'm thinking of it as more of . . .

**Harrison:** I'm not putting it down, I'm just not putting it up.

**Rowland:** I guess maybe the virtue I see of it is more a compositional virtue, that they're like just really . . . you know, the virtues of, like, making every note count, which is ultimately what . . .

**Harrison:** Well, even if it's only one note, at least so that it gives you maybe a little twitch.

**Rowland:** Yeah. Ultimately, I guess it's what hits you emotionally, whether it's some fabulous lick or not.

**Harrison:** The "Disease of Conceit."

**Rowland:** That was a great album [*Bob Dylan's* Oh Mercy].

**Harrison:** Very nice. Great songs. That's the main thing.

**Rowland:** Since we're moving in that direction, I wanted to ask you a few things about the Wilburys. It struck me that in some ways the Wilburys was . . . the myth that was created for the Wilburys, in a way, was sort of like the fantasy—your fantasy—of how wonderful it would have been to have had that with the Beatles, with all the good stuff but with the anonymity and without the burden. Is that sort of . . . ?

**Harrison:** In a way. But I think more than that, the thing that went on in the past, there was a big craze in the late '60s and '70s where they started having these things they called "supergroups" and "supersessions" and "super jams," and everybody was super-duper. And after a while . . . first of all, just by getting somebody famous or a couple of "super people" together, [*that*] didn't really guarantee it was going to be a success. And more often than not, it was just a clash of personalities and just a big ego detour. And so I thought, "What we should do is play it down; we don't want a big fanfare saying, '*Bob Dylan! Roy Orbison! Tom Petty!*' and all that." I think they're going to know who it is eventually, but I think rather [*that*], than, like, the record company's natural choice, [*which*] would be [*adopts a sleazy, huckster tone*] "Look who we've got!"

It took a while to give them the idea that, let's just play it down and then just have a joke . . . lighten up a bit, because everything is so serious. I mean, even the picture on the front, I love that picture, but we only had . . . I realized there was going to be only this one day the five of us would be together, and quickly got our guy, took some pictures, and they were really quick, and they weren't that good. But that picture, we just blew it up, made it all dirty, threw it on the floor and stepped on it a bit and ripped it up, and it became much better. [*Chuckles.*]

**Rowland:** Especially the one in the back where you can actually see the crinkles in the paper. . . . Everything just seemed to fall in place I guess.

**Harrison:** That would be a little miracle really, the fact that we just all happened to be there smiling on the same day. When we do another Wilbury album, it's going to be just as much fun, otherwise I'm not doing it. But the thing is, it can't be *as* spontaneous because we already know about it. But I think the songs can be spontaneous, and we can make it with the same vibe and the same atmosphere in which the way we wrote the songs and recorded them. But there's got to be an element where people are already primed to it now, and so, like . . . I remember the second Beatles single that ever came out; *New Musical Express* reviewed it in England and said, "below-par Beatles."

**Rowland:** That explains the line in "Cockamamie Music" [*"Cockamamie Business"*].

**Harrison:** Exactly, yeah. So I'm sure they're going to say, "Oh, it's not as good as . . ." or maybe they'll say, "Oh, it's gotten much better now." That isn't . . . the point is to be able to keep on going and have fun and lighten up a bit. You know, that's what I think. Everybody is so serious.

**Rowland:** You were kind of a central character I guess in getting . . . because you were working with Jeff [*Lynne*], and then . . .

**Harrison:** Because the first song of the Wilburys was really for an extended single for my *Cloud Nine* album.

**Rowland:** Oh, I see. Which was . . . which one?

**Harrison:** They were putting out a single, I forget which one it was, it was probably . . . "This Is Love," I think it was. And in England and Germany, they have to have this twelve-inch version of an extended mix. If you haven't got an extended mix, you've got to give them another song to put on it so you have three songs. So I didn't have an extra song in the can, and I didn't have an extended version because the song was conceived like *that*. I mean, [*indistinct*] and I hate that, where . . .

**Rowland:** Yeah, you have to create something.

**Harrison:** I tried to do it with one of them, and it was just like a pig's . . . nose. So what I did was, "I'll write a song tomorrow and just do it." And that's what happened. I just found—I got Jeff, because he was there having dinner with me; Roy was there and he said, "Can I come?" And, you know, we couldn't find a studio at that time, so we went to Bob's house and did it, and he happened to be in. . . . So in that respect, cause it was my project I was doing, that got it started. And then the record company heard it and said, "Oh we can't put that out. . . . It's too good." [*Laughter.*] I thought, "Well, what do we do? We'll just have to do another nine and make an album," and so I got them all to agree to do that.

**Rowland:** So you did it all in a pretty quick period of time.

**Harrison:** Oh, yeah. We did the other nine by writing them like the first one. We're going to write one and do it tomorrow, right, and then we just did that for nine days. And it's like the Rutles, you know, "The first album took 20 minutes. The second one took even longer."

**Rowland:** One of the nicest things was that it was all shared credits completely on it. Did it really work that way? I mean, was it all just, you were all sitting in a room?

**Harrison:** Yeah. We broke it down a bit. Like, for example, "Tweeter and the Monkey Man." Bob wrote much more of that than any of us did. But, you know, it's all proportioned. Everybody is included on everything, but it's all proportionate in the songwriting thing to what we did. We worked out a formula so that when you put it across the whole record, maybe I got a bit more for this one, he got a bit more for that one, and everybody got something for being in it anyway. It just worked out; everybody was happy about that.

**Rowland:** "Handle with Care" was great because you could really hear kind of your signature writing at the beginning and then Roy's and then Tom Petty's . . .

**Harrison:** Oh, there's a lot of Bob in there. It's those lyrics, some great and funny words.

**Rowland:** Can I ask you, did you know Tom Petty at all before?

**Harrison:** Yeah. I actually met him just before he got on Shelter Records. I met him at Leon Russell's house back in 1970-something.

**Rowland:** When he was Leon's house songwriter.

**Harrison:** I just met him one night there, but when I remet him again, I had forgotten that I actually met him before; Tom reminded me about that. But once I was reminded, I do remember that big studio Leon had in his house. But the tour they did, Tom and Bob were on the road for a couple years together, and when he came to England I think it was about '86 . . . no, it was '87, because it was right when I was making *Cloud Nine*, or just finishing. And they came and we went and hung out with them a couple of nights. And then we came here, I think it was Christmas of . . . '87, then I met Tom again. Actually, I took some of the promo guys who worked on my album for lunch with Jeff Lynne. This was right before Christmas, and Tom happened to be in the restaurant as well. And then he wanted to get together with Jeff, and then they went off and started that album while Jeff was already, he was going to do Roy—he'd been trying to so some stuff with Roy for years.

**Rowland:** Well, now, you've known Roy, at least off and on, for many years.

**Harrison:** Yeah, 1965, I think, or '64. No, it might have been '63.

**Rowland:** Yeah, '63, I think, was your first headlining tour, and he was on the bill as well.

**Harrison:** Yeah, we toured England with him. I hadn't seen him, though, through the years. I think I've met him a couple of places in between, but I haven't seen him for a long time.

[*Quiet pause.*]

**Rowland:** . . . It's really too bad. [*Orbison died in December 1988 —Ed.*]

**Harrison:** . . . Yeah. But you know, it's all just a dream anyway. It is. This life is a dream, you know, from birth to death; it's only just the coins flipped over onto the other side for a bit. You know, I'm not afraid of death. I'd like to die peacefully, nicely, somewhere. I don't want to get impaled through by a Boeing 707 or something silly. But at the same time, death—it is the only guarantee that you have in life.

**Rowland:** Yeah, some people don't even get taxed, so I guess it's really the only one left. I kind of agree with that.

**Harrison:** The art of dying.

**Rowland:** Uh-huh.

**Harrison:** All things must pass.

**Rowland:** Mm-hm. At the same time—I don't know how to even phrase this question, but I'm going to try it—it must have been a particularly hard thing to come to grips with the way that—

**Harrison:** With Roy?

**Rowland:** Well, I was thinking of John, really.

**Harrison:** Well, it was because it was such a waste by some stupid person. If John had been killed by Elvis or something, it would have been, you know, at least . . . but killed by somebody who was, like, pointless and didn't have any . . . and in such a violent way and also in such a sneaky way. You know, I mean, that thing—I've just read about it and at times I flash on that when people call my name from behind, you know: "Mr. Lennon, will you sign this." It's such a shitty thing.

**Rowland:** I know. It's so insidious.

**Harrison:** And also, he cast—that guy Chapman—cast a very dark cloud over any fan who happens to be standing on the pavement when you come by . . . because you just don't know who's crackers and who isn't.

The idea of John not being here doesn't bother me so much because he *is* here to me. You know, "life flows on within you and without you." And although he's not here in his physical body, but . . . that's what the whole life of Christ was to show people, you dug him now, you know, you dug him then, redig him now. The reincarnation, you know, in order to realize that it's the spirit, not the body. I've learned that over the years that that's it: you don't need . . . in a way you don't need a living guru right in front of you, because he's in front of the spiritual eye every time you close your eyes. And you just go inside, and it's like that. They're all there, all our loved ones and all our friends and relatives; everybody is all there in their astral bodies.

**Rowland:** Mm-hm. I think that's a really great. . . .

**Harrison:** So the way he died was tragic, but [*sings opening couplet of Bob Dylan's "This Wheel's On Fire"*] "If your memory serves you well, we were going to meet again and wait . . ."

**Rowland:** Was it at all . . . at the time it happened—you guys had been really close for a long time, but it sounds like there had been a little bit of a rift at the time that it happened. Did that make . . . ?

**Harrison:** Well, we've been close and, you know, distant. The fact that he was living in New York meant that I never saw him for a long time. I saw him once, I don't recall which year, it was probably about 1978; I think the autumn of '78 was the last time I saw him when I went up to the Dakotas. And then I just was never in New York. You know, he'd send postcards occasionally. But that's like the Rutles, too—like Leggy Mountbatten, the Rutles manager.

**Rowland:** [*Laughs.*] Yeah, right, right. Sending a postcard.

**Harrison:** In a way, to me, I'm in England and I can still think of John still in New York, because I never saw him anyway for so long. He could still be there for all I know, you know? So I mean, it's like, they can kill the man, but they can't kill his spirit, and they can't kill what he meant to you.

**Rowland:** That's right, that's really true. One thing I really loved in your song for him [*"All Those Years Ago"*] was that idea of living with the bad and the good. I always looked up to kind of like not mythologizing him but really *keeping* . . .

**Harrison:** Well, that's the problem that's happened since. You know, okay, John *was* special, but there's a lot of other special people, too. If you die . . . they made people like Janis and Jimi Hendrix and all them people who died, suddenly became like these super incredible people.

But I think it's harder to *live* in a way. It's much easier to die than it is to live. And in fact, dying and living are the same thing. We're half-dead anyway. The moment you're born you start the road to death.

**Rowland:** Some days you feel it, too.

**Harrison:** And I don't mean it in a sort of ugly, pathetic way, I just mean that's reality. But John, you know, he was a good lad, he was—there was a part of him that was saintly, that *aspired* to the truth and great things. And there was a part of him that was just, you know . . . a looney! [*Laughter.*] Just like the rest of us! And he had his mood swings and that, but he was basically very honest. If he was a bastard one day, he'd say, "Ah well, fuck that, you know, I'm sorry, I was wrong." And he'd just deflate any feeling you had against him, any negative feeling. Not like some other people I know who sit on walls . . . and don't come clean.

**Rowland:** Just to round this out a little bit, I know you guys can't discuss the details of the "Long and Winding Settlement" . . .

**Harrison:** You know why we can't? Because it was it was about ten foot thick, you know. I don't think anybody other than the lawyers read it.

**Rowland:** Can I ask you . . .

**Harrison:** It's a good feeling . . .

**Rowland:** . . . to be done with it?

**Harrison:** Yeah, because you know, it went on for a long, long time, and it's like this thing now I feel about all the problems and stuff that goes on in life. It's like your life is all these little knots that you try to undo before it gets too late. And it's just another incredibly big knot that's now gone away, and I'm sure Capitol and EMI are relieved. And I know we certainly are. The funny thing is that most of the people who were involved with the reason why that lawsuit came about aren't even *in* the companies anymore, and so I'm sure other people at Capitol and EMI had to take on the karma of their predecessors. And so I'm sure they were relieved too. I don't hold any animosity against anybody.

**Rowland:** Does this also end the suits between . . . amongst the Beatles themselves?

**Harrison:** Yeah. Well, because, you know, everything was hinging on everything else. It was a very sort of complicated state of affairs. I'm sure people have talked about it. It was talked about in *Rolling Stone* and all that. But it gets rid of that too. It doesn't, in a way you can't just wash away some of the causes of the politics of it, the things that caused it, although it's settled now. It's a weight off the mind, but some of the original causes can't go away in my mind. Because there's certain things that should never have happened in the first place.

**Rowland:** Meaning what?

**Harrison:** Meaning that . . . if I stab you in the back and you happen to get to a hospital and don't die, it may mean that you might still not like me or you may not want to see me again, you know, in case I did it again.

**Rowland:** So what kind of relationship do you and Paul have these days?

**Harrison:** We don't have a relationship.

**Rowland:** Really?

**Harrison:** I think of him as a good friend, really, but a friend who I don't really have that much in common with anymore. You know, sort of like you meet people in your life who mean a certain thing; it's just like you're married, and then you're divorced, and you wish the other person well, but life has taken you to other places, to friendlier . . . whatever the expression is . . . confines.

**Rowland:** You're not planning to go to his show or anything?

**Harrison:** No. You mean, just because I happen to be in LA while he's here? No, I don't want to go to his show because I've heard all them tunes anyway. And secondly, I was not in town when Ringo did his show and I would have loved to have really seen that, and I don't want Ringo to think that I'm not supporting him and I'm supporting Paul. And at the same time, I'm here anyway; I've come to town to do what I've got to do. But I wish him well, and there's always a place in my heart for Paul and Linda . . . and Hamish [*Wings guitarist Hamish Stuart*]. [*Rowland laughs.*] But you know, I . . . don't look back.

**Rowland:** I know you're getting antsy, so I'll drop that. Just a few more questions if you'll indulge me. Before I forget, so at some point there will be another Wilburys record is what you're saying . . . ?

**Harrison:** Yeah, there will be as far as the Wilburys are concerned. I think today, as I speak right now, I would say it's just a matter of when and where. Because Jeff is just making his solo album, and Tom is just on his tour now, and Bob's got his album and his never-ending tour, and if the time is right, I think in the new year for us—if we want to do it. Everybody was very happy about it. We're all still friends, I believe. I think so, unless I read about it in the paper here, and maybe they can send me a fax if there's any change of plans. [*Rowland laughs.*] But I look forward to it. I had a lot of fun on that one.

**Rowland:** Because you guys are all kind of spread to the winds at different times. How do you all keep in touch about something like that?

**Harrison:** Postcards. [*Rowland begins a surprised response, then laughs instead.*] . . . Faxes. Telephones.

**Rowland:** Is there any desire [*to replace Roy*] . . . ? I'm asking because it's just a question that I think people want to know.

**Harrison:** The fifth Wilbury. Well, I don't know. It's like when you go back to the Beatles. There were so many fifth Beatles, there were probably about five hundred fifth Beatles and likewise there could be, there's many, I mean, what I saw as the Wilburys—it was an attitude really. Basically, it was an attitude. And I see loads of people out there who have what I would say . . . you know, there was somebody who wrote in a New York paper, I forget which paper it is, maybe you can find it from the press department, there was this great article and it said . . . I don't know how they got into it . . . but it said things like, "Little Richard is a Wilbury, somebody else isn't. Madonna wouldn't be a Wilbury but . . . Cyndi Lauper is a Wilbury." That kind of thing. It was quite funny.

It's just like an attitude and there's loads of people—I can make a list right now and put twenty people on it who, to me, would be wonderful in the Wilburys. But the thing is, the way it happened, it happened on its own.

And, like we just talked about, the next Wilbury album's going to be more, because everybody knows about it now, it's not going to be . . .

**Rowland:** Less spontaneous.

**Harrison:** Yeah. And I think to start, like, planning it, I don't think you need a fifth Wilbury for a start. And if we do, it will be the fellow, the woman, or whoever it is, who happens to walk in the door and be right. And not because they read in the article and figured out where—knock, knock—like that. But we could have maybe the Wilbury B team as well. I can do that, I could get, like, "We Are the World," you know, "We Are the Wilburys" and just have the big giant Wilburys. I'd love to do that. There's some great people out there.

**Rowland:** It's a sweet way of kind of keeping a musical community together while deflating the whole kind of superstar apparatus of it. I see the appeal of that to you as well.

**Harrison:** But you can't, you know, just to finish off about the fifth Wilbury, you can't replace Roy Orbison. Now Roy just happened to be there, like we happened to be there, on the day, and it was right, and it was brilliant. It's not every day you can form a group with all these legends. And you can't replace *him*. But that's not to say there aren't many other Wilburys floating about out there. But at the moment the four of us, we have to just talk ourselves, really. And then I think we just should do it and see what happens.

**Rowland:** Mm-hm, that sounds right.

**Harrison:** You know, keep as much openness about it—and the more you try and conceive what it's going to be . . . I mean, maybe it shouldn't even be the Wilburys, maybe it will be the Trembling Wheelbarrows . . . or the Smegmas . . . Betty, Doris, Syl, and Gladys Smegma, volume seven.

**Rowland:** [*Laughs.*] A few volumes might have gone out of print by the time the next one comes out.

**Harrison:** I think so, definitely. Then we'll have the bootleg version.

**Rowland:** That reminds me—what about . . .

**Harrison:** Or what about the Silver Wilburys? Have you heard of those?

**Rowland:** Yeah, the very early session.

**Harrison:** Some people have got a nerve.

**Rowland:** As you know, there's always bootlegs that have come out in the past and recently. It would seem now that this ten-inch-thick settlement has reached its fruition that it might make sense to go and actually collect it and put it out in a nice way.

**Harrison:** Of the Fab Four, you mean?

**Rowland:** Yeah, coming back to that.

**Harrison:** Oh yeah, we've got a few things that's going to come out anyway, but we've got the real versions of some of the ones that were bootlegged.

**Rowland:** That's what I'm wondering about.

**Harrison:** Yeah, we've got plans to put all that out, because now it's not just getting the lawsuit out of the way, but it means . . . let's face it, the Beatles catalogue will go on forever with Capitol and EMI. And there is a lot of stuff that can come, and it just means that it's easier now to deal with that. How can you deal with the future if you haven't tied the past up? So this really clears the way, and it's great because all kinds of things can come out.

I just realized I've got a really great bootleg tape of the Beatles, and it's never been out before either. It's just demos that we made at my house.

**Rowland:** Like around when?

**Harrison:** It was of the *White Album*.

**Rowland:** Oh really?

**Harrison:** It's "Back in the USSR" and "Julia" and all them. I've got them on an Ampex four track.

**Rowland:** So that's what it sounds like, that there's a lot of stuff in the vault, or in your vault. . . .

**Harrison:** Yeah, and the BBC. They have a lot of stuff.

**Rowland:** It's mostly outtakes and things; it doesn't sound like there's really any songs that didn't get on records?

**Harrison:** I don't know. There's mainly different versions of stuff, and there's probably a lot of stuff which is stuff that people know as bootlegs from our club days. [*Indistinct; Rowland laughs.*]

**Rowland:** I know you were writing stuff recently. Somebody had told me that they heard that there were hundreds of hours of Abbey Road stuff.

**Harrison:** Oh, well, I don't know many takes they made. I think that's a bit of a cheat when they take something which is just the take before. It's really exactly the same virtually, except maybe the performance wasn't quite as good. 'Cause that was the reason why you chose whatever take it was.

**Rowland:** So you mentioned before, as you just mentioned, this catalogue is going to go on forever. Because of the fact of that, and really the greatness of the music, you're kind of a keeper of a legacy, now, for now and forever. Is that something that you can pretty much accept or come to terms with?

**Harrison:** Yeah, well we're not really the keepers of it because we don't own the masters. [*Laughter.*] Sad to say, EMI and Capitol still own the masters. But you know, they are the keepers now, but at least with our relationship with them, you know, things when they come out, at least, maybe they come out so that everybody is happy. There was a period when we finished our original contract with them, and then things would be . . . we used to take so much care of the running order and which tracks were on what and packaging, and then when it came to America it all just gets split up and changed and different covers. And then when our contract expired there would be all this weird stuff coming out. Occasionally they'd send you a copy and say, "Here's your new album."

**Rowland:** I know, I was so amazed because I grew up here, when they finally reissued the CDs as the original albums, to get these records. I was saying, "Gee, you mean *Help!* wasn't just really five songs and a soundtrack to a film?"

**Harrison:** We used to have at least twelve or fourteen tracks on every album, and none of the albums would have the singles on them. We'd do the singles separately. We were so naive in those days. Then they said, "Oh, they don't pay you for more than twelve or ten or something." That's why they took them off and used the singles. . . .

**Rowland:** Okay, I just have two more quick questions, and then I'm going to let you go. What do your kids think about your music?

**Harrison:** Well, I've got just a boy, one boy.

**Rowland:** I'm sorry. I always thought you had a boy and a girl for some reason.

**Harrison:** Well, I don't know . . .

**Rowland:** [*Laughs.*] I guess not—if you don't think so, I guess you don't.

**Harrison:** Uh . . . all inquiries to the above address. He's like most kids; I realize that most kids get into the Beatles because when they're around the age of three or four or five, they always see *Yellow Submarine*. See, I never told my boy anything about the Beatles, until one day he said, "Hey Dad, how does that piano riff go on 'Bulldog'?"

I went, "Geez, you know, if he's going to know a Beatles song, how come he knows that one?" Then I realized it's on *Yellow Submarine*. You know, he's not really that impressed. I mean, it was a long time ago. He's more into the Wilburys. He's exposed to all this other stuff. Actually, you know who he really likes is Iron Maiden. [*Laughter.*]

**Rowland:** That headbanging stuff.

**Harrison:** Well, yeah. Because he's into skateboarding, so it's all that kind of stuff. Mike McGill and Tony Hawk. But he learned piano, and he's been exposed to, you know, everything: classical Indian music, dance. I always tried to play him . . . if he says listen to this, and then I'd say, "Yeah, but have you heard this?" And then playing like an old version of whatever it is, or let him be aware, so he's got a great broad . . .

**Rowland:** Expand his ear.

**Harrison:** You know, even silly Hawaiian music and stuff like that, "Wicky-Wacky-Woo." I mean, when he was five he could play the solo from "Minnie the Moocher" on his kazoo perfect, note for note.

**Rowland:** Hey, that reminds me, everyone asks what kind of music did you listen to when you were a kid—what movies did you watch when you were a kid?

**Harrison:** When I was a kid all I could remember was *Bambi* and the forest going on fire. I don't know, I can't remember in my early childhood. I remember when I was a school boy and I used to sag off school and go watch all the horror movies in Liverpool, but I suppose the films that have given me the most pleasure would have to be . . . I think my favorite film of all time has got to be *The Producers*. I just love that. Every bit of dialogue is very . . . I love Mel Brooks. I think he's just wonderfully crazy. But that one in particular of his is the best film.

I love the Blues Brothers movie because the music was great, and the story was good, and it was packed full of action.

**Rowland:** Were you much a fan of *Beguiled* [Bedazzled, *1967*]?

**Harrison:** I don't know if I saw that.

**Rowland:** Dudley Moore and Peter Cook.

**Harrison:** I don't think I've seen that.

**Rowland:** Oh. I think you might like it.

**Harrison:** It's like, I've seen so many movies, especially on TV and that. I can't ever remember what they were about. I know some of the things we made, like I mentioned *How to Get Ahead in Advertising*. I love that because it's just so outrageous.

**Rowland:** Yeah, I want to find that—that sounds great.

**Harrison:** You know, there's films which are interesting because, like, for instance, I did that song for *Lethal Weapon 2*, and although it was so amazingly violent, Mel Gibson is so great, and it had a few messages in it, and it was very entertaining.

**Rowland:** Yeah, now is that something where you saw the film and then wrote the tune, or had you been contracted to write a tune?

**Harrison:** I did see it before I wrote the song, and I think because my friend was doing the score to it and he was, I think, trying to get me involved because Eric was going to do some music with David Sanborn, and he showed me the rough cut of it with no sound on it at all—just the live sound, no dubs. The reason I did that I think basically was because Michael Kamen was doing music to it, and he wanted me. And then I met Dick Donner, who is very nice; I liked him a lot. And then when he heard the song, how we'd done it—we started to do it with Eric for his album. Dick heard Eric's rough version of it, and he wanted the song badly, and so he asked me if I'd do it because Eric wasn't interested in doing it for the film.

It's hard to think just on the spot like that, what movies . . . I don't think I've seen something that really just blew me away. You know, there's bits and pieces in things. I hate the arrogance of film, and I hate the way . . . it's sort of like painting by numbers—if you have this person or that person. It's all like that now, all this packaged stuff. And I know you have to do that, but I hate to think that, well, "You've got this great film, but I'm not letting my client be in it because he's only going to be in films that my other client's going to direct. And your little film can't afford $6 million for this asshole actor. . . ." [*Sighs.*] Well, it's a cockamamie business.

**Rowland:** Exactly, that's what it is. That's what I like about so many of the HandMade films: they go against the grain of that. They're very entertaining and unprepossessing. They kind of catch you off guard. And I think that's the magic of movies.

**Harrison:** They don't clean up at the box office, though. But I don't care about that—as long as we can just get by. It would be nice to suddenly make 200 million out of the T-shirts of *How to Get Ahead in Advertising*, but until that day—as long as we can get by.

**Rowland:** What are your plans, basically, for the future? The lead up to that actually is, is there a particular reason why you put out the *Best Of* at this time?

**Harrison:** Well yes. There's two reasons basically. Well, first of all, I had a five-record deal with Warners: five records and repackage. So it was part of my obligation. But secondly, if I'm going to repackage those five albums—which I've done—I might as well do it *now* while people at least know who I am. Not to say, though, they'll necessarily buy it or not.

But the other reason is that I didn't want to do too much work this year because I was really tired after the last couple of years of writing and then doing *Cloud 9*, and then I went straight from that into the promotion of it, and straight out of *that* into the making of the Wilburys. And the Wilburys really wiped me out because, in a way, I was the Wilburys' manager. All the time we were in the recording studio I was doing everything—all the art work and coordinating, making it so everybody was happy and figuring out their publishing deals and trying to get the record deal—just all that stuff. And I was, like, *so* stressed out at the end of that Wilbury period I just thought, "Well, the next year I'm just going to soft pedal."

And it's a perfect time. I'll just compile that album that I owe the record company, and I'll do a couple of new tunes for it. Because I'm waiting, really, for Bob and Tom to get off the road and for Jeff to do his album, because really that's what I want to do; I don't really want to do a solo album, not at the moment. I like being in a group—share the responsibility and you can all have a laugh.

**Rowland:** It's kind of coming around full circle in a funny sort of way. . . . That's really great. I think we can probably wrap it up.

# PART V
# 1992–2001

# RADIO INTERVIEW

Scott Muni | July 21, 1992 | WNEW-FM


Of the three former Beatles active in the 1980s and '90s, none was more averse to touring than Harrison. The primary reason was the stinging, negative reviews of his 1974 US tour when he had lost his voice. Over the years, whenever the '74 tour was referenced, he openly acknowledged its shortcomings, yet felt the criticism was unnecessarily harsh. There was another reason the road never seemed to call Harrison: he never established a consistent working band—rehearsed and tour-ready, familiar with older material and up-to-speed with Harrison's latest as well.

There are many musical benefits that come from touring with the same lineup night after night: the songs begin to breathe and mature, becoming fresh, more developed versions of the studio originals. The band itself starts to take chances, loosening song structures, playing off each other, inspired by the reaction of the audience. One of the tragedies of the Beatles' story is that the music they created after their last US tour in 1966 was never performed publicly, save for a brief rooftop "audition" in 1969.

Harrison's old friend Eric Clapton was aware of all of this when, in late 1991, with a dozen dates in Japan on the horizon, he invited Harrison to join his tour for that limited run. It would not be arduous, and he would benefit from an all-star lineup that knew his songs and could do them justice: guitarist Andy Fairweather-Low, keyboardists Chuck Leavell and Greg Phillinganes, bassist Nathan East, drummer Steve Ferrone, and Ray Cooper on percussion.

Harrison said yes, choosing a number of his own songs he had seldom, if ever, performed live—"Taxman," "Piggies," and "What Is Life"—and the tour happened.

One can imagine the disappointment among millions of American and British fans that Harrison and Clapton did not bring the show home. To appease them, several nights were recorded, and Harrison released *Live in Japan* in mid-'92; it was only his second live album. To help promote the record, Harrison agreed to a number of interviews, including a telephone chat with an old friend: New York City rock deejay Scott Muni, who had a habit of speaking in complex sentence structures and referring to himself as "professor."

The following transcript is of a typical, polished broadcast on WNEW, one of America's leading classic rock radio stations in the heyday of that format. The program was artfully produced from a brief telephone chat, with Muni re-recording his questions later. —Ed.

**Scott Muni:** The George Harrison is standing by, because rarely does he feel like and do an interesting conversation, which is coming up in just a few minutes from now, on 102.7 WNEW-FM, and 107.1, eastern Long Island. . . . We'll pour it on with George Harrison, moments away.

———————————

**Muni:** All right, George Harrison is well aware that WNEW-FM has the most curious and intelligent rock audience in the world, and so, in our attempt to have our discussion with him, we wanted to let him know that we were all *both* educated and curious, of course, about the tour and what it would be like with Eric Clapton, and how much *we*, as rock fans, love the whole idea of *Live in Japan* and that album.

**George Harrison:** Good. I'm happy about it anyway. I thought it turned out good; it's got a really good sound considering live isn't the easiest thing to record and mix and hold onto the kind of—you know, because you've got so much *power* on the stage with all the amplification, but to put it back into a CD and try to have it sound as powerful, it's not that easy. But I think it came out pretty good.

**Muni:** George, you love to play music and you love to record music, but I think one of the problems with, uh, George Harrison, from our standpoint, the public, we want to hear you all the time, right? So it's not possible that you're going to be recording all the time, nor is it possible that you have a group. So how did this thing happen with Eric Clapton? Do you want to tell me?

**Harrison:** Yeah, sure. Eric has been touring for quite some time, and in 1990 he was doing a world tour, and he reckoned that wherever he was going, certain people would ask him what I was up to and why wasn't I doing stuff.

Then when I talked to him around the time he was at the Albert Hall in the beginning of 1991 doing the *24 Nights* [tour], and he was saying, "Look, the rest of this year the band are off, so if you wanted to do something with us, then we could back you up and it saves you the problem of getting a band together and all this. Why don't you think about it?"

And I kept meeting Eric over that period of time, and it just seemed like it was a good idea actually. It was quite a generous thing for him to offer, and I just thought a lot about it, and I went through the "yes-no-yes-no." And then finally I decided, "Yeah, I ought to do it, because if I don't do it now, next year Eric will be busy again with his band. The opportunity won't arise, and I've got to do something sooner than later, otherwise I may never, ever do a tour."

**Muni:** And you want to, and I know that, but it's—

**Harrison:** Yeah, well, I think—

**Muni:** Where do you get an Eric Clapton? Where do you get somebody you can work with, and make it work out right, so everybody feels good and you do a great show? So I think it's just perfect.

**Harrison:** It was perfect. It's a great band, and those guys are really good, and they're very enthusiastic and nice people to hang out with. I'd heard them numerous times at Eric's concerts, and I kind of knew most of them anyway, so it made a lot of sense to do it.

**Muni:** Well, so anyway, we know about George Harrison and Eric Clapton and old friends and *close* friends through the years. So we're going to leave that part out. It's great to have you guys back. Now, what comes out is George Harrison *Live in Japan*, a two-CD set with Eric Clapton and the band, and what must have gone through your mind is like, "What . . . what songs am I going to do?" [*Chuckles.*]

**Harrison:** Yeah, well you got to get a set together, obviously, but it was not that difficult. What I did was I chose songs that had been singles or hits or ones that had been meaningful during like the Beatle period, or just songs of my own compositions from Beatle periods. I put together a cassette of maybe thirty songs, gave it to all the musicians, and then they kind of went through it. When we met for rehearsals there were the obvious ones that we were going to do, like I couldn't really avoid doing them, things like "Something," "Here Comes the Sun," "Guitar Gently Weeps." And I wanted to add some songs.

A lot of the songs that I had done, I had wrote them and then I recorded them, I sang it that *one* time on the record, and never, ever done them since. So to me they're like new songs—like "I Want to Tell You" and "Old Brown Shoe," even "Taxman," I've only ever sang it the one time. "Piggies," you see, I've never really done that one before, and all my new songs like "Cloud Nine" and "Cheer Down," "Devil's Radio," even something like "Isn't It a Pity" has been around since 1970, that song from *All Things Must Pass*. But the first time I ever performed it. It's really good for me to . . . see, it's like singing new songs.
[*Music plays.*]

**Muni:** Yes, and we've only just begun our conversation with George Harrison, and as you can tell by him speaking, he had plenty to say and a lot of looseness here, so our conversation with George Harrison on 102.7 WNEW-FM will continue in just a couple of moments.

---

**Muni:** The professor with you at rock's higher institution of learning, 102.7 WNEW-FM, and a wonderful conversation with George Harrison. And I asked George, it's kind of tough after all those years to get back together and start to work on some songs with somebody like Eric Clapton, and I guess sort of to gravitate to things that might be familiar or unfamiliar and find something that would be the *right* song.

**Harrison:** Well, the obvious one when Eric and I get together, which is the first song that we ever did together, which was "While My Guitar Gently Weeps," and I'm particularly happy about the way it came out on the live version. It's far superior, I think, to the original studio recording, and Eric just plays his butt off. It's really good.
[*Music plays.*]

**Muni:** We're talking to George Harrison. George, the traveling now, and even though this was not a long tour, and out of it the George Harrison *Live in Japan* CD set that we have to enjoy, and with Eric Clapton in the band. You don't, as we said, you don't get the opportunity to travel or tour—and especially with people you want to—that often, but now that you have, what was it like compared to the last time you toured?

**Harrison:** Well it was much easier, I can tell you. Because in '74, I'd done so much work that year, I produced I think three albums and a concert tour of Europe of Ravi Shankar and this Indian orchestra. Plus, I'd had numerous meetings with people about . . . there was a musical I was trying to write at the time with this guy called Jerzy Kosinski. I had a very busy year, and then I was trying to make my own album at the same time, and this tour was happening at the end of the year, so by the time I started the tour I was already wiped out. That was the tour where I lost my voice in the rehearsal.

But also, that went on and on for weeks and weeks. This tour that I've just done, it was only really twelve dates in Japan. Once we got over the jet lag of flying into Japan, everything else was taken care of on the bullet train. So we didn't really have to get on a plane, and the train in Japan is very nice to travel on—very quiet, on time, [*Muni chuckles*] it's quick and efficient. So it was really very, very simple, the traveling part.

**Muni:** Okay, so, selfishly—from my audience's standpoint—selfishly I could say, "Okay then, we like that too. Do you think it's possible you might do some more? Some more dates?"

**Harrison:** Yeah, I think so. It's just a question of when and how.

**Muni:** Great.

**Harrison:** Obviously it's easier for me if I did it with Eric's band again . . .

**Muni:** [*Laughs.*] Sure!

**Harrison:** . . . because it would save a lot of time rehearsing, but at the same time I'm not against forming a new band, or with some of the musicians I've played with in the past. And it's just a question of how to do it so that I don't end up on one of these six-month or two-year tours, like it seems to be, the thing that happens when you gear up for it; it becomes such a *big* thing. So much expense that the people end up going on the road for so long, and I don't want to do that. I'd love to just do, say, ten dates somewhere and then have a break and then do ten dates somewhere else, and, you know, like that.

**Muni:** Sure. And you know what—I think that the guy you're talking about, Eric Clapton, wants to do the same thing. There's no question about it, he doesn't—I don't think most people really want to go out for a year and a half or something like that.

**Harrison:** But the problem is that when you get all the trucks and the stage and the mics, and it's such a big thing, really, to organize, but there's [*also*] obvious expense involved. Once you've got it wound up and moving, you might as well just keep on going and make it all pay. That's what I've got to try and come to terms with, some way of doing it so that it's enjoyable. It's not just going to break my neck, you know.

**Muni:** And the pocketbook, right?

**Harrison:** Exactly.

**Muni:** Well, okay, question now, the rumor mill is working on George Harrison. And you've made reference to 1974 and you lost your voice and all that. Then Eric Clapton came along, and you guys worked this thing out, and he said, "This is a chance for you not to lose your voice because if you stop smoking on this tour, then maybe you won't lose your voice." Is that a rumor? Is that true, did that happen? [*Chuckles.*]

**Harrison:** Well, actually—no, what it was, was . . . I've been smoking for years, and I was trying to give up smoking for probably twenty years. And on many occasions, I did, whether it be for a day, a week, or in some cases maybe even a month, but I always got back on it. I was thinking part of the reason for me to do the tour was that I had to . . . if I was ever going to sing again, I had to *really* stop smoking because I was getting to the point where it wasn't a joke. And so I thought—I did it the other way around, most people end up smoking on tour, I did it the other way—I said, "If I'm going to be able to tour, I'm going to have to give up smoking." So I booked the tour on the basis that it would give me a very *big* reason to make the effort, just to get myself together.

**Muni:** Did it work a little bit?

**Harrison:** Oh yeah, absolutely. I haven't smoked for a year, and I have no desire. To me now, it's the most disgusting thing in the world.

**Muni:** Are you serious?

**Harrison:** Absolutely. I haven't smoked for a year . . .

**Muni:** I need it!

**Harrison:** . . . and I'm so happy to be free of that.

**Muni:** Hey, I have a lollipop and some chewing gum with me, because I have now gone ten weeks. The reason I had to ask you [*is*] because I'm going crazy, as you know. I mean, you said you tried stopping, so did I, but I've been smoking so long. I was smoking before they had regular cigarettes even. [*Chuckles.*]

**Harrison:** Well I was smoking from when I was thirteen to when I was forty-eight, so you figure that out.

**Muni:** I was little longer than that. Yeah, me too. That's great! OK, now you're helping me a little because I've only got ten weeks so far.

**Harrison:** Ten weeks, well you can do it! The main thing is . . .

**Muni:** But I'm not on tour . . .

**Harrison:** . . . musicians who smoke, I mean, they all recognize the syndrome. You can smoke, whether you smoke twenty a day, you go in the studio, you end up smoking *forty* or *sixty*.

**Muni:** At least . . .

**Harrison:** And it's not just cigarettes, you end up smoking everything.

**Muni:** Yes, I know. [*Laughs.*] OK, I thought that was a rumor, but I think that's great.

**Harrison:** And the band . . . The Wilburys. God, every one of them smoked, and there was five of us all smoking, and so the guy who is working with us, he ended up going and buying, you know, about ten different brands of cigarettes. So every room you walked in, there was all these cigarettes everywhere. I thought, "Geez, it should be called the Smoking Wilburys." [*Music plays.*]

**Muni:** George Harrison, before you leave, the Wilburys now. Keep Wilburys in your mind, because on this album, George Harrison *Live in Japan*, the two-CD set, there are two producers: Spike and Nelson

Wilbury. Now, I know that there was hookie-dookie and skullduggery involved in the Wilburys' names, but if I'm not mistaken, Spike *and* Nelson were kind of the same person. Are you trying to tell me that you're the producer and that there aren't two producers, or am I missing a message?

**Harrison:** No, you've got it.

**Muni:** I did get it, OK, good. [*Laughs.*]

**Harrison:** The thing about all this, it's just—to me it sounded kind of boring when you just keep putting your name on everything. I could have just done that—"Produced by me"—but I just thought it was a cute way of getting . . .

**Muni:** It is, it's great. So Spike and Nelson both produced it, great.

**Harrison:** Right, yeah.

**Muni:** Okay, before you get out of here, before we leave our concert. You're really on the move, and I'm glad we got together to talk about some stuff and some things from the album. Let's [*have*] you take me into this two-CD set and, in your own [*words*] there, introduce something that you thought you really liked of the collaboration of the band and your stuff and so forth, another song from you and Eric.

**Harrison:** OK. Well, I should tell you also that a couple of people have asked me how the CD resembles the actual show. Well, this is the exact show that we did, and it's also in the exact same running order that it was on stage. The only minor change, and it's not really a change, but in the concert, I would finish the first half of the set with "Piggies," Eric would do four tunes, and then I'd come back on with "Got My Mind Set on You." But to make the disc one and disc two kind of similar length, we just moved "Got My Mind Set on You" onto the end of the first disc. [*Music plays.*]

**Muni:** Yes, a conversation with George Harrison on 102.7 WNEW-FM. George, as you mentioned, the new CD, *Live in Japan*, is pretty much the way the concerts went, in that particular order. How about another example of you working with the band and Eric Clapton?

**Harrison:** There's a song here, when Eric was doing the *Journeyman* album, and I wrote this song for him, but he didn't use it. I think we made an attempt at it, we just ran through the song, and at that time he was working with Michael Kamen doing the music to *Lethal Weapon 2*, and the director Dick Donner heard this song, and he wanted it in the film. And Eric didn't really want it—he didn't want to have a single out from the movie—so Dick Donner asked me if I'd record the song, which I did. I wrote it for Eric originally, and Tom Petty helped me write the lyrics to it. It's called "Cheer Down." So this is one of my newer songs that was included in the *Live in Japan* set.

[*Music plays.*]

**Muni:** So, of course, we were not able to enjoy that *Live in Japan* concert with George Harrison and Eric Clapton and the band. But George, our audience, of course, has the opportunity with this new CD set, pretty much the way things went. But the possibility of the many songs you talked about, old, new, and then different, was there a particular song that you never sang live before that was kind of special to you?

**Harrison:** This one that I wrote originally back in 1980, I believe, when John got killed. It was called "All Those Years Ago." It was particularly nice to do this one because it's got a lot of parts to it, a lot of little synth parts and a lot of stuff, and it shows the band up, the arrangement, and all the parts and also it's got a good solo in the end with Eric. So we played "All Those Years Ago."

[*Music plays.*]

**Muni:** Well of course, that song, "All Those Years Ago," happens to be close to me and to everybody. I think it's wonderful. I think it just shows that the performance, the Eric Clapton band and you guys, it seems that you wore everything really well—the earlier stuff from early Beatle years, George Harrison originals, the blending of Clapton and your guitar and everything. It seems like it fit really well, and you seem to sound that way, that it really worked, didn't it?

**Harrison:** It did, yeah. I'm very happy. You know, all the time I was mixing the record, as I said earlier, it's not that easy mixing trying to get the *feel* of the show onto disc, but I'm very happy how it turned out. The engineer, John Harris, was excellent, and I thought, because I was being precautious, I think it turned out even better than what I was expecting. And it was a great band to work with, and I just hope I can do it again sometime.

**Muni:** We do too, because I know you love to play, you love to record, but you really love to perform, too. Hopefully for all of us in our area here that love you so much we'll get a chance to see you and again you'll be performing soon live, I hope. Meanwhile everybody's got the *Live in Japan* two-CD set to listen to and know the fun that you guys had. I really appreciate you calling, hope I'll see you in London . . . or New York, or . . .

**Harrison:** Well, OK . . . it's been good to talk to you Scott, and all my best wishes to the listeners, and I look forward to coming to New York sometime, maybe Madison Square or something like that.

**Muni:** Love it.

**Harrison:** I'll see you there Scott, all the best.

**Muni:** Stay well.

**Harrison:** OK, bye-bye. . . .

**Muni:** From his lips to our ears, hopefully—you heard him say "Madison Square Garden" and all. Very soon I hope to hear again from George Harrison and again from his friends, from Ringo and from Paul. Keep up to date with everybody and what they're doing, and if we get lucky, we will have maybe that collaboration of George Harrison and Eric Clapton and the band, or something similar to that coming to our area. Would that be OK? You bet! Scott Muni, at the place where rock lives—102.7, WNEW-FM, in New York!

# RADIO INTERVIEW

Bob Coburn | August 24, 1992 | *Rockline*

From the 1980s and well into the 2000s, a national network of popular FM radio stations helped tie together the American rock scene—one of the country's most vibrant and lucrative musical communities. It was the heyday of well-produced programs distributed by satellite feed, often combining music and talk with the history, news, and inside stories of the rock world. *Rockline* was one of the leading shows of this period: a weekly call-in radio program created by the Global Satellite Network and hosted by Los Angeles radio personality Bob Coburn. The show's simple format—conversation, music, and questions from listeners—made it enduringly popular with rock stars and their fans, and Coburn was part of that winning formula. He was informed and engaging, welcoming to his guests and listeners. By the end of its thirty-three-year run, it seemed every rock musician of weight had been on the show, including Robert Plant, Keith Richards, and Paul McCartney—even Bill Clinton and Al Gore had stopped by during their first election run.

Harrison's turn came in August 1992. As the transcript of his visit reveals, *Rockline's* format was tailor made for his personality. He's comfortable with Coburn and gracious and funny with his fans, willing to tease and be teased. It's clear he's aware of how music styles are changing, of hip-hop and sampling, and half-seriously suggests that Ice-T cover one of his tunes. He even points out how the sound of digital synthesizers had improved since their advent in the '80s.

*Rockline's* listeners seem to have been equally up to date. The lucky few who got to speak with Harrison expressed excitement about his new album, *Live in Japan*, as well as projects still in development, such as the Beatles documentary *The Long and Winding Road* (which eventually became the 1995 UK television series *The Beatles Anthology*). One caller started a discussion about Harrison's recent efforts for abandoned orphans in Romania, Romanian Angel Appeal, which Olivia Harrison had spearheaded in 1990 and George supported with the all-star album *Nobody's Child*.

469

Coburn, after hosting *Rockline* for so many years, eventually purchased the program outright from its corporate owner, even as a new generation of fans were turning from broadcast radio to the internet for music news and, eventually, music itself. He created an online archive to chronicle the program's 1,650-show history and an FAQ list as well. The last question on the list is a three parter:

What are the three most common questions asked of host/owner Bob Coburn?

3. Who is you least favorite guest ever?

2. Who is your favorite guest ever?

1. Can I have your job?

Answers:

3. No reply.

2. George Harrison

1. You *are* kidding, right?

—Ed.

**Bob Coburn:** Good evening, nice to have you here. Congratulations on the double CD, it came out really nicely. You've got to be proud of it.

**George Harrison:** I'm glad you like it. Thank you.

**Coburn:** I understand you just came back from Hawaii.

**Harrison:** Yeah, I go down there occasionally.

**Coburn:** That's odd because I leave for there tomorrow, so . . . I'll take your place. In fact, give me your address, and I'll be happy to take your place. [*Chuckles.*] Why did you limit the tour to Japan? Why did you decide to go there and keep it just there?

**Harrison:** Originally, it was just to be a short tour. Eric suggested to me earlier in the year, if I wanted to get out on the road, because he had been around the year before. Wherever he'd been, he said people kept saying to him, "Where's George? Why isn't he doing anything? Tell him to do a show!" So he said, "Why don't you use my band? It's easy for you—you don't have to think about anything. You just step into my band, we'll do a few weeks rehearsal, and just go and do a few weeks touring. Just to get you, you know, back into it."

So I thought about it. And he said, "We can just go to Japan." He loves to go to Japan; he goes every year. So I just said, "Okay, I'll go to Japan. I haven't been there for years."

**Coburn:** Now what about North America? All your fans here want me to ask you that. What about touring North America? Is that a possibility?

**Harrison:** It is definitely a possibility. I mean, Japan, really, Eric chose that because he thought the last thing I needed, after not going on tour for seventeen years [*Coburn whistles quietly*], was to get a hostile audience. [*Laughter.*] So that was a bit of training. But I'm ready for hostility now.

**Coburn:** You can handle the hostility now, huh? It *has* been a long time since you were on the road. Has the technology changed dramatically, or about the same?

**Harrison:** It's probably pretty much the same. I think it might have improved the quality of the sound systems, certainly the quality of the samples on the . . . keyboard synthesizers has improved. Sounds is much better.

**Coburn:** There is a little bit of sampling throughout the CD, here and there.

**Harrison:** Yeah, well you can't bring cello players and hundreds of saxophone players with you, really.

**Coburn:** That's true.

**Harrison:** The band is quite big as it is, I think a ten-piece band.

**Coburn:** Now what about a new studio LP? I understand you're thinking about creating a new studio work.

**Harrison:** Well, this is my next problem. As you say, am I going to tour the States? I have to try to decide. See, I believe I can tour without actually putting out a new album because . . . I've never toured, so it's like they haven't even heard the *last* album.

**Coburn:** It's not like you're overexposed.

**Harrison:** Yeah, exactly. But at this point, you know, some people in the record company said, "Well, maybe you should wait and just do an album, put that out, and then tour off of the album." I don't know, I'm trying to make that decision. I'm talking to my agent.

**Coburn:** That's a tough one to make. Go out on the road now? Make a new record? What do you do?

**Harrison:** Well I think, you see, had Eric's band been available after this new year, the beginning of the new year, I probably would have just continued straight on with that situation, but it was always put to me as a situation that was just for, like, November-December, when Eric was free. After that he said—[*audio skips around briefly*]—been on the tour this year, then it would have been perfect for me just to continue. But having had this break, I'm now lapsing back into the old kind of, you know, forgetting what it's like to be on the road. I don't particularly . . . you know, I'm not brilliant at taking care of my career. I'm not very career-minded, you know? And touring is something which I can take it or leave it, and I think I need that push. If I was in a band it would be easier, but I need the push, and that's why I thanked Eric for actually getting me this far.

**Coburn:** We're going to play a track right now from *Live in Japan* by George Harrison. It's "Taxman." A little sampling at the beginning of this, right off *Revolver*, huh?

**Harrison:** Yeah, the keyboard player, Chuck Leavell, he went out and bought *Revolver* for the rehearsal and sampled it onto it. It actually delayed the release of the record because I had to get permission to use it.

**Colburn:** Did you? Oh, that's right, you don't have the rights anymore, do you?

**Harrison:** Well, I don't think we had them in the first place.

**Coburn:** [*Laughs.*] Let's listen to it now. "Taxman," George Harrison. [*Plays song.*]

**Coburn:** *Live in Japan*, George Harrison, "Taxman." A reminder: everyone who gets on the air with George tonight receives the brand new *Live in Japan* CD that we're playing this evening, along with a *Live in Japan* poster, courtesy of Warner Bros.' Dark Horse Records, and a copy of the *Best of Dark Horse: '76–'89* CD, brought to you by Columbia House Music Club. Look for our ad in the upcoming issue of *Rolling Stone* to get more information about our offers. Columbia House: entertaining America, one person at a time. I know you want to talk with George. Your turn is next—toll-free, 1-800-344-ROCK!

---

**Coburn:** And welcome back to *Rockline*, I'm Bob Coburn. It's an evening with George Harrison, and the first call for George tonight from Columbus, Ohio: it's Dan, a listener of Q-FM96. Dan, you are on.

**Dan:** George, this is the honor of all honors to be able to talk with you.

**Harrison:** Thank you, Dan.

**Dan:** The live album is very much worth the long wait, and I can't wait to see if you hit the States.

**Harrison:** Well, good. Thank you.

**Dan:** My question: it's pretty common knowledge that you're a fairly private person, and I was wondering, with all the multitudes of books and articles and films and TV specials and everything else that's been documented about you—and the Beatles, of course—does it ever bother you to think that there's so many people that know so much about you probably better than you know yourself?

**Harrison:** That side of it doesn't bother me, really. It's a long time now that this has been going on, and so I got used to it back in the '60s. The thing that does bother me is the information that they know, whether what they *think* they know about me is correct, because a lot of the time you're reading stuff which is absolutely wrong, and you get an impression, or a writer has given you the impression, that his *concept* of what I am. And that's the only problem, that's the thing that bothers me.

**Coburn:** What do you do in those cases? Sometimes just let it slide, and others you go, "Hey, I can't put up with this . . . "?

**Harrison:** I think, ninety-nine percent of the time I've let it slide. Because the moment you get uptight [and] I start saying, "Hey, that book stinks, it's not true," all I do is give the book more publicity.

**Coburn:** Right. Call more attention to it.

**Harrison:** It's easier to just let it go, just turn the other cheek.

**Coburn:** Dan, thanks for starting us off. It's Rick's turn—we're headed to Atlanta now, 96.1 WKLS-FM, our affiliate there. Welcome to *Rockline*, Rick.

**Rick:** Hello, George.

**Harrison:** Hello, Rick.

**Rick:** I hope to see you out again soon because I've loved your music for the last twenty-eight years now, and I'd like to thank you for all the great music for all these years.

**Harrison:** Great, thank you. I didn't realize it had been so long.

**Rick:** I've also enjoyed your involvement with the movies, and my questions are: what would you consider an ideal movie project, if there is such a thing? And also, what's your involvement with the *Long and Winding Road* movie project?

**Harrison:** Right. Well, generally, about my involvement with HandMade Films, we've had a little spell where we haven't made anything since *Nuns of the Run*. But we've got a lot of projects right at this moment; in fact, this afternoon I had some business meetings specifically about HandMade Films. So we've got about eight projects that we've been working on that [*we*] have, as they say, on the back burner. But now we're trying to get them on the front burner. So I couldn't really tell you what they're about because there's a variety of subjects, and all I can say is it's not that easy to be able to get a film, to get a major distribution deal, to get the actors and the directors. One thing's for sure though, these films won't be like the films we made in the past, in as much as they were always small-budget films, made out of England, that didn't necessarily have any named actors or a name director. I think that kind of market is largely gone, and if we want to stay in the film business, I think we have to kind of follow the Hollywood thing.

It's unfortunate in one way, because I think you always need to have some kind of *alternate* subjects rather than the usual Hollywood stuff, but hopefully we'll be able to get some good stuff. We've got some good ideas and good films, and maybe we can slot them in and get them made.

As to *The Long and Winding Road*, that is a tentative title. I don't personally want it to be called that because, you know, I want it to be a bit broader than that. But anyway, that film which is . . . you know, we've had footage for years and years. We didn't complete it because, you know, everybody knows we, the Beatles, had personal problems and managerial problems. Then, of course, along came all the other people who put out a lot of videos and films of the Beatles that was, more or less, a lot of the footage that we had, that was public domain or hijacked material. And now we've approached it from a totally different angle, because the only people who really know the Beatles story is the four of us.

Unfortunately, there's only the three of us now, and there's going to be a slight gap in as much as you don't have John's up-to-date personal dialogue. You have a lot of stuff that we're using in the film where we've gone back to his interviews and—taped interviews—so that we can use that to illustrate certain points.

We've also gone back to our birth really, because the influences that influenced the Beatles were really from when we were born. So actually, there's—well, the guy who is putting it together, he got on the first video reel . . . he was up to forty-five minutes and Pete Best hadn't even joined the band yet, so . . . [*Coburn laughs.*] We're talking about maybe a ten-cassette kind of show.

**Coburn:** That sounds like a long-running documentary. It's like the Civil War series on PBS! [*Laughs.*]

**Harrison:** It is, it certainly is. It's long . . . I don't know if it's winding.

**Coburn:** Rick, great call, thanks. Let's move onto Indianapolis. Vince is on the line, a listener of Q95. Hi.

**Vince:** Hi, George.

**Harrison:** Hi, Mario . . . oh! I mean Vince.

**Vince:** Mario! [*Laughs.*] I'm a lifetime fan, so this means a lot to talk to you. Off the subject a bit, I know you're a big Indy car fan, and have you ever thought about turning a practice lap at Indy?

**Harrison:** Oh no, I wouldn't want to do that. That's the last thing . . . maybe if you would have asked me that twenty years ago I might have said, "Yeah!" But it's the last thing I would want to do at this time of my life. A good friend of mine actually hit the wall doing 220 miles an hour, and I don't like to do that. He's someone who has raced all his life so I wouldn't do that.

**Coburn:** What were you going to say, Vince?

**Vince:** How about becoming a future car owner, possibly? Have you ever thought about that?

**Harrison:** Well, they say, first of all, if I had the sponsorship money—because the last thing you do is use your own money, I found that out. They have a saying, or they used to ten, fifteen years ago in Formula One racing. They'd say, "How to make a million in Formula 1? You start with thirty million."

Because all it is, nowadays the budget for one year is, like, maybe $30–50 million. It's hard to imagine. It's the biggest waste of money, but I enjoy it from that point of view. But the main people who have that kind of money to throw around is cigarette companies.

**Coburn:** There you go, Vince. Thank you very much. And of course, he called from Indianapolis, and the Brickyard is there. You look at it, and it looks kind of simple. "Ah, I'll just tool around the yard one time, you know." . . . Man, 220 miles an hour, I don't think so.

**Harrison:** Yeah. I hear Emerson [*Fittipaldi*] won yesterday. Good old Emmo. Anyway, off we go.

**Coburn:** Off we go to *Live in Japan*. Another song from George Harrison—"What Is Life" on *Rockline*.
[*Plays song.*]

**Coburn:** Well, thank you—George Harrison, *Live in Japan*, "What Is Life?"—from *All Things Must Pass*, originally. That of course [*was*] the live version of that. We're headed to Chicago, Mike is on the line, a listener of The Loop. Mike, you're on *Rockline*.

**Mike:** A very nervous Mike. How you doing, George?

**Harrison:** I'm as nervous as you are Mike.

**Mike:** I remember the first time you were on you had a couple of Dos Equis to slow you down. [*Indistinct*] . . . iced tea, here.

**Harrison:** That's right, I'm not doing that now. I'm drinking hot tea.

**Mike:** One of the things over the years that made me almost as proud [as] musically what you guys have accomplished is socially what you've been able to do over the years, hence my question. I know this took place a year or two ago . . .

**Harrison:** Remind me, what have we done? I can't remember.

**Mike:** How successful have been the efforts of the Roman Angel Appeal?

**Harrison:** Romanian.

**Mike:** Has there been any marked improvement in the conditions there, and how did you and Olivia find out about this in the first place?

**Harrison:** Well, you know we found out in the first place because I think somebody again from the British newspaper or the BBC television came out of there with the footage, just the same as it usually happens. But, yes, it's been very good, and the appeal was very good. They made a lot of money from . . . in fact, just through one newspaper in England alone, the *Daily Mail*—the readers gave a million pounds, which is incredible.

In America, I think they've got something like $100 thousand, plus there was the record that we managed to get together and put out. And so the record has paid quite a lot of money. I don't know exactly, I know I saw one check for a half-million dollars, and I think they might have had a couple more smaller checks since then. So you know, obviously to do anything you really need the money. They're organized very well now. They've got about thirty people, maybe even more, down there in Romania, and they've also now employed some Romanian workers because the cost, it's much cheaper down there. You don't pay them so much money as you would to send people from Britain.

**Coburn:** People are flocking over there to adopt children as well.

**Harrison:** Well, I'm not too sure about that. There was, at the beginning, that kind of thing happened but from what I understood the government stopped that. They tried to put in a lot of red tape, or maybe they needed to, because you never know, you've got to check to see what's going on.

But anyway, generally speaking, it's going very good and actually in fact, my Mrs. is having a meeting tomorrow about it in Los Angeles, about the American side of it. So it's going very well, and she's still very much involved as are all these many other kind people, and that's about as much as I can say at this moment.

**Coburn:** What about this other project with Olivia and Billy Connolly—Parents for Safe Food. What is that about?

**Harrison:** Well, that thing was, I don't know if . . . It was really Pamela, who is Billy's wife, she was mainly in charge of that. And it was a thing that came in Britain, as in America, they had the Alar problem—you know, all the apples were all sprayed with pesticides, and all the crops are sprayed with pesticides. And I think—I don't know if it was Meryl Streep, somebody started it in America, but the same kind of thing happened in Britain, and a lot of kind of celebrity people did this to attract the attention. But they had also a guy who used to work for the government, I forget which department he was, but he knew all of the ins and outs. Generally, it was just to try to get some controls on the food, at least to make them label the food that had the poisons in them. Because in Britain it was even more lax than in America. I believe everything has to be indicated on the packaging as to what is exactly in it.

**Coburn:** For the most part, yes, yes.

**Harrison:** In England, though, they didn't have that. You could just buy something; you just didn't have a clue.

**Coburn:** You didn't know what it was. Mike, thank you very much. It's Glen's turn. He is in Austin, Texas. KLBJ FM 94, a station there. Hi.

**Glen:** Hello, George.

**Harrison:** Hello.

**Glen:** Listen, my question is, are you ever going to write another book, maybe?

**Harrison:** Uh . . . I don't know. Well, actually, I've got a book that I'm associated with that's coming . . . you know, I did this book which was really to show off the talents of this artist, and I did a book of illustrated lyrics, and actually, the part two of that is coming out. When you say "to *write* a book"—the first book that I did, I didn't actually write it, what we did was just talked into a microphone, and people asked me questions, and then you write it down, and you read it back, and you edit it and add to it and take bits away. I don't know . . . maybe someday, maybe when I get old.

**Coburn:** [*Chuckles.*] Thank you very much, Glen. We are taking a time out. We are just getting started here so give us a call, toll-free, at 1-800-344-ROCK. I'm Bob Coburn; it's *Rockline*, with George Harrison.

---

**Coburn:** We are back on *Rockline*, live via satellite from Hollywood. I'm Bob Coburn. Next week, Dana Strum from Slaughter will fill in for me as I vacation. His special guest will be Joe Satriani and his band—they will play live—and also Bonham. Both have hot new CDs out, and Joe is going to bring his guitar and play a couple of tunes for ya, and I'm sure Dana will update everyone on what's going on with his band as well, with Slaughter. Joe Satriani, Bonham, hosted by Slaughter's Dana Strum—one week from tonight on *Rockline*.

Tonight, it's an evening with George Harrison. We have a call from Manchester, New Hampshire. Derek is on the line, a listener of Rock 101 WGIR. Here's George for you, Derek.

**Derek:** Hi, George, how're you doing?

**Harrison:** Fine, thank you, Derek.

**Derek:** I can't believe I'm actually talking to you. I'm one of your biggest fans, but I bet everybody tells you that. [*Laughs.*] First of all, I want to say that your double-album CD is fantastic, and I hope that when you do go on tour, New England is in your schedule.

**Harrison:** Thank you. Well, you know, if I ever get on this tour I'm just going to go everywhere, more or less.

**Derek:** The question I have is, I heard when you played Japan back in December that your son Dhani was up on stage during the encore of "Roll Over Beethoven" at some of the shows. I was interested to know if he's musically oriented. Are you teaching him guitar, and is he into your music?

**Harrison:** Yeah, well, he was there for a couple of shows as was another friend of mine's boy who also plays guitar, and I just thought it was good for the kids because they had been there for three days at the Tokyo Dome, and they just loved the musicians and the band, and we just got them on there for the last segment just so they could have that buzz, you know. But he is. He loves music, he loves the guitar, and I don't really teach him. I tried to show him a few things if he wants to know, but he's got a teacher in school. It's a guy who comes in and teaches the few kids guitar, and it's much nicer than [when] I was at school. You know you couldn't learn guitar in my day. But this fellow, he comes and he says, "Tell me what you want to learn . . ." And he says, "I want to learn the solo to [*Dire Straits'*] 'Sultans of Swing'!" And then the guy shows him, and he comes home and practices it. It's cool, it really is!

**Coburn:** That's great. That's really great. Who is the other person, do you mind mentioning who it was?

**Harrison:** It was my friend Brian Roylance, who's actually the publisher who did the leather books—those kind of limited edition books that I was involved with. It was his boy Nicky. He came on with us.

**Coburn:** What a great shot for him too. Derek, good call, thanks. Let's move on to Orlando, Florida, and by the way, we are thinking of everyone in South Florida and of course the Gulf area here in the United States as that hurricane blows through. We hope everybody is OK. Brian is in Orlando—should be safe up there. He's listening to Rock 100 WDIZ. Hi, Brian.

**Brian:** Hi, Bob. Good evening, George, nice to talk to you.

**Harrison:** Evening to you too.

**Brian:** My question tonight was in regards to your songwriting. You've collaborated with Ringo Starr, Ron Wood, Bob Dylan, Jeff Lynne—even before all of you were Traveling Wilburys.

**Harrison:** Tom Petty!

**Brian:** Now, are you working with anyone, in terms of songwriting, that we haven't heard about yet? And in regards to the songs that you've written for other people, are you ever going to represent them on studio recordings or in live recordings?

**Harrison:** Well, the first question is, no—at the moment I need to get back into writing some more songs. I haven't really written much lately. I thought that when I went off on the road that that would kind of stimulate me into . . . I thought, "Well, by the time I finish this tour I will have written about twenty tunes," but actually I never wrote a thing. [*Laughter.*] I just didn't have time, I was always on the train or something. Anyway, the answer to that is, no, I haven't really been writing lately, but I have a feeling I'm going to try and start doing something now.

I haven't specifically got anybody that I'm writing with, but you never know. I think I need to get myself started first, and then I'd like to maybe write a couple with Tom, you know, because he's fun to write with.

**Coburn:** Yeah, and a great musician too. He's tremendous. Brian, thank you very much. You look at this CD *Live in Japan* and you realize how many great songs George has written over the years, and one of these originally appeared on *Abbey Road*. Here's the live version of "Here Comes the Sun" by George Harrison, on *Rockline*.
[*Plays song.*]

**Coburn:** Yes, indeed. "Here Comes the Sun." You know what I like about that version? You didn't rush through it. It would have been easy to play that really fast, but you want to breathe, you know; you kept the tempo and the pace there.

**Harrison:** Yeah, I think that's just getting relaxed. Well, the best thing, really, is these days I don't have to count it in anymore. Steve Ferrone, who's the drummer with Eric's band, he sets the tempo during rehearsal on his little box, and so right before we start the tune he checks our tempo and that's it. Which is really good because there is a tendency to get a bit speedy.

**Coburn:** You kept it under rein, so to speak. Good old Steve, on his little machine, the magic machine. We're headed to Tulsa, Oklahoma. Our next call for George Harrison is Rick, a listener of 97.5 KMOD. You are on, Rick!

**Rick:** Hi, George!

**Harrison:** Hi, Rick.

**Rick:** How are you doing, sir?

**Harrison:** I'm good, thank you.

**Rick:** I would like to say first, it's such a big honor to have the privilege to talk to you this evening. I never would have guessed this would have ever happened in my lifetime. And the question I have for you is just how did the Traveling Wilburys come about, and can we look forward to any more projects from the Wilburys?

**Harrison:** Well, I thought we covered the story about how they came about, I'll just tell you quick . . .

**Coburn:** Let's do the second part then.

**Harrison:** The second part. I was just hanging out with all them guys, and we just did it; we did one tune, and then we thought, "Well, we might as well do nine more and make an album." [*Coburn laughs.*] Whether we'll get together again, I think from what I can guess, we haven't really talked about it; everybody has been off busy doing their own thing. But I'm sure the four of us . . . it's just a matter of the timing because I think we all enjoyed it so much. And, yes, I think we will, it's just a matter of timing.

**Coburn:** That's good news. That's a good combination of people. Rick, thanks for the call. We're going to LA right now. Mike is on the line, listening to 95.5 KLOS. You're on the *Rockline*, Mike.

**Mike:** Hi, George.

**Harrison:** Hi, Mike.

**Mike:** I was wondering if you had any plans to release any videos, maybe something live from the last tour, or maybe a compilation of music promos that you did?

**Harrison:** Yeah, I think eventually . . . I don't know if I've got enough really to put together to make a compilation. But yeah, I believe I will eventually put out whatever the videos that were put on, like the MTV kind of videos.

Unfortunately, the show in Japan, there was a chance to video it—there was a kind of deal with the TV station—but when I talked to the people, they were going to just do it really with three cameras and do it live and put it out. They were really more interested in doing it quick and cheap, and I thought, "Well, maybe I'll just pass on that and try and do it properly." Because once it's out, it's really the only . . . you don't want to see two versions of the same thing really, so I thought I might as well do it properly someday. So I think when I do the next tour, I'll make a video of the show as well.

**Coburn:** All right. There you go, Mike, thanks. We're going to play another song from *Live in Japan*. George Harrison with "Dark Horse" on *Rockline*.

[*Plays song.*]

---

**Coburn:** Welcome back to *Rockline*. I'm Bob Coburn. It's an evening with George Harrison. You can call George at 1-800-344-ROCK; that's the number that Eric called in Auburn, Alabama. He's a listener of Rock 103 WVRK in Columbus, Georgia. And Eric, you're on the show.

**Eric:** Hi, Bob and George, how are y'all doing?

**Harrison:** Fine, thanks.

**Eric:** George, I wanted to know if you enjoyed that performance at the Hard Rock Cafe in London that you recently did with Carl Perkins, and what prompted you to do that?

**Harrison:** Well, I'm glad you asked that because I know Carl is listening in tonight, and I'd just like to say, "Hi Carl and family." What it was, was . . . the only reason I went there, I mean I don't normally go to the Hard Rock; I went there purely because Carl was in town, and it was my chance to get to hang out with him for an evening, and so I went there and then, I don't know, he just asked me if I'd get up and go up there with him, so I did it.

**Coburn:** And how can you say no when Carl Perkins asks?

**Harrison:** You know, I'm not mad about just jumping up anywhere when I'm unprepared. I'm not that keen on it, but at least I know Carl's tunes. [*Laughter.*]

**Coburn:** There you go. Thanks for the call, Eric. We're going to move to Syracuse, now. We have Dave on the line, a listener of 95X. Welcome to the show, Dave.

**Dave:** George Harrison.

**Harrison:** How you doing?

**Dave:** What an honor. This is incredible. I've been a fan of yours since I was about four years old. I've been listening to your music forever.

**Harrison:** How old does that make me?

**Dave:** It makes me twenty-two, I don't know. I was born in 1970, I just missed the whole Beatles thing unfortunately, but I listen to your stuff every day. And, uh, well, let me get to the question—I was listening to a documentary that you were on last night where you mentioned when you were composing "Something," you had Ray Charles in mind.

**Harrison:** Yeah, that's right.

**Dave:** You had an idea of him singing some words to the chords you were just banging out, and I was wondering—because I remember, on a show called *Sesame Street*, I think it was, Richie Havens had a version of "Here Comes the Sun"—I was wondering if you can imagine anyone else performing or recording anything that you've ever done, who would you like to hear do some of your work and why?

**Harrison:** Ice-T, I'd like to hear him doing . . . what could he do? Yeah, just something like that, really. Actually, the best thing that I've ever heard of something I did myself is—unfortunately it's not that well known, but—it was done in 1972 as the B-side of "Think," which was a re-recorded version of "Think" by James Brown, and on the B-side was "Something," and it's the most incredible version. I think they should put it out as a single.

**Coburn:** Oh, I can imagine. . . .

**Harrison:** It's incredible.

**Coburn:** I remember last time you were here, too. . . .

**Harrison:** I said, "Did I write that?"

**Coburn:** Not that way, yeah.

**Harrison:** He could have put his name on it, I wouldn't have known. And it's beautiful.

**Coburn:** Remember last time you were here, you mentioned that you first got an inkling that maybe the Beatle thing was coming to an end when you were in one studio doing "Something," and Paul was down the hall doing, "Why Don't We Do It in the Road?" [*Chuckles.*]

**Harrison:** Right, well—

**Coburn:** It's kind of . . . *different* songs, you know.

**Harrison:** No, what it was, though—we ended up . . . it was the *White Album*, and we ended up that there were so many tunes that, you know, the recording sessions had been going on for so long that we were try-ing to . . . we were all in different studios as they were empty. The one person was in [*studio*] number two in Abbey Road singing something—I don't mean the song, somebody singing a tune. And I think John was in number one doing something else, and that kind of thing was happening. We were trying to get a lot more done quickly, and it was during that period, I was in an empty studio, I just went in and I kind of wrote that tune. It just came about like that.

**Coburn:** Here's the live version by George Harrison on *Rockline*.

[*Plays song.*]

**Coburn:** Mm, nice indeed. A little slide guitar in there.

**Harrison:** No, it wasn't slide. That was fingers.

**Coburn:** It wasn't slide? Sounds good.

**Harrison:** "Cheer Down," that's the slide one.

**Coburn:** All right, we'll get to that in a minute. That of course is *Live in Japan*, George Harrison. I'm Bob Coburn. Next call from Albuquerque, Paul is on the line. 94 Rock, our station there. Hey, Paul.

**Paul:** Hare Krishna, George!

**Harrison:** Yeah, Hare Krishna to you too, Albert, I mean . . . Albert-querque.

**Paul:** [*Laughs.*] How are you doing, sir?

**Harrison:** I'm doing very well, thank you.

**Paul:** Great. OK, my question is, in the past it seems as though you've tried to distance yourself from your time with the Beatles. In your '74 tour, you did very few of your Beatle-era songs. But on your recent tour of—

**Harrison:** That's not true, actually . . .

**Paul:** I beg your pardon?

**Harrison:** I don't think that was true, really. I didn't do as many tunes as I did on this, but I did. I actually did "Dark Horse." . . . Oh, that wasn't a Beatle tune was it? [*Laughter.*] Yeah, right, but I am longer on this tour, you see.

**Paul:** Right, more tunes. OK, but on this tour you perform many of your Beatle-era songs. Here we are twenty-two years after the Beatles breakup; are you now more comfortable with your Beatle past than you were, say, in 1972 when all the hassles and legalities were going on?

**Harrison:** That's true, in fact I'm so comfortable with it I don't even remember it. It's like, to me, those tunes, if the Beatles hadn't have existed I would have written them tunes, and if the Beatles were still going today then, you know, "Cloud Nine" would have been on a Beatle record. It's just like that. So to me they're just my songs whether I was in the Beatles or not.

**Coburn:** That's great. Paul, thanks for the call. We're headed to LA again. We have Amy on the line, 95.5 KLOS our station. Here's George for you, Amy.

**Amy:** Hi. George, it's a pleasure to talk to you.

**Harrison:** Hi, Amy.

**Amy:** I have a short, simple question. Do you still play the sitar?

**Harrison:** A little bit now and then, just occasionally. I don't practice it every day like I did during the period of about, I think it must have been 1967–'68, that period. I was kind of heavily into it every day. But I played it a little bit on "When We Was Fab," that record, and I played a little bit on a song I did for a little animated TV film which is called *The Bunburys*—similar to the Wilburys, but it's rabbits.

**Coburn:** *The* Bun*burys*. [*Laughs with Harrison.*]

**Harrison:** I did one about the Indian rabbit called Rajbun, and I played a lot of sitar on that one.

**Coburn:** Somebody told me you would have been just as happy being in Monty Python as the Beatles. Is that true? [*Chuckles.*]

**Harrison:** Well, I did like them a lot. I still do actually.

**Coburn:** Then you could have been a Rutle.

**Harrison:** I was a Rutle!

**Coburn:** [*Laughs.*] That's right, you were, weren't you!

**Harrison:** I was, I was one of the original Rutles.

**Coburn:** Amy, thanks. We're taking a time out. We're coming back with George Harrison in just a moment. More rock 'n' roll from *Live in Japan*. More phone calls with you and George and *Rockline*, on the global satellite network.

---

**Coburn:** Welcome back to *Rockline*. I'm Bob Coburn. It's an evening with George Harrison, playing some great music tonight off *Live in Japan* by George Harrison, taking your calls as well. Going to play one right now that was cowritten by Tom Petty—it's called "Cheer Down"—on *Rockline*, on the global satellite network.
[*Plays song.*]

**Coburn:** Yes. "Cheer Down," George Harrison, on *Rockline*. I'm Bob Coburn. The next call for George from Richmond, Virginia. It's John, a listener of XL102. Welcome to *Rockline*, John.

**John:** Thanks. Hi, George.

**Harrison:** Hi, John. You thought Santo and Johnny had finished, didn't you?

**John:** What?

**Coburn:** Santo and Johnny! "Sleep Walk," right? Go ahead, John. . . .

**John:** First, I just got to say, "Wow, I'm actually talking to you!" I have written down on a piece of paper: "You are John Flowers. You are talking with George Harrison." I'm a bit nervous.

**Harrison:** I'm John Flowers, or you are? We all are, we're all John Flowers.

**John:** My question is . . .

**Harrison:** Any relation to Johnny Appleseed?

**John:** Yeah. [*Laughs.*] My question is, what were some of your influences in rock? I mean, like, what made you want to pick up a guitar and start playing?

**Coburn:** Yeah, who did you like when you were growing up as a kid?

**Harrison:** Well, the main influences for rock were the obvious ones, really. I remember specific records, hearing them. You know, like, when I was about eleven or ten, I heard Fats Domino, "I'm in Love Again." A couple of years later, I remember riding on my bike and hearing "Heartbreak Hotel" coming out of somebody's radio. You know, specific things like that. It was Elvis, Little Richard, Eddie Cochran, Chuck Berry, and Buddy Holly.

**Coburn:** Carl Perkins.

**Harrison:** Carl Perkins, of course, and Jerry Lee, you know; it was all the good stuff. I still think that's the best stuff that I hear occasionally on the oldies station. I heard Little Richard doing "Rip It Up" the other day, and it's just *incredible.*

**Coburn:** Oh, man. And he does *rip it up,* doesn't he?

**Harrison:** You know, nobody is doing rock 'n' roll anymore, to my concept of rock 'n' roll. There is none, there's none left, except all that old stuff. I don't even think the Beatles did rock 'n' roll, really. We took music, popular music, into other areas, but . . . we could *rock* when we did live shows and stuff, but I don't think our music was rock, not like Little Richard. That was the greatest stuff. Larry Williams? Can't beat it.

**Coburn:** "Bony Moronie," Larry Williams—and a ton of other good ones too.

**Harrison:** Sure, "Short Fat Fannie," "Dizzy Miss Lizzy," "Slow Down," yeah.

**Coburn:** Wonderful. John, thanks for the call. Let's move on. So many people want to talk with George. We're going to try and get as many in as we can. We have Larry on the line now in Exeter, New Hampshire. He's listening to 100.3 WHEV in Portsmouth. And, Larry, you're on.

**Larry:** Hi, George.

**Harrison:** Hi, Larry.

**Larry:** I'm a big, big fan of yours. This is a great honor of mine. My question is, how do you feel about the reissuing of *Bangladesh* on CD, and are you pleased with the packaging and how things are going with that?

**Harrison:** Yeah, I'm happy about that. It took a long time, really, to get it out, and I'm pleased that it's out, because it just means that the fund keeps on getting topped up a little bit.

**Coburn:** There you go, Larry. Thank you very much. We'll take a brief time out. We're coming back with more rock 'n' roll by George Harrison and more of your phone calls. The number is toll-free from anywhere in North America—1-800-344-ROCK. *Rockline* on the global satellite network, with Bob Coburn and George Harrison.

---

**Coburn:** Hey, thanks for coming back, I knew you would. George Harrison's here on *Rockline*. I'm Bob Coburn. We're playing songs from *Live in Japan*; we're about to play a song that was on *Cloud Nine* originally, "Got My Mind Set on You." This was recorded very well. Who engineered this record, and what kind of guy was he?

**Harrison:** He's a guy from New York, and he's called John Harris. Hello, John, if you're listening. Very good. He's worked a lot on live recordings, and he actually recorded Eric's *24 Nights*, so it was very suitable to have him because he knew the band; he'd worked with them a lot. And anyway, so he came, did it, and we mixed it together later in February. It's come over good, I think.

**Coburn:** It does, and it sounds like this. "Got My Mind Set on You."

*[Plays song.]*

**Coburn:** "I've Got My Mind Set on You," George Harrison, *Live in Japan.* You know, we would have played "While My Guitar Gently Weeps," but it's so *long.* We wanted more time to talk with you.

**Harrison:** Yeah, but the point of why it's so long is because, well, you know, for guitar players it's a great tune to play guitar on. And Eric, it's a kind of special one, because Eric always plays good on it—I mean, he played great on it . . .

**Coburn:** Back on the *White Album,* yeah.

**Harrison:** Right. I don't know, that song for me is becoming more meaningful the older I get, and he particularly plays good on that take. In fact, we did six takes, six shows we recorded. Unfortunately, there was some performances which were actually better than the ones I got to use on the album, but things happened, like the PA system fed back and squeaked all over the track and spoiled it. So this was the version we ended up using, but it's an incredible solo. I love the way Eric plays on it.

**Coburn:** More reason for the *Rockline* listeners to go out and buy the double CD, see.

**Harrison:** Do they still do that? Do people still buy records?

**Coburn:** People still buy—not records much anymore—but they buy CDs and cassettes, that's for sure. We got Phil on the line, George. He's in Albuquerque listening to 94 Rock.

**Phil:** Wow, two calls from Albuquerque.

**Coburn:** Amazing isn't it?

**Phil:** Figure the odds! First, I want to say I'm a little nervous, I've never talked to a living legend before, and it is a great honor to speak to . . .

**Harrison:** Icon . . . living icon.

**Phil:** . . . Bob Coburn. Aww, you blew my joke, George. I said, "I'm glad to speak to Bob Coburn." [*Laughter.*]

**Coburn:** More like a *dead* legend, Phil, but go ahead.

**Phil:** Well, what can you do? You stole my question too, Bob. I was going to ask about Monty Python, and I wondered if you hung out with the guys from Monty Python back in the early '70s when the *Flying Circus* was on the air and how close you—I know you've worked with Eric Idle and stuff since then, but I was curious if you were into it back then when you were younger.

**Harrison:** I think by the time I met them they'd actually finished the television series. I met them, actually, when I was making this record. I think I was making the record that was called *Living in the Material World.* I met them at that point, I met a couple of them, Michael Palin and Terry Jones. They were trying to master this album, which had—it actually had the spiral of the cut on the vinyl record, it actually had *two beginnings* . . .

**Coburn:** Oh, that's right!

**Harrison:** . . . and they were trying to master that down at Apple Records, and it kept bursting through, you know, it kept cutting through from one track to the other. And they eventually got it done. I don't know if they got it done at Apple, but I met them then, and then later I met them when they were premiering the *Holy Grail* movie.

**Coburn:** What a concept to put two things on one side of a record. Depending on where the needle falls you get one or the other.

**Harrison:** You get a whole side of the album different, not just one track.

**Coburn:** No! [*Laughs.*] That's amazing. Phil, see you made a better question out of it, Phil. Thanks for calling, and thanks for the joke too. We have Dennis on the line now in Lynn, Massachusetts, Rock 101 WGIR in Manchester, our affiliate there. Dennis, got George Harrison here for ya.

**Dennis:** Hi, George.

**Harrison:** Hi, Dennis.

**Dennis:** I have one of the largest collections of Beatle original photos in New England, and one thing I always wanted to ask, there was one shot that was taken from a rooftop with a 600mm lens of you, John, and Elvis. I always wanted to ask, were the photos taken in the home that you were at?

**Harrison:** I'd like to know how you talk from under the water, first of all. No, but I don't believe that photograph was actually real. I haven't seen it myself, but we certainly never were on a rooftop, John and I, with Elvis. It probably was Paul McCartney! He looks like Elvis.

**Coburn:** [*Laughs.*] Dennis, there you go, thanks for being on. That's it everybody. Thanks for listening and calling. What a fun night this has been! Coming up in the next few weeks on *Rockline*—REM, Def Leppard, Ozzy Osbourne, Sass Jordan, Delbert McLinton, Slaughter, and Joe Satriani, hosted by Dana Strum; Bonham will be there as well. Thanks tonight to Clyde Bakkemo, also Larry Butler at Warner Bros. Records, to Patty Oates, to Anita Safran, and especially to our guest this evening, Mr. George Harrison. A great, great night—congratulations on the record. It's great to have you out playing live again.

**Harrison:** Thanks Bob, thanks all. . . .

**Coburn:** [*Song begins to play.*] We have something special George has chosen to close with. Tell us what this is, please, George.

**Harrison:** Well, we tried to play this last time we were on. This is a special request for Bette Midler. It's "Kalimankou Denkou," by Yanka Rupkina—it's *The Mysterious Voices of Bulgaria* [*Le Mystère des Voix Bulgares* (Nonesuch, 1987)].

**Coburn:** . . . I knew that.

# MAGAZINE INTERVIEW

Timothy White | November 15, 1992 | Interview Transcript

Harrison came to know many music journalists over the years but grew close to a very few. Timothy White, who came up through the ranks of music reporting in the 1970s and '80s, was on that short, privileged list. His byline appeared most notably in *Musician*, *New York Times*, *Playboy*, and *Rolling Stone*. He eventually became editor-in-chief at *Billboard* magazine, earning a reputation as a deep researcher, a meticulous editor, and a biographer of such legends as Bob Marley, the Beach Boys, and James Taylor.

White and Harrison first met in the late '70s and crossed paths repeatedly through the '80s and '90s, resulting in some great interviews and memorable interactions. One of White's favorite stories was of a spur-of-the-moment invitation from Harrison to attend a Ravi Shankar concert while White was on a London trip with his wife Judy. The musical performance was followed by a taxi trip through late-night London. White recalls many anecdotes from that night: watching Harrison autograph the only loose piece of paper the taxi driver had—a ten-pound note ("Would I do that to the Queen?" Harrison asked before signing his name across her likeness); hearing of Harrison's ongoing legal battle with former film business partner Denis O'Brien and the song he was thinking of writing about the debacle ("O'Brien is Lyin'"); and listening as Harrison begged the manager of a Chinese restaurant to stay open for a few more minutes, never mentioning who *he* was, but saying, "Please understand, *Ravi Shankar* is coming and hopes to have dinner! This is *Ravi Shankar*, one of the world's greatest living musicians! I'm sure you understand. It'd be terrible to disappoint him."

The following Q and A is pieced together from White's typewritten transcription of the interview he conducted with Harrison—later substantially edited—for the 1992 issue of *Billboard* that put Harrison on its cover, marking him as the first recipient of the magazine's

Century Award. The annual honor was created by White and the magazine's publisher to celebrate musicians with careers of longevity and chart-topping achievement, as well as social engagement and overall influence. Tony Bennett, Stevie Wonder, Buddy Guy, Emmylou Harris, and Annie Lennox have been among the recipients since.

The unedited conversation between Harrison and White preserves a strong sense of their familiarity, as well as their willingness to plunge down the many rabbit holes of Harrison's career that most journalists had neither the time nor the inclination to investigate.

When Harrison died in late 2001, White wrote a very personal farewell in *Billboard*: "Through his recordings, he prayed for the human race. Perhaps, in the days to come, each of us—in his or her own way—might spare a moment to pray for him."

A little more than six months later, White himself passed away from a heart attack at the age of fifty. His British publisher, Chris Charlesworth, wrote a eulogy for White in the *Guardian*, closing with a tantalizing snippet from their last conversation: "He told me about his idea for a biography of Eric Clapton and George Harrison, tracing their intermingling lives." —Ed.

**Timothy White:** What was your room like at 25 Upton Green?

**George Harrison:** It was very sparse, really. All it had was a bed and a sideboard.

**White:** You used to have racing car photos on the wall, right?

**Harrison:** That was after I was about twelve, yeah. I had some pictures. But it's not like you imagine these days, where you see *E.T.* and it goes in the kid's bedroom, and it's all full of posters of Arnold Schwarzenegger and that. Or even like my boy's room now. It was very austere, really, in the '50s. We didn't really get lots of magazines. I had a few I cut out—I don't know if I had them on the wall, though—of Jane Russell and Marilyn Monroe. They were my first pinups when I was about fourteen, fifteen.

**White:** What I'm getting at is, I wonder where you would first sit as a youth and play guitar on your own?

**Harrison:** Well, what I used to do is I used to sit downstairs in the kind of dining room of the house, and we used to have this old upright piano that nobody played. A lot of houses would have a piano that nobody ever played, and they would always be out of tune, and we had one of them. And then sometime later it got chopped up and got chucked away when the junk man'd come around; he took it.

So there was just a little table there, and a sideboard for the dishes and stuff, and this upright piano. And I used to just sit there later when everyone had gone to bed and polish my guitar, and play—try and practice bits that I'd seen other people playing and try and figure out chords.

There was a very important man, actually, that I used to go to see with my dad. And when I started playing guitar my father remembered this guy. He was called Len Horton, and he's never, ever been mentioned in any interview, and I often remember him and think, "Wow, that guy was very helpful to me." My dad would call him up and say that I was trying to learn the guitar, and could he help me? And so this guy, who owned an off-license—which was like a shop that sells liquor but they're only open at specific time periods of the day—and this guy used to be closed on a Wednesday night. So I used to go to his house where he lived in a little apartment that was above the shop. And he had this guitar, and on that he would show me all this kind of old songs like from the '20s and '30s, mainly. Like "Whispering," "Stardust"—those kinds of songs.

**White:** Might that have been where you started to become a fan of Hoagy Carmichael?

**Harrison:** Well, yeah. At that period my mother was into that. I think that was a big hit just around 1941–'42; a little bit before I was born, "Hong Kong Blues" was a number one hit, I believe.

But it was mainly like the kinds of songs that would be called dance band music in those days. And they had all those kinds of old chord changes. And he [*Horton*] used to show me those, like [*sings*] "Dinah, is there anyone finer . . ." You know. [*Laughs.*] That kind of stuff, basically.

Basically, I was more influenced in my growing-up period by things like the Ink Spots, Hoagy Carmichael, those kinds of singers, and Cab Calloway kind of music. And then I also heard a lot of Django Reinhardt from when I was about thirteen years old.

**White:** Do you remember what kind of guitar he [*Len Horton*] had?

**Harrison:** Yeah, he had this guitar that looked really great in those days, [*compared*] to what I had. It was—I think they're made in Germany—Hofner, like the bass Paul ended up having, the violin bass, right? That company, Hofner. And he had the top of the line; it was called the Hofner Committee, and it was in birds-eye maple, a blond guitar. They were modeled after the Gibson 400s, the big cello, f-hole style of guitars. And he'd let me play on his guitar as well.

**White:** Sounds like a good sport.

**Harrison:** He was, and I'd just go and spend a couple of hours at his house, and then say, "Thanks a lot, Len. I'll see you next week."

I don't know how many times I actually did that, because I'd forgotten totally about it until just a couple years ago, and then I suddenly remembered. I've often thought, "I wonder if that guy is still alive?"

**White:** And he was a close friend of your dad's?

**Harrison:** He used to be a friend of my dad's when they went to sea. That was around the early 1940s, and then when he stopped doing that, and there wasn't any work doing that, and the war was on or something, and then he'd kind of lost touch with him.

**White:** Do you remember your first acoustic and electric guitars?

**Harrison:** The first guitar I bought, it cost me £3.50. It was a very cheap guitar, a little round-holed acoustic guitar that I bought from a guy who used to go to the school I went to; he was called Raymond Hughes. I must have been about thirteen years old, just thirteen. Then I played that and learned a little bit on that. And then, it was such a bad guitar, all the frets buzzed, and you couldn't get certain notes out of it because of the action, where the strings were hitting the fingerboard. So the moment I realized that I was learning a few chords I thought, "I've got to get a decent guitar."

My mother, she was the sympathetic person in the family, and I said to her, "I've got to get a better guitar!" I think she might have helped me buy this next guitar, which again was a Hofner. It was an f-hole, down-market version of this guy Len's guitar. It was called a Hofner President. It wasn't electric but it was a cello-style, cutaway, f-hole guitar. And I used to chunk along on that for quite a while. That really made me improve my playing quite a lot, by having a decent instrument.

And I traded that with a guy from a band in Liverpool that later became known as the Bluegenes.

**White:** The Swinging Blue Jeans?

**Harrison:** Yeah, but it was before that. They were some kind of a trad band or something, and this guy, I swapped him for an electric guitar, which again was a Hofner! They were, I suppose, the most popular guitars because they were available in England from Germany.

**White:** And what did that first electric look like?

**Harrison:** Well, it was a little Hofner. I've got one actually now. It's a great looking guitar. It's not a solid. You would think it's a solid, about the size of a Les Paul, but it's not solid; it's hollow-bodied, but it doesn't have any f-holes. And it's got two little black pickups on it, and it was called a Club 50.

A pretty neat guitar, now. When you pick it up it feels like a typical '50s big neck, but it's a nice little guitar. It was blond. They used to always make it in what they called a blond or brunette, and the brunettes were kind of like the sunburst, but not three colored, just maybe two-color sunburst. And then the blond would be a natural kind of yellowy finish.

I think the first person who really got me interested in guitar was Jimmie Rodgers—"The Singing Brakeman." And my father had some records, and he used to go away to sea, and he brought back this big wind-up gramophone and Jimmie Rodgers records. "Waiting for a Train," it was called, and "Blue Yodel." And so I always remember that from when I was a little kid of about eight or seven. I remember hearing that with that scratchy needle. And you'd open the front doors on this thing, and you'd have slats making, like, a loudspeaker, and just hearing that guy playing the guitar and yodeling.

Later, when I was a little bit older than that, there was this guy from Florida, and he was a huge success in England during the '50s, and he was called Slim Whitman. Again, there was a singer with a guitar. And then it turned into Bill Haley.

And then in Britain we had this big craze called skiffle music, which came out of a traditional jazz, which is kind of Dixieland jazz. There was a jazz band, Chris Barber, and the guy Lonnie Donegan was the banjo player in Chris Barber's jazz band. And he would do his own spot in the show, and then he played guitar with the bass player and then this woman, Beryl Bryden, who used to play the washboard with thimbles on her fingers, and that became known as skiffle. He was an enormous hit and sold a lot of records; "Rock Island Line" was actually number one in America too.

He did a lot of touring, and as a forerunner to the rock'n'roll bands that came out of England in the '60s, he was a big influence on those kids like myself. Everybody got a guitar, and a washboard, and a tea chest bass with a broom handle and a piece of string on one of these wooden pegs. And the music was simple, two chords or three chords at the most.

When the skiffle faded out, all of the people who were left with their guitars who still wanted to play became the rock and roll bands of the '60s. So he was a big influence in that way.

And I heard some stuff by Big Bill Broonzy and Leadbelly. They got a lot of play, I believe, because of Liverpool being a port.

But the main thing that really buzzed me, I remember, even before I heard Elvis, was Fats Domino's "I'm in Love Again." I can even see exactly where I was when I heard that. There was this little place near where I was born called Wavertree—a district. And right there at that point there's a thing called the Picton Clock Tower. And it was just this tower in the middle of the road with this clock on it. And then there used to be this big old art deco cinema called the Abbey. And I was just walking across the road there somehow, and I was somewhere around there when I heard Fats Domino: [*sings*] "Yes it's me, and I'm in love again!" It must have been on a radio or record player somewhere.

And that was like when I [*later*] heard Ravi's music. It touched somewhere deep in me.

When I heard Elvis's "Heartbreak Hotel," I was on my bike passing somebody's house, and they must have had a gramophone playing. I couldn't *believe* the sound of that record.

**White:** It's like Saul on the road to Damascus.

**Harrison:** And it's the same, I suspect, for everybody! . . . But you've got to remember that in the 1950s, America was more cool than Britain, with everybody having their little Chevys or Cadillacs. We were coming out of a world war, and it was depression. So for us, that was like the sound of hope.

But it's character building when you've been bombed! [*Laughter.*]

**White:** Do you remember the very first song that you ever wrote?

**Harrison:** Sure, that was the one on that second Beatle record. It's called "Don't Bother Me." I had never tried writing songs before that.

**White:** That's a pretty mature song for your first song.

**Harrison:** The thing was, you see, I'd been with Paul and John writing all the time, and I think it took me a while to pluck up the courage to actually write one, because we'd already had a bunch of hits with Lennon-McCartney songs, and they'd been writing songs for some time. I don't know, it must have been a couple of years. They were getting what seemed like quite expert at it. And for me I just had to try and write something that was acceptable and I wouldn't just get laughed out of the room with. So that was the first one I'd ever written.

**White:** Did it take you very long to write?

**Harrison:** Not really, no. It just took half an hour or an hour. I remember it well, because we were doing a summer week at this place [*Gaumont Cinema*] in Bournemouth in the south of England, this little holiday town. And I had some kind of flu, some kind of bug, and I was sick. And so I was staying in bed all day long. The doctor had been called, and he gave me this medicine; in those days they had this medicine that had morphine in it, this medicine that you would drink, swallow, that had a morphine base. You could buy it over the counter; I'm sure it must've got banned over the years. But I remember he prescribed it. And I was taking that stuff and in bed, all feeling weak and tired but trying to reserve my energy so I could get out of bed each night to do the concert.

We would just play like twenty-five minutes, the Beatles. That was our show in a kind of two-hour mixed cabaret of people; that's how it was in the early '60s, it was still kind of music hall. They'd have jugglers, comedians, and people who play xylophones, and then a couple of other singers. And on top of the bill would be, "the Parlophone recording artists, the Beatles!"

This was '63, and we'd only probably had "Love Me Do" come out and maybe "Please Please Me."

**White:** So the song was written about your mood when you needed a doctor?

**Harrison:** Yeah, right! So it was the first thing I thought of, really [*laughs*] as a lyric. And I never really thought it was a great song. I was quite happy that I had written it, because that was the thing. I just thought, "I'm going to see if I can write a song because *they're* writing them."

**White:** Nice song, strong mood, unconventional.

**Harrison:** It's kind of a strange song. He's all uptight because she's gone away. It's pretty embarrassing stuff, really—although I could imagine doing it now and could make it sound pretty good. But in those days we didn't know much about how to put a song over.

**White:** What made you sing "The Sheik of Araby" at the Decca audition in '62?

**Harrison:** Well, it was always a popular song in England. Everybody knew that song. This guy who's a friend of ours, called Joe Brown, he actually recorded and had a hit with a rock version of it [*in 1961*]. And so I was thinking of doing a cover version of a song that'd been kind of a popular song in the past and would now be redone as a rock song.

**White:** Joe Brown, he had the Bruvvers?

**Harrison:** It's like "the brothers," but with a cockney accent it comes out as a "v," you know, the Bruvvers. I did a couple of Joe's records in live shows in them days.

**White:** What did Decca think of the audition?

**Harrison:** They didn't like us, did they? Because they didn't hire us. Instead they hired Brian Poole and the Tremeloes. And that was the famous quote that Dick Rowe, the head of [*singles A&R at*] Decca Records at the time, said, "Guitar groups are on the way out, Mr. Epstein." [*Laughter.*] That's brilliant, isn't it?

**White:** The poor bastard.

**Harrison:** Aha! Well, did you ever see the Rutles movie? They said, "You're the man who gave away the Rutles." He said, "You gave up the chance of all those royalties, all those gold records, and all that." And he says, "Yes, that's right." And he says, "What's it like to be such an asshole?" [*Laughter.*] I believe Dan Aykroyd played that part.

**White:** What was it like doing *The Rutles*? You seem to have had a great time being involved in that project as a consultant and playing the part of an interviewer.

**Harrison:** Now we're all pretty much at ease about the Beatles, because so much time has lapsed. But there was a period when we were persecuted for years by the public and the press, and then we persecuted ourselves with all the lawsuits and stuff, until there was a point when just a mention of the word "Beatles" used to make my toes curl.

In that period, when Eric Idle was doing *The Rutles*, I fed him videotapes of all this footage of us. We're still only just putting it together, finally now, as the Beatles documentary. But we've had a lot of this footage on a thing that was tentatively called *The Long and Winding Road*, but we're not having it called that anymore, I'm glad to say, because in a way that title's been haunting us for years.

So anyway, I gave Eric Idle all this footage, and he used to analyze it and then write the Rutles story. That's why with a lot of the scenes in the Rutles film, the art director, they came up with everything, all the costumes and guitars all painted the same, and little nuances of things the public might [*not*] have known. Like there was a shot of us coming into New York in the back of a limousine, and somebody had given us these little Coca-Cola or Pepsi-Cola radios—they looked like little Pepsi or Coke machines, and they were radios. And Paul's holding it up, and you hear the radio's saying, "And the Beatles are going to be here read-ing their own poetry . . ." And Paul looks around and says, "Oh, yeah?" And in *The Rutles* is that shot where he's saying, "And the Rutles are coming to town to talk about their trousers!" There's a lot in the Rutles that is really spot on. And anyway, it was good for me because I could follow the growth of the Rutles. I still am friends with Eric Idle, and it, in a way, kind of exorcized the things about the Beatles that bothered me in that period of time.

**White:** One more question from your boyhood. Do you recall the first album that you bought?

**Harrison:** I can tell you something that was a real disappointment. I'd got the money and I wanted "Rock Around the Clock" by Bill Haley, and I asked somebody to get it for me, somebody in my family, and I couldn't wait to get that record. They said they'd buy it for me, because I was so into wanting this record. Because for me, all the saxes and Franny Beecher, that guitar player on the Bill Haley record, was just unbelievable.

And they came home, and they gave me this record and said, "Oh, they sold out of Bill Haley so I got you this one." It was the Deep River Boys. I thought, "Aw no, fuckin' hell!" It was such a disappointment. That was the first record I didn't get.

Before I had any money, my brother had a record player, but he had records like *West Side Story* and music like that. I think I got a Lonnie Donegan record. But I didn't really have any money until after we'd been to Germany. By that time, it was '62 and I was getting records at Epstein's shop, and then we were just trying to get everything.

I had a friend in school who had a sister who was married to an American. And I used to think he was so lucky. He'd have all these cool jeans and leather jackets, and things like that, that his brother-in-law would bring him from America. He also had all these records, the EPs and an LP of that Elvis album with the pink and the green [*cover*].

He was my mate anyway, so I used to get to hear stuff through him. I didn't have any money anyway until the Beatles got going really.

**White:** You were forerunner of the world-music initiatives with your involvement with Indian music. No one in rock 'n' roll had ever tapped into another culture's music to such an effective extent. What made you get involved in it?

**Harrison:** In retrospect, it's easier for me to say. The thing was we made that movie *Help!* Somebody came and said, "Well, we've got this script," and OK, off we were doing it. But there was this whole thing in the script about this Indian god, Kali, it was called, and the sacrificial ring, and all the music had sitars. I remember us doing a scene in the restaurant where they come and try and chop the table, and the guy gets thrown in the soup. And there were a few Indian musicians playing in the restaurant.

When we were waiting to shoot the scene, I remember picking up the sitar and trying to hold it and thinking, "Wow, this is a funny sound." But in a way that was just a kind of incidental thing. It wasn't a very memorable thing; it was just something during one day of shooting. It didn't stick in my mind until the thing that happened next, which had something to do with smoking reefer or taking LSD, and . . . I'd hate to say it.

But somewhere down the line there was a point where I heard Ravi Shankar's name, and then I heard it again, and then the third time I heard it I thought, "Wow, this is like a funny coincidence, this name Ravi Shankar." And I talked about him with Dave Crosby from the Byrds. And *he* mentioned the name. And I said, "Yeah I keep hearing this name— I've gotta get a record." I went and bought a record; I put it on, and it just seemed to me like it hit a certain spot in me that I can't explain. My intellect didn't really know what was going on, but it just hit a spot where it seemed very familiar to me. The only way I could describe it was my intellect didn't know what was going on musically, and yet this other part of me really identified with it.

I mean, I'm not sure, maybe I'd heard it. We used to have short-wave radios, you know, when I was growing up, and all evening the radio would be on, and my mother was always tuning it into all kinds of weird—whatever you could pick up on it. So maybe I'd heard it from Algeria or somewhere, or maybe I heard it in some other lifetime! [*Laughs.*] Who knows?

It was something that was like it just called on me, and I just heard it, and I felt very familiar with it. And then the more I listened to it, I thought, "Wow, I'm gonna to meet this guy, Ravi Shankar." And sure enough a few months elapsed, and then I'd met this guy from the Asian Music Circle, and then he said, "Oh, Ravi Shankar's going to come to my house for dinner. Do you want to come and meet him?" I said, "Sure," and that's it, you know.

In those days, all you had to do—and, I mean, it's still the same now to a degree—you only have to think of something, and you can actually make it happen. It just happens.

**White:** The Asian Music Circle?

**Harrison:** That was a little organization amongst the Asians in England. There's one now—I don't know what happened to the Circle—called the Asian Music Circuit. It's a much bigger thing now because it's more organized. There's more Indians in Britain, and because of the influence that's taken place and the years that have elapsed, many more musicians can come. They all come and go through to America and go through Europe and Britain, and there's lots of gigs for them to play. A lot of them don't play big gigs. There's still only a few like Ravi who can play Carnegie Hall or the Festival Hall in London, but there's a lot of little halls and little gigs all up and down the length of these countries, which is now organized by the Asian Music Circuit.

**White:** Did you study with Ravi in England or India?

**Harrison:** At this dinner I had with him, we talked and talked and then he said, "Do you want me to show you? I'll give you some instruction, then." And he came to my house the following day with Alla Rakha, the tabla player. Well, actually Alla Rakha came a bit later.

But we sat there, and he showed me how to hold the thing. Hey, I got started straightaway into the basic lessons: doing scales up and down, the correct posture, everything to do with the pick, the right hand and what you do, the left hand and what you do, and how you're supposed to position yourself to play it. And then we started learning exercises.

And then that evening, after a couple of hours of that, Alla Rakha came and Ravi wanted me to invite a few friends, and Ringo and John came over. And they gave us just this little private concert. That was far out!

Alla Rakha was and still is the most incredible tabla player.

**White:** He's amazing. His hands seem so strong.

**Harrison:** I know! And when you see him and you're just sitting like five inches away from him, it's the most unbelievable thing. I still, to this day, am fascinated with the tabla players.

**White:** It's amazing how they can do those finger rolls.

**Harrison:** The sound is an incredible amount of different noises that's coming out of it! And yet the playing is only from the wrists, the hand movements. Nothing much else is moving! You know, once I was told that Ravi played in Moscow for Khrushchev with Alla Rakha. Apparently when Ravi came on and starting playing, he [*Khrushchev*] got up and came down to the front, and after they finished playing, he made Alla Rakha open the skin, take the skin off the table, because he couldn't believe it; he thought it was some kind of computer or something, and he wanted to see what was inside that was doing it. [*Laughter.*]

And Ringo, he was just blown away. For me, it sucked me in and made me want to know more about it and learn a bit of it. Ringo just didn't want to go near it, because to him it was just so far out, it just made him back off. But he said something to that effect: "Wow, it's just unbelievable!"

**White:** What was the first song you did with sitar?

**Harrison:** First of all, there was "Norwegian Wood (This Bird Has Flown)," because I'd gone out and bought one. This was before I'd met Ravi. They used to have these shops in London called Indian Craft, and you could go and buy all these little carved bits of ivory and little carpets and brass work of all kinds of craftwork from India. They had a sitar in the shop—it was just a kind of cheap sitar but, anyway, I bought it—and I had it at that session, for what must have been *Rubber Soul*. And I just played it on "Norwegian Wood"; it kind of fit onto that song.

And then I wrote a song for the next album, *Revolver*, called "Love You To." And that was one which I actually wrote on the sitar. It's mainly just sitar and tabla, but it does have guitars on it as well. And then "Within You Without You" was the big one. More than just sitars and tabla, it had all the *sarangis*. And that was quite a complicated one at the time because it was done in three sections, and then I edited the three sections together. It had a solo instrumental in a 5/4 kind of tempo, which was very unusual. I suppose Dave Brubeck was the only person who ever played out of 4/4 or 3/4.

See, this is the thing. In Western music, basically the tempo goes 4/4 or 3/4, and that's it. In Indian music they have a hundred-and-eight rhythm cycles, and they can even play in things like 7½. [*Laughs.*] It's quite complex, but I did learn this little piece, one of my exercises that I used to practice, that was in a 5/4 timing. So I did the solo in "Within You Without You" into a 5/4, just to show how clever I was. [*Laughs.*]

**White:** "The Inner Light" on the flip side of "Lady Madonna" was an Indian-influenced, lovely song too.

**Harrison:** I like that one myself. I actually recorded all of that, apart from the vocals, in Bombay, when I was doing the *Wonderwall Music* album. That's finally come out again; they finally put the old Capitol catalogue out.

**White:** *Wonderwall?*

**Harrison:** Well, in talking about this world music, because of my fascination with Indian music—and by that time I'd been to India a couple of times—when I did that music, what I was trying to do was a mini-anthology of Indian music. I was trying to show within the score of that film as many different aspects of what had turned me on in Indian music. And so I used all different instruments: *shehnais*, which are these incredible wind instruments, and *surbahar* which is like a deep version of the sitar, and all the tablas, various drums. And there's a fantastic instrument called the *santoor* which has got 116 strings or something, and it's played with little wooden . . . it's the equivalent to the cimbalom, which is the Western instrument. It's a bunch of strings strung over a box, and you play it with little hammers that you hold between your first and second finger and your thumb.

All that stuff to me was so exciting. To me the sound was kind of new in one way, and yet you could hear how ancient it was. So I tried to show that with *Wonderwall Music*.

**White:** What was the story behind "The Inner Light"?

**Harrison:** At the time we were doing TM, that guy David Frost used to have a TV show, and John and I were on that show, and they had done interviews with the Maharishi. And they had an audience made up of people who were for and against meditation. In the audience there was a guy who was called Juan Mascaró, and he was the Sanskrit teacher from Cambridge University. He's written the Penguin Classics books, the Bhagavad Gita and the Upanishads, and various Vedic literature.

Somebody had played him "Within You, Without You," and he thought it was such an inspiring song. He wrote to me, and he said, "I hope you will go on and write more of these kinds of songs, and I'll send you this little book I've written called *Lamps of Fire*." They were all translations from various different philosophies, and he said, "This one on such and such a page would probably make a good song." I turned to the page, and it was called "The Inner Light." His translation of a thing from [*the Chinese classic text*] *Tao Te Ching*.

And so when I read this little thing, it was very nice, and I had a little extra time after I'd finished the music for *Wonderwall*. I got the band of Bombay musicians, and I just made that tune up to fit the words of "The Inner Light." I took the tape back to England and then put the vocal on that.

**White:** This was twenty years before Paul Simon or Peter Gabriel or David Byrne got interested in other cultures and making it accessible without diluting it, making people curious.

**Harrison:** It was such a buzz for me. The whole thing about Indian was somehow awakened for me after I had LSD. It unlocked this enormous big door in the back of my consciousness. That music and the whole idea of Indian; I just had this thing inside of me saying "Indian." And Ravi, he was like my contact. And then I went off into India with him, and I started checking out the yogis of the Himalayas; basically, the music was part of the thing.

I don't want to get too soppy, but in the Indian philosophy the music has been very important. Different instruments are shown being played by different gods. The percussion instruments—there's an instrument called *damaru*, and it's played by Lord Shiva; it's a little drum that has these little strings with lead weights on them. They swing it 'round, and the little lead weights rattle on the skin. [*Makes rapid purring noise.*] So that represents the percussion. And there's this Goddess Saraswati that plays this stringed instrument known as the *veena*, and the *veena* is the forerunner to the sitar. And consequently all other stringed instruments come from out of that.

But then the woodwind is represented by Krishna, who plays the flute, a wind instrument. Now, if you read in the philosophy of Lord Krishna, it explains how through Krishna's flute—it's symbolic—one by one we are awakened by the divine music of the Lord. He wakes us up. And when people get turned on to something, that's what happens.

In a way, when I heard "Heartbreak Hotel" by Elvis coming out of somebody's radio when I was a kid on my bike, *that* is still Krishna's flute. The music is still that mystical sound that's saying, "Hey, come on!"

For me that sitar music, it was such a turn on. And it wasn't just because I'm interested in string instruments or because I thought Ravi was good. It was a very deep thing. Something was calling me. And I'm still trying to head in that direction.

**White:** It's like that "Wake Up My Love" song, that music is such an agent of awareness.

**Harrison:** In India, Ravi did a movie in 1967 called *Raga*, and in that film he said, "Music is the only language I really understand, for I believe in *nada brahma*, meaning 'the sound is God.'" All sound and all music is created deep in the cosmos. The sound that's manifest is the original sound. "In the beginning was the Word." As they say in the Bible, "Thus spaketh the [*Lord*], amen." And that is Om, the basic sound vibration. And all other sound is coming from that.

And the music, whether it's very subtle or it becomes more gross into the physical world and into the radio stations, it's still based upon that original sound vibration. The subtlest manifestation of God is the Word, and then the Word turns into time and the atom, and then it keeps going until it ends up as all this big dream that we're in now.

**White:** In Egyptian theology, in the beginning was the word, and the word was God, and the word was with God. Were you raised in the Catholic Church?

**Harrison:** My mother was. My father wasn't. So it wasn't that strict. It wasn't like, "You've got to go to church." But I still went there a bit as a kid. Usually when you're young, you don't have much option, because you're just going with your mother wherever she goes. And I went there up until I was about eleven. Around that time, I thought, "Wait a minute. I don't really like this." I could see on the wall they had the paintings of the Stations of the Cross, and I thought, "Something really *heavy*'s going down here."

And yet when I looked around the church, it just looked stupid, all the people just—it was like bullshit. And so I got out of it. By the time I was twelve, I didn't really count myself very religious at all. I shy away from the word "religion," actually.

India, in a way, turned me back on to Christ. The Christians have never been able to explain Christ. What they do, they do because of their own inability for realization, because basically that's what it was all about: trying to tell everybody how to have that consciousness. Because it's political isn't it, the whole Christian Church was based on politics— "We couldn't get rid of this guy, and he won't go away, so let's cash in on him," and that's basically where it came from.

**White:** And it's been a power struggle for the last two thousand years.

**Harrison:** And there's a few books I've got, and I keep thinking I'm just going to go down to the Vatican and have big boxes of these books and throw them through the window, saying, "Read this, you bastards!" So I got out of the church because I couldn't relate to it.

**White:** It's based on a lot of fear. As you say, there's very little spirituality in religion.

**Harrison:** This gets to why I wrote "My Sweet Lord," because after going to India, I wanted to know about the swamis and yogis, and I got a book off of Ravi by the first Indian swami who ever came to the USA, who was called Swami Vivekananda. *Vivek* means discretion; *ananda* means bliss. And he was a great swami. He came to Chicago in about 1890, I believe. Anyway, in his book he said, "If there's a God we must see him. If there's a soul we must perceive it. Otherwise, it's better not to believe. It's better to be an outspoken atheist than a hypocrite."

And when I read that after all that stuff I'd been through with the Church, with "You just believe what we tell you. And don't ask questions." Whereas the Swami's saying, "If there's a God we must see him." I thought, "Right on, that's the one for me!"

If there's a God, I want to see him. There's this thing about people who are great believers, but they've got no proof, the Billy Grahams of this world who rant and rave and yet have had no contact, no direct perception. Religion is supposed to be about how to have direct perception, so it no longer is an argument whether it is or it isn't—you just *know* because you've had your *own* experience.

But how do you do that? They can't tell you how to do it in Christianity. In India, they can show you: this is how you do it.

**White:** Christianity doesn't teach transcendence.

**Harrison:** And also, Christianity, they lost the disciplical [*sic*] lineage, you see. As soon as Christ's disciples were dead, that was it. It's all hearsay. In India, you can follow a lot of those Krishnas on the street who are actually in direct disciplical [*sic*] line with Krishna. You can follow their guru back to Vedanta, his guru, and just keep going back. That's how it was taught in India, and they never even wrote it down for thousands of years. They just taught it to the other people, just as Christ had his master and became a realized master himself. And then he had his disciples. It's all passed down by becoming that thing, by realization. And in Christianity the disciplinal line got broken right after Christ. So that's why it was never as pure as it is in Vedic culture. I say that, as opposed to Hinduism.

**White:** Do you have a favorite song or composition that's sometimes overlooked?

**Harrison:** There's one I liked a lot called "Life Itself." But it's not a rock and roll song; it's a mystical kind of lyric. And I like that one you mentioned, "Wake Up My Love." I got the idea for that from a Paul Robeson song. I'm happy I've written a rock'n'roll song like "Devil's Radio," which is actually saying something.

**White:** "Teardrops"?

**Harrison:** That's quite a nice song. That could be done by some black group, because you could make a good dance routine to that one. There's one song I wrote [on Gone Troppo] called "Baby Don't Run Away." It's not a good production, but it could be a good R&B song. "The Pirate Song," that was one I wrote with Eric Idle: "I'd like to be a pirate, a pirate's life for me/All my friends are pirates and sail the BBC!"

There was one called "Your Love is Forever," which was quite nice, a nice melody, on the album I did with Russ Titelman.

**White:** Other musical genres you're interested in?

**Harrison:** There was a guy in England called George Formby—it's a peculiar north-of-England style of singing where he came from, not far from Liverpool. He played a ukulele banjo. He's gotten a lot of publicity recently because last year was like thirty years since his death, and they put on a big exhibition of his songs and memorabilia.

He wasn't that much of an influence on me. It's just that you couldn't escape him growing up in England around the '40s and '50s. He was a big movie star and made like twenty-four British movies. And his father was a very famous stand-up monologue player who'd do these characters. In fact, Charlie Chaplin took his character the tramp from this guy's father, George Formby Sr.; he had a character of a tramp with the big shoes and the clothes that didn't fit. Charlie Chaplin came to him and asked if he could borrow the character.

But I got into the ukulele banjo, an amazing little instrument. I recorded with it on some stuff I haven't got out yet; I've written a few songs with it. I carry one around because it's such a funny instrument;

it makes you laugh when you hear it. It's very limited [*as*] to what you can do, although there are players who can play classical stuff on it. I've seen people play, like, the "William Tell Overture" on the ukulele banjo.

For me, It's the narrowness of the chords. You play all these little basic chords, and there are only four strings, and they're all around the same positions, but it gives you a kind of an interesting way of looking at the same chords you know from the guitar. It's the same tuning as the guitar. It's a high sound because in the fourth string, instead of it being low, it's actually an octave above where it would be on the guitar.

But I've written a couple of good tunes on it. When you mix it in with Wilbury music, it's actually a neat sound. The song I've made a demo of is one of the old records of this George Formby, but the version I've done of it is more like an early Ry Cooder tune.

And I've spent some time in Hawaii and been influenced by the ukulele. Basically the ukulele is just a little tiny guitar that you can put in your pocket. They have a sweet sound to them. And in Hawaii I've bought all kinds of new ukuleles. There's big ones that are concert size, and they make six- and eight-string ukuleles which have got the most lovely sound with nylon or gut strings.

And the instrument of the ukulele banjo interested me as a historical thing. The Portuguese, when they went out in the 1800s to Hawaii, they took their instrument, which is called *cavaquinho*, which is really a little ukulele, and they started making them. And the king of Hawaii, King Kamehameha, saw these people playing and he said, "Ukulele!" *Uku* means "flea," and *lele* means "to dance." So he was commenting on how quick their fingers were going, like a dancing flea. And then ships started going to Hawaii, and Hawaiian music became a fad for a period of time, from about 1926 to 1932. And all the dance bands did Hawaiian-style songs. And I believe the country and western steel guitar came from the Hawaiian. There was a song that won the Grammy called "Sweet Leilani," by Bing Crosby, and Harry Owens wrote it.

But this guy called [*Kelvin*] Keech took the ukulele and the banjo—which can be traced back to the Far East—and he hybridized this as the banjolele or the ukulele banjo. I wanted to get some, and I found out they were only made between 1926 and 1932. So anyway, I got involved with this George Formby Society mainly to get the instrument.

**White:** Any plans for the next solo record?

**Harrison:** I keep trying to write the songs, just, lately, I wish I could do it quick like a Wilbury record, but solo albums are much more difficult. But the idea I would really like to achieve would be to get it out and then do this famous tour I'm supposed to be doing and get that out of the way. If I had gone straight from Japan and toured the world that would have been it for me, but I couldn't use that band once we'd finished Japan because Eric was working.

I'm just going to have to do a tour on my own. And then I can finally retire. [*Laughter.*] But I don't know if I can get an album out by next summer and then tour next winter.

**White:** You invented your own job with a freshness and a heartfelt originality that made it so much more rich than a mere career.

**Harrison:** See, I never really did much [*as*] far as a career. There's a lot of people out there who really plan what they're doing. They got their publicists and their managers and they plan their tours like a Desert Storm campaign. But mostly it's just me. . . . It's all just been haphazard.

# TELEVISION INTERVIEW

**John Fugelsang | July 24, 1997 | VH1**

Whether or not this is indeed Harrison's last televised performance is less important than realizing that 1997 was the year he was first diagnosed with throat cancer. Radiation treatments initially seemed to stem the threat, and now and again he would make an appearance—especially when it came to supporting Ravi Shankar, who was promoting a new album, *Chants of India*. Despite a slightly drawn appearance, Harrison displays an undeniable spirit and strength in this conversation with one of VH1's more insightful hosts at the time, the comedian-turned-TV-journalist John Fugelsang.

At the time, VH1—MTV's sister channel—had remained more committed to music-focused programs while MTV had shifted their priorities to shows like *The Real World*, which would lead to the reality TV revolution. On the day Shankar and Harrison were scheduled to stop by the VH1 studios, Fugelsang had been scheduled to fly to London to interview Paul McCartney. He delayed his flight and quickly prepared for what was expected to be a brief chat with Shankar and Harrison. What VH1 got was a four-hour visit that included an extended chat about spirituality, the concert for Bangladesh, and a bit about the Beatles—and a few songs sung on an acoustic guitar that happened to be on hand.

The conversation is refreshingly loose and informal—like when Harrison asks where all the good hippies of the '60s have gone, and Fugelsang comes back with "driving Volvos, George." But Fugelsang's respect for Harrison's lifelong spiritual search is obvious, as he gives Harrison ample room to explain what he has learned over the years. One cannot help but compare this televised discussion with Harrison's encounter twenty-six years prior with Dick Cavett: the way Harrison warms up over time as host and guest get their timing in sync, how Harrison keeps mentioning Shankar, who sits patiently on his left. Yet, whereas

Cavett wanted to discuss the Beatles while Harrison was more inclined to discuss spiritual matters, Fugelsang was more in tune with Harrison's priority.

"I wanted to talk about God, and meditation, and what happens when you die, and the soul," Fugelsang told journalist Chuck Daly in 2013. "And the whole time the producer's in my ear saying, 'Get him to talk about John Lennon!'" Looking back fifteen years later, Fugelsang admits that he is less than impressed by his younger self: "I was making inappropriate jokes, I was cutting him off, I was stammering, I couldn't shut up, [*but*] I think it was my lack of polish that made him enjoy the experience, actually. And the fact that I was into the stuff he was into talking about." Fugelsang adds:

> So, the day George died, VH1 aired—all day long—an interview with George and some twenty-five-year-old kid talking about God and the soul, and what happens when you die. It helped me realize, "Oh, I'm not that same young person anymore." And it helped me grow, spiritually—the experience of meeting George and doing that.

The following transcript combines the original VH1 program, which aired on July 24, 1997, with excerpts from the extended program that was broadcast on November 30, 2001, the day the news arrived of Harrison's death. —Ed.

**John Fugelsang:** It's been a great year for music fans. Last year saw the release of Ravi Shankar's four-CD boxed set *In Celebration*, and this year has brought us the release of the new album *Chants of India*, produced by George Harrison. And it's a great thrill for me to be here today with two of the greatest living artists in music, from the East and from the West, Ravi Shankar and George Harrison. Thank you both for joining us.

**George Harrison:** Thank you.

**Ravi Shankar:** Thank you.

**Fugelsang:** George, how did you first come to meet Ravi and discover the music?

**Harrison:** During the days when there was the mania, the Beatlemania, well I got involved with the records, you know, I bought some of Ravi's records, and I listened to it, and although my intellect didn't really know what was happening or didn't know much about the music, just the pure sound of it and what it was playing, it just appealed to me so much. It hit a spot in me very deep, and it was, you know, I just recognized it, somehow. And along with that I just had a feeling that I was going to meet him. It was just one of those things. And at the same time, when I played the sitar—very badly—on a Beatle record, then Ravi was coming to London. A lot of press were trying to set it up that we'd meet, but I just avoided that. No, I didn't want it to, you know, be on the front page of a newspaper as a gimmick, because it meant more to me than that. So I thought, "Well, I'll wait and meet him in my own time." And that arrived on an occasion—there was a society called Asian Music Circle, and the fellow who ran that, who I'd got to know, he said Ravi's gonna come—he was in London—he was going to come for lunch, and we met like that way. Then he came to my house and got me to learn how to hold the sitar and put me through the basic lessons of sitar.

**Fugelsang:** Ravi, I've always wanted to ask you: how did you feel the first time you heard "Norwegian Wood"? What did you honestly think of George's sitar playing?

**Shankar:** When my niece and nephews, [*laughs*] they made me hear this—and that was after I met George, I hadn't heard anything before that—and I was not much impressed by it, you know. But I saw the effect on the young people, I couldn't believe it, even in India. It was not only in the West, but it seemed they were just lapping it up, as you say. [*Laughs.*] You know, they loved it so much.

**Fugelsang:** How did the other guys in the Beatles react when you started bringing this . . . when you brought this instrument into the studio?

**Harrison:** Well in those days, you know, we were growing very quickly, and there was a lot of influences that we were . . . I mean that was the best thing about our band. We were very open minded to everything, and we were listening to all kinds of music, you know, like avant-garde music—later became known as "avant-garde a clue" [*i.e.,* "*haven't got a clue*"; *Fugelsang chuckles*]—and various things like that. So you know, they just thought, "Well, that's good," they liked the *sound* of it. And on "Norwegian Wood," it was one of those songs that just needed something to give it that little extra, and the sitar I'd bought—a very cheap one in a shop called India Craft in London—and even though it sounded bad, it still fitted onto the song, and it gave it that little extra thing, so they were quite happy about it.

I went to India to be with Ravi, to see India, to learn some music, and just to experience India, but I also wanted to know about the Himalayas. *That* is the thing that's always fascinated me about the idea that . . . um, I mean it may sound like a lofty thing to say on VH1 but basically, you know, what are we doing on this planet? And I think through the Beatle experience that we'd had, we'd grown so many years within a short period of time. I'd experienced so many things and met so many people, but I realized there was nothing actually that was giving me a buzz anymore. I wanted something better. I remember thinking, "I'd love to meet somebody who will really impress me." And I don't mean because, somebody like Burt Lancaster because he was in a movie. I mean, I met Burt Lancaster, and he impressed me on that level. But I meant someone who could *really* impress me.

That's when I met Ravi. Which was funny, because he's this little fella [*Shankar smiles; Fugelsang chuckles*] with this obscure instrument, from our point of view, and yet it led me into such depths. And I think that's the most important thing; it still is for me.

You know, I get confused when I look around at the world and I see everybody's running around, and, you know, as Bob Dylan said, "He not busy being born, he's busy dying." And yet nobody's trying to figure out what's the cause of death and what happens when you die. I mean that, to me, is the only thing really that's of any importance. The rest is all secondary.

**Fugelsang:** Do you think pop musicians are afraid to deal with subjects that are so big, or it just doesn't occur to them? Or do people think, "Oh it's not commercial enough, who wants to talk about life itself?"

**Harrison:** I don't know what anybody else thinks, and as the years have gone by, I seem to have found myself more and more out on a limb as far as, you know, that kind of thing goes. I mean, even close friends of mine, you know, they maybe don't want to talk about it because they don't understand it, but I believe in the thing that I read years ago, which I think was in the Bible; it said, "Knock and the door will be opened," and it's true. If you want to know anything in this life you just have to knock on the door, whether that be physically on somebody else's door and ask them a question or, which I was lucky to find, is meditation, is, you know, it's all within.

Because if you think about it, there isn't anything—I mean, in creation, all of creation is . . . *perfect.* There is nothing that goes wrong with nature—only what man does, then it goes wrong. But we are made of that thing, the very essence of our being, of every atom in our body, is made from this perfect knowledge, this perfect consciousness. But superimposed on that is through—if I can use the word—the tidal wave of bullshit that goes through the world.

**Fugelsang:** It's cable, you can say that.

**Harrison:** Yeah, so we're being barraged by bullshit. But not only that, the way the world is structured, or the way creation is structured, we have duality which says, "yes-no, good-bad, loss-gain, birth-death"—and it's a circle that you get trapped in; it's like the [*Bob Dylan tune "Stuck Inside of Mobile with the*] Memphis Blues Again." And that's the hardest thing to understand: what is causing both of these things. What is causing day and night, good and bad—it's all the cause, and this is the effect.

So, I mean, we're getting really transcendental here—

**Fugelsang:** Well, no—

**Harrison:** . . . but to say our physical being is really—on a very, very subtle level—it's just like the sap in a tree, it runs throughout all parts of the tree, now, it's like that. Our bodies are manifesting into physical bodies, but the cause—the sap—is pure consciousness, pure awareness. And that is perfect knowledge, but we have to tap into that to understand it.

And that's really why, for me, this record's important, because it's another little key to open up the *within,* for each individual to be able to sit and turn off, um . . . "turn off your mind, relax, and float downstream," and listen to something that has it's root in a transcendental . . .

because really even all the words of these songs, they carry with it a very subtle spiritual vibration. And it goes beyond intellect, really. So if you let yourself be free to let that have an effect on you, it can have an effect, a positive effect.

---

**Fugelsang:** Ravi, you said a very beautiful thing a couple of years back in an interview; they asked you what it was like for you to become a big rock star—quote, unquote, a big pop star, as it were—and I recall you saying that it was easier for you because you were older at the time, as opposed to someone like George who was in his early twenties when it happened.

[*To George*] Do you think *that* may be a reason why you found a search for something deeper in life? I think about you embracing Eastern philosophy; I think about Dylan becoming born again. Do you think it drove you to search for something deeper because you were worshipped by millions, and why do you think it drove you to search for something deeper as opposed to someone like Elvis who had a hard time handling it?

**Harrison:** Actually, Elvis, I think, looked for something deeper too, because I know at different times he was involved with different organizations. It was sad about Elvis—I think compared to the Beatles, Elvis, I always saw the problem for him was that he was the only one who had that experience, whereas [*indistinct*] hippies, you know—it takes more people to share that experience. I mean the four of us all had that experience, and we gained strength and supported each other in the turmoil. But, yeah, I think fame is a good thing in terms of giving you heightened experience, or at least more experience, but then it's what you do with that, or what that uncovers. I think for me, you know, as I say, I realized I just want more—this isn't it. This isn't it. Fame is not the goal, money—although money's nice to have, it can buy you a bit of freedom, you can go to the Bahamas when you want—but it doesn't . . . it's not the answer. The answer is how to get peace of mind and how to be happy. That's really what we're supposed to be here for, and the difficult thing is that we all go through our lives and through our days, and we don't experience *bliss*—and it's a very subtle thing to experience that, and to know how to do that is not just something you stumble across. You've got to search for it.

**Fugelsang:** Did you experience bliss onstage or in the studio—in a way, did performing put you in touch with that bliss?

**Harrison:** Well, we had happiness at times but not the kind of bliss I mean, where like every atom of your body is just *buzzing*, you know. Because, again, it's beyond the mind. It's when there's no thought involved. It's a pretty tricky thing to try get to that stage because it means controlling the mind and being able to transcend the relative states of consciousness: waking, sleeping, dreaming—which is all we really know. But there is another state that goes beyond all that, and it's in *that* state—that's where the bliss and the knowledge that's available is.

---

**Fugelsang:** Ravi, how was it for you when you first met George? What was your take on Beatlemania?

**Shankar:** I'm ashamed to say that I knew almost nothing about them when I first, you know, met them, excepting that they're very popular. And meeting them in the parties, I was so impressed by George at that time, who looked so much younger; he was so inquisitive, asking about so many different things. Mostly music, sitar, and, of course, along with that certain spiritual . . . and the only thing . . . I felt that his enthusiasm was so real you see, and I wanted to give as much as I could—through my sitar of course, because that is the only thing that I know of. The rest . . . I cannot express. He talks so beautifully. He is used to words. He *writes* poems. He *writes* songs. I do sometimes, foolishly, but I'm not that much . . . I express myself through notes, musical notes, so it's a different way of . . . but anyway.

As you said, when I met him, and we started off immediately, after a few days, as he said earlier, to sit properly, how to hold the sitar and, you know, how to handle the finger position and all that, the basic things. And he was so interested, and he was so quick in learning, and then we fixed immediately for him to come to India, and he came. We fixed it for six weeks, but [*chuckles*] unfortunately it didn't happen because people recognized him after a week or so, and there was such a commotion in Bombay that we had to run away to Kashmir and live in a houseboat and all that. But unfortunately, he had to leave. There was some . . .

**Harrison:** I believe *Sgt. Pepper's* or something was getting . . .

**Shankar:** Then I thought, my God, I couldn't believe that any four people could create such a storm all over the world.

**Harrison:** The Spice Boys. [*Harrison and Fugelsang laugh.*]

**Shankar:** And it was not that I was unknown or anything. I was playing concerts in Carnegie Hall and different places, but as a classical Indian musician. But the moment it was known that he has become my disciple, it was like a wildfire. You know, I became so popular with the young people all of a sudden, and I was rediscovered, as they say, and then I took that role of superstar for a number of years because of him. Because, you know, the whole thing was going a bit not to my liking because of the association of drugs and things like that. So I really had a very difficult time for the next few years to put my music in the right register or right place, but because I did *that* is why I am here today, also, sitting with you. Otherwise I wouldn't have been here. People have really come to understand the depth and the seriousness of our music along with all the, you know, enjoying part of it, the entertainment part, that is there, but the true root—and that's what is also projected in this particular record.

---

**Fugelsang:** I want to talk about the early 1970s, the concert for Bangladesh. Now, how did this all come about? Was it Ravi who set it in motion?

**Shankar:** Yeah, it was that period when Eastern Pakistan and the Pakistan government had problems, and they wanted to get separate, and they wanted to name it Bangladesh. It was mainly the language issue. It started with that and then became a big political issue. But our concern was . . . my concern was that many of my relatives were there. They came as refugees, a lot of children. So all that was very painful to me, and I was at that time planning to give a benefit show and maybe raise 20,000 . . . 25,000 . . . 30,000 dollars and send it, you know as . . . and

George happened to be in Los Angeles at that time, and he saw how unhappy I was, and I told him. He said, "That's nothing, let's do something big," and immediately he, like magic, you know, he phoned up, fixed Madison Square Garden and all his friends, Eric Clapton, Bob Dylan, and it was magic really. Just . . . [*Snaps.*] And he wrote that song also, "Bangladesh." So overnight that name became known all over the world, you know.

**Harrison:** America was actually shipping armaments to Pakistan, who were, you know, just massacring everybody, and the more I read about it and understood what was going on, I thought, "Well, we've just got to do something," and it had to be very quick. And what we did, really, was only to point it out. That's what I felt.

**Fugelsang:** When you think about all the talent you assembled and all the money you raised for the album, it was a very controversial thing in Bangladesh. John Lennon used to get in trouble all the time for his activism. Did anyone tell you, you know, "It's a little bit hot, don't go there"? Were you discouraged at all by people for pursuing it?

**Harrison:** No, not really. I think that was one of the things that I developed, just by being in the Beatles, was being bold. And I think John had a lot to do with that, you know, cause John Lennon, you know, if he felt something strongly, he just did it. And you know, I picked up a lot of that by being a friend of John's. Just that attitude of, "Well, we'll just *go* for it, just do it."

**Shankar:** This was something unique. The whole spirit was so beautiful, Bangladesh concert.

**Harrison:** It was just pure adrenaline, and, you know, it was very lucky that it came off because all musicians weren't there for rehearsal. We rehearsed bits and pieces with different people, but we didn't have everybody all on at one time until the show itself. And so we were just very lucky, really, that it all came together.

When Ravi said to me . . . you know, he wanted me and Peter Sellers to come and introduce the show, and he could make $25,000. Straightaway I thought of the John Lennon aspect of it, which was: film it, and make a record of it, and, you know, let's make a *million* dollars. . . . And I think that boldness was by having that fame, by learning through the Beatles, that you get a bit more clout if you're well known.

**Fugelsang:** Let's talk about the concert because it was such a *great*—it's credited as being the first all-star benefit concert, the precursor to Live Aid and all the benefit concerts of the '80s. How did you go about getting the talent who showed up—Eric Clapton, Ringo, Bob?

**Harrison:** I just got on the telephone in Los Angeles. There was a fellow . . . there was an Indian astrologer who I'd met in LA, and so I said to him, "Hey, is there any good particular day to put this concert on," and he said, "August the first or August the second." And I thought New York was the best place to put it, just because of all the media and it's in between Europe and LA, and I checked Madison Square Garden, and I found it was vacant on that day, was it the first or the second?

**Fugelsang:** It was the first. . . .

**Harrison:** And I just got on the telephone and I started calling people, and it was certain people I knew I could rely on, who was Ringo and [*Jim*] Keltner, the drummers, and we got Badfinger to be the acoustic guitar players. I was hanging out a lot at the time with Leon Russell, and Leon said he'd come and bring Don Preston. Leon actually was very helpful with the song itself, "Bangladesh." I kind of wrote the song, but he suggested to me to write that intro, where it kind of sets up the story. . . .

**Fugelsang:** "My friend came to me. . . ."

**Harrison:** Yeah, and then Leon of course played on the single—we quickly made the single to try and get it out to . . . you know, get it on the radio.

**Fugelsang:** How quick was it?

**Harrison:** Oh, we did it in one night I think.

**Fugelsang:** Wrote it, recorded it . . . ?

**Harrison:** I wrote it one day and a couple of days later assembled the people who played on it, and then came off to . . . oh, and then I was calling Eric all the time; Eric was in a bad way at that time. He had a slight . . . [*makes a motion as if tossing a bottle over his shoulder and smiles*] drinking problem or something . . . but he managed to make it eventually. But that's why we ended up with Jesse Ed Davis, because he was around, so we started showing him the songs that we were going to do in case Eric didn't make it, and then Eric came so we decided to have both on, because we couldn't chase Jesse away.

**Fugelsang:** Three guitarists in one show—that's terrific.

**Harrison:** Yeah, and Don Preston as well, actually, Leon's guitar player. And then Bob . . .

**Fugelsang:** Tell me, how did you get Bob? *How* did you get Bob out of seclusion up in New York State to come down and do the show?

**Harrison:** I just asked him really, and, I don't know, my relationship with Bob is . . . I don't know, it's . . . I've always tried to be straight with him because he's also been surrounded by a tidal wave of bullshit. [*Chuckles.*] I just always tried to be straight with him, and he responded. The night before the show, it was a bit tricky because we went down to Madison Square where they were setting it up, and we stood on the stage, and suddenly it was a whole, frightening scenario, and Bob turned to me and said, "Hey man, I don't think I can make this, I got a whole lot of things to do in New Jersey," or something like that.

And by that time I was so stressed out because I'd just been on the telephone for like, I think it was three weeks about, three weeks of setting the entire thing up. I'd been on the phone about twelve hours a day. And at that point I said, "Look, don't tell me about that. At least you've been onstage on your own, that's all you've ever done. You know, I've never— I've always been in a band—I've never stood out front, done that. . . ."

**Fugelsang:** You had never done a tour before. . . .

**Harrison:** ". . . So, you know, I don't want to know about that." And right up till he came on the stage, I didn't know if he was going to come.

**Fugelsang:** When the show began you didn't know if he . . .

**Harrison:** Yeah, and I had a list on my guitar, and I had the bit that said, "Bob—question mark." If you look in the film, I turn around to see if he's around, and he's so nervous that he's just coming on even before I announced him.

**Fugelsang:** He hadn't been onstage in a long time.

**Harrison:** He delivered and that really, I think, it really made the show—by having . . . you know, Ravi and myself was one thing, but Bob just gave it that extra bit of clout.

---

**Fugelsang:** I know the one benefit concert you've done in England in the past twenty years or so is the for the Natural Law Party back in '92, I believe. What brought that about?

**Harrison:** Well, it was . . . one of the things that made it easier was I'd just done a tour of Japan with Eric Clapton's band, so I was kind of up to speed with the songs that I was doing and the band was there that knew all the material. But that was, I think there was a general election going on, and as far as I'm concerned, whichever . . . there's Neil Innes, you know, from *The Rutles*, he wrote a song once, and it said, "No matter who you vote for, the government always gets in." And it's like that. In England, you always get—as far as I was concerned—the left, the center, and the right, they're all really the same. They're all different shades of the same grayness. And although it was a long shot . . . you know, Maharishi tried to get these people to form together into a party which would be called the Natural Law Party. Maharishi Mahesh Yogi. And the idea behind it, really, is to have consciousness as the basic thing, because if . . . really, we get in government, or we get in any situation in life, we get the reflection of our own consciousness. We can't really complain about what we have because that is us. It's a reflection of our own being.

Now, if we could have people who were actually conscious, in a spiritual sense, then all the underlying problems to society—I mean it would be able to change overnight, but over a generation or two generations—you could have things where, for instance, say, in England, and I'm sure it's the same here, you get disease, so you've got a lot of expenditure on hospitals and on fixing up people who have disease. Now the problem is that most doctors, they study disease—they don't know about *health*, so you'd need to reprogram stuff so you teach people about how to be healthy. That way you don't spend so much money on disease. People would be healthier. You wouldn't have such a requirement for all these various things that take up all the money; you'd be able to use that money for something else.

So the natural law that operates on this planet, or in this universe, everything—as I said earlier—everything works in a perfect order, and there's a scheme to things, which has a certain intelligence that drives it and makes everything work. Now, if we as individuals could go to that level of consciousness, where we can bring it into our being, and as Maharishi Mahesh Yogi once said, for the forest to be green each tree must be green. So it's no use just one or two people being like this; you'd have to make the whole of society [*so*] they had that understanding. And that's what I think, really; you'd have to school people, right from being children, teach people about their health, about their bodies, about consciousness—because it's all to do with consciousness.

Raise the level of consciousness, and then everything automatically becomes better.

**Fugelsang:** Do you think it can happen, or do you think people are totally on autopilot too much?

**Harrison:** It can happen but it's something which will take a long, long time, generations of people. I mean, if you look now, just through, say, from the '60s or the '50s, there's a lot more people, thanks to Indian music, thanks to rock'n'roll music, who have got much more understanding. You go out there on the street now, you can find Indian spice shops, Indian restaurants, and places to go for yoga and meditation. There's a much higher awareness, generally, on those kind of things. And so it *is* seeping through. I mean, where did all the really good hippies go when they all dropped out?

**Fugelsang:** [*Smiles.*] They're driving Volvos, George.

**Harrison:** No, I don't think all of them are. I think a lot of them are . . . have, you know, brought up—there's probably two generations of kids now, who are much more open to that type of consciousness. And they're being brought up being vegetarian, or whatever, that helps the society become much more balanced. It's all to do with the balance—you know, we've got too much *extreme* going on.

**Fugelsang:** You're optimistic.

**Harrison:** You have to be optimistic, yeah.

**Fugelsang:** Me too, it's so funny because when you talk to people, it's down the middle. Those that think it's getting better, those that think it's getting worse, and those that think its reflected in the music, in all cases.

**Harrison:** It is getting better and worse, because that's the nature of relativity. You know, good and bad, good and bad. But the individual—if the individual gets on that consciousness, then it doesn't matter because in a way you can retain the balance between the good and the bad. You know, because, really, good and bad are the same—they are. It's the same sort of thing. So in the middle is the safe path.

---

**Fugelsang:** Wanna try one of the Beatles' tunes? [*Harrison strums guitar and smiles.*] You wanna try "Something"? A Bob song? A Carl Perkins song? I'll take a Rick Astley song, George. [*Harrison laughs.*] I'll take a Spice Girls medley, George.

**Harrison:** I'll play one of mine if I can think of one.

[*Voice off-camera says, "All Things Must Pass."*]

**Harrison:** Really? [*Laughter.*]

[*Harrison plays and sings two verses of "All Things Must Pass."*]

---

**Fugelsang:** I'd like to start off talking about the *Chants of India* album, cause it's a real beautiful CD, record, whatever we call them these days. Do you think that an American audience is going to be able to relate to the music on the album?

**Harrison:** I think so. It's like, first of all it's not really like sitar music; I know Ravi's sitting here with his sitar, everybody knows him from sitar music, but it isn't really sitar music. I mean, it's basically spiritual music, spiritual songs, ancient mantras, and passages from the Vedas, which are the most ancient text on the earth. And so it's these ancient songs, which are all spiritual music, but trying to put it in a context where it doesn't change it from what it basically is—but at the same time, the instrumentation to make it palatable to not just westerners but to everybody.

**Shankar:** Well, I always had in my mind not to make it so difficult for hearing for people who are not used to our music at all, for instance. But apart from the words which are very old and they all mean almost the same thing, you know: peace, love, for ecology, for trees, for nature, for human beings, body, spirit, everything. About thirty years, forty years ago these were absolutely not heard. You were not permitted to even . . . you had to give it only to your disciples and that also privately in the ear, not loudly. But now books are all printed. Everything is out even in network, you know. [*Chuckles.*] So as far as the words are concerned, they are open now, but the tune—that I had to give, or add in slight orchestration in the background, [and it] was with this very thought, that it should *match* this old sentiment of whole spiritual context that it has. At the same time not be too much or sound very ritualistic or fundamentalistic or anything like that. That's the main thing that I tried.

**Fugelsang:** Well, for a kid from Long Island, I never thought I'd get to say this on TV. Please welcome, performing "Prabhujee" from *Chants of India*, joined by Ravi Shankar's wife Sukanya, please welcome Ravi Shankar and George Harrison.

[*George, Ravi, and Sukanya perform "Prabhujee."*]

# PUBLIC STATEMENT

**George Harrison and Olivia Harrison | January 2000**

Around 3:30 AM on December 30, 1999, George and Olivia Harrison were the victims of a home invasion. A mentally ill, thirty-three-year-old man named Michael Abram broke through a window in their Friar Park mansion with a knife and a mission to cause deadly harm. As he later explained to the police, he was convinced the Beatles were "witches" and had to be stopped.

Olivia called the police while Harrison, fearing more for the safety of his wife and mother-in-law than his own, confronted Abram with only his bare hands to defend himself. A desperate struggle ensued: Harrison grappled with the intruder as Olivia repeatedly bludgeoned Abram's head with a brass lamp. Within fifteen minutes, the deranged man was cuffed and in the hands of the police, and the injured couple were in an ambulance speeding to the hospital. Harrison had been stabbed more than forty times, suffering major blood loss, a pierced lung, and cuts to his left hand.

There was a shared, dispirited reaction once the news got out, a feeling of "*not again*"; one could not help but be reminded of John Lennon's fatal encounter with a fan nearly twenty years before. The headlines later mentioned how *another* intruder—an unbalanced woman named Cristin Keleher who claimed to have a "psychic connection" to Harrison—had broken into his Hawaiian home earlier in the month, expecting him to be there over the holidays.

As the couple recovered physically and spiritually, and headed into the new year, they remained resolute and chose to welcome 2000 by responding to the outpouring of support they had received. When others in a similar situation might have turned inward and gone into lockdown, the Harrisons reached out with a simple note—expressing their gratitude and a prayer for the future. —Ed.

Thank you for your kind thoughts, flowers and messages of concern and compassion for our ordeal. Your kindness and love were a great help and a desperately needed contrast to our unfortunate experience.

*We would like to wish you and your families a happy new year and hope it will be a peaceful and loving one. We hope to see you again soon.*

George, Olivia and Dhani Harrison

[*The card is signed with the Om symbol.*]

# ONLINE Q AND A SESSIONS

**George Harrison | February 2001 | Yahoo!, MSN**

If Harrison's battle with cancer in his final year had any effect on his energy and spirit, his work schedule did not betray it—not until the waning months anyway. At the start of 2001, he was working on a new album (*Brainwashed*, which would be released posthumously in 2002) and promoting the release of a thirtieth anniversary, remastered edition of *All Things Must Pass*. The original three-LP set was refitted to a double-CD format, with five new tracks added, including a partial rerecording of "My Sweet Lord." It came out on Gnome Records, an imprint created specifically for this release and distributed by Capitol.

Harrison welcomed the usual battery of interviews and appearances and acceded to one additional venue then just beginning to realize its potential: the Internet. In 2001 the role of websites, online sales, and social media was still being worked out, and chats with celebrities were still a novelty.

Harrison embraced the coming of new media: he launched a website specifically focused on *All Things Must Pass* that was described by *Goldmine* magazine as featuring "graphics and sounds and little Macromedia-created gnomes dancing and giggling and playing guitars in a Terry Gilliam-esque world." He participated in creating an EPK that included audio and video bites of himself and other album participants—his son Dhani, coproducer Jeff Lynne, drummer Jim Keltner—speaking about the project. And for the leading online destinations of the day, Harrison participated in a few online chats.

The chats that took place on two leading sites of the day—Yahoo! and MSN—follow. In these Q and A sessions, Harrison reveals himself as a man still full of life and plans. There's a palpable energy that rings with the freshness of the medium. He's still an undying fan of Indian music and Hoagy Carmicael, still happy for a good punchline ("What's Eminem?"), and open to discussing even the near-fatal attack in his house. —Ed.

## Yahoo!

**ChatYahoo_Lisa:** Welcome to Yahoo! Chat. We are here with George Harrison.

**george_harrison_live:** Hello! It's nice to be here! It's my first time on a computer . . . I'm pretty illiterate.

**yahoomusic asks:** What made you decide to re-issue *All Things Must Pass* now?

**george_harrison_live:** It's the 30th anniversary and I'm in the process of remastering my entire catalog, which I want to get back into the stores. So we started with that one, and hopefully during the year we'll be able to come with the next batch and so on, so that everything I have ever done will be available.

**morvyon asks:** George, are you planning a new studio album?

**george_harrison_live:** Yeah. I hope to put out a new studio album, possibly in November, and I have at the moment many songs in various states of completion—possibly 35 songs that I have been working on over the years.

**yahoomusic asks:** Do you surf the internet much? What types of things do you do online?

**george_harrison_live:** No, I never surf. I don't know the password.

**willowy_blonde asks:** Hi, my boyfriend wants to know, he's a musician, what's your fave electric guitar, and do you still have "Rocky," your '61 Fender Strat?

**george_harrison_live:** Hello willowy blonde! I still have Rocky! And he can be seen at Cyril's rare guitar shop on allthingsmustpass.com.

**timbarwick asks:** Will you be releasing *Living in the Material World* in a remastered/extra tracks version?

**george_harrison_live:** Well, as I said before, that will be the next one to be remastered. I have to get into my tape library to find out if there are any alternate versions of anything.

**silbeat asks:** Hi George! Glad to hear from you again! Are you planning to do any live performances? If so, where would you like to play? (Please include Argentina!!!). With love from Argentina. Sole, Mara, Silvi, Vale, Gilda, Ale, Sami and Graciela.

**george_harrison_live:** Hello Argentina! At the moment I have no plans for live performances. If I do later, I will certainly come to Argentina.

**rbortega2001 asks:** What did you think of Bob Dylan getting nominated for an Oscar?

**george_harrison_live:** I think he should win it! I think he should win ALL the Oscars . . . all the Tonys . . . all the Grammys.

**pcpalmiere asks:** How has *The Rutles* influenced your career?

**george_harrison_live:** I got all my ideas from *The Rutles*! Particularly, the 12-string Rickenbacker and slide guitar styles I got from Stig O'Hara. I met him once and he is a super chap.

**oldmanalex asks:** Hello from Russia, George! Russian fans invite you to play in Moscow! Can you tell, will the Traveling Wilburys reform? Are there any plans to record something with Tom Petty, Bob Dylan and Jeff Lynne?

**george_harrison_live:** Thank you, Russian fans! I'll be there after Argentina!

**nattyrobbo asks:** Hi George! I'm Natalie, an 18 y.o. girl from Australia, and I'm a HUGE fan. Any hints for a budding guitarist???

**george_harrison_live:** Yes. Buy a ukulele!

**mike_n_tex asks:** George, do you ever see a reunion tour with you and Paul and Ringo?

**george_harrison_live:** Stranger things have happened.

**flatcat65 asks:** George, which version of "My Sweet Lord" do you like best, your original or the new version?

**george_harrison_live:** I like the new version better. Because it's new! And I like Sam Brown singing it.

**ChatYahoo_Lisa:** Why did you re-visit it?

**george_harrison_live:** At the time, the song was so popular and also so controversial that the most important thing about it for me was that it, in its small way, conjured up a touch of spirituality—something we are very short of . . .

**ChristopherClause asks:** Hi George! Christopher here! Thank you for being such an inspiration! What was it like working with Phil Spector? Although I can hear his influence, your "influence" and leadership in the production is clear. God bless you, George!

**george_harrison_live:** Phil Spector was prob the greatest producer from the '60s and it was good to work with him because I needed some assistance in the control box. Phil is very funny—loveable. We love him.

**mebissy asks:** I have several teenage friends who've just discovered *All Things Must Pass*. They were wondering about radio airplay. I explained that this was a re-mastered, etc. album—a re-release, essentially. They, however (as do I) feel the music is just as cool as it was when you first released the work. Wouldn't it be great if a single was selected and the whole cycle could start again?

**george_harrison_live:** It's nice to know that teenagers find *All Things Must Pass* *cool.* As far as a single goes, I suppose that's really up to Capitol Records. I have no objection!

**melissay1 asks:** Hi, Mr. Harrison, how do you feel about the *Beatles 1* album being top of the charts?

**george_harrison_live:** It's very nice. It's also nice that young children seem to be hearing it for the first time. And I think, as an alternative form of music for today, it has its place alongside all this other stuff.

**captainwombat_2000 asks:** Out of curiosity, why the garden gnomes on *All Things Must Pass*?

**george_harrison_live:** Originally, when we took the photo, I had these old Bavarian gnomes which I thought I would put there, like, kinda . . . John, Paul, George, and Ringo. Gnomes are very popular in Europe, and these gnomes were made in about 1860. So, while building the website the gnomes just seemed to get into it, and we just couldn't stop them!

**gearfabasitwere asks:** Is Indian music still a big influence on your music?

**george_harrison_live:** Yes!

**ChatYahoo_Lisa:** Anything particular?

**george_harrison_live:** Check out U. Srinivas, a South Indian electric mandolin player. Eat your heart out, Van Halen!

**moosefalva101 asks:** Following the incident at your house on Dec. 1999, has your outlook on life changed at all?

**george_harrison_live:** Yes and no. Adi Shankara, an Indian historical, spiritual, groovy-type person once said, "Life is fragile, like a raindrop on a lotus leaf." And you better believe it!

**Nicole_Paul asks:** I am curious about your website and the way the cover photo is altered by adding roads and urban development to the picture. Does that symbolize anything?

**george_harrison_live:** Yes. It symbolizes that our world is being concreted over. Haven't you noticed?

**bluejeanbaby42001 asks:** George, you have quite a reputation as a gardener . . . What are some of your "pride & joy" plants? Love, Dianne.

**george_harrison_live:** Well, for the cooler climates (as in England), the current trend is definitely toward Miscanthus. You'll find many lovely varieties; try the Zebrensis and also the Malepartis. However, if you're gardening in the tropics I think you'll find a lovely little ginger called Kahili.

**a_t_m98 asks:** Mr. Harrison . . . what is the opening chord you used for "A Hard Day's Night"?

**george_harrison_live:** It is F with a G on top (on the 12-string), but you'll have to ask Paul about the bass note to get the proper story.

**hari_girl asks:** What do you think of Eminem's Grammy nomination?

**george_harrison_live:** What's Eminem? Aren't they chocolates or something?

**beatles_lvr asks:** You started the "band aid" movement; who would you help today? Love you, George!!

**george_harrison_live:** Bob Geldof!

**Moyette asks:** What did you record with Bill Wyman last month?

**george_harrison_live:** An old Ketty Lester song called "Love Letters."

**sharonconcannon2000 asks:** Why was "I Live for You" left out of the original mix? (I think it's lovely, thank you for putting it out at last!)

**george_harrison_live:** I didn't think that we had got a good enough take on it. Except for Pete Drake, the pedal steel guitar player. At that time, I had so many other tracks as well, so we just left it off. It did need patching up in the drum department.

**pcpalmiere asks:** How close are you to releasing that boxed set of unreleased songs and demos you talked about in *Billboard* some time back?

**george_harrison_live:** Well, hopefully during this year I should at least get out a new album and all the other boxes of unreleased demos could possibly follow in 18 months. I'm trying to get everything that has ever been done out there. It'll just take a little time.

**nikolaidisgm asks:** George, what do you miss most about John Lennon?

**george_harrison_live:** John Lennon.

**michaelcalcina asks:** George: In the *Anthology* book, you talk about the unwound G string. What is that? I play guitar and I'm not sure what you're talking about.

**george_harrison_live:** It's one of those little things that goes up your butt so that people can't see your panty lines. No, It's actually a 3rd string that doesn't have a winding around it.

**spongeweed70508 asks:** Does Paul still piss you off (tell us the truth)?

**george_harrison_live:** Scan not a friend with a microscopic glass—you know his faults—then let his foibles pass. Old Victorian proverb. I'm sure there's enough about me that pisses him off, but I think we have now grown old enough to realize that we're both pretty damn cute!

**incantataa asks:** Mr. Harrison, I was wondering if you might tell us a bit about your ideas on love. Romantic love, that is. I recall you having written some of the Beatles' most beautiful love songs. It would be interesting to hear how your religious attitudes have impacted your beliefs concerning romanticism.

**george_harrison_live:** Well, the lover that we miss is actually God. The beauty that you see within each other is actually God. So, Krishna was the greatest romanticist. He had girlfriends on every corner! I can't separate the two—a beautiful girl is the divine mother, a beautiful man is the manifestation of potential.

**fabzzy asks:** You're joking in a most Pythonistic manner tonight, George . . . it's great to hear you online!!!

**george_harrison_live:** PISS OFF!! You nosy bastard!

**i_arcos asks:** Is it true that you recorded "Homeward Bound" with P. Simon?

**george_harrison_live:** I recorded that with Paul Simon on *Saturday Night Live* back in 1853.

**tnntxx asks:** George, given the drug experimentation of the '60s, how do you feel about the legalization of pot?

**george_harrison_live:** Well, I saw someone on TV last night pulling out huge loads of pot out of various fields in California. My feeling is . . . as long as you can go into a store and buy whiskey, bourbon, and all the rest of it, then a little grass is nothing. The authorities are just causing the price to be high—'scuse the pun.

**ckeavenyuk asks:** Have you any tips to budding songwriters? Do you, as John apparently advised you, stick at it until you have finished it?

**george_harrison_live:** Try and write some melodies. And some words that mean something. It is true that if you are on a roll, then it's best to finish it in one go. That's what Johnny said.

**kdtash asks:** Any chance that the Dark Horse material, esp. *Shankar Family and Friends* will be released on CD?

**george_harrison_live:** Well, along with my own catalog of records, the other Dark Horse records hopefully will be finding a new home and coming out on CDs (remastered) sometime in the future.

**mp0071999 asks:** Hey George, will you be ever be back on Yahoo?

**george_harrison_live:** Possibly. It's pretty painless for me.

**kyntire2001 asks:** Happy Birthday (a little early). During your recent Internet video promoting *All Things Must Pass*, you pointed to an engraving on the back of your guitar. What did the engraving say?

**george_harrison_live:** It's a Maclaren Strat, and it had a metal chassis number plate on the back. Thank you all! May God bless you all. Don't forget to say all your prayers tonight. Be good little souls. Lots of love! —George.

**ChatYahoo_Lisa:** Thank you sooo much for joining us. . . . Pretty please come back soon!

**george_harrison_live:** Check out allthingsmustpass.com for further entertainment!

**ChatYahoo_Lisa:** Bye everyone!

## MSN

**Digital Dish Diva says:** Welcome to MSN Live! Tonight MSN Live and allthingsmustpass.com present a very special event with former Beatle George Harrison, who is celebrating the re-release of his hit album, *All Things Must Pass*. It's hard to believe thirty years have passed since *ATMP* topped the charts with hits like "My Sweet Lord." Join us tonight as we talk about music history with legend George Harrison. George, it's an honour to meet you, sir. Welcome to MSN Live!

**George Harrison says:** Hello, good evening! How's your father! How's your uncle?

**Digital Dish Diva says:** George, the Internet was not a part of your promotion last time around for *All Things Must Pass*. What part does the Internet play in promotion for *All Things Must Pass* now?

**George Harrison says:** I suppose the fact that it is just like this. And everyone is listening. It eliminates the time of someone printing up a newspaper.

**SR says:** Is it true that you were really asked to join the Beatles because you knew all the chords to "Twenty Flight Rock"?

**George Harrison says:** No! Paul knew "Twenty Flight Rock," but I did too.

**Spockmiester55 asks:** What is the difference between the old and new release if any?

**George Harrison says:** The new release is remastered and is much, much better [*compared*] to the record that existed up until now, and it has five bonus tracks on it. It also has new packaging.

**Sherwood asks:** Will your other past releases receive the deluxe treatment as *All Things Must Pass* did?

**George Harrison says:** It depends really. They will all be remastered. Whether the artwork will change, I don't know. It depends what we feel at the time and what the record company feels at the time.

**jerryfender asks:** Don't you miss the old packaging with albums versus CD's? *All Things Must Pass* was great because even the box was huge!

**George Harrison says:** Twelve-inch square artwork gets you more scope and greater impact. Those days the album cover used to be part of the overall package. It seems to become less important because it is smaller and not so many people are interested in the artwork.

**doodah asks:** Where were you spiritually then when you wrote the lyrics for "My Sweet Lord," and where are you now spiritually? Have you grown?

**George Harrison says:** Swami Vivekananda said, "If there is a God, we must see him. And if there is a soul, we must perceive it." In the West they still argue if God really exists. Basically, I am in the same place. The song really came from Swami Vivekananda.

**iluvgeorge asks:** Will you be touring?

**George Harrison says:** At the moment, no.

**lidbaby asks:** Any musicians you like right now?

**George Harrison says:** Hoagy Carmichael, but there are many, many, many musicians.

**babe asks:** Is most of what's been written about you pure rubbish? Is there any one book that's more accurate than any other?

**George Harrison says:** The one that is the most accurate is *The Beatles*, by the Beatles. When a book is written by someone who doesn't like you, it may not be very good.

**WildingTangent asks:** Are you still writing and recording songs? How would [*you describe*] your style of music these days?

**George Harrison says:** I am still doing that, yes. Hopefully, there will be one coming out at the end of the year.

**tedsblues asks:** Re: recording . . . analog or digital?

**George Harrison says:** I have always recorded analog except when I was in a live concert. Generally, I record on analog, but I hear that digital these days is getting better. The bandwidth is getting better.

**arainyfriday asks:** Looking back, how do you view your book *I, Me, Mine*? If it were to be rereleased, would you make changes based on perspective you have gained over the years?

**George Harrison says:** It was OK for the time. I thought it was well made. It was an excuse to have a nice leather book like the Bible.

**liam0241 asks:** What was the inspiration for the song "Run of the Mill"?

**George Harrison says:** There was an expression that came from a place called Yorkshire, where they made fabric. Run of the mill just means average. I was using that phrase more or less, because, the Beatles were just splitting up. I don't know if they had that expression in America.

**sasha asks:** Hi, Mr. Harrison. My dad and I like your site. Did you do it?

**George Harrison says:** I am not a technician. But I sat with people from Radical Media. They came to my house and set up the computers. The technicians did it and I kept thinking of ideas. I didn't have a concept of what a website was, and I still don't understand the concept. I wanted to see little people poking each other with sticks, much like Monty Python.

**Digital Dish Diva says:** You can check out George Harrison's website at allthingsmustpass.com

**rico asks:** What do you wish you could do, that you haven't done already?

**George Harrison says:** Dematerialize my body.

**OKRichH asks:** I consider this a great privilege to chat with you. Was the recording of *All Things Must Pass* a fulfilling outlet for you?

**George Harrison says:** Yeah, at the time it was very fulfilling—a chance to do a record of my own material.

**Brit asks:** What's the most popular misconception about you that people have?

**George Harrison says:** That I am serious. Pisces are depicted as two fish going in opposite directions. Many people do not see my humorous side.

**Beat asks:** Are you interested in all in the different sounds that electronics can add to guitar sounds, or are you more of a "back to basics" advocate?

**George Harrison says:** More of back to basics. I really like the sounds they had in the '50s. Now you just buy something and plug it in. You can sound like Jimi Hendrix or whoever and everyone sounds the same.

**jediprincess00 asks:** What would you like to say to the younger generation that looks up to you?

**George Harrison says:** Try to realize what the purpose of being in a body is. There is only one purpose really and that is what you have to try to not forget. "Who am I? Where did I come from? Where am I going?"

**Digital Dish Diva says:** And on that note, George, it has been a pleasure having you as our guest tonight!

**George Harrison says:** Lots of love and kevlar to everyone! It has been nice talking to you. Please enjoy the website!

# LAST WORDS

George Harrison | November 2001

In mid-2001 reports began to circulate that Harrison was gravely ill; the cancer he had valiantly fought for a years had returned. In May he entered the Mayo Clinic in Minnesota to remove a cancerous growth from a lung; in July he was beset by a brain tumor and moved to Switzerland—purchasing a villa—to be close to the clinic where he was being treated. In October the time had come for last-ditch measures; emaciated and in pain, Harrison moved to New York City to be near his oncologist at Staten Island University Hospital.

By mid-November all possible treatment was deemed futile. The illness and various treatments took their toll, and Harrison was only able to speak with great difficulty. He searched for a tool to help him communicate and deflect the seriousness of his situation; being a fan of Austin Powers movies, he found a Dr. Evil talking doll to serve as a proxy. And in an effort to maintain his privacy, Harrison relocated once more—to Los Angeles, settling into the home of a longtime friend and security consultant, Gavin de Becker.

There in the company of very few people—including his wife, son, and two fellow Hare Krishna members—he passed away on November 29, 2001. The death certificate listed the cause as "metastatic non-small cell lung cancer."

These are among the last words, written and spoken, of George Harrison. —Ed.

[*Excerpt from a note written to Mike Myers, received late November 2001 during primary shooting of* Austin Powers in Goldmember. *—Ed.*]

. . . Sitting here with my Dr. Evil doll . . . I just wanted to let you know I've been looking all over Europe for a mini-you doll.

Dr. Evil says "frickin'," but any good Scouser [*Liverpudlian*] will tell you it's actually "friggin'," as in a "four of fish and finger pie," if you get my drift.

Thanks for the movies, so much fun.


*[Spoken to Olivia and Dhani Harrison in George's final days, to be shared with the world. —Ed.]*

Everything else can wait, but the search for God cannot wait, and love one another.

# ABOUT THE CONTRIBUTORS

**Michael Aspel** is a British actor and radio and TV personality who has hosted such popular UK programs as *Crackerjack, Give Us a Clue, This Is Your Life, Antiques Roadshow,* and *Aspel & Company*. He began his career as a newsreader for the BBC in 1957, and after many roles and programs, hosted *Aspel & Co.* for ITV from the '80s up to 1993. He is currently retired, though he does make appearances on special occasions.

**Charles Bermant** was a freelance reporter and music journalist in the 1970s and '80s, contributing to Washington DC's *Unicorn Times* and Canada's *Globe and Mail* and writing a regular column on rock video for the *San Jose Mercury News*. He eventually turned his focus to new media and computer technology and now lives on Bainbridge Island, Washington, writing occasional music and tech articles and hosting radio station KPTZ's *LIVE! and Kicking* program.

**Dr. Jenny Boyd** is the British-born ex-wife of rock drummer Mick Fleetwood, sister of George Harrison's ex-wife Pattie, a former model, a licensed psychotherapist, and a mother of two. She is also the author of two books—*Jennifer Juniper: A Journey Beyond the Muse* is soon to be published—and currently resides in California.

**Mick Brown** is a freelance British journalist and broadcaster noted for his investigative reporting on cultural and political affairs. His byline has appeared in a wide variety of publications over the years, including the *Sunday Times, Guardian, Observer, Rolling Stone,* and *Crawdaddy,* and he is now a regular contributor to the *Telegraph* magazine and *Daily Telegraph*. He is also the author of a number of books, including *Richard Branson: The Inside Story*, *American Heartbeat: A Musical Journey Across America from Woodstock to San Jose*, and *Tearing Down the Wall of Sound: The Rise and Fall of Phil Spector*.

**Dick Cavett** is a comedian, writer, author, and television personality and host who, from the late 1960s through the 2000s, developed and produced a number of talk shows that were unusual in welcoming both mainstream and countercultural figures. Cavett was also noted as for engaging his guests with in-depth and extensive discussions.

**Maureen Cleave** is a freelance British journalist who was known for her profiles and interviews for various publications with such luminaries of the mid to late '60s as the Beatles, Bob Dylan, Mick Jagger, Joan Baez, Marc Bolan, the Everly Brothers, and others.

**Bob Coburn** was a rock deejay and longtime host of *Rockline*, a nationally syndicated call-in radio program that aired from 1981 to 2014. He began his career in the late '60s on various stations around his hometown of Dallas, before moving to San Diego and eventually joining KLOS-FM in Los Angeles in 1980, where *Rockline* was produced. Coburn died of lung cancer in 2016.

**Anthony DeCurtis** is a noted music journalist, critic, biographer, and educator, best known for his years on the masthead of *Rolling Stone* and contributing to such publications as the *New York Times*, *Relix*, and others. His career straddles the world of journalism and academia; he holds a PhD in American literature and is a senior lecturer in the University of Pennsylvania's creative writing program. He remains a contributing editor at *Rolling Stone* and has authored and edited a number of books, including anthologies of his own writing, collaboration on Clive Davis's autobiography *The Soundtrack of My Life*, and the recent biography *Lou Reed: A Life*.

**Elaine Dutka** is a journalist and cultural reporter specializing in film and the arts. She has served as *Time* magazine's West Coast Show Business correspondent and on staff at the *Los Angeles Times*; her writing has appeared in the *New York Times*, the *International Herald Tribune*, *Los Angeles Magazine*, and the *Huffington Post*. She currently resides in San Francisco.

**David Frost** was an independent television commentator, writer, and talk-show host based primarily in London who became known—through the variety of programs that he hosted—for being unusually in tune and relatively evenhanded in his coverage of cultural upheaval in the 1960s. He also held a reputation for hosting hard-hitting conversations with politicians. In 1977 he became famous in the US for his extended interview with former President Richard Nixon, who had remained largely out of the public eye after resigning from the White House. Frost remained active as a journalist and speaker until he passed away in 2013.

**John Fugelsang** is an actor, comedian, TV host and political commentator whose name and face became associated with music news coverage on MTV's sister channel VH1 during the 1990s. Since then he has expanded his career to a wide range of acting and hosting opportunities and, since 2015, has led Sirius XM's talk show *Tell Me Everything*.

**Mitch Glazer** began his career in the 1970s as a music journalist writing for *Rolling Stone* and *Crawdaddy*. Since then, he has achieved renown as a screenwriter and film producer of consequence; *Scrooged* (1988), *Great Expectations* (1998), *The Recruit* (2003), and a number of television productions have all profited from his creative flair.

**Mukunda Goswami** (born Michael Grant in Portland, Oregon) was one of Sri Prabhupada's earliest American disciples. After meeting Prabhupada in 1965, he helped establish ISKCON's first temple in San Francisco and served as a bridge between ISKCON and the burgeoning rock generation. He moved to England in the 1970s and continued to rise within the organization, creating and running ISKCON's communication office in Los Angeles and writing a number of books on spirituality. Goswami moved to San Diego in the 1990s, then New Zealand, and finally Australia, where he lives in the ISKCON New Govardhana community.

**Dave Herman** was a rock radio deejay who rose to prominence in New York City, known primarily as a host on WPLJ and later the city's leading rock station, WNEW. Though Herman has been praised and awarded for his many years hosting rock radio programs and conducting interviews with leading musicians, his end was less laudatory; he was arrested for criminal sexual activity in 2013 and died in custody the next year.

**David Hull**, aka "The Hullabalooer," is a Los Angeles radio personality who rose to prominence during the 1960s on the pop music station KRLA and contributed articles and interviews to the station's music publication, *KRLA Beat*. He later expanded his career as a game-show host and voiceover specialist for TV and radio commercials. Now retired, he lives in Palm Springs, California.

**Carroll James** was a radio deejay on the Washington DC station WWDC known for interviewing the Beatles before their famed concert in 1964, as well as introducing the group to an early fan—Marsha Albert—who had phoned and requested their music a few months prior. Though subsequent research has shown that Beatles singles had been programmed by various US stations before WWDC, James is nonetheless credited with playing a key role in kickstarting Beatlemania in the States—and almost certainly was the first to honor a fan's request for the band's music. Over the course of his career, James served as a disc jockey for stations in Washington, Baltimore, and Norfolk Virginia until becoming a freelance announcer in the late '60s. He passed away in 1997.

**David "Kid" Jensen** is a Canada-born deejay who joined the staff of British pirate radio broadcaster Radio Luxembourg in 1968 and by the 1970s was producing various programs in and around London. He eventually joined BBC Radio 1 in 1976, hosting *Roundtable* and other programs. In years since, he has continued to appear on a number of broadcasting services and programs and can be heard today on the online radio station UDJ.

**Nick Jones** is a music journalist who joined *Melody Maker* at the age of sixteen in 1965, following in his father's footsteps at the same publication. After a number of years reporting on the London rock scene, Jones worked the "indie" side of the music industry. Most recently, he continues to pursue a passion for promoting local free gigs and runs a music and arts charity based on England's South Coast.

**Larry Kane** is a legendary broadcaster, author, and TV news anchor best known for his years hosting nightly broadcasts in Philadelphia. He is also renowned for being the sole broadcast journalist to witness every one of the Beatles' appearances on their historic 1964 and '65 American tours, which he attended when he was just twenty-one and working out of a Miami station. He has since written a memoir, a novel, and several books about his experiences with the Beatles: *Ticket to Ride, Lennon Revealed*, and *When They Were Boys*. Today he is semiretired, contributing occasionally to KYW News Radio.

**Monty Lister** was a popular Liverpool-based radio deejay whose career rose as the Beatles' fame drew attention to the region. He managed Radio Clatterbridge, a hospital radio station, where he hosted two weekly music shows until 1967 when he joined BBC Radio Merseyside and began presenting the long-running Sunday-morning request program "Tune Tonic." He passed away in 2019.

**Kurt Loder** is a rock journalist, film critic, and TV personality who served in the 1980s as editor at *Rolling Stone* magazine. In 1987 he joined MTV News, becoming their primary on-air reporter and host of many regular and special news programs. He currently hosts the music-focused talk show *True Stories* on Sirius XM.

**Ray Martin** is an Australian television journalist, on-air host, and entertainment personality whose long and awarded career has found him fulfilling many different roles in front of the camera from 1965 to the present day. The majority of his career he has been affiliated with Australia's Nine Network, with a long tenure as host of *Midday with Ray Martin*.

**Barry Miles**—best known simply as Miles—was a central figure in London's counterculture crossroad of music, drugs, spiritual explorations, and intellectuality. In 1966 he cofounded Indica Books and Gallery—where John Lennon first met Yoko Ono—as well as *International Times*, Europe's first underground newspaper. He interviewed many of the music scene's leading personages—including various Beatles, Mick Jagger, and Pete Townshend. In years since, he has authored *Hippie*, a reflection on '60s and '70s counterculture and a slew of major musician biographies. He currently lives in London.

**Scott Muni** was a rock deejay and radio producer whose career stretched from the heyday of pop music stations on the AM dial to the rise of rock radio on FM. He began broadcasting in 1950 while serving in the army, came to New York City to host programs on commercial stations in the late '50s, and worked for a litany of progressive rock stations during the '60s, until finding his longtime home at WNEW-FM in 1967. Muni passed away in 2004.

**Sir Michael Edward Palin** is a British actor, writer, and TV presenter best known as a member of the era-defining, early '70s comedy troupe Monty Python. He has starred in a variety of films, primarily in comedies such as *Monty Python and the Holy Grail* (1975), *Monty Python's Life of Brian* (1979), *The Missionary* (1982), and *A Fish Called Wanda* (1988). In the decades since he has travel-blogged extensively, written several books, and provided voiceovers for and acted in numerous productions. In 2019 he received a knighthood for his cultural contributions.

**Sri Prabhupada**, also known as A. C. Bhaktivedanta, was a Calcutta-born spiritual teacher and Vaishnava monk whose followers are collectively known as the International Society of Krishna Consciousness (ISK-CON)—or, more familiarly, the Hare Krishna movement. Prabhupada founded ISKCON in '66 as a means of spreading his teachings to the West. By '68, his following had spread to a number of major American cities as well as London, where the guru met the Beatles. During his lifetime he produced more than sixty translations of Vedic scriptures that remain well regarded in religious and academic circles alike. Though he passed away in 1977, his teachings and influence are still felt today in the activities of his followers.

**Mark Rowland** spent a decade as executive editor of *Musician* magazine in the late '80s and '90s and wrote narrations for the best-selling multi-media books *And the Crowd Goes Wild* and *We Interrupt This*

*Broadcast*. Turning his skills to television, he became co-executive producer of TV One's award-winning music documentary series *Unsung* and served as chief writer and supervising producer of BET's documentary crime series *American Gangster*. To date, he has produced and written over a hundred one-hour episodes of documentary programs for television, for such acclaimed series as Fox Sports' *Beyond the Glory*, History Channel's *Modern Marvels*, ESPN's *Sports Century*, and VH1's *Behind the Music*.

**Marcia Schafer** (now Raubach) is a media specialist who—when she was seventeen and still in high school—hosted a weekly local radio show in her hometown of Benton, Illinois. In 1963 she claimed the historic distinction of being the first member of the American media to meet and interview a Beatle.

**Howard Smith** was the New York City–based *Village Voice* reporter who covered the rise of the counterculture in New York City from 1966 into the '80s in his column *Scenes*; he also hosted and produced a weekly radio show for WABC/WPLJ. Smith's career later led him to pursue the role of documentary producer, in which he created an Oscar-winning portrait of Bible preacher Marjoe Gortner (*Marjoe*, 1972). Smith later collected his interviews in an anthology of transcripts titled *The Smith Tapes*. He passed away in 2014.

**Sylvia Stephen** was a culture reporter working the London scene in the early 1960s writing for *Fabulous*—a pop pin-up music magazine first published in January 1964 that rode the wave of popularity that the Beatles kicked off. *Fabulous* changed its name in June 1966 to *Fabulous 208* after joining with Radio Luxembourg, the commercial radio station broadcasting popular music into the UK in the 1960s. During her time with the magazine, Stephen wrote pop profiles of several Beatles, the Swinging Blue Jeans, the Kinks, and the Rolling Stones.

**Derek Taylor** began his career as a journalist in his hometown of Liverpool and became an early champion of the Beatles after writing about them for the *Daily Express* in early 1963. His enthusiasm earned him the position of the Beatles's first press officer, which eventually led him to move to Los Angeles where he continued to amplify his role as a writer, framer, and media specialist for the rock music scene. He remained close with the Beatles, particularly George Harrison; he contributed to Harrison's autobiography *I, Me, Mine*, and when he authored his own biography, *Fifty Years Adrift (In An Open Necked Shirt)*, Harrison returned the favor. Taylor died of cancer in 1997 while working on *The Beatles Anthology*.

**Alan Walsh** became the news editor of *Melody Maker*, one of the UK's two primary music-focused publications during the 1960s, after a long climb up the journalistic ladder from his native Liverpool to London. His seven-year run in that position—from '64 to '71—coincided with the Beatles's years at the top and afforded him the chance to witness and report firsthand on the rise of youth culture, rock music, and the London scene in general. He went on to found a number of other music publications in the '70s, including *Sounds* magazine and *Kerrang!*, and died in 2015.

**Timothy White** was one of the premier rock journalists and music-magazine editors in the 1980s and '90s. He came up through the ranks of music reporting in the 1970s, his byline appearing in *Musician, New York Times, Playboy*, and *Rolling Stone*. He eventually became editor-in-chief at *Billboard* magazine and wrote biographies of such legends as Bob Marley, the Beach Boys, and James Taylor. White died in 2002 at the age of fifty.

**David Wigg** is a British journalist and BBC One deejay famed for his extended interviews with various rock groups and personages, including Mick Jagger and Queen. Wigg hosted the popular *Scene and Heard* program and over the course of his career has written for such UK publications as the *Daily Express* and the *London Evening News*. Today he still writes for the *Daily Mail*.

# CREDITS

Deepest gratitude to everyone who gave permission for material to appear in this book. Every reasonable effort has been made to contact copyright holders. If, however, any error or omission has been made, please bring it to the attention of the publisher.

Interview with Monty Lister, *Sunday Spin*. Broadcast October 28, 1962, on Radio Clatterbridge. Printed by permission.

Interview on *The Mersey Sound*. August 28, 1963. Printed by permission of British Pathé.

Interview on *The Public Ear*. Broadcast October 3, 1963, on BBC Radio. Printed by permission.

Interview with Marcia Shafer, *Redbird Notes*. September 1963. Printed by permission of Marcia Raubach Schafer.

Columns by George Harrison, *Daily Express* (UK). January–August 1964. Reprinted by permission.

Excerpts from *Ticket to Ride: Inside the Beatles' 1964 and 1965 Tours that Changed the World*, by Larry Kane, 2004. Printed by permission of Larry Kane.

Interviews on *The Public Ear*. Broadcast March 22, 1964, on BBC Radio. Printed by permission.

"Teledate: Sylvia Stephens talking to George Harrison," by Sylvia Stephens. Published June 13, 1964, in Fabulous (UK). Reprinted by permission of Rock's Backpages.

Interview with Dave Hull and Derek Taylor. Broadcast April 7, 1965, on KRLA-AM. Reprinted by permission of Rock's Backpages.

"How a Beatle Lives Part 3: George Harrison—Avocado with Everything . . ." by Maureen Cleave. Published March 18, 1966 in *Evening Standard*. Reprinted by permission of Rock's Backpages.

"The Way Out Is In: An Interview with George Harrison," by Barry Miles. Published May 19, 1967 in *International Times*. Reprinted by permission of Rock's Backpages.

"The George Harrison Interview," by Alan Walsh. Published September 2, 1967 in *Melody Maker*. Reprinted by permission of Rock's Backpages.

"Beatle George and Where He's At," by Nick Jones. Published on December 16 and 30, 1967, in *Melody Maker*. Reprinted by permission of Rock's Backpages.

Interview with David Wigg on *Scene and Heard*. Broadcast October 8, 1969, on BBC Radio. Printed by permission.

Room Conversation with Sri Prabhupada, John Lennon, Yoko Ono, and George Harrison. September 11, 1969. Text courtesy of the Bhaktivedanta Book Trust International, Inc. www.Krishna.com. Used with permission..

Interview with Howard Smith. Taped May 1, 1970. With kind consideration of The Smith Tapes, 2019.

Interview with Dick Cavett. Broadcast November 23, 1971 on *The Dick Cavett Show*, ABC-TV. Copyright ©1971 by Global ImageWorks. Printed by permission.

Conversation with George Harrison, Sri Prabhupada, and ISKCON Members. July 22, 1973. Text courtesy of the Bhaktivedanta Book Trust International, Inc. www.Krishna.com. Used with permission.

Interview with Dave Herman. Broadcast April 19 and 20, 1975 on WNEW-FM. Copyright © 1975 by Entercom. Printed by permission of WNEW 102.7.

"The George Harrison Interview," by Mitch Glazer. Published February 1977 in *Crawdaddy*. Reprinted by permission of Mitch Glazer.

Interview with David "Kid" Jensen on *Roundtable*. Broadcast February 9, 1979, on BBC Radio 1. Audio from the radio documentary "When George Met Michael," presented by Paul Gambaccini and produced by Richard Latto. BBC Radio, 2019. Printed by permission.

"A Conversation with George Harrison," by Mick Brown. Published April 19, 1979 in *Rolling Stone*. Reprinted by permission of Rock's Backpages.

Interview with Mukunda Goswami. September 4, 1982. Text courtesy of the Bhaktivedanta Book Trust International, Inc. www.Krishna.com. Used with permission.

Interview with Charles Bermant. September 17, 1987. Reprinted by permission of Rock's Backpages.

Interview with Anthony DeCurtis. August 27 or 28, 1987. Reprinted by permission of DeCurtis and *Rolling Stone*.

Interview with Elaine Dutka. August 25, 1987. Reprinted by permission of Elaine Dutka.

Beatles Rock & Roll Hall of Fame Induction Speech. January 21, 1988. Printed by consent of the Rock & Roll Hall of Fame Foundation.

Interview with Ray Martin. Broadcast February 10, 1988, on *Midday with Ray Martin*, Nine Network, Australia. Printed by permission of Nine Films & Television Pty Ltd.

Interview with Michael Aspel. Broadcast March 5, 1988, on *Aspel & Company*, ITV. Printed by courtesy of the ITV archive, 2019.

Excerpts from *It's Not Only Rock 'n' Roll: Iconic Musicians Reveal the Source of their Creativity*, by Jenny Boyd, 1988. Reprinted by permission of Dr. Jenny Boyd.

Interview with Kurt Loder. Broadcast October 18, 1988, MTV News. Copyright ©1988 by Viacom. Printed by permission.

Interview with MTV News. January 1989. Copyright © 1989 by Viacom. Printed by permission.

Interview with Michael Rowland. November 27, 1989. Printed by permission of Mark Rowland.

Interview with Scott Muni. Broadcast July 21, 1992, on WNEW-FM. Copyright © 1992 by Entercom. Printed by permission of WNEW 102.7.

Interview with Bob Coburn. Broadcast August 24, 1992 on *Rockline*. Printed by permission of Rockline, LLC 2019.

Interview with Timothy White. 1992. Printed by permission of Judy Garlan.

Interview with John Fugelsang. Taped July 24, 1997, VH1. Copyright © 1997 by Viacom. Printed by permission.

Online Q and A on MSN Live, February 2001. Printed by permission of Microsoft.

Online Q and A on Yahoo!, February 2001. Printed by permission of Oath/Verizon Media.

Press conferences and public statements are in the public domain.

# INDEX